A timber bridge provides an oriental atmosphere and the perfect place from which to view koi.

THE TETRA ENCYCLOPEDIA OF

KOI

A comprehensive introduction to keeping and displaying these magnificent ornamental fish, from choosing healthy stock to installing a fully equipped koi pond. Plus a full-colour survey of all the major varieties.

Tetra Press

16097

A Salamander Book

Credits

Editor: Anne McDowell
Design: David Jones and Stonecastle
Graphics.
Color reproductions: Scantrans Pte.
Ltd.
Filmset: SX Composing Ltd.
Printed in Hong Kong.

A stone wall will screen the pond and enable children to watch koi safely.

寄稿者
CONTRIBUTORS

This encyclopedia embraces the experience of a team of professional koi dealers, the insight of enthusiastic hobbyists and the expertise of specialists in associated fields. The main contributors are as follows:

Bernice Brewster
(Koi anatomy, Water quality and filtration, Health care)

Nicky Chapple
(Buying koi, Koi varieties)

John Cuvelier
(Pond and filter construction)

Mark Davies
(The history of nishikigoi, Feeding koi, Breeding koi)

Deri Evans
(Pond and filter construction, Seasonal care)

Glyn Evans
(Pond and filter construction)

Keith Phipps
(Showing koi)

Yvonne Rees
(Landscaping and water gardens)

Peter W. Scott MSc., BVSc., MRCVS, MIBiol.
(Health care consultant)

目 次
CONTENTS

Greenery, rockwork and Japanese artefacts create a restful, oriental setting for these koi ponds.

PART ONE

PRACTICAL SECTION

A fascination with koi often develops into an obsession, but enthusiasm for collecting and showing these beautiful fish must be coupled with a clear understanding of what makes them 'tick' and how you can provide the ideal environment for them. The chapters in this practical section of the book reflect and enhance these priorities.

After a brief introduction to the history of koi, our attention turns to the anatomy and basic physiology of koi as members of the carp family. The next two sections offer guidelines on providing the most appropriate physical environment for koi – with practical advice on designing and constructing suitable ponds and filters – and an all-important look at the biochemical aspects of maintaining water quality. These are followed by three chapters that consider in turn the subjects of buying, feeding and seasonal care. In these sections, you will find essential guidance on how to look after your koi on a day-to-day and season-by-season basis.

Since a koi pond can be a decorative addition to your garden, the next chapter takes up the challenge of landscaping and water gardening in the widest sense, with practical suggestions that embrace both Western and Oriental influences. It is a sad fact, however, that even in the best systems koi are prone to ill-health from time to time. How do you cope? This is the subject addressed in the chapter on health care, which includes a detailed survey of all the common pests and diseases that could affect your koi, together with sensible advice on prevention and cure. The final two chapters provide basic information on breeding koi – a pursuit rapidly spreading from the exclusive domain of professionals into the growing world of enthusiastic hobbyists – and offer a 'behind-the-scenes' look at showing koi.

Selecting prize-winning koi at a national koi show.

THE HISTORY OF NISHIKIGOI

The many beautiful koi varieties we know today are, in fact, all descendants of the black fish known as Magoi. Although early records of koi (i.e. common carp) date back some 2,500 years, their farm cultivation is much more recent. Colour mutations first appeared some two hundred years ago and by the end of the 19th century many of the varieties we know today had been established. However, it was not until the 20th century that koi-keeping as a hobby began to flourish. The development of road and rail links and, more particularly, the advancement of air travel, facilitated the transportation of koi, and these beautiful fish soon attracted a huge following in other parts of the world, particularly in the USA and UK. Since the first days of the culture of nishikigoi – as fancy koi came to be known – many farmers have invested much time and effort in developing new varieties. Although Japan still leads the world, other countries are now producing koi for their own home markets, and it is probable that the most beautiful nishikigoi are yet to be seen.

A tea house, strong green foliage and large boulders create the Japanese atmosphere in this water garden.

THE HISTORY OF NISHIKIGOI

Contrary to common belief, koi are not indigenous to Japan. They originate from eastern Asia – in the Black, Azov, Caspian and Aral Seas – and from China, where the earliest written record of these fish is found. At his birth, the first son of the great Chinese philosopher Confucius (551-479? BC) was presented with a koi by King Shoko of Ro. Confucius named his son after this fish because it was considered to be a symbol of strength; allegedly, it was the only fish able to swim up the falls of the Yellow River. In 533 BC, a Chinese book entitled 'Yogyokyo' set out methods of breeding koi. At this time, colour variations were limited to red and grey. Since koi at this time were cultivated solely for food, however, such variations were not considered seriously in the ornamental sense.

Koi were introduced to Japan with the invading Chinese, and the first account of them being kept in Japan, apparently by an Emperor, dates back to AD 200. From here, the story moves forward to the 17th century, when rice farmers of Yamakoshi go, a village in the Niigata prefecture on the northwestern coast of mainland Japan, introduced carp into their irrigation ponds to supplement their diet of rice. The area is situated high in the mountains, where snow fall of up to six metres made access difficult, if not impossible, during the winter months. Such an isolated position forced the inhabitants of Yamakoshi go to rely on the resources they had, and the attention they devoted to breeding carp led to the Niigata region becoming established as the centre of the growing koi 'industry'.

Colour mutations were first noticed between 1804 and 1830. These mainly involved red koi, white koi and light yellow koi (the latter being improved to become the first single-coloured Kawarimono) and, later, the tortoiseshell-patterned koi – all mutations from the black common carp, known as Magoi. Around 1830-50, cross-breeding of red with white carp produced what could be described as the first Kohaku. Early koi varieties, such as Asagi, Higoi and Bekko, were cross-bred until, in the 1880s, many of the varieties we know today were fixed. Certain varieties consistently reached high standards of quality over a period of several generations and, in this way, lineages became established.

Asagi and Ki Utsuri were first produced in 1875. These varieties were highly prized and began to exchange hands for very large sums of money. This led to a temporary ban on the industry, as the local authorities thought that such carp breeding bordered on speculation. Fortunately, as the local villagers had no other means of livelihood or pastime, the ban did not last long.

Meanwhile, in Central Europe, a mutation arose in the late 18th century that was to exert a striking influence on koi 'design'. The mutation affected the scales, resulting either in scaleless, so-called 'leather' carp or 'mirror' carp with large shiny scales along the dorsal line. These fish, which became known as 'doitsu' from their Germanic/Austrian origins, were originally bred for the table, being easier to clean than fully scaled fish. Some doitsu carp were introduced to Japan in 1904 and from these individuals the first Shusui (which are doitsu Asagi) were produced in 1910.

Breeding fancy koi was restricted to the Niigata region until the beginning of the 20th century. Indeed, it was not until

Below: *The many beautiful koi varieties we admire today are all descendants of the black common carp, known as Magoi, shown in this old illustration. This fish, which is still in existence, has a history of some 2,500 years, and originates from the seas of Eastern Asia and China.*

1914 that koi were introduced outside this area, when Hikosaburo Hirasawa, the Mayor of Higashiyama Mura (now Yamakoshi Mura), sent 27 koi to the great Tokyo Exhibition to promote the economic circumstances of the poverty-stricken people of the Niigata region. These koi were awarded a second prize at the exhibition and eight of them were presented to the Emperor Taisho's son. This marked the beginning of the flourishing koi industry as we know it today.

Unfortunately, after several good years, during which the Kohaku and Sanke varieties were stabilized, an economic depression in 1920 caused the koi industry to fall to a low ebb. During the period up to the Second World War, several more varieties, including Shiro Bekko and Showa, were successfully established, despite another depression in the industry, this time caused by food shortages. Koi breeding continued to thrive in Niigata, and the industry grew as the area became more accessible, with the building of the Shin-etsu Railway and the National Highway Route 17.

Above: *The bright colours and patterns of these beautiful koi are the result of nearly two centuries of selective breeding. Today, there are hundreds of different varieties in existence and new and unique koi are continually appearing, principally in Japan.*

To a certain extent, the boom in the breeding of koi that took place at the end of the Second World War was made possible by the commercial development of air travel. Transportation of koi all over the world was then possible and a huge international market developed. For example, koi were first shipped to San Francisco in 1938, to Hawaii in 1947, to Canada in 1949 and to Brazil in 1953.

Koi-keeping outside Japan has increased dramatically, particularly during the 1980s, and many koi are now being produced in other countries for their own home markets. Although at present Japanese varieties outshine those produced in other parts of the world in terms of range and quality, it is conceivable that new varieties will eventually appear for the first time outside Japan.

Above: *It was here, in the Niigata prefecture of Japan, that koi were first bred, initially for food but later for their beautiful colours and patterns. The region remains at the heart of the koi-breeding industry.*

KOI ANATOMY

Before considering any health-related problems to which koi may be subject, it is vital to understand a little bit about their basic anatomy. After all, few people would consider tackling a faulty car engine without having some idea of how an engine is put together. In the same way that understanding the structure of an engine and how it works enables a mechanic to detect and repair any faults, so appreciating how koi are 'built' and 'what makes them work' is a necessary first step in tackling any problems associated with their health.

This section considers the body shape of koi and then the very basic anatomy in two natural categories: the external anatomy, which includes all the visible parts of the body; and the internal anatomy, which embraces the organs and tissues and the systems that 'connect' them inside the body.

This Beni-goi (top) and Doitsu Purachina (bottom) combine beautiful coloration with a streamlined shape.

KOI ANATOMY

Body shape

In common with most fishes, koi are broader at the front than at the tail end. Such a shape streamlines the koi and minimizes turbulence as it moves through the water. If a cone is placed with the pointed end turned into a current of water, the water swirls at the rear flattened surface, creating turbulence, or drag. If the cone is reversed, so that the flat surface meets the current, the flow of water around it is less turbulent and actually assists its passage through the water. The movement of koi through the water is similar to that outlined for the second cone.

The external anatomy

The external anatomy of koi includes the scales, fins, operculum (gill cover), vent, eyes, nostrils, barbels and lateral line.

Scales These form a lightweight, pliable suit of armour over the surface of the fish. Each scale is an extremely thin but flexible plate of bone-like material. The front end of the scale is inserted into a deep pocket of skin; the back is quite free and overlaps the front of the scale behind, just as roof tiles overlap. There are two distinct types of scale pattern found on koi: completely scaled, and the so-called doitsu, in which the scales are enlarged and arranged along the midline of each side of the body and, usually, at the dorsal and anal fin bases. The scales of doitsu koi are entirely embedded in the skin. (We look more closely at scalation, and, in particular, at the various types of doitsu scalation, in the varieties section on page 125.)

Covering the scales and, indeed, the whole body of the fish, is a layer of mucus. This mucus is mildly antiseptic and is secreted by special cells in the skin. It gives fish their characteristically slimy feel and literally 'lubricates' the body as the fish moves through the water, helping to maintain a 'slippery', hydrodynamic shape.

Fins Koi have five sets of fins: the dorsal, anal and caudal (or tail) fins, which are single, and the pectoral and pelvic fins, which are paired. Fish swim using the body muscle, (as explained on page 18), and the fins play an important role in maintaining stability in the water. When erected, the dorsal and anal fins prevent rolling and yawing, and the pectoral and caudal fins control pitching. The pectoral and pelvic fins also control fine movement by counteracting the propulsive forward motion caused by the exhalation of water from the gill covers, thus enabling the koi to remain motionless.

Operculum (gill cover) This is a large bony plate that protects the delicate gills (see page 20). It is free at the rear and lower edges and acts as a one-way valve, allowing water to leave the gill chamber but preventing any backflow of respired, oxygen-deficient water to re-enter the gills. It articulates with the skull and the large hyomandibular bone. (In fishes, this bone forms part of the suspension for the lower jaw; in humans, it is tiny and forms the stapes in the inner ear.)

Vent Just in front of the anal fin is a large pore, usually termed the vent. The gut and the ducts from either the testes or ovaries terminate at this point. This is not a cloaca, which is a term used to describe a common opening for the digestive, urinary and genital systems. Just in front of the vent there is a smaller opening, which receives the urinary ducts from the kidneys.

Eyes Koi have fairly good eyesight for fish. The position of the eyes on the head gives them almost total 360° vision, enabling them to see above and behind, as well as in front and below themselves. The ability to see above and behind is particularly important because it enables koi to watch for the approach of enemies while they are feeding.

Nostrils On either side of the snout are a pair of nostrils, i.e. four in all. In cross

External features of koi

The streamlined shape of a koi is typical of the carp family of fishes to which it belongs. The strong, high-backed body and well-developed fins give the fish speed and manoeuvrability in the water. Note the two pairs of sensitive barbels.

Nostrils

Operculum (gill cover)

Barbels (two pairs)

Pectoral fins

section, the nostrils are seen to be joined by a U-shaped tube. The water flows in through the front nostril and out through the rear one. The floor of the tube is folded into a series of ridges, which are then arranged in the form of a rosette. The ridges are coated in a skin that is peppered with olfactory, or 'smelling', cells. These cells are able to detect extremely small quantities of dissolved substances in the water, even from quite distant objects. In fact, the sense of smell is more important to the koi than eyesight for finding food.

Barbels Koi have one pair of barbels on each side of the mouth, a small barbel on the side of the upper lip and a larger one

more or less at the corner of the mouth. These fleshy structures are moved by muscles that once operated parts of the jaw and palate and are covered with taste buds that literally allow koi to taste anything the barbels contact. Like their ancestors, the wild carp, koi are bottom feeders, using their barbels to locate grubs, insects, crustaceans, worms and water plants in the substrate. (Koikeepers generally feed koi with floating pellets and sticks, but this is simply to enjoy seeing their spectacular livery as they surface to feed). Thus, koi use their sense of smell to locate an area where food is to be found, and then detect the individual particles of food using the very sensitive taste buds on their barbels.

Lateral line organ Along the middle of each side of the body there is a row of scales, each pierced by a small pore that connects by way of a small tube to a canal that lies in the skin beneath the scales. This system of canals and tubes forms part of the lateral line organ. On the head, the lateral line organ runs beneath the eye to the snout, its passage being marked by conspicuous pits. In some doitsu koi (see page 125), the lateral line may be seen as a conspicuous line that runs along the middle of the fish, from just behind the operculum to the tail. Although the sensory cells of the lateral line are similar to those found in our internal ear, it is difficult to interpret precisely the sensation these cells impart to

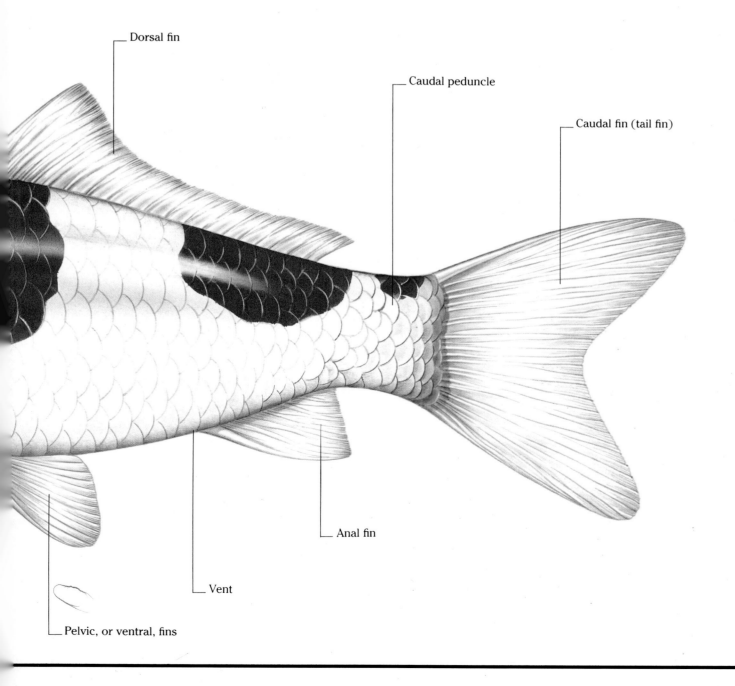

Dorsal fin

Caudal peduncle

Caudal fin (tail fin)

Anal fin

Vent

Pelvic, or ventral, fins

KOI ANATOMY

the fish. It seems that they are sensitive to water movement, waves and disturbances in the water, enabling koi to avoid other fishes, objects and the pond walls.

The internal anatomy
The internal anatomy is more complex than the external anatomy, not only because of the number of different organs involved, but also the way these various organs interact.

Skeleton One of the most important features of the internal anatomy, but one which receives the least consideration, is the skeleton. Koi are members of a group of fish known as teleosts, literally meaning 'bony skeleton'. The skeleton has several major functions: it forms a protective and supporting framework for the internal organs and tissues, and enables the fish to move by providing a series of flexible joints and attachment

points for muscles.

Parts of the first four vertebrae of the backbone are modified to form the Weberian ossicles, a system of tiny bones that link the swimbladder to the inner ear. Sounds travelling through the water cause the swimbladder to vibrate and the ossicles amplify these vibrations and transmit them to the sensitive hair cells within the liquid-filled semicircular canals of the inner ear. With such an apparatus, koi can undoubtedly 'hear'.

Teeth Koi, like all other members of the cyprinid family, lack teeth in the jaws. Their few teeth are large grinding devices on plates of bone in the throat.

Muscle The bulk of the koi body is formed from four large blocks of muscle, two on either side of the body. These blocks are subdivided into V-shaped muscle segments. The muscle segments

of the throat and gill arches are very well developed to control respiratory movements. The jaw muscles cover most of the cheeks and exert their force in closing the jaws. The muscles of the paired fins are simple in construction, although those controlling the pectoral fins are very extensive.

Heart The heart, situated just behind and below the gill arches, is a large muscular pump consisting of four consecutive chambers. The first chamber is simply a thin-walled sac with very little muscle. The second chamber, or atrium, is also thin walled, but expandable. The third chamber, or ventricle, has thick muscular walls and is largely responsible for the pumping action of the heart. The fourth chamber is also thick walled and has special non-return valves in it, preventing blood flowing back into the preceding chambers.

Koi skeleton

This skeleton, drawn from life, clearly shows how it forms a framework to support and articulate the body of the fish. The vertebral column is literally the central axis of the koi's skeleton, providing attachment points for the major blocks of muscles that give koi their power and agility.

The circulatory system

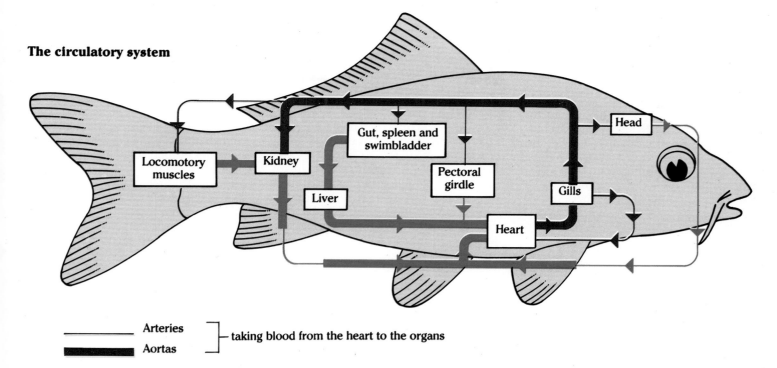

Arteries ⎫
Aortas ⎬ taking blood from the heart to the organs

Veins ⎫
Major veins ⎬ taking blood back to the heart

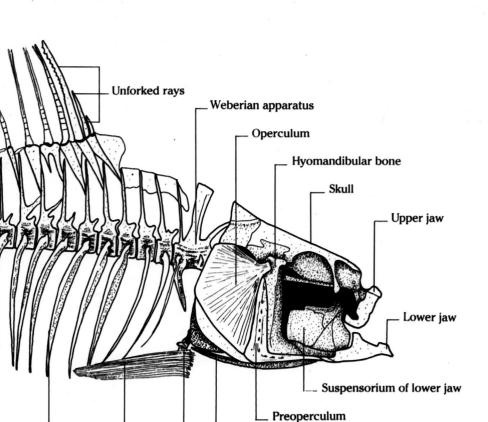

Unforked rays

Weberian apparatus

Operculum

Hyomandibular bone

Skull

Upper jaw

Lower jaw

Suspensorium of lower jaw

Preoperculum

Branchiostegal rays

Pectoral girdle

Pectoral fin

Ribs

Circulatory system This is the transportation system by which nutrients and oxygen reach the cells of the body and waste products are removed from them. It is an embracing term that includes the blood, plasma and vessels through which these body fluids flow. The heart provides the pumping force to move the blood through these vessels, first to the gills and then to the brain and the remaining parts of the body, before returning once again to the heart. The vessels that carry blood to and from the gills, to the brain and then body are arteries; those that return the blood to the heart are veins. (See the diagram shown above.)

Generally, the most important function ascribed to the circulation is transporting oxygen from the gills to the tissues and removing carbon dioxide from the body via the gills. However, it also supplies a constant stream of food materials from the gut or liver to the tissues. As the tissues process the foodstuffs, they produce nitrogen-containing waste products, which are poisonous to the tissues. Some of these nitrogen products, together with any excess water, are transported in the blood to the kidneys, where they are extracted and 'processed' into urine. As in other bony fish, most of the nitrogenous wastes leave the body in the form of ammonia, which diffuses into the water from the gills.

Blood The blood consists of three main elements: the plasma, red blood cells and white blood cells. The plasma is a watery fluid of complex structure. The red blood cells contain haemoglobin, a red pigment that binds with oxygen. Thus, the red blood cells flowing from the gills carry oxygen to the tissues, where they ex-

KOI ANATOMY

change their oxygen for carbon dioxide, the waste gas produced during the process of metabolism.

The white cells in the blood have an equally important role to play, but mainly in terms of protecting the fish from infection. There are several different types of white blood cell, their precise function varying according to their type. All accumulate in injured, inflamed or infected areas of the body, where they repel bacterial or viral invasions, remove dead or damaged tissue, and assist in repairing damaged tissues.

Blood cells have a short lifespan, new ones being produced primarily in the spleen and kidneys.

Gills The gills are the equivalent of our lungs; they provide a large surface area of tissue where carbon dioxide is exchanged for oxygen. In addition to carrying out this process of gaseous exchange, they are an important site for osmoregulation (i.e. controlling the salt/water balance and excretion).

To the naked eye, the gills appear as rows of very fine, finger-like projections arranged on a series of curved arches. There is a double row of delicate filaments in a V-shaped arrangement along the posterior surface of each arch. The surface of the filaments is highly folded, enormously increasing their surface area, and the skin is extremely thin, allowing intimate contact between the blood and water. As water flows over the gill filaments, oxygen is extracted and carbon dioxide released – a process of 'external respiration'.

The osmoregulatory role of the gills is made possible not only by their large surface area but also by an outer layer of special cells that absorb salts from the water. (Salts is used here in the chemical sense, rather than simply referring to sodium chloride, or common salt.) Since the body tissues and fluids of a koi contain a higher concentration of salts than the surrounding fresh water, there is a tendency for water to be absorbed and salts lost through the gills. (The processes at work here are osmosis and diffusion. Osmosis is the process by which water passes through a semi-permeable membrane – in this case, the gill membrane – from a weaker to a stronger solution. Salts move by diffusion in the opposite direction. Water and salt movement stops when the solutions are equally concentrated on either side of the membrane.) The excess water absorbed through the gills is excreted in copious amounts of dilute urine produced by the kidneys. The special cells in the gill membrane selectively absorb salts back from the water, thus helping to maintain the correct salt balance within the blood and body tissues of the koi.

Gut The gut performs three major functions: physical breakdown and mixing of food (i.e. by the teeth); chemical breakdown (i.e. by digestive enzymes); and absorption of the food materials. In koi, there is no stomach; food is digested in the very long intestine. Once the nutritive content of the food has been absorbed into the bloodstream, the remaining solid, undigestible material is voided.

Spleen The spleen, a compact purple-red organ, lies very close to the gut and liver. It is important for the formation and storage of red and white blood cells.

Liver The liver in koi is very large and consists of several lobes. Its main function is to store glycogen – a stored form of glucose – and, to a lesser degree, other food products. As glucose and other simple sugars are used up by the working tissues and organs of the body, the liver releases the stored glycogen, which is broken down into glucose and 'fuels' the working cells.

The liver also breaks down old and damaged blood cells. The product is known as bile and collects in the gall bladder. From here it drains through the bile duct into the intestine, where it is mixed with the solid waste.

Pancreas The pancreas is a soft tissue, similar in appearance to the liver, that produces a number of digestive enzymes, which it releases into the intestine to chemically break down food.

Kidneys The kidneys are paired organs that lie in the dorsal (upper) region of the body cavity on either side of the vertebral column, or backbone. Each kidney is basically a construction of tubules, closely surrounded by a network of tiny blood vessels, called capillaries. The tubules are connected to a system of ducts that merge into a single one, the ureter, which runs from the kidneys to a pore just in front of the vent, where the urine is voided.

The intimate contact between the capillaries and the kidney tubules allows waste products to pass from the blood into the tubules in a continuous filtering process. The waste products involved are simple nitrogen compounds formed in the tissues during the metabolism of proteins. These compounds would prove poisonous to the cells if they were not carried away in the bloodstream and removed by the kidneys (and via the gills).

The kidneys also regulate the water content of the body – urine is largely water – and control the type and quantity of salts retained by the koi.

Reproductive organs In males these are the testes; in females, the ovaries.

The testes tend to be rather compact and more regularly shaped than the ovaries and, although subject to seasonal change, they show no marked difference between the resting and breeding condition. The testes produce sperm cells, many millions of which may be released during the breeding period.

The ovaries are relatively large and irregularly shaped organs in mature female koi. Eggs may be found in the ovaries throughout the year but the number of mature eggs present is very low when the fish is not in breeding condition. When the female is ready to breed, the ripe eggs burst into a central cavity in the ovary, then pass into the oviduct and are shed at the vent.

Swimbladder As its name suggests, this organ helps the koi to swim by providing buoyancy in the water. It is an elongated oval sac that lies along the top of the body cavity, just beneath the vertebral column and kidneys. It is almost sub-

Internal anatomy of koi

This generalized view shows how the major organ systems lie within the body cavity. Note the long kidneys that lie close to the swimbladder near the spine.

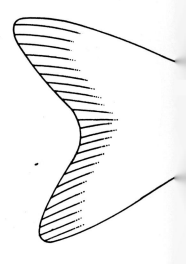

divided into two parts by a narrow constriction. At this point there is a duct, which connects the swimbladder to the gut. Indeed, in embryo koi the swimbladder develops as a minute outgrowth from the gut. This connecting duct enables koi to 'top up' the swimbladder by gulping and swallowing air at the water surface. The air bubble passes into the gut and is 'pumped' into the swimbladder by a duct. The mixture of gases within the swimbladder is more or less the same as air.

Brain The brain is a very soft, pink organ encased by the bony skull. During the development of the embryo in koi, the brain and spinal cord are formed as a tube. The front portion subsequently enlarges to form the brain, the hollow within the tube persisting as fluid-filled cavities, or vesicles. The brain consists of three regions: the fore-, mid- and hindbrain.

At the front of the forebrain are the olfactory lobes, one lobe for each pair of nostrils on each side of the head. They receive the nervous impulses from the nostrils and interpret them as smells. The forebrain also incorporates the light-sensitive pineal organ and hormone-secreting pituitary gland. During the development of the embryo, part of the forebrain is responsible for forming part of the eyes, their associated nerves and the pineal organ. (Interpreting optic nerve signals as sight is a function of the midbrain.) The pineal organ, located on the upper surface of the forebrain, is light sensitive and is thought to represent the remnant of a second pair of eyes on top of the head in some remote ancestor of vertebrate animals. In koi, the pineal organ senses changes in daylength and stimulates the release of reproductive hormones during the breeding season. The pituitary gland produces hormones that stimulate growth and reproduction as well as activating other glands, such as the thyroid.

The main function of the midbrain is to interpret messages relayed to it by the nerves, particularly those concerned with movement and the attitude of the body in the water. The midbrain also acts as the 'seat' of memory, learning and intelligence, although it is very difficult to assess or quantify degrees of learning and intelligence in koi. On top of the midbrain are two oval optic lobes that interpret nervous signals from the eyes and thus provide the sense of sight.

The function of the hindbrain is unclear, although it appears to act as a coordination centre for movement, equilibrium and posture.

Spinal cord The spinal cord is the posterior continuation of the brain, its fluid-filled central canal being the vestigial remnant of the embryonic tube from which the brain develops. The spinal cord extends almost the entire length of the body and is connected to many of the major nerves. As in other vertebrate animals, its main role is to act as a 'through route' for nervous impulses travelling between the body and the brain (see also below).

Nervous system Apart from the brain and spinal cord, which can be considered as the central nervous system, a complex network of nerves extends throughout the body of the koi. This system relays sensory information, such as touch, taste and smell, to the brain and activates the tissues, glands and muscles. There are two quite clearly defined types of nerve systems: the autonomic system and the motor system. The autonomic nervous system controls the 'unconscious' activity of organs such as the gut, gills and certain glands. In effect, the fish is unaware of their 'background' functioning. The motor nerves, on the other hand, carry signals to initiate conscious activities, such as the contraction of muscles to achieve movement.

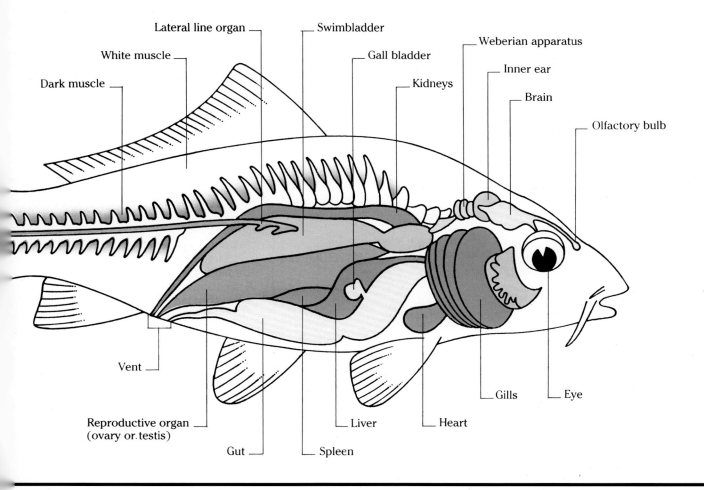

Lateral line organ — Swimbladder
White muscle — — Gall bladder
Dark muscle — — Kidneys
— Weberian apparatus
— Inner ear
— Brain
— Olfactory bulb

Vent —
— Gills — Eye
Reproductive organ —
(ovary or testis)
Gut — — Liver — Heart
— Spleen

POND AND FILTER CONSTRUCTION

Once you have decided to build a koi pond, your first task must be to give a great deal of thought to just what type of pond you require, both from your own point of view and, even more importantly, from the point of view of its future inhabitants. Whatever your circumstances and capabilities as a builder (if you are doing the job yourself), constructing a pond pleasing to the eye, that is easy to maintain and, last but not least, provides a safe and permanent home for your koi, is a considerable feat of civil engineering and should certainly not be entered upon lightly. Bear in mind that creating a pond that consists of a stark rectangular hole in the ground, perhaps surrounded by boulders or even a brick or stone wall, intended solely for the purpose of displaying koi, requires exactly the same degree of care in its design and construction as does the more informal pond intended to blend in with the rest of the garden, complementing the dry land plants with its display of waterborne flora. In this section, we explore first the design and logistic decisions involved in planning a koi pond and its filter system. Then we concentrate in more detail on the basic construction techniques involved in building a pond and a simple multichamber external filter.

Pond construction on the grand scale – placing rockwork around the edge of a large koi pond.

POND AND FILTER CONSTRUCTION

Initial planning

Sitting down to design a koi pond is probably the most important aspect of the whole operation. If you do not get it completely right or forget to make allowances for some vital component or aspect, the actual construction could become a nightmare rather than a pleasure – in addition to increasing the expense of your pond out of all proportion! The secret of avoiding such disasters lies in checking and double checking at each successive point in your design, both at the drawing stage and during the actual construction.

Before you become absorbed in detailed design considerations, you will need to think about, firstly, how much space you have available for the pond and its filtration system and, secondly, your financial budget for the project. Be careful not to set your sights too high – these things have a habit of growing in size and, consequently, in cost! Remember that the time that you spend at this stage on the initial planning, and later on more detailed pond and filter design, will save you time and money both during the construction process itself and, subsequently, in maintaining the completed system on a day-to-day basis.

Working out a budget

Should you be in a financial position to be able to have your pond constructed by a professional firm, you would be wise to insist upon a written estimate for the job, then add, say, 10 percent for contingencies. Also, ask for details of other ponds your selected company has built, bearing in mind that the custom building of pools specifically intended for koi-keeping is a relatively new industry. And remember that house builders, or even landscape gardeners, are not necessarily professional koi pond builders.

If you are taking the DIY route, working out the cost of your proposed pond should be relatively easy, even if the result is frightening! The supplier of items such as liners will provide exact costings according to your measurements (accuracy is essential), be it in sheet or box-welded form. A building supply company will be able to provide delivered prices for concrete blocks, bricks, cement, sand, etc. It is in the area of 'sundries' that your problems can really start! Plumbing can run away with a great deal of money, for example, and here you must make the crucial choice between using 'domestic' or high-pressure pipe for the bottom drains and associated filter network (see page 31). The difference in cost can be substantial.

In costing your pool, you should also take into account all the mundane things like the hiring of a skip or a cement mixer. In fact, it could be more profitable to buy a small electric cement mixer outright; if you look after it properly and clean it regularly during your building operation, you could re-sell it and lose less than the cost of hiring one.

Also consider the cost involved in preparing drawings. If you have no knowledge of how to lay out your ideas, then find somebody who understands the principles and detail and can translate your plans into a set of drawings you will be able to work from. Money spent at this stage will save you a lot more in the long run. Starting to construct a new koi pond without a full set of drawings can be a costly mistake.

Which style to choose?

Obviously, your first decision must be the type and style of pond you wish to build and, unfortunately, this is where many prospective koi-keepers fall at the first hurdle. Having seen koi displayed at various retail outlets, usually in plain, unrelieved display tanks, naturally enough all attention is focused on the dramatic colours and patterns of the koi, with scant attention being paid to their surroundings. Your first question to yourself must be: Will such a tanklike pond be in keeping with my garden, or should I aim for a more informal and decorative style?

Thus, choosing the style of your pond is probably the most important, and yet one of the most difficult, decisions to make. Before deciding on whether to build a formal or informal pond, first consider how it will look in your garden. Although the finished pond will undoubtedly form the centrepiece of your garden, do make sure that it blends in with your surroundings. Consider as many aspects as you can and take the time to study as many garden and landscape books and magazines as possible before you begin to plan the style of your pond. These will give you new ideas to add to any thoughts you may already have.

Try to choose materials that blend or contrast with any rockeries, walls or

Above: *A rectangular pond is relatively easy to design, construct and maintain. It creates a formal shape in the garden, but its hard edges can be effectively softened with suitable rockwork and planting.*

Below: *This is a fine example of an informal koi pond, complete with wooden decking over the filters, planted borders, pebble beach and Japanese stone lantern.*

paths already in your garden. Bear in mind, however, that very ornate finishes can be difficult and extremely costly to produce, and are also difficult to maintain. Try, therefore, to keep your designs and finishes as simple as possible – as the Japanese would say, 'simple is beautiful'.

Should you wish to concentrate solely on building up a collection of exhibition-class koi purely for the pleasure of viewing them in isolation, then the clinical 'hole-in-the-ground' type of pond should suit you admirably. However, while it might please you, consider the feelings of your future charges! Will your koi feel at home swimming around hour after weary hour in gin-clear water, unrelieved by any other form of life, lacking shelter from the sun, unable to rest for a while in the shade of water lily leaves, or to browse among the stalks of irises and other marginal plants? Before you make your final decision, contrast this scenario with the natural habitat of the carp family, to which koi belong. Their idea of heaven would be a muddy, heavily planted pond in which they could happily grub around searching for those succulent morsels of plant, crustacean and insect life which abound in that type of natural aquatic environment!

Obviously, for the hobbyist, such a 'natural' pond is totally impractical, but a semi-formal, planted pond with clear water does at least strike a happy medium, pleasing to the viewer as well as to the koi. Many people believe that koi and plants cannot live together satisfactorily, a belief which is quite incorrect. It is perfectly true that koi are extremely efficient plant destroyers, capable of uprooting well-established plants in their never-ending search for food but, provided that plants are correctly installed in koi-resistant planters, there is no reason why both should not flourish together in a well-organized koi pond.

What shape is best?

Having decided on the general style of your pond, the next question is: What shape should it be? Here, of course, a great deal depends on the space available and the surroundings that will form a backdrop to the finished pond. In addition, choosing a specific type of construction material will raise some immediate limitations on your options concerning shape. If you opt for one of the liner materials, the pond shape will be restricted to one in the range of square, rectangular, elliptical, oval, or round. The square and rectangular shapes can be ordered 'box welded', thus obviating the unsightly and dirt-gathering folds that bedevil liner ponds.

If you aspire to a more intricate shape of pond, then you will need to select an alternative method of construction. However, try to avoid designing a pond that is too complicated in shape. Although a pond of very irregular outline might look very attractive and natural, you could well run into difficulties with areas of 'dead' water, which will allow dirt to collect, encouraging the growth of anaerobic bacteria and the proliferation of disease organisms. Such stagnation can occur very easily in a very irregularly shaped pond, where it is difficult to ensure that water returning from the filtration system is mixed sufficiently with the water in the pond. This type of pond will also be more difficult to maintain and, more importantly, could create prob-lems if and when you need to catch the koi – for disease treatment, for example.

A surprising omission on the part of the majority of pond designers, particularly of larger ponds, is the use of an island in their design. Properly constructed, an island can really add the finishing touch to an otherwise very ordinary pond, especially when a nicely constructed bridge is incorporated. With a little thought and a tiny amount of extra plumbing, it is even possible to incorporate a small rockpool which cascades water back into the pond. An island should be located off centre in the pond, thereby creating a channel of faster flowing water that koi seem to enjoy. Of course, it is important to avoid making this channel an area of stagnant water.

Suitable pond shapes

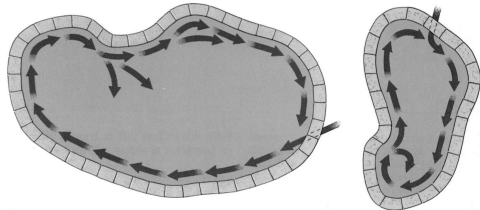

Above: *Large open designs such as this, and more formal squares and rectangles, are ideal for koi ponds. Sensibly placed, this design could include an island, as long as it does not create areas of 'dead water'.*

Above: *Even a relatively small pond can be fine for koi, as long as the water is deep enough and its flow is unobstructed. Even in rectangular ponds it is advisable to 'round' the corners for this purpose.*

Unsuitable pond shapes

→ Good Water flow

↯ Stagnant areas

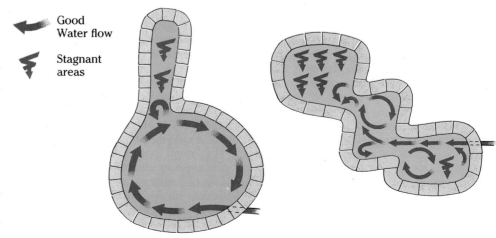

Above: *The narrow neck in this otherwise suitable design will invariably become an area of stagnant water 'marooned' from the water flow. This will ultimately affect the environmental quality of the whole pond.*

Above: *Complex shapes like this may look impressive in the garden but the dead ends and narrow channels create areas of stagnation and prevent thorough mixing of filtered water returning to the pond.*

POND AND FILTER CONSTRUCTION

Surface area of the pond

There is one golden rule to follow when deciding on the surface area of the pond; irrespective of shape, always aim for as great a surface area as possible. In so doing, you will obtain maximum air/water interface and oxygen absorption, oxygen being the life force in any water ecosystem. As an example, compare two ponds each with a surface area of $10m^2(1076ft^2)$, one of which is 2m(6.6ft) deep and the other 1m(3.3ft) deep. The first pond contains twice as much water as the second, yet both ponds are only able to absorb the same amount of oxygen from the atmosphere via the water surface. Thus, pond surface area is an extremely important consideration, and providing a larger volume of water is of no benefit without adequate surface area. (But consider this in relation to the advice on depth that follows.)

Depth of the pond

There are many differing opinions on the correct depth of water for successful koi-keeping, most of which have been based on empirical reasoning. Some koi-keepers have had resounding success with ponds only 1m(3.3ft) deep, but these are the exceptions rather than the rule, with climatic conditions and straightforward luck often playing a part. The majority of enthusiasts have ponds 2m(6.6ft) deep, and even 3m(10ft) deep, in some cases. In order to fully promote growth through exercise gained by swimming, deep water is certainly essential for koi, but just how deep is deep? Generally, you should consider 1.5m(5ft) as the minimum depth and 2.4m(8ft) as the optimum depth for a koi pond. (If you live in a climate that is not subject to lower temperatures, i.e. below 5°C(41°F), then such a deep pond may not be essential.) Any depth between 1.5 and 2m(5-6.6ft) is probably an acceptable compromise in most circumstances; depths in excess of this merely make life difficult during the excavating process and after completion, when pond maintenance and/or catching your koi can become problematical.

Another important consideration when deciding on the depth of your pond is that of temperature fluctuations. If there is one thing likely to distress koi, it is rapid changes in environmental temperature. The deeper your pond is in proportion to its surface area, the less susceptible it will be to temperature

Right: To calculate the volume (and therefore water capacity) of your pond at the design stage, consider it in terms of simple shapes and follow these guidelines.

Calculating approximate pond volume

Simple rectangular shapes

Calculating the volume of a square or rectangular pond is simply a matter of multiplying the length x width x depth (in metres) to produce the volume in cubic metres (m^3), which is equivalent to the weight of water in tonnes. To convert the volume into litres, multiply this figure by 1000. To convert litres to US gallons, multiply by 0.26; to convert litres to Imp. gallons, multiply the figure by 0.22.

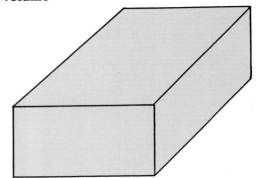

Ponds with shelved areas

The easiest way to calculate the volume of a pond with a shelf is to treat the shelf section and the remaining pond section as two separate portions. Thus, use the above formula to calculate the volume of each of the rectangles and add the results together.

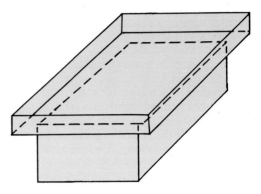

Shapes with a benched bottom

Here, we consider ponds with angled sides in the bottom section. Let's assume for simplicity that the angle is 45°. Calculate the volume of the main rectangular body of the pond using the formula in the first example. Next, consider the centre section along the bottom as another rectangle and treat it in the same way. Then, add the two opposite triangular sections together as a long thin rectangle and add the volume of this to the volume of the other two sections. Also, do the same for the triangular sections running across the width of the pond at each end – not shown here. For simplicity, these calculations do not include the small triangular sections at each bottom corner.

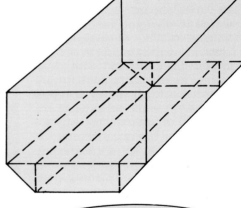

Straight-sided circular shapes

Here we need to introduce a new formula to calculate the surface area. This is radius squared (i.e. half the diameter multiplied by itself) x 3.14 (which is an approximate value for π). If the pond is straight sided and has a constant depth, multiply the surface area by the depth to calculate the volume.

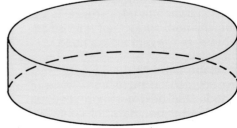

Conical shapes

Tapering sides are found on many koi ponds and so it may be necessary to estimate the volume of a conical shape. The shape shown here is not a cone but simply has a bottom area smaller than the surface area. In this case, calculate the average radius of the two circles by adding them together and dividing by two and use this in the calculation given above.

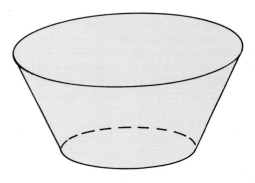

fluctuations. Bear in mind that, even in warm climates, temperatures can fall dramatically overnight, severely chilling shallow ponds, and this may be followed by a rapid rise to very high temperatures the following day. Koi should not be subjected to fluctuations of more than 1-3°C(2-5°F) in a 24-hour period. The larger the volume of water, the slower the dissipation of heat loss into the surrounding ground, but remember that heat loss will be higher if the surface area is larger. Thus, the chill factor of a 1m-deep pond will be twice as great as that of a 2m-deep one, even if both hold the same volume of water. At a water depth of 1.5m(5ft) or more, temperature changes are insignificant, whatever the ambient air temperature. During a hot spell of weather, the temperature in a deep pond will rise, but only slowly, causing no distress. The reverse applies in cold weather, again with no ill-effects.

In very deep water, such as is found in natural lakes, a phenomenon known as a thermocline develops. This is the level below which no variation of temperature takes place whatever the surface air temperature. To a lesser degree, a similar state of affairs exists in a koi pond, where temperature changes reduce as depth increases. (The exception to this rule is the situation when water is being removed from the pond bottom for filtration, when surface and bottom temperatures will eventually almost equalize.) A simple way of appreciating the impact of ambient temperature upon a pond is to consider it as a giant storage heater, being slow to both gain and lose heat in response to external influences.

Shallow ponds not only offer an unstable environment in terms of temperature, but they can also affect the koi's security, preventing them from escaping from a potential threat. How often have you seen skittish koi in confined shallow ponds darting about and probably damaging themselves in the process? Shallow ponds, especially those with ledges, also create a perfect feeding place for the domestic koi's largest predator – the heron. Try to avoid building such inviting feeding haunts into your design; if they have easy access to a food supply, herons and other predators will continue to visit a pond until the supply runs out. If, however, the pond creates dangers for them and they are unable to take food easily, they will soon move on to easier opportunities, leaving you and your koi in peace.

Koi, like most animals, need exercise to maintain their muscle tone and body shape. They achieve this by swimming vertically in the pond, not horizontally.

Where vertical swimming is restricted, koi become fat, and such effects are often seen in koi that have been kept in shallow ponds for long periods. The higher water pressure found at depth is also important to koi for maintaining their shape.

Pond and filter capacity

Working out the surface area, volume and capacity of your pond is essential to enable you to choose the correct size of filter, set stocking levels and establish effective dosages for treating the pond against disease and parasites. The formulae and estimating techniques described in the panel will help you to arrive at these figures before you start work on constructing the pond. Of course, deviations will occur in the building process – even minor changes will alter your initial results – but getting close to the final expected capacity will at least enable you to arrive at the all-important figure for the capacity of the filter system that you will be planning in parallel with the pond.

We will be considering the selection and design of filters later in this chapter.

Right: *With the cover removed, it is clear that the capacity of this filter is at least one third the size of the pond it serves. This is the ideal minimum ratio between filter and pond, and applies for either internal or external filters. A filter cannot be too big.*

Below: *The same pond photographed from a different angle with the filter covered up with wooden decking. This rectangular koi pond measures 5.2x2.4x1.5m deep (17x8x5ft) and contains about 30 koi of various sizes. Its capacity is about 19m³.*

At this point in the planning process, it is a good idea to apply the general rule of allowing space for your filter equivalent to one third of the surface area of the proposed pond. In other words, a pond with a surface area of 15m² requires a filter with a surface area of 5m². This general rule applies equally for external and internal filters and should be regarded as a minimum. In Japan, some hobbyists actually go as far as having filter systems as large as the ponds they serve. Certainly, you need not be concerned over building too large a filter; quite the opposite as, where koi pond filters are concerned, big is beautiful!

Confirming how much water your pond and associated systems hold on completion is a simple matter of hiring a flowmeter when you first fill them up.

POND AND FILTER CONSTRUCTION

Selecting a site

Having finalized the design of your pond, your next objective must be to choose a suitable site in which to install it. Deciding on a position will depend on several factors, including its proposed size and style, and the decision must be a balance between common sense and prudence. Be prepared to compromise, because it is only very seldom that what you want and what you can have will coincide. The chances are that on the very spot that you would like to locate your pond there is a sewer inspection cover, a telegraph pole, or even a block of concrete supporting your washing line! Such things are sent to try you! And when you start digging, also be prepared to find that your chosen site also proved attractive to the builder of your house as a dump for all his surplus materials and rubbish! Forewarned is forearmed!

Also consider the safety angle when planning the position of your pond, particularly where young children are concerned. You may need to put up a strong fence and a gate with a substantial lock to keep inquisitive children at bay (see the pond shown on page 27). It is worth noting here that a shallow pond is not necessarily any safer than a deep one, as children can fall in and knock themselves out on the hard bottom of a shallow pond. And remember, too, that small children who can swim are just as much at risk when they instinctively panic.

Above: *This square pond enjoys an open setting with a boundary along one edge. A planting scheme based on low-growing conifers allows easy access to the pond, an unobstructed view and few problems from leaves, making maintenance an easy task.*

Buildings, walls and fences

Ideally, your pond should be easily viewed from the house but should not be located closer than 3m(10ft) to the building to avoid disturbing the integrity of the property. If you do want to build nearer than this, you should take professional advice. In fact, consider this 'safety margin' as applying to any wall or fence near the pond. This distance will also allow ample 'walking round space' for maintenance of your pond, something often overlooked until it is too late.

If you cannot avoid siting your pond in a position where the full force of the prevailing wind strikes it, then do consider installing some form of windbreak, such as a trellis fence or screen block wall, or even a row of slow-growing conifers upwind of, and not too close to, the pond. A solid wall type of barrier, such as a close-boarded fence, would be quite useless, as this would simply create turbulence on its leeward side and not break up the wind pattern and reduce its velocity as would pierced blocks or a hedge.

Trees

Consider carefully before building a pond close to trees. Trees have various types of root structure, and siting a pond close to a tree with spreading roots could cause considerable problems. The classic and graceful weeping willow, for example, loves water and its rooting system can travel 20m(65ft) or more, and will break through the side of a pond with the greatest of ease! Not only may tree roots affect the finished pond, but if you damage an existing tree's roots during the construction process, the tree may become unsafe and fall into your pond or, worse still, onto your house or an adjoining property. So, if you are obliged to build close to an existing tree, be sure to establish what sort of root structure it has before you start digging.

If you are starting with a bare site, the best advice is to avoid planting trees close to the pond from the outset. Everyone has a mental picture of a garden pond surrounded by lawns and with a tree or two languourously dangling over the limpid water. After a few sessions of clearing leaves, branch tips – even cones – from the water, plus dredging out grass clippings every time the lawn is cut, this idyllic picture quickly loses its attractions! Compromise must be the order of the day; you will be just as happy with a few less vigorous shrubs and a garden seat strategically positioned on a 'buffer zone' of patio slabs. Needless to say, there are certain circumstances where leaf fall simply has to be tolerated, such as when your neighbour has several

trees, the leaves of which inevitably blow in the direction of your garden. In such cases, all one can do is to grin and bear it rather than start a mini-war by requesting the removal of the offending objects!

Surveying the site

Once you have decided on the style and size of your new pond and its position in the garden, you will need to carry out a detailed survey to establish the levels and actual position of the pond and any external equipment, such as filtration systems and standpipe chambers.

While marking out positions is a simple operation, establishing levels may be an unfamiliar and somewhat daunting task. If you are unsure about this aspect, take professional advice to avoid difficulties later on. If you are using the services of a pond builder, they will have all the necessary levelling equipment and will carry out the survey for you. If you intend to do the job yourself, you should be able to pick up what you need from a local hire shop.

Whatever levelling technique you use, you will need an accurate, long tape measure, a club hammer and a supply of wooden stakes (say 38mm/1.5in square) of various lengths from 30cm(12in) up to 1m(39in). Mark out and measure the pond shape and size using the wooden stakes; you may find that you need to do this a few times before you position the stakes correctly. Then do the same for any externally sited equipment. Once you have completed this procedure, stand back and make sure you have created what you had in mind. If you are considering an informal pond, it will help to trace out the shape on the ground using a length of hose.

If you want to be absolutely precise, when you are 'staking out' your pond, measure the distance between your first stake and a convenient fixed point (technically known as a datum), such as the edge of a wall, and then record the positions of the remaining stakes in relation to each other. Making a note of this will enable you to reposition any stakes that become misplaced.

The next stage is to establish the levels of the ground. If you have an extensive site and you contemplate building a large pond, you may consider doing this the 'professional' way by using a surveyor's level of some kind. A dumpy level is ideal. This consists simply of a bubble tube (for levelling the device) and a telescope (for sighting). A calibrated staff will be supplied with the equipment and you can use this to read off different heights. To carry out the survey, first set up a tripod in a suitable position, where you can see all areas of the pond and other sited equipment, and mount the levelling device on top. Use the bubble tube to set the device level. The first task is to establish a datum height. This can be the first marker, but a fixed object, such as a wall, would be better, just in case a peg is accidentally moved or knocked out of the ground. Sight through the lens towards the staff (held vertically by a willing assistant) and establish the reading to give you your datum height. Use a chalk to mark this datum position on the staff for future use and write it down on a table. Make sure you keep the staff upright when taking these sightings, otherwise you will obtain false readings. You can now proceed to establish the heights at all your peg positions and record the difference compared to your datum height. Keep this data sheet safe – you will need it when you are drawing up the detailed design of the pond system and to establish levels during construction.

A simpler method of establishing levels over long distances is to use a hosepipe with a funnel attached to each end. Fill the hose with water and adjust the funnels until the water reaches the brim of each funnel, indicating that they are level with each other. Then measure the distance from each funnel to the ground below. Ensure that one funnel stays in the same position (as a datum) and only move the other funnel, otherwise you will obtain a false reading. (Alternatively, use a clear plastic hose so that you can see the water level inside and align the meniscus with a mark.)

The most (literally) 'down to earth' way of establishing levels, and one which is ideal at the building stage, is to use an accurate spirit level and a straight edge (or a series of both) to check the level between the tops of pegs driven into the ground short distances apart. We will see how this technique works in practice on page 38, under *Preparing to build*.

The basic principles involved in the above surveying processes are reflected in the panel shown below. This has been a very brief explanation of what is an extremely important stage in designing and installing a koi pond. If you have any doubts about your own abilities in this respect, be sure to seek expert advice rather than make unfortunate errors.

Establishing ground conditions

Before you decide on the type of construction, you will need to establish the ground conditions. These vary considerably; the ground may be clay, flint, sand, rock, or a combination of two or more of these natural substrates.

A high water table can also be a problem; you may dig down just a few centimetres and find water. This can become an almost impossible hurdle to overcome. If you have a stream or natural pond in your garden or close by, you can assume that the water table is fairly high

Using a surveyor's level

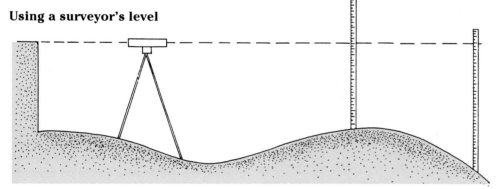

Using surveying equipment to establish levels may seem complex, but the general principles involved are very simple. To use a dumpy level – literally a sighting telescope levelled on a tripod – establish a datum height on a nearby fixed object, such as a wall, by holding up the calibrated staff and sighting through the telescope. Mark this height on the staff using chalk and then ask someone to hold the staff vertically at various locations and mark the staff at the line of sight. The difference between the datum and each location height shows how the levels vary. Keep a table of results.

Using a water-filled hosepipe

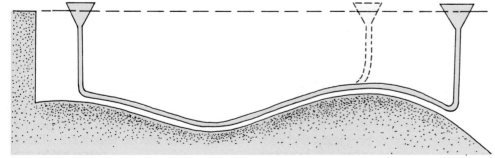

This method makes use of the purely physical property of liquids finding their own level. You can use a clear hosepipe and check the level against a mark on the pipe or, as here, fit funnels at each end and check for these being full up to the brim. The method again involves setting up a datum height and keeping one end of the hose in a fixed position while the other end is taken to various locations around the site. Measuring the distance from the brimming funnel to the ground provides a series of comparative heights around the site.

Using pegs, spirit levels and straight edges

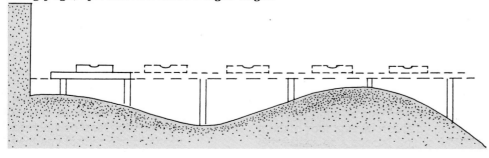

Using a spirit level is perhaps the most familiar way of checking levels. Try to buy or borrow a good-quality, long spirit level (ideally two) of the type builders use and arm yourself with an assortment of sturdy wooden pegs of various lengths, plus some straight and true pieces of hardwood. Drive in the first peg with its top at the desired height, and using the straight edges and spirit levels, set out a series of pegs with their tops at the same level as the first. Allow for a peg every 30cm(12in) for accuracy. You may need to flatten bumps.

POND AND FILTER CONSTRUCTION

(i.e. close to the surface), although this may vary at different times of the year. If you live at the top of a hill, however, it is highly unlikely that ground water will cause you any problems. In any case, it is best to assume nothing until you have checked the ground conditions yourself and are satisfied that you are safe to proceed with the excavation.

The best method to ascertain the ground conditions is to use a hand sampler, or auger, (basically, a large 'corkscrew' device that removes a plug of earth for examination). These are normally available from a plant hire shop. Alternatively, just make sample excavations near the centre of the proposed pond. Removing two or three spadefuls of earth from around the site gives a better knowledge of the conditions prevailing, preferably to the full planned depth of the pond, but this is not always possible.

If you do find a high water table, coping with it will create extra cost, since you may need to use special equipment in order to prevent the excavation continuously filling up with ground water. The cheapest, and easiest, method of removing ground water is to hire a large mechanical pump that can cope with sludge. Connect this to a pipe and discharge the water as far away from the excavation as possible. This method has its disadvantages, however. If the flow is fairly fast and the ground is of a light substrate, such as sand or gravel, or very heavy, like clay, the side walls of the excavation may collapse, which will create further problems and may be dangerous. A second, though considerably more expensive method, is to freeze the ground. This is achieved with a compressor and spiked probes, which are driven into the ground around the pond edges and act in a very similar way to a domestic refrigerator. Once the ground has frozen, a barrier is created to inhibit the flow of water into the excavation.

Providing services
You will need to allow in your design for the provision of services, such as electrical power, mains water and drainage. (Of course, you will also need to discover the location of existing services before you start excavating.) While you can be flexible with regard to the route taken by electricity supply cables and mains water pipework, the positioning of the pond and filter drain plumbing must be governed by the accessibility of your nearest sewer inspection chamber. To ensure that pond bottom drains operate at maximum efficiency, the outlets must enter the sewer at the lowest point pos-

sible, i.e. at the base of a sewer inspection chamber. Should you not have an inspection chamber or sewer within easy distance of your proposed pond, you have a problem. In that case, do not be tempted into thinking that a rubble-filled sump will suffice as an alternative; it won't! A surprising amount of 'muck' is washed out of a pond each time a bottom drain is operated, and this would quickly render a sump useless. You would be well advised to omit a bottom drain(s) and to rely on a vacuum system for cleaning the pond. The waste can then be piped to wherever there is access to your sewer system.

With regard to pipework, nothing detracts from the overall visual impact of a pond than a conglomeration of visible pipework and cables. In a properly designed pond, there should be nothing visible in the way of pipework, apart from the vertical air intake of a venturi and the overflow/skimmer outlet.

When considering a supply of mains water for pond cleaning and topping up purposes, it is much more acceptable to have a dedicated separate supply permanently installed, which can usually be obtained by plumbing a 'tee' into the supply for an outside tap. This type of installation has the benefit of being easily fitted with a de-chlorination cartridge, together with a spraybar injection system to 'gas off' any small amount of residual chlorine remaining. Such a system is much neater and much less trouble than using a hosepipe for every maintenance. Do check with your local water supply company to ensure that you comply with local byelaws, and there will probably be a small annual fee to pay.

Unless you are suitably qualified or experienced, do not tackle the electrics yourself. It is much safer to consult an electrician in the early stages, who will advise on suitable cables and assist with planning a route for your cable. Do not be tempted to merely plug your pond electrical apparatus into the nearest socket. Remember that water and electricity form an extremely dangerous combination. It is important – and legally required in many countries – to fit a residual current circuit breaker to the electrical circuit. Such a device will automatically switch off the current in a matter of milliseconds should anyone touch a live part of the circuit. (We look at this aspect again at the building stage.)

Choosing building materials
Possibly the most important decision you will make during the design stage is the choice of building material. Every material has advantages and dis-

advantages, depending upon your point of view. If at all possible, do not be influenced by the question of cost. Far better to spend a little more and take slightly longer over the construction, and end up with a pool that delights you, rather than to go for a lower cost option that will always be a cause for regret! As for the materials, all you can do is read the following descriptions, make comparisons, weigh the pros and cons, and come to your own conclusions.

Precast ponds
Probably the simplest, although not the cheapest, size-for-size pond you can 'build' can be obtained ready made in glass-reinforced plastic. These are available in a range of sizes and shapes, and, can be installed at ground level, partially above or fully above ground level. They come fully finished apart from the fitting of services. They are excellent in their own way, but, of course, you are limited to the chosen shape of pond. Where space is limited, one of these precast ponds could well fill the bill. Be sure to choose one that is deep enough for keeping koi (see the recommendations about depth on page 26).

Liners
The liner is far and above the most popular material used in the construction of ornamental ponds. The principal advantage in using a liner is undoubtedly the time factor; a liner pool is quite capable of being completed over a weekend – if sufficient labour is available.

What liner materials are suitable? Polythene sheeting is not suitable, as many would-be builders have found to their regret! Not only is polythene fragile, it also degrades rapidly under exposure to sunlight. It is fine for use as an underlining 'skin', but nothing else. There are a

Above: *This is a sample of the butyl rubber sheeting widely used to line ponds. This example is 0.75mm(0.030in) thick and will provide a service life in excess of 20 years. Black is an ideal colour for koi ponds.*

number of proprietary liner materials available, most of them based around PVC (poly vinyl chloride), some of which have woven nylon reinforcement and offer colour variations. These are reputed to have a service life of between five and ten years, which is a relatively short timespan.

Butyl rubber is undoubtedly the best material for use as a liner, but, of course, it is much more expensive. For a square or rectangular pond, butyl liners can be supplied 'box welded' to fit the buyer's measurements, which must be accurate. The heavier grades of butyl have a reputed life of up to 50 years, even the standard grades being good for 20 years.

This material is ideal for the type of pond desired by koi-keepers who are not interested in the idea of incorporating plants or interesting contours into their ponds. Butyl can be used for informal ponds, but suffers from the disadvantage of being unable to accommodate curves without forming pleats and folds, which can be a nuisance by collecting dirt and mulm at a remarkable rate, in addition to being unsightly. Fitting service outlets and flanges, etc., is relatively simple, although it is vital to take great care to ensure that the various holes are accurately positioned.

Once filled, a butyl liner pond will not take kindly to any stress the weight of water might place on the material around an inaccurately positioned pipe flange. It can be most offputting to find the liner has torn through this cause! There have also been cases where the family dog has fallen into the pond and, in its panic-striken struggle to escape, has literally shredded the liner. Another disadvantage with liner ponds is that the inevitable growth of algae or blanketweed cannot be scraped off, and vacuuming is also a problem, as the liner tends to be sucked onto the end of the vacuum tube in the process. Nevertheless, despite all its apparent shortcomings, the liner remains in the forefront of a long list of pond building materials and is certainly worth considering.

Fibreglass
Well known among the pleasure boats and yachting fraternity, fibreglass is being increasingly used as a finishing coat on concrete ponds. Unfortunately, it is appallingly messy to apply, and one can only recommend that the application be left to a professional company! Successive layers of glass matting and resins are applied, building up to a thickness of approximately 5mm(0.2in), with a final coloured gel coat, preferably black, finishing the job. Correctly carried out,

Above: *Applying resin to a layer of fibreglass matting in a large commercially built koi pond. The resulting layer of bonded fibreglass provides an excellent, if expensive, lining. The final coloured coat should be black or dark green.*

the fibreglass pond is probably the ultimate attainment, giving infinite durability, colossal strength and, in the event of a crack developing in the concrete, simple to repair by means of patching.

As it is apparently so good, why don't we all use it? The short answer is that it is expensive, being more than double the price of the concrete pond to which it is applied! However, an ingenious technique may well signal the end of the price barrier! Specialist companies are now able to spray simultaneous jets of fibres and resins straight onto a suitable excavation, thereby eliminating the pre-coating building work. Using this system, the most exotic pond shapes are obtainable and the fibreglass pond is well worth consideration!

Concrete
For the average DIY builder without funds available for the more exotic materials, concrete must be the best choice. It has to be admitted that, in the past, concrete ponds have gained a bad reputation for springing leaks and developing cracks. Nowadays, however, thanks again to advancing technology, these problems are a thing of the past. The secret lies in the use of tiny plastic fibres added to the concrete and rendering mix which enable the mix to contain a much higher proportion of cement powder.

Once the chemical reaction with water has taken place, cement alone is a very strong material but, in drying, tiny hairline cracks develop, weakening the finished product. Sand is added in various proportions in order to reduce

the shrinkage as the concrete dries, but the result is a fairly porous and relatively weak product. By adding fibres, the proportion of sand can be reduced dramatically and the concrete or rendering has incredible strength once it has dried. It is impermeable to water and, most important for pond use, is highly resistant to damage by frost.

Building a concrete pond now merely consists of laying a floor of lean concrete, erecting dense concrete blockwalls and rendering the whole thing with a 5mm(0.2in)-thick coat consisting of two parts sand and one part cement plus the fibres mixture. The resulting pond is long lasting and very cost effective when compared to other methods. Coupled with the fact that almost any shape and contour is possible in concrete, this type of building material must be a very strong contender!

Choosing pipework
The suppliers of high-pressure PVC/ABS pipe are likely to advise you that only this pipe will withstand the continuous pressure of water remaining within it i.e. rather than simply flushing through it. They may dissuade you from using domestic-grade plastic pipe because it simply isn't up to the job. Even encasing in concrete may not guarantee its integrity, since the concrete may crack and allow water leaking from a fractured pipe to escape. The conclusion of this line of reasoning is that, yes, pressure pipework and its associated fittings are expensive, but so are your koi. Something you may reflect upon when you discover them high and dry in an empty pond.

The converse argument weighted from the DIY point of view is that in the average pond and filter pipework arrangement, the head or pressure encountered will be well within the handling capabilities of ordinary domestic soil pipe, which is available in 10cm and 15cm (4in and 6in) diameters, the orange-brown variety being suitable for in-ground use. The rubber seals which are an integral part of the fittings used with this piping form a leaktight union and have the advantage of being easily removable should you find during assembly that your measurements are incorrect. With solvent-welded, high-pressure pipe, getting it wrong can be an expensive mistake.

The golden rule is to ask around for advice. What you hear may save you spending out unnecessarily on expensive pipework or, conversely, persuade you that saving money in the short term will only lead to inevitable disaster in the future. (In the building section, we explain how to use both types of pipework.)

POND AND FILTER CONSTRUCTION

Designing for water

Here, we look at the design aspects concerned with water and the movement of water, starting, appropriately enough, with bottom drains.

Bottom drains

Bottom drain filtration is probably the most underestimated of filtration and pond cleaning systems. Remember that your pond is the biggest settlement chamber you have and a considerable amount of debris will collect on the bottom, including leaves from surrounding trees, dust, fish waste and uneaten food from within the system.

Bottom drains take the heavier, 'dead' water and debris from the bottom of the pond to a separate chamber, where it is either passed through the filtration system or discharged into the main drainage system. Recirculating bottom water through the filter is only recommended when the stocking level of the pond is low and you want the nitrifying bacteria in the filter system to obtain as much 'food' i.e. nitrogenous wastes, as possible. When stocking levels are high, the water should be released through a valve or standpipe to a drainage system.

To be really effective, it is essential to scallop the bottom of the pond and position the drains in the centre of these dished areas, which help to guide dirt and mulm into the drains. Many people make the mistake of installing bottom drains on a flat surface, and even drains installed above the lowest point in the pond are not unknown!

How many bottom drains should you install? Here, again, the answer is influenced by what is financially and/or practically acceptable to you. In practice, the more bottom drains you install, the better your overall filtration/cleaning will be. On a 'money-no-object' basis, you should aim to incorporate a bottom

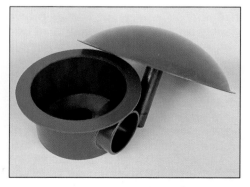

Above: *A bottom drain fitment suitable for a concrete or fibreglass pond. The drain is set into the concrete foundations and rendered or fibreglassed up to the lip. The domed 'lid' shown alongside fits into the recess in the base, leaving a gap around the edge.*

Using valves to switch filter feeds

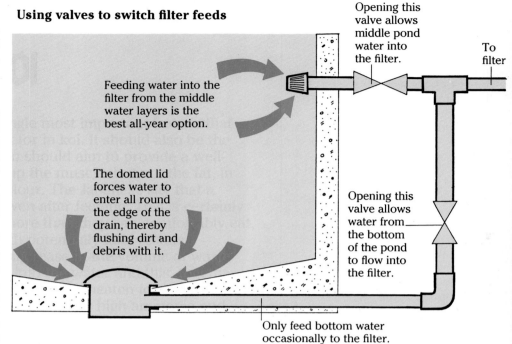

Opening this valve allows middle pond water into the filter.

To filter

Feeding water into the filter from the middle water layers is the best all-year option.

The domed lid forces water to enter all round the edge of the drain, thereby flushing dirt and debris with it.

Opening this valve allows water from the bottom of the pond to flow into the filter.

Only feed bottom water occasionally to the filter.

drain every 1.5-2m (5-6.6ft), i.e. the centres of each dished area should be this distance apart. By this reckoning, a koi pond measuring 6x3m(20x10ft) should have eight bottom drains. Obviously, this is not always possible. In financial terms, it would add a very large amount to the cost of your pond, as each bottom drain requires a dedicated length of pipe and a separate 'pull tube' or ball valve. (If you connect two drains to a common outlet, remember that the effective suction 'pulling power' of each drain is halved.) A more 'economical' suggestion would be to avoid having bottom drain centres more than 3m(10ft) apart. On this basis, in an average pond of $14m^3$ capacity (approximately 3080 Imp. gallons/3640 US gallons), one bottom drain should be adequate, with an additional drain recommended for each further $10m^3$(2200/2600 gallons) of planned pond capacity.

If you do not install bottom drains, or have not installed enough to cope adequately with your pond, you will need to vacuum the bottom of the pond regularly to avoid build-up of waste, using either a hand vacuum or electric pump with vacuum attachments. You will also need to make regular water changes – in practice, a daunting and very time-consuming task.

Helping water flow

When deciding on the shape of your pond, you will need to think about how water flows within it. Water will flow in a straight line until either it loses momentum and velocity and becomes stagnant,

Above: *How a system of valves can be used to divert either middle or bottom water into the filter. Opinions vary, but it seems advisable to use middle water most of the time, with the occasional use of bottom water when the filter is bacterially 'low'.*

Below: *Bottom drains and their associated high-pressure pipework in place during the construction of a large commercial koi pond. Each drain has its own dedicated pipe leading to the standpipe chamber.*

or until its direction is changed by other influences, such as other moving water currents or a fixed structure, such as the pond wall. Obviously, if it hits a flat wall at 90°, its momentum and velocity are reduced significantly, as the water is displaced in 360° from the point of impact. If, however, it strikes the pond wall at a shallow angle then the water is deflected in the same direction as the flow, albeit at a reduced velocity. Therefore, if all corners of the pond are radiused, or 'faired out', velocity losses will be greatly reduced. (There are frictional losses as

Above: *The radiused, or 'faired', corners of this koi pond help to promote good water flow – an important design feature that pays dividends when the pond is fully stocked and operational. Such shapes mimic the rounded contours of natural watercourses.*

Right: *In the sides of this professionally built koi pond under construction, the filter feeds are positioned at different heights and locations, providing a variety of options for taking pond water into the chambers of the external filter system, shown on page 35.*

the water rubs along the wall of the pond and as it shears on slower moving water, but we will ignore these.) So, when designing your pond, always allow for 'faired corners'.

Vertical movement and pond returns

As we saw earlier, ponds with narrow necks are unsuitable, as they inhibit water flow and create eddying currents, leaving stagnation points. Vertical motion of the water is also important. Most ponds are constructed with shallow water returns (pumped water is returned either at the surface or just below it). But where ponds exceed 1.2m(4ft) in depth, deep water returns are advisable if there are no waterfalls to create downcurrents. This is because water returning to the pond at, or near, the surface will shear, leaving deeper water reliant on movement from bottom drains. A deep-water return will allow control of water movement deeper in the pond.

The number of returns to a pond should be proportional to its volume and surface area. For example, a pond measuring 3x1.5x1.5m deep (10x5x5ft), with a capacity of $6.75m^3$, would need only one return, while a pond 9x4.5x2.4m deep (30x15x8ft), with a capacity of $97.2m^3$, would need two or three surface returns plus a waterfall, or one or two deep-water returns. You should be able to control these by using a valved bypass. This would be used to turn off the deep water returns in winter, when pond temperatures drop and koi become inactive. (Any fast-flowing, deep-water returns would disturb the koi and use up their reserve energy, weakening them when they are unable to feed, see also page 78.)

Filter feeds

Filter feeds must be considered during the pond design stage, since, depending upon the type of filter feed you choose, you must allow for the pipe runs in the plan. There has been much argument as to the various advantages and disadvantages of using pond middle water or bottom water for feeding a filter. There can be no doubt that the optimum solution is to have the option to use either, exerting control by means of valves. In order to accommodate the necessary valves, etc., be sure to allow for a suitably sized valve chamber and consider carefully the layout of piping needed to make the system operate efficiently. During the cold winter months, feed middle water to your filter, thereby avoiding any chilling of the deeper parts of the pond. During the summer months, you can choose to valve off the middle water outlet and feed bottom water to your filter. In line with our comments under *Bottom drains* on page 32, however, we recommend that water from the bottom drain is only fed to the filter occasionally when the nitrifying bacteria population is low. In effect, it is quite acceptable to use middle water all year round.

Of course, you may wish to consider using a vortex chamber as the first stage in your filter chain. Feeding water from the bottom drain into the top part of such a chamber sets up a spinning current that allows the sludge to fall to the base, where it can be run off to waste, while the 'cleaner' water in the uppermost layers is fed into the filter proper. Such chambers, although expensive, do offer a solution to clogging problems that may arise when using bottom drain water as a filter feed.

Watercourses and waterfalls

One of the most attractive features of a properly designed koi pond is undoubtedly the spectacle of moving water. If space permits, consider fitting a watercourse between your filter outlet and the point of re-entry to the pond. In addition to the visual impact of a stream, the ecological benefits to the natural balance of the pond are considerable. Planted out with suitable plant life – watercress is ideal – the stream becomes an extension of the filter system, finishing off the purification process carried out in the filter. A waterfall is also a very important part of any water ecosystem, adding as it does much needed oxygen to the water. But beware of creating excessive noise; complaining neighbours may compel you to switch off a noisy waterfall at night, at the very time when oxygen demand is at its highest! (See page 51 for more details.)

Above: *In a small corner of a grander scheme, a waterfall not only provides a focal point but also helps to keep the water aerated as it flows from one pond to another. Such an attractive and beneficial water feature should be part of every pond.*

POND AND FILTER CONSTRUCTION

Filter design

Many newcomers to koi-keeping imagine that the function of filtering the koi pond is merely to obtain clear water in which to view the fish. In fact, the clarity aspect is of secondary importance. The primary object of filtration is to enable the pond to support a greater number of fish than would be possible in an unfiltered pond, by removing the toxic end products of the natural bodily processes that take place within the fish. Even a dozen large koi occupying a relatively small pond will, in the course of 24 hours, excrete a considerable amount of waste. Ammonia and other toxic chemicals will quickly build up to a point where the fish will suffocate on their own waste, unless these toxins are continuously converted into less harmful products.

We discuss filtration from the biochemical point of view in *Water quality and filtration*, starting on page 48. Here, we look at the 'nuts and bolts' of filter design, including both ready-made systems and the DIY alternatives.

Internal (undergravel) filtration

Although very popular at one time, undergravel filters are no longer regarded as an efficient means of filtration and should only be considered as a last resort when lack of space precludes the use of external types. In its simplest form, an internal filter consists of a matrix of pipework laid on the floor of the pond and covered with a layer of gravel ranging from 25 to 50cm (10-20in) deep depending upon the size and type of gravel used. (As a rough guide, use 25cm of 6mm(0.25in) gravel or 50cm of 15mm(0.6in) gravel.) A pump attached to one end of the pipe matrix pulls water down through the media, where debris is trapped and biological action strips the toxins from the water before it returns to the pond.

When first matured, this type of filter is undoubtedly very efficient, but it suffers from the inescapable drawback of area 'blocking' caused by a build-up of heavy solid waste products and the formation of colonies of anaerobic bacteria. Raking the gravel surface is only a short-term remedy, as the dislodged solids will merely settle elsewhere and start the process all over again. After perhaps two years in service, an internal filter will also prove disappointing because continual digging by koi leads to heavily 'coloured' water loaded with suspended solids. In most cases, your only option will be to remove your fish to a holding tank while you dig out and wash perhaps a couple of tonnes of extremely dirty gravel – a back-breaking and unpleasant task that will do you and your koi no good at all, thanks to the upheaval involved.

Should you be unable to avoid using an undergravel filter, then ideally your pond should be flat bottomed or, preferably, the filter can be contained within a walled-off area of the pond. In either case, the filter area should be approximately one third the pond surface area.

Use piping of a minimum diameter of 38mm(1.5in) – plastic domestic plumbing pipework is fine – and construct the matrix of pipework in such a way as to ensure maximum drawdown through the media. Once the matrix is assembled, drill 5mm(0.2in) holes throughout the length of the matrix at approximately 40mm(1.6in) centres along the piping.

Above: *A hobbyist's pipe matrix in place on the filter bed section of a liner pond. It is important to design the grid so that water is drawn down evenly over the whole area. This will prevent channels developing in some parts of the gravel bed.*

Ideally, drill these holes on the underside of the pipes at the 4 o'clock and 8 o'clock positions. Put the matrix in position and cover it with a sheet of plastic mesh with 12mm(0.5in) apertures – this will slow down the clogging process – and then spread gravel to an even depth over the whole area. You can use either 'sharp' or 'smooth' gravel, but ensure that the particle size does not exceed 15mm(0.6in).

As with any filter, do not switch off an undergravel filter for more than 12 hours, otherwise the oxygen-dependent nitrifying bacteria will start to die and you will end up with a serious pollution problem.

External filters

Although external filtration systems are considerably more expensive to build and more complicated in their construction, they are far more effective and maintainable. Although they, too, may be

A typical undergravel (internal) filter

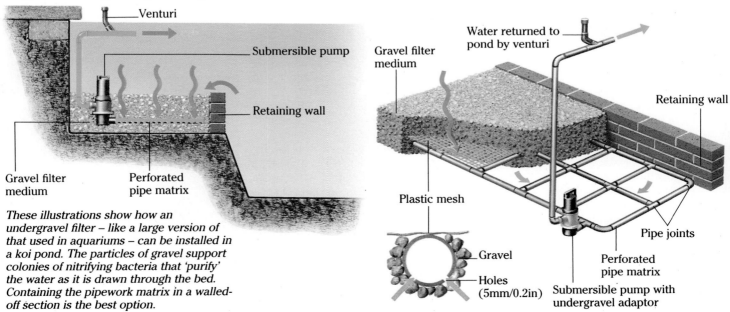

Venturi

Submersible pump

Retaining wall

Gravel filter medium

Perforated pipe matrix

These illustrations show how an undergravel filter – like a large version of that used in aquariums – can be installed in a koi pond. The particles of gravel support colonies of nitrifying bacteria that 'purify' the water as it is drawn through the bed. Containing the pipework matrix in a walled-off section is the best option.

Gravel filter medium

Water returned to pond by venturi

Retaining wall

Plastic mesh

Gravel

Holes (5mm/0.2in)

Pipe joints

Perforated pipe matrix

Submersible pump with undergravel adaptor

Right: *This represents a typical example of a single-chamber, external filter fed with water from a submersible pump. In some designs, the water flows upwards.*

Pump-fed external filter

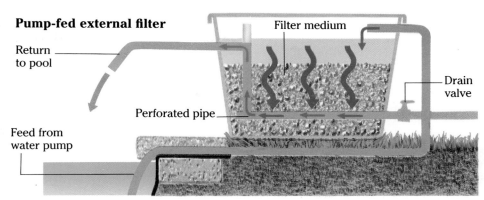

Filter medium

Return to pool

Feed from water pump

Perforated pipe

Drain valve

susceptible to blocking, the time involved in back-flushing to clean them is minimal in comparison to the internal system. Draining debris is simple and analyzing water quality and condition is easy. Taking all things into consideration, an external filter is by far the best option, and it is worth considering this type of system, even if you have to opt for a smaller pond to keep within your original budget limits.

External filters fall into two main groups, those which are pump fed and those fed by gravity.

Pump-fed external filters

There are a number of small, single 'tank' filters available commercially which use a variety of systems and medias to achieve the same aim, that of producing pure water. You should be prepared to accept the premise that when a large body of water requires filtering, there is no way that a small tank containing media of whatever type will be capable of doing the job properly. Having said this, there is every possibility that a system using multiples of these miniature units could be assembled into an effective system. Problems may arise with the plumbing, however, as the majority of these types of filter are pump fed, the water entering at the top and percolating down through the medium (or having reached the bottom, percolating up through the medium). Rather than tackling the filtration in such a piecemeal manner, however, it would be more advisable either to opt for a larger commercial 'modular' filter or to build a suitable filter from scratch.

Gravity-fed multichamber filters

There can be no doubt that the most popular and proven system of filtration is that of the gravity-fed, multichambered variety. With this system, the filter body is constructed or installed at the same physical level as the pool so that the water level in both is identical. Therefore, if water is drawn from one end of the filter, gravity carries a fresh supply to the filter. Irrespective of how many chambers are used, water will flow from chamber to chamber, passing through successive 'blocks' of media as it progresses. (This is why it is so important to establish correct levels throughout the system during the design and construction phases.)

Water is transferred from chamber to chamber via transfer ports, and these must be of sufficient size to ensure there is no restriction of flow. The larger commercial modular filters use full-width transfer ports, which are greatly superior to those using, say, 10cm(4in) piping. These larger commercial filters are usually constructed in glass-reinforced plastic and are truly excellent, being provided with drain ports (for cleaning the media) and the correct size of inlet and outlet piping where required. Unfortunately, their excellence is reflected in

their relatively high cost. Here, once again, DIY design can come into its own; anyone capable of laying concrete blocks accurately can design and build an equally effective filter system at a fraction of the cost, as we shall later when we consider how to build one on page 46.

Above: *Part of an extensive multichamber filter system serving a large koi pond. These are commercial units that can be plumbed together in various configurations to suit any type and size of koi pond. They are expensive but highly effective.*

Below: *This schematic cross-section shows the working principles of a basic DIY multichamber filter system, featuring two settlement chambers and four media chambers. This design is featured in the construction phase, starting on page 46.*

Basic multichamber filter design

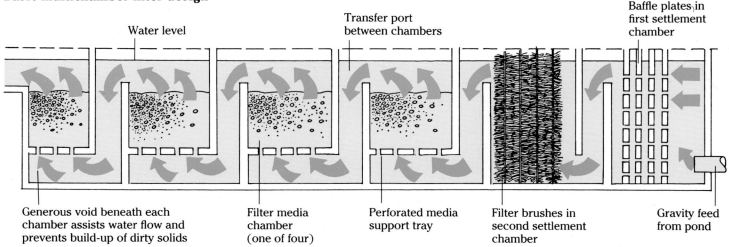

Water level

Transfer port between chambers

Baffle plates in first settlement chamber

Generous void beneath each chamber assists water flow and prevents build-up of dirty solids

Filter media chamber (one of four)

Perforated media support tray

Filter brushes in second settlement chamber

Gravity feed from pond

POND AND FILTER CONSTRUCTION

Filter design parameters

If you are thinking of building your own multichamber external filter, consider the following design parameters and interpret them in the light of your own requirements.

Pond to filter ratio

It is obviously important that your filter is large enough to cope adequately with the demands of your pond. There are many different formulae for calculating the designed pond to filter ratio, but the most commonly used are related to the surface area of the pond and filter system, and the rate at which water passes through the filter – which is a function of contact time and turnover rate.

Surface area As we have seen, the general rule is that the surface area of the filter should be one third of the pond surface area. You can regard this as a minimum, however, because there is no

upper limit to the size of a filter. Literally, the filter could be as big as the pond – it's just a question of space and finance!

Contact time This is the time taken for a given volume of water to pass through the filter system from the point of entry to exit. The contact time of filter water should be between 10 and 15 minutes.

Turnover rate This is the number of times that the total pond capacity should pass through the filter per day. The turnover rate through the filtration system should be 8-12 times the total pond capacity per day. Remember, however, that pump outputs are affected by the length of pipe runs, bends in pipes, and the height at which the water leaves pipes. Venturis may also affect turnover rate. If you are unsure of the effect of these factors on your designed system, consult your local dealer or the pump manufacturer for guidance.

Water flow through the filter

When considering water flow through your filter, your primary objective should be to set up obstruction-free flow paths. An important aspect in achieving this is the sizing of transfer ports, which should occupy about one fifth of the chamber volume. Another way of promoting freedom of flow is to limit the depth of media in each chamber. There is no point in having a media depth of greater than 50cm(20in). There is no evidence that biological efficiency improves with more media; the bacterial population responds to the nitrogenous loading.

Below: *A basic configuration of a koi pond and external filter system. The set-up is simplistic and is intended to highlight how the various elements fit together. The scheme is shown in plan view on the righthand side, with cross-sections through the standpipe chamber, pump chamber and settlement chamber of the filter arranged down the lefthand side.*

Typical arrangement of koi pond and external filter system

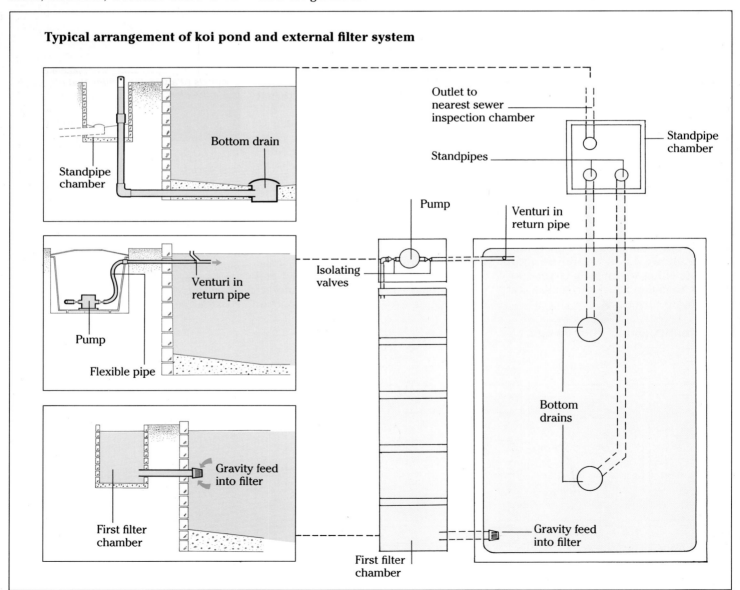

Whichever type of media you decide to use, it will require some means of support in the chamber. Here again, the correct choice of media support will ensure freedom of flow. Possibly the simplest media support is perforated PVC sheeting, which is available from dealers. Whatever you decide to use as a media support tray, mount it in the chamber in such a way that a void of at least 20cm(8in) is left underneath the media. The purpose of having a void is twofold: to assist freedom of water flow, and to prevent pockets of dirty solids gathering, which could encourage the growth of unwanted anaerobic bacteria.

Water levels
In gravity-fed systems, the top water level in the filter must equal that in the pond. Achieving this in practice relies on careful planning and surveying at the initial design stage (see page 28) and following these plans through accurately during construction.

Maintenance
You will need to clean the void spaces in your filter on a regular basis, particularly if your design does not incorporate a bottom drain system. Inserting a vacuum pipe down through the transfer port and under the void space is quite effective, which is another good reason for having large ports and voids.

Settlement chambers
It is vital to provide adequate settlement areas in your design. It might appear to be a waste of space having two or three empty chambers apparently doing nothing, but after seeing just how much solid waste will collect at these points rather than proceeding into the filter proper, the benefits of settling chambers will quickly become obvious. It is also an advantage to fit two or three baffle plates in the first settling chamber to reduce the natural turbulence of the water as it enters the chamber. A few rows of long filter brushes should also be fitted as an additional means of trapping solids.

Vegetable filtration
If your pond design does not include an area devoted to a stream for watercress or similar plants to flourish, you might like to consider adding a chamber at the end of your filter chain for this purpose. Since your filtered water will be very rich in nitrates, a bed of 'greedy' aquatic plants will consume a great deal of this before the water returns to the pond.

Type of pump
It is important to decide at an early stage in the design process on the type of pump to use. The choice comes down to submersible or external. (We will be considering the practical aspects of installing pumps on page 43.)

Submersible pumps, although simpler to install, are usually rather more expensive to both buy and run and are certainly not as reliable in the long term as external pumps. Should you elect to use a submersible pump in a multichamber external filter, install it in the final chamber of your filter chain, and conceal the return outlet pipework leading back to the pond. In this configuration, the pump effectively 'pulls' water through the filter system by gravity as it continuously pumps water from the final chamber into the pond.

External pumps are designed to pump water rather than to pull it, and so they must be installed at as low a level as possible relative to the level of water in the filter. This will ensure that a constant positive head is available – 'head' being the term used to denote the height of water above the pump inlet point. You will need to build a dry, but well-ventilated, chamber to house an external pump. The ventilation is essential to dissipate the condensation caused by the heat of the motor windings; otherwise the motor would soon burn out. Also allow space in the pumping chamber for isolating valves, so that you can turn off the water flow through the system in order to service or replace the pump.

Above: *A view looking from the last chamber of an external filter (at the bottom of the photograph) along the mazelike channels of a vegetable filter that ultimately leads the cleaned water back into the pond. The aquatic plants growing in the channels absorb excess nitrates from the water.*

Below: *A multichamber filter system next to a koi pond, with the pump chamber clearly visible in the foreground of the photograph. Note the isolating valves fitted on either side of the pump to enable it to be serviced or replaced. Good design speeds maintenance.*

POND AND FILTER CONSTRUCTION

Preparing to build

Whatever type or style of pond you have elected to build, you'll need a basic 'kit' of tools and equipment to complete the job. Make sure everything is to hand before you start; there is nothing worse than having to stop while you track down a vital piece of equipment. Therefore, make a list of what you will need and be sure to obtain everything in good time! If you are fortunate enough to be able to engage a professional builder to construct your pond, such mundane matters need not concern you as your contractor will doubtless know just what is required. For the DIY builder, however, there is quite a formidable list of equipment to consider.

In the majority of cases, most of the spoil from your excavation will need to be disposed of, and for this you'll need to hire a skip. Don't run away with the idea that your proposed rockery or landscaping will swallow up all you dig out; spoil from an excavation has an almost magical ability to more than double in bulk once removed from the hole! You'll also need a good wheelbarrow to get the spoil into the skip, which itself will require some means of access in the form of a very strong ramp from the ground up to the edge of the skip, which can be as high as 1.2m(4ft). Make the ramp as long as possible; a barrow load of soil can be extremely unwieldy, both to push to the top of a ramp and then to lift and tip. If at all possible, get a helper to do the barrowing while you do the digging and filling, and then take it in turns to relieve the monotony.

The only other large item of equipment you need worry about is a concrete mixer. If you are hiring one, then preferably choose a petrol-driven model, as it is not unknown for a power failure to occur just when a mix has been started, leaving a rapidly solidifying mess to be cleared from a 'powerless' electric model. If you feel confident about your electricity supply then it could be worthwhile to buy an electric mixer and re-sell it after the job is complete, as we mentioned earlier on page 24.

An assortment of chisels for working stone and brick is an absolute must, as you will find during construction that bricks and blocks will always need trimming. If you have access to one, a disc cutter (like a hand-held electric circular saw with a stone-cutting disc) will prove very helpful. A disc of 12.5cm(5in) diameter being adequate for most jobs. Be sure to use goggles when using a disc cutter; no pool, however impressive, is worth damaging your eyes for!

Perhaps the most important items of equipment you will be using are spirit levels – ideally, a 30cm(12in) and 120cm(48in) level – plus an assortment of straight edges (lengths of straight and true hardwood). For establishing very long levels, you can use a length of clear plastic hose filled with water, as we have described on page 29. Depending upon the size of your proposed pond, you will need a number of wooden pegs when setting levels out. Preferably, make these from 38mm(1.5in)square hardwood, pointed at one end to make them easy to drive into the ground. Allow for a peg at not more than 30cm(12in) intervals to ensure accuracy when setting out. The ideal length of the pegs will vary according to the type of ground; for solid clay a length of 30cm(12in) will be fine, whereas crumbly and friable earth requires double this length.

Should you be unfortunate enough to strike a layer of stone when excavation is underway, an electric jackhammer (a portable pneumatic hammer drill) will be essential. You can hire this from a plant hire company, but, again, be sure to wear goggles when you use it.

Building a liner pond

Here, we look in detail at the sequence of steps involved in building a liner pond. Starting on page 45, we will review the basic differences involved in building a concrete pond.

Installing a concrete collar

The first step is to install a concrete collar, or 'ring beam', which will form the 'skeleton' of your pond. The simplest method of visualizing this collar is to imagine it as a large concrete 'washer' lying in the ground, the inside of which represents the finished diameter of your pond. Be sure to check your plans!

You can use a length of hose to mark out the shape of your pond, pinning it in position temporarily with wire hooks driven into the ground. Dig a trench along the outside of this area approximately 45cm(18in) deep and 30cm(12in) wide, removing the spoil as you go, otherwise you will quickly find yourself working in a quagmire! Your trench should have vertical sides and a clean, debris-free base. You will find it an advantage to check the level of the trench base as you go along, rather than wait until you've finished.

Before pouring any concrete, and assuming the trench base is level, install lengths of hardboard around the inner edge of the trench, smooth side facing outwards. This will ensure a smooth surface for the liner to rest against. Hold these hardboard strips in position with transverse lengths of wood. Remove these when you pour in the concrete and tamp it down in the trench.

Drive a series of pegs along the base of the trench, following the centre line at approximately 30cm(12in)-intervals, setting the first peg to the depth of the finished collar. Follow this level all the way round with subsequent pegs. Take your time; a mistake or a little carelessness at this stage can ruin the completed job! Provided that you have adjusted these pegs to the correct height, your finished collar, and consequently the pond, will be exactly level. (You can leave these pegs in position when pouring concrete, or you can drive them into the ground after the collar has set and fill the holes with wet concrete.)

Below: *The first stage of constructing a concrete collar to establish a firm edge around the pond. Here, work has started on digging the trench to receive the concrete.*

Having finished preparing the trench, you can now begin the actual construction. Start mixing the concrete early on in the day so that you can finish filling your collar trench before dark. Spreading this operation over two days will result in a weak collar, because concrete does not bond to itself very effectively. Make the mix from one part cement to six parts by volume of mixed aggregate (sand and gravel). Add water carefully. The ideal mix should be quite 'stodgy', with no tendency to 'slump' or run; too wet a mix will dry weak and be prone to cracking. Shovel the mix into the trench, working it well into the bottom and sides. Treading it in with heavy boots can be quite effective, the object being to expel as much air as possible from the mix. If it makes you feel happier, hire a vibrating poker for this job.

Having filled the trench and tamped it down, you can now begin the task of obtaining a smooth, level surface, using the tops of your pegs as guides. A large plasterer's float is an excellent tool for this purpose. Once this task is completed, go away and forget about it for at least 48 hours to give the initial 'set' a chance to take place undisturbed. (It will take anything up to a month for the concrete to cure fully, so be warned and tread carefully during the next operation.) If your concrete has been mixed to the correct consistency without too much water, now is a good time to remove the sharp edge from the inside rim of your collar in order to prevent later damage to the liner. This is easy to carry out by running the point of a trowel along the line of the hardboard shuttering, removing a little concrete and leaving a slight chamfer along the edge.

The main excavation

Following the initial 48-hour setting period of the concrete liner, you can now begin the task of digging out. There is a right and a wrong way to tackle this job; the following suggestions employ a little logic but still require the same muscle power! Start your digging in the centre and work in straight lines, progressing a spade's width at a time but leaving a spade's width all round the edge. Having removed the first layer of topsoil and stacked it somewhere for later use, now remove the last spade's width from around the edge. Do this carefully, avoiding any undercutting of the collar and ensuring that the excavation sides remain vertical. Carry on in this manner until you have reached the required depth, bearing in mind the recommendations about optimum depth made on page 26. Eventually, you will reach a point at

Left: *Smoothing off the surface of the wet concrete collar with a plasterer's float. Try to do the whole concreting operation in one day; new and old concrete will not bond very well if you split the job over two days. Let the concrete set for at least 48 hours before digging out the pond.*

Below: *Digging out the soil from inside the collar. Dig in straight lines, starting at the centre and working outwards, removing one level at a time. Be very careful to keep the sides of the excavation vertical and avoid any undercutting that may cause collapse.*

which it is physically impossible to lift the spoil out of the excavation. At this point, enlist the assistance of a helper armed with a couple of buckets suspended on ropes – slower, but most effective!

At this point, we should introduce a few words of caution on the question of safety while digging. If the terrain is at all crumbly, do be aware of the danger of slippage; the sides of an excavation can collapse inwards without warning, with dire consequences. Should you suspect that this could happen as you dig deeper, be sure to change your plans, not only for your own safety while digging but also to preserve the stability of the finished pond. The best way to cope with this is to incorporate brick or block walls. It will be too late to embody these after the liner is installed and filled with water. Unprotected in this way, the walls of an unstable pond could subside during a very wet spell. (This can happen even to long-established ponds.)

Installing bottom drains

Having excavated the hole to your liking, the time has arrived to install your bottom drain(s). While it is possible and quite common practice to install these devices straight into the ground, do con-

sider laying a concrete base with the bottom drain encased in it. Not only is this a much more workmanlike method, but it also has the advantage that should you, as many others have done, decide that a liner pool is not for you after all, you have a sound base all ready for laying blocks to construct a concrete pond (see page 45). Either way, the installation procedure for the bottom drain is identical, apart from the height difference depending on whether a concrete base is used.

Together with its associated pipework, a bottom drain is a very expensive item and any mistake made during its assembly is uncorrectable, so take a long look at all the components and carry out a 'dry run' before attempting the installation proper. The best-quality components are moulded from PVC/ABS plastics and are intended to be solvent welded together. This technique involves coating both mating surfaces with a solvent cement and inserting one piece into another. As the name implies, the cement welds the two surfaces together – virtually instantaneously. Theoretically, there may be five seconds in which to make any adjustment of position but, to be on the safe side, you should assume that there will be no time at all!

POND AND FILTER CONSTRUCTION

Cut all the pipework and fittings to exact size and assemble them 'dry', marking them to ensure that they will fit together accurately at the cementing stage. The easiest way to mark your components is simply to scratch a series of lines on each component where it meets its partner. Do this once everything is assembled 'dry' and when you have checked that each length of pipe is truly horizontal and vertical. Due to the moulding process, it is not unknown for some components to be unacceptably tight at the dry-fit stage. To avoid assembly problems once the solvent cement has been applied, check each joint for fit and, if necessary, 'dress' the surfaces with the finest grade of abrasive paper until an easy slide fit is obtained.

Having cut everything to size, assembled the various components 'dry' and propped them in position as necessary to take measurements, you can now begin the task of trenching the ground for your pipe runs. By now you should know exactly where the termination point for the waste pipe will be and will have dug out the chamber ready to receive the standpipes, etc. Dig the trench from your standpipe chamber so that it terminates about 30cm(12in) from the pond wall. Then make the final breakthrough from within the pool to minimize damage to the soil under the collar. Where a change in direction occurs, allow for the larger diameter of any bends or elbows. Also allow for the vertical run of pipe from the bottom drain during trenching.

Once the trenching is complete, assemble the drain and pipework 'dry' *in situ*, just as a final check, placing blocks under the drain and pipework as necessary to achieve the correct positioning. All being well, you can now begin the jointing process. To carry out this task properly and without undue mental stress really requires two or three pairs of hands, so don't be tempted to go it alone, however much you want to get on with the job. A hasty mistake could spell disaster! Assembling solvent-welded systems involves cleaning each male and female connection with solvent cleaner, applying solvent cement to each jointing face, lining up your marks and inserting one component into the other with firm pressure. Provided you have applied the solvent cement generously, there is no need to insert them with a twisting motion; this may lead to positioning problems for the 'first-timer' using plastic jointing technology. Having made the joint, just run a finger around the outside of the joint to spread any surplus cement and form a small fillet. Within the space of five minutes or so, the integrity of the

Fitting the bottom drain pipework together

Side view

Standard bottom drain fitting

Vertical pipe to standpipe chamber

Blocks to support the pipework in position while you check fit and measurements

Plan view

Ensure that your marks on the pipe and elbow match

A length of standard 10cm(4in) high-pressure PVC/ABS pipe

Above: *It is vital to 'dry-fit' the pipework components together before you solvent weld them; mistakes can be impossible to rectify later! Use blocks to support them.*

joint will be sufficient for you to manipulate it within reason while making the next connection.

Once the assembly is complete, you can now manoeuvre it into its final position within the pool, temporarily securing it with a collection of odd bricks, blocks, etc. Then you can fix it permanently by placing a stiff mix of concrete in the trench around the piping and leave it for a couple of days to set. If you are intending to use a separate filter feed, say for middle water, you will need to repeat the whole exercise in order to install the pipework, but by now you should be feeling something of an expert!

Concreting the pond base

Having completed the pipework, the next job to tackle is laying the pond floor. First and foremost, set your level around the outer edge of the pond excavation, once again using wooden pegs set at about 30cm(12in) centres. Aim for a minimum concrete depth of 15cm(6in), this depth being constant right across to the bottom drain. If you did not allow for a slight slope towards the bottom drain during excavation, it is quite acceptable to incorporate this now by returning some of the removed spoil as necessary and compacting it into position before driving in the level pegs.

Whatever size of pool is involved, you will need a considerable quantity of concrete for the floor and, as with any concreting, this is best completed in one working day. Should you have any doubt about achieving this timescale, you might wish to consider taking a delivery of ready-mixed concrete. There are cer-

tain advantages to this method; for instance, when placing the order, you can ask to have a waterproofing additive in the mix. The only major problem with bulk concrete delivery is one of time. Most delivery drivers expect to simply drop and depart, although some are prepared to unload the mix into a wheelbarrow, as long as there is a rapid turnround made possible by, perhaps, three helpers each with a barrow. As concrete can become unworkable quite quickly, especially in warm weather, the ready-mixed option also requires extra help with the pond for laying the stuff, so some organization is called for.

Use the same laying technique as for the collar, but on a somewhat larger scale. Shovel the concrete into position and work it well in with the shovel, particularly in any areas around exposed pipework, then tread it in with large boots and finally smooth it off with a plasterer's float. Of course, you will reach a stage when you are trapped in the excavation with the part under your feet waiting for concrete. Exit by means of a pair of steps or small ladder and complete the concreting from outside the pool, if necessary, by being held by the feet over the edge.

Positioning the liner

The moment has now arrived when the liner can be offered up to the excavation – better known as the moment of truth!

Even for a modestly sized pool, a folded liner can be incredibly heavy, so don't bank on being able to cope singlehandedly, quite apart from the danger of abrading or tearing your liner by dragging it across the ground.

Depending upon the size of liner involved, you should have at least four people to place the liner in position. If you are installing a box-welded liner, do ensure that you have the thing the right way round; if you get it wrong, it can prove quite difficult to lift out and turn. Lay the flat sheet type of liner across the excavation, ensuring that there is an equal amount of overhang around the edge. The easiest way to get the liner into its hole is simply to run water into it but, as the weight begins to pull the liner down, do ensure that the overhang does not become unbalanced, resulting in a lopsided configuration.

The weight of water will eventually pull the liner down until it touches the floor. At this point, the procedure to follow is identical for both box-welded and flat-sheet liners, and involves a volunteer going for a paddle, preferably barefooted to minimize the risk of damaging the liner. Whatever grade of liner being used, there will be a certain amount of stretch in the material but not enough to prevent pleats and folds developing. All that can be done is to manually persuade the liner to take up a position as free from pleats and folds as possible. Since this can only be done while filling is in progress, someone has to get wet! The more water you can get into the pond, the better will be the final lie of the liner, even though you will need to empty the pond when you make the various pipe connections.

With the pond as full as possible, lay the surplus liner flat around the edge and weight it down with heavy blocks; leave these in position until the pipefitting work is complete. Avoid placing any tension on any part of the liner that is still exposed, as this could lead to later problems, such as tearing. You simply have to endure any wrinkles that are visible, although many of these will not be seen once you have added the finishing touches. Leave the water in the pool overnight to allow the liner to settle into its position ready for the next operation.

Fitting drains and pipes to the liner

You are now about to enter the area of most risk when building a liner pond, that of attaching the liner to the various drain and pipe flanges. This is risky because any error in positioning may lead to the liner tearing due to the stress placed upon it by the weight of water.

Pump out the water from your pond down to a depth of perhaps 30cm(12in) and place three or four concrete blocks broad-face down around the site of the bottom drain. This will prevent any movement of the liner relative to the bottom drain while you are paddling around carrying out the fixing operation. When these are in position, pump out the remaining water before you start to cut and attach the liner.

You are probably now wondering how to set about cutting the liner accurately so that the centre hole and all the screw holes are correctly aligned? This is where the concrete blocks show their worth! After completely drying the area of liner around your bottom drain, take a piece of chalk, preferably the type used by tailors, and rub briskly around the face of the bottom drain flange, which you should be able to feel through the liner. This will leave an imprint of the centre hole and screw holes on the liner. Carefully cut around the centre with a sharp knife and expose the bottom drain sump. To make this task easier, hold the liner flat against the flange and cut with downward strokes, using the inside of the sump as a guide. Remove the circular section of liner and perforate the screw holes using either a leather punch or a small soldering iron, but be careful!

Clean all the mating surfaces carefully and assemble the flange using the appropriate mastic compound, if required by your particular bottom drain. (This should have been supplied with the drain.) Now tighten the screws in an even manner, ensuring that none is tightened more than the others. It might be helpful at this point to call it a day, run some water into the pond and mark the level, ready to check for leaks the next morn-

Fitting a liner to a bottom drain

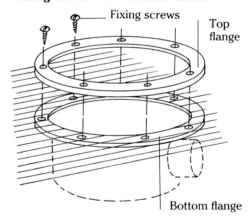

Above: *Cutting and fitting the liner around a bottom drain demands a good deal of care. Mark the position of the hole and flange screws using chalk, cut out the centre, perforate the screw holes and tighten the screws evenly to ensure a secure seal.*

Above: *Placing the liner in the excavation is a tricky operation needing lots of willing help – at least four people for a large liner. Try to arrange an even overlap around the edge of the pond, with plenty to spare.*

Right: *Running water into the hole is the best way to bed the liner into position. If necessary, get into the water and manually sort out pleats and wrinkles.*

POND AND FILTER CONSTRUCTION

ing. If you have followed the above sequence of instructions to the letter, there should be none!

Mark out, cut and fit the filter feed pipe connection in the same manner. If you are using one of the threaded types of connection here, wrap some PTFE tape on the threads to ensure a watertight seal. (Plumbers use this kind of tape.) When fitting these attachments, it is vital to ensure that the weight of water in the finished pond will not stress the liner at these attachment points. Otherwise, there is a real risk of a tear developing.

However impatient you might be to get on with the job, pause at this point and take stock. Fill the pool yet again and leave it overnight to check for leaks.

Finishing off the edge

You have now reached the exciting part of your project, finishing off the edge of the pond. Whether you intend building an ornamental wall around the pond or just placing large rocks around the perimeter, the requirements are identical. In broad terms, you should lay the excess liner flat around the outside of the pond, set your wall or rockwork on top and cement it into position. The weight involved will hold the liner in place, but be sure to let the mortar set before continuing, otherwise all your good work could be undone!

The object is to fold the liner up behind the wall or rockwork in such a way that the liner remains watertight far above the proposed top water level. The aim is to hide the edge of the liner from view by arranging for the water level to be above the point at which the liner changes from the vertical to the horizontal axis.

If you are constructing a wall, make this double-skinned and run the liner between the two layers. Achieving the same effect with rockwork can be a little more difficult. With very large stones, you can still fold the liner up, cement it and hold it in position with a gravel path or paving stones. If you fancy something slightly different, consider fitting sections of tree log around the edge as shown below. Do

Left: Sawn logs provide a natural-looking edge to a koi pond. Do ensure that the wood preservative used is not toxic to fish. This type of edging is just one of the many options for finishing off your pond.

beware of using any materials which have been treated with preservatives, however, as these chemicals are invariably toxic to fish! You may wish to incorporate a shelf for marginal plants, but do try to avoid any sharp edges on which the koi can damage themselves when swimming, particularly at spawning time. All that now remains is to remove any excess liner with a sharp knife and to leave the pool filled to allow any cement in contact with the water to lose its alkalinity and harden off completely (see also page 46 for more on alkalinity).

Building the standpipe chamber

The standpipe assembly normally used on koi ponds is a commercial assembly consisting of a sleeve and socket with a neoprene 'O' ring for sealing purposes. A pipe long enough for the top end to be above the top water level in the pond is inserted into the sleeve; a cross piece, or 'tommy bar', allows the pipe to be withdrawn. With this pipe in position, the pool water finds its own level by gravity. Pulling out the pipe (with a twisting motion) causes a difference in level be-

Variations on edging a liner pond

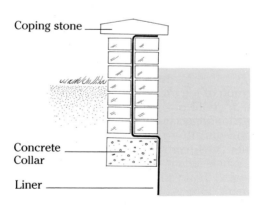

Coping stone

Concrete Collar

Liner

These are a few ideas for finishing off the edge of a liner pond. The aim is to secure the liner above the water level and hide it from view. Sawn and treated sections of log are particularly effective and will fit in well around an informal pond. If you build a marginal planter, either leave the pond edge low enough for water to splash onto the soil or, better for koi, build up the edge but leave out the occasional perpendicular joint to allow water to reach the roots. Slope any paving or turf slightly away from the pond to prevent pollution from the garden.

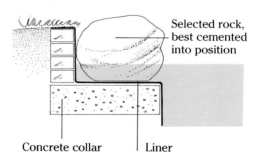

Selected rock, best cemented into position

Concrete collar   Liner

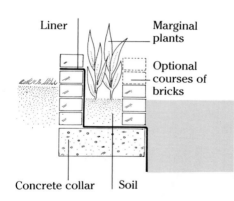

Liner

Marginal plants

Optional courses of bricks

Concrete collar   Soil

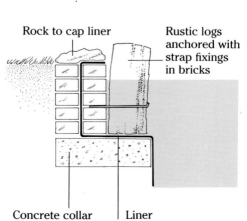

Rock to cap liner

Rustic logs anchored with strap fixings in bricks

Concrete collar   Liner

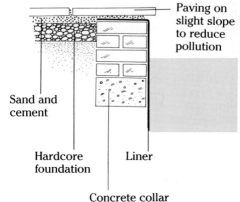

Paving on slight slope to reduce pollution

Sand and cement

Hardcore foundation   Liner

Concrete collar

tween the pond and the standpipe chamber and water flows by gravity into the chamber. The flow comes from the bottom drain and carries with it any debris within the suction area around the drain. This rush of water is propelled by the head of water in the pond and will continue to flow until either the standpipe is replaced or the water level in the pond falls to the level of the standpipe socket. The pond cannot be completely emptied via a bottom drain unless the standpipe socket is at the same level as the bottom drain itself.

You can build the standpipe chamber either from concrete blocks, and then render it, or from engineering-quality bricks. Do not use ordinary house bricks, as these will quickly deteriorate under the action of water. In addition to an entry point for the pipe from the pond, there must also be an access out of the chamber to your main sewer, which means breaking into the nearest sewer inspection chamber. (You may need to seek advice on this, depending on your local building regulations and byelaws.) Ideally, use standard clay sewer piping from the standpipe chamber to your sewer inspection chamber, as it is much easier to achieve a watertight seal with cement, this being a drawback with plastic piping. Arrange for the entry into the inspection chamber to be as low down as possible to ensure that the maximum head of water is available from the pond.

From a technical point of view, the standpipe is a rather crude device. A much more efficient and reliable method of releasing waste water from the pond is to use an industrial ball valve of the same diameter as the bottom drain pipework. Needless to say, these valves are very expensive, particularly the motorized versions. But what price perfection for the committed enthusiast?

Attaching the filter feed

By now, attaching the filter feed pipework should seem to be child's play. If you are using the same industrial-quality piping as on the bottom drain, this will merely be a matter of fixing a flange at the point of entry into the filter and cementing a suitable length of pipe into position. You might find it easier to cut the pipe to length and cement the flange on the end of it first. Then you can adjust the position and height of the filter carcass before drilling the holes for the flange-fixing screws.

If you have elected to build your own filter system from cement-rendered concrete blocks (see page 46), you could run into difficulties obtaining a watertight seal at the flange connection, as cement

does not adhere very well to plastic pipe, even if the surface is roughened. Various methods have been used to overcome this problem, their success rate depending upon the skill and perseverance of the individual. One method is to make a hole in the blockwork large enough to accommodate the feed pipe, then to liberally coat the flange-bearing surface and the inside of the hole with fibreglass. Once this has all dried and been checked for flatness (most important), attach the flange using a suitable mastic compound as a seal. Then cement a short length of pipe from the inside of the filter so that it butts up to the inside of the flange, and spread a fillet of gap-filling cement on the inside of the pipe where it touches the flange. Finally, paint the whole area with a waterproofing paint. It might seem rather clumsy but it does work! If you like spending money, you could attach a flange at both sides of the blockwork, thus reducing the risk of seepage.

A more economical alternative to using industrial pipework and fittings for the feed pipe – and one which has worked successfully on many ponds – is to use domestic drainage systems. These consist of 10cm(4in)-diameter plastic tubes, fitted together with push-on units sealed with neoprene gaskets. Once assembled, these systems can withstand quite a considerable head of water without seepage. Connecting this class of pipe to a concrete construction poses no problems at all; adaptor sleeves can be used to couple the plastic pipe to the un-glazed clay pipe, to which cement adheres readily. For the pool end, one of the complementary ground boxes and screens can be easily fitted to the liner and will work quite satisfactorily.

A cautionary word about electricity

Your pond and associated systems are going to require a source of electricity and you should think seriously before tackling this yourself. Electric current and water form an extremely dangerous alliance and on no account should you tackle this job unless you are really confident or suitably qualified.

Do not expect one domestic socket to serve the needs of your pond. A little thought should tell you that your pump will need one, a vacuum pump will need another and, during winter, you might well wish to run a heater to keep a small area of water free of ice. As an absolute minimum, you should aim for a double socket or even two doubles, of the switched variety and of the 'metal clad' construction. These should be housed in such a position that rainwater cannot drip upon them and they should prefer-

ably be hidden from the view of the casual visitor. Consider housing your electrics in a lockable metal cabinet, for example, for safety and security.

Statutory regulations governing the installation of external electrical circuits vary from country to country, but all are designed to protect you and yours from a lethal electric shock. Where appropriate, the most important of these regulations requires the fitting of a residual current circuit breaker to any new outdoor circuit, a device that shuts off the supply instantaneously in the event of a circuit, or equipment connected to that circuit, developing an earth fault and becoming 'live'. If you already have an outside electrical supply to a greenhouse or garage, for instance, do seriously consider fitting such a circuit breaker; it could save your life! There are also regulations governing the depth at which outside circuit cables can be buried in the ground, as well as the type of cable and methods of installation. Taking all these factors into consideration, there really is a good case for calling in an electrical contractor and having this part of the job carried out professionally.

Installing pumps

At the heart of any koi pond is a pump. Unfortunately, there is an absolutely bewildering assortment of pumps available, and buying an unsuitable one can be both frustrating and expensive. As we have seen on page 37, the pumps with which you will be concerned can be divided into two groups: the submersible type for direct immersion into the water to be pumped, and the external pump intended to be installed remotely.

Taking a look firstly at the submersible type, you might be forgiven for thinking that, on the face of it, nothing could be more simple than dropping such a pump into your pond, coupling it up, switching it on and running the system up to full

Above: *A typical pump chamber located close to a koi pond, showing its associated pipework. Properly installed in a dry, ventilated chamber, external pumps are preferred over submersible ones for long service life and ease of maintenance.*

POND AND FILTER CONSTRUCTION

power. So what are the snags? Firstly, submersible pumps are more expensive to buy, usually more expensive to run, and, finally, may not prove extremely reliable. The higher purchase price can be explained by the fact that the electrical and mechanical components need to be well insulated from contact with the water, which entails the motor windings, bearings and internal connections being contained within a sealed pot that is usually filled with oil to cool and lubricate the motor. Another drawback is that the perforated screen fitted in order to prevent debris from entering and clogging the impeller (the part which actually moves the water) can quickly become matted with blanketweed, etc., necessitating frequent removal of the pump for cleaning, which can become a most boring chore! From an aesthetic point of view, the pump, its cable and its outlet piping are virtually impossible to conceal, and will certainly detract from the visual pleasure of your pond.

Some submersible pumps can be purchased complete with an adaptor plate that fits over the inlet screen, allowing direct connection to pipework associated with undergravel filters. The one place where a submersible pump can be used with advantage, however, is in the final chamber of a filter chain, where, of course, it is invisible, along with its cable and piping. When used in a filter chamber, this type of pump is sometimes simply placed on the surface of the final layer of gravel that gives the filtered water a last 'polish'. Here, you must take precautions to prevent fine grains of gravel being sucked into the pump, where they will play havoc with the bearings. It could well be an added advantage to buy the type of submersible pump fitted with an automatic switch that shuts the pump down in the event of a disaster with your plumbing which could result in your pool being pumped dry, with obvious consequences for your koi. (An example of this would be a fracture occurring in the return pipe from the filter to the pond, allowing water to leak away. An 'automatic' pump has a sensor that shuts it down when the water level drops by a certain amount, thereby preventing the pump from completely emptying the pond.)

The externally mounted pump undoubtedly has a number of advantages over the submersible variety. The most important of these must be that of purchase and running costs. The water in a great number of koi ponds is now circulated by central heating pumps, better known in the plumbing industry as 'circulators'. The difference in cost can be quite staggering; three small central heating circulators can be bought for the same cost as one submersible pump, for example. Some of these circulators have a variable speed control, which can be useful during the winter months, when full circulation is not really necessary – thereby saving on running costs.

The only real drawback with external pumps is that they need to be properly housed in a dry, well-ventilated chamber if you are to avoid condensation problems. However, once properly carried out, these precautions will pay for themselves over and over again in that your pumps will give years of trouble-free service. One relatively simple method of housing an external pump is to use a domestic polypropylene water tank placed in the ground. Use 38mm(1.5in) diameter plastic piping for your pumping circuit. (This is an internationally accepted standard, making spares always easily available.) Connect the inlet and outlet pipes by means of 'tank connectors' used with domestic plumbing systems. Screwed pump connections are also easily available using the same size and type of piping. When deciding on piping sizes, always remember that even a small reduction in the diameter of pump pipework can have a serious effect on the efficiency of a pump, quite out of proportion to the reduced diameter.

Selecting the most suitable size of pump can be difficult, as the information given in pump literature can be misleading. For instance, the pumping output figures provided for a given pump and head are based on the unit pumping against an open end; such parameters as pipe size and any change of pipe direction are not taken into account. As an example, a pump rated at, say, 4500 litres (approximately 1000 gallons) per hour at 1.2m(4ft) head may only deliver 80 percent of that when connected to pond pipework with perhaps a venturi connected at the outlet end. Therefore, when selecting a pump, always consider both the pipe size and the number of pipe bends used in the system. To maximize pump efficiency, always try to limit the number of bends in the output pipework by sensible location of your pumping chamber (see the scheme on page 36).

Above: *The smaller of two ponds in an extensive koi pond complex at the block wall stage. Note the three standpipes for the bottom drains set in the base.*

Above: *The same pond after the walls have been rendered into smooth curves and fibreglassed. The base around each bottom drain has been dished to aid water flow.*

Above: *Part of the multichamber filter system under construction that will serve both this relatively small pond and the larger informal koi pond featured at various stages on the opposite page.*

Right: *The small pond on completion and stocked with fish. Brick, stone and log edging complement each other and blend in well with the overall style of the garden.*

Take care when comparing the running costs of various pumps, as the figures quoted for power, whether expressed in watts or horsepower, invariably relate to the output power rather than the actual energy consumed when pumping. Thus, a pump whose data plate quotes a power figure of, say, 60 watts, could use anything up to twice this figure in electrical consumption.

When installing your pump or pumps, do remember the advice given on page 37 regarding the fitting of isolating valves to enable the pump to be removed for servicing or replacement. A point to remember when siting your pump is that pumps are designed to propel water rather than suck it, so any pump must be installed at the lowest point possible relative to the normal top water level. This will ensure a constant positive head of pressure is available at the inlet, or suction side, of the pump.

Building a concrete pond
Constructing a concrete pond generally follows the same techniques as for a liner pool, the excavation and laying of the base, as well the installation of bottom drains, being identical.

If you have laid your base level, then it is merely a matter of building a wall from concrete blocks. If the terrain is heavy – solid clay, for example – you can erect these block walls flush with the sides of the excavation. If the terrain is at all crumbly, however, it will be better to leave a gap that can be backfilled with hardcore or even concrete as the work proceeds. When building in solid terrain, use dense concrete blocks measuring 45x23x10cm(18x9x4in), and in loose terrain, use hollow blocks measuring 45x23x23cm(18x9x9in). As you lay each two courses of blocks, backfill as necessary, but only up to the halfway point of the last block laid so that the layers of backfill do not coincide with the weaker mortar joints. To cope with acute corners, cut the blocks into smaller segments and work mortar well into the joints, particularly at the rear. Tackle the inlet and outlet points for pipework in the same way as for a liner pond, using unglazed clay pipe with adaptors for plastic pipe where appropriate.

Rendering a concrete pond
The traditional method of finishing a concrete pond was to apply two separate rendering coats, each approximately 20mm(0.8in) thick, containing a high proportion of sand to reduce cracking. Unfortunately, the result was inherently weak, with a high porosity and extremely vulnerable to frost damage. The modern

Above: *An early stage in building a large informal pond. The concrete base is underway and metal rods are already in place to reinforce the block walls.*

Above: *Bottom drains and connecting PVC/ABS pipework in place before the floor is built up around them. Each drain has its own pipe to the standpipe chamber.*

Above: *Making the dished areas around each bottom drain involves shaping the concrete within these circular templates. The aim is to avoid areas that will not drain.*

Above: *The block walls are now in place and both these and the base have been contoured and rendered. The smooth curves will promote water flow in the pond.*

Above: *The interior of the pond after it has been fibreglassed and painted. This dark green colour is ideal for koi ponds and will show off the koi colours well.*

Above: *Now the attention turns towards finishing off the edges of the pond, with brickwork, stonework and a shallow pebble beach in preparation in the foreground.*

Above: *The newly finished pond, with new areas of planting just beginning to get* established. *It will be several months before the pond fully 'matures' in all aspects.*

POND AND FILTER CONSTRUCTION

method involves applying just one coat of 5mm(0.2in)-thick rendering made from a 2-to-1 sand/cement mix with the addition of the plastic fibres mentioned on page 31. Where there is any uneveness, such as at the corners, you can apply the rendering material as thick as necessary to give a smooth contour, there being no tendency for it to slump or fall away. Cover the whole pond, including the floor, in one continuous operation. Spreading the job over two days is not recommended, as the material is so impervious to water once dry that successive coats will not bond. If you render the pond in very hot weather, take precautions to prevent it drying out too rapidly, either by providing a cover over the pool or by spraying it periodically with a fine mist of water. After a couple of days, fill the pond. Concrete cures much more evenly under water, it being a little known fact that concrete continues to cure for many weeks after laying.

If you intend to coat the pond with a fibreglass skin, you can carry this out without further preparation, but be sure that it is completely dry before you start. As we mentioned previously, this is really a task best left to the professionals.

Coping with alkalinity
For a normal concrete-finished pond, there are just a couple more points to consider. Firstly, with such a high level of cement being used in the rendering, the level of alkalinity will also be proportionally higher and this could make the pool uninhabitable for fish if it is not neutralized. This is possible by chemical means or even by repeated washing with clean water, but the end result will be a pond of a most unnatural appearance, as the rendering will be almost white in colour. Painting is the best solution.

Painting the pond
The most popular method of finishing off a concrete pond, and at the same time affording protection against alkaline pollution, is to paint it. Here again, cost must be the controlling factor in your choice of which paint finish to use. The best – and the most expensive – option is to use a two-part, water-soluble epoxy paint. This is a completely non-toxic product that has a texture very similar to emulsion paint and was first developed for sealing drinking water reservoirs. It dries with a hardwearing and slightly glossy finish that, to some degree, discourages the growth of algae. Applying a thinned-down coat, followed by two full-strength coats, produces a virtually everlasting finish, which even resists the action of a scraping and cleaning operation! An

alternative and much cheaper option is to use a suitable bitumen-based paint. This contains a high percentage of sand, so the finish is not up to the standard of the previous material, and applying it is quite a messy operation. On no account be tempted to use one of the many paints advertised for use as roof repair mediums; most of these are highly toxic to fish. Check and double check before buying paint for your pond!

Before starting to paint, you must overcome the problem of surface fibres. The rendered surface will contain many of the reinforcement fibres and these will 'peak' when paint is applied, resulting in lots of needle-sharp points just waiting to gash any passing fish. The remedy is simply to pass a blowlamp over the rendered surface to dissolve any stray fibres. After applying the first coat of paint, carefully go over the whole surface of the pond with the flat of your hand to find any fibres you have missed. As the paint will have hardened these, a quick rub with sandpaper will remove them. Be sure to carry the painting up as far as is necessary to cover any mortar used to secure ornamental rockwork around the edge of the pond.

What colour paint should you use? Black is the best choice. Avoid light colours; it is a well-known fact that the colours of koi do fade against a light-coloured background. In the epoxy paint range there is a clear variety available which is ideal for coating any cement work that is not underwater and visible to the viewer. This is a useful precaution against rainborne alkaline runoff from ornamental rockwork, and for protecting the joints in waterfalls, cascades, etc. from leakage.

Building an external filter
If you are installing a ready-made module, the procedure couldn't be more straightforward; simply excavate the site, arrange the pipework and drop the carcass into position. When budget considerations preclude the use of such a 'luxury', one alternative option is to build a simple multichamber filter in concrete. Here, we look briefly at the steps involved in building such a filter.

Building the carcass
To build the filter carcass, use the same techniques and materials as for the concrete pond. Excavate the hole, making the sides as vertical as you can, and create a flat, level floor. Break through the walls of the excavation in the appropriate positions to accommodate the pipework, not forgetting to allow for the thickness of the base and walls.

Above: *Another view of the 32,000-litre (7000-gallon) pond shown on page 86, this time with the covers taken off the filtration system, cleverly positioned beneath the pavilion. The multichamber filter system includes a sand filter at extreme left.*

Using a set of level pegs as before, lay a 15cm(6in)-deep concrete base of 6-to-1 aggregate/cement mix and allow it to set. Once the base will bear standing on without damage, build up the walls using dense concrete blocks suitable for the terrain. Use your spirit level constantly to ensure correct levels throughout. Leave gaps in the blockwork to accommodate the pipework, and make these good with a strong concrete mix after the piping has been installed. Ensure that the walls extend 10-15cm(4-6in) above the planned top water level.

Render the inside in one operation with the 2-to-1 sand/cement mix with fibres added, to a uniform thickness of 5mm(0.2in). Carefully seal around the piping with the rendering mix and apply the same rules as for the pond with regard to premature drying.

Making and fitting the partitions
Providing and installing backwash and drain valves in a concrete filter is such a difficult business that it is best to omit these in favour of making extra wide transfer ports that enable a vacuum pipe to be passed down and under the media support trays for periodic cleaning. (If you use ring media in the filter, such as plastic hair rollers or similar, this material is easy to lift out and clean anyway.)

Make the partitions within the filter body by casting them from a fibre-reinforced mix of 1-to-1 sand/cement. The extra strength provided by the higher proportion of cement is necessary because the flat sheets you will cast will only have a nominal thickness of 12mm(0.5in). These concrete sheets will be used to form two kinds of partitions within the filter body: those fixed off the base to allow water to flow beneath them and equivalent ones on the upstream side that rest on the base with water flowing over the top. To avoid any confusion, let us call the first type 'partition sheets' and the second type 'transfer port sheets'. (The diagram opposite clearly shows how these are arranged.)

Cast these parts in a simple, one-sided mould made from a flat sheet of exterior-quality plywood with a framework made from lengths of 12mm(0.5in)-square timber screwed onto the face. The inside measurements of this removable frame should be identical to the size required for your partitions. You can afford a little latitude in this measurement, but avoid making them too big; the method of fixing will cater for any slight undersizing.

Casting your sheets involves applying a quantity of the cement mixture onto the mould frame, taking care not to leave any spaces around the edges or in the corners, and scraping off any surplus cement with a straight edge to leave an even surface. It is a good idea to lay the mould on a hard, flat surface, such as a garage floor, and to rest a concrete block or two on the edges of the framework while the cement is setting. This will discourage any tendency for the mould to warp. After three days, unscrew the framework and carefully remove the cement sheet from the backing plate. Stand it on edge to allow it to dry completely. Depending on the size and number of chambers in your filter, casting the partitions is obviously going to be a lengthy task and so you might prefer to make a number of moulds in order to speed the job, bearing in mind that this type of plywood will always be useful in the future and not just be wasted.

Fixing the partitions into the filter carcass is quite straightforward, but does require careful use of a spirit level. First establish at what height the underside of the partition sheet is to be above the base; 15cm(6in) is ideal, with the top of the partition being level with or slightly below the top edge of the filter carcass. Find something to lay on the filter base to act as a temporary support, two pairs of house bricks laid side by side will provide the correct height, and lower the partition into position until it rests on the support. Check it for level and compensate for any discrepancy by inserting thin packing material between the sheet and the support.

Now tap small wooden wedges into place between the sides of the sheet and the filter wall; these will effectively hold the sheet in position while you complete the next operation. Mix a quantity of cement mortar of a fairly dry consistency and apply a fillet of this to all four corners of the partition in contact with the filter wall. You can leave the wedges in posi-

A basic DIY multichamber filter

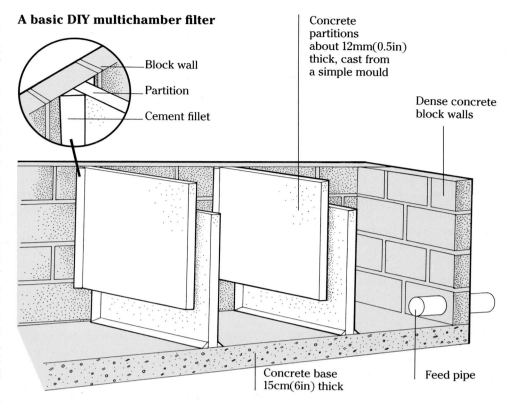

Block wall
Partition
Cement fillet

Concrete partitions about 12mm(0.5in) thick, cast from a simple mould

Dense concrete block walls

Concrete base 15cm(6in) thick

Feed pipe

Above: *A cutaway view of the DIY concrete multichamber filter featured in the text and shown in 'functional' cross-section on page 35. At this stage, the partitions and transfer port sheets are being installed. Be sure to allow sufficient time for the concrete to set at every stage. Site the filter system so that the water level matches that in the pond.*

tion and cover them with the mortar. Repeat this operation for each partition in the filter. After about three days, gently tap out the supporting bricks.

Since the transfer port sheets rest on the base of the filter, no temporary support is required, but you might find that a little packing is required to get them level, depending on how good your building skills were! Don't forget that these sheets are located at the upstream side of the partitions you have just installed, i.e. towards the pond inlet end. Leaving a gap of 15cm(6in) from each partition sheet, fix the second sheets with wooden wedges and fillet them with cement as before. In this case, however, also apply cement along the sheet at base level to prevent unwanted leakage of water between the chambers.

Adding supports for media trays
Once all these have dried to your satisfaction, you must provide some means of holding up the media support trays. Two courses of engineering-quality bricks laid around three sides of each chamber, leaving the opening free to the transfer port, is probably the easiest strategy. You can lay these bricks dry, if you prefer but, for the sake of a little time, it is better to cement them into position. If you are using a rigid tray for the filter media, the lack of support at the front end will not be a problem, particularly if you intend using lightweight plastic ring media. If you use more flexible support trays with perhaps gravel media, then you will need

to provide additional support along the fourth side – a couple of bricks laid longitudinally should be fine.

Adding baffle plates
Should you decide to fit some baffle plates in the settlement chamber(s) you can make these using the same 1-to-1 sand/cement mix in the moulds. Use a short length of plastic pipe like a pastry cutter to make holes in each sheet before it sets. Since these baffle plates do not require permanent fixing in the chamber, wooden wedges alone will hold them in position quite satisfactorily.

Finishing and painting
The final stage of construction consists of painting the filter using the same materials and sequence as with the pond. As fish will not be in contact with the filter surfaces, there is no need to remove the fibres, but do be careful when setting up and maintaining the filter as the upstanding painted fibres can be rather sharp.

Although the above may appear to be a rather daunting marathon of work, the finished result will be a superb filter, every bit as efficient as its commercial equivalent but at a tenth of the cost.

水質と濾過

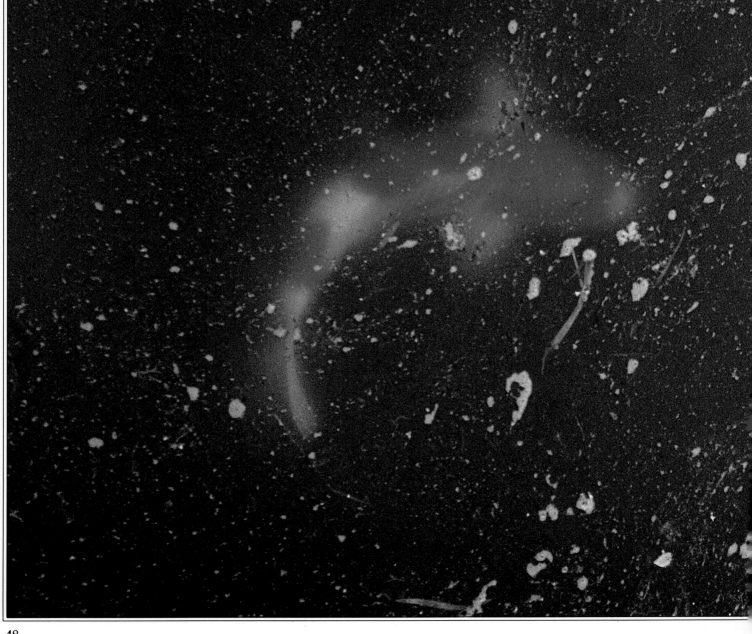

WATER QUALITY AND FILTRATION

Of all the pets we may choose to keep, fish are among the most demanding; in addition to feeding them and caring for their general well-being, we must also closely control the environment in which they live. Water is an alien medium to us and it is not easy to know whether the water in the pond is of the right quality to keep our koi in the best of health. Clear water is not always an indication of purity; it may contain colourless dissolved impurities, such as ammonia and nitrite, that are harmful and may even kill our koi. In this section, we explore the vital subjects of water quality and filtration, with special emphasis on the nitrogen cycle and the underlying principles of biological filtration. We also review the common types of filter media used in koi ponds, including those that exert a chemical influence on the water. For the application of filtration processes in practical terms, including how to build a simple multichamber design, see *Pond and filter construction*, starting on page 22.

Excessive protein waste in the water can cause an obvious scum, but even clear water may not be pure.

WATER QUALITY AND FILTRATION

Water quality

Water is one of the earth's most abundant compounds; more than two-thirds of the surface of the world is covered in water and it is essential for all living organisms. Koi, like their wild ancestors, are freshwater fish, and we need to understand the quality of their natural environment in order to simulate it as nearly as possible in the pond.

Water quality embraces a number of parameters, such as temperature, pH value (degree of acidity or alkalinity), hardness (and salinity), oxygen content, and the levels of ammonia, nitrite, nitrate, chlorine and chloramine. Water may also be contaminated by algae and/or by pollutants, such as pesticides and herbicides. Here, we look briefly at these important parameters.

Temperature

Koi are basically extremely hardy fish, being able to survive a temperature range of 2-30°C(36-85°F). In their native Japan, the winters are cold but relatively short. In Northern Europe and North America, the severe conditions experienced in very long winters may cause problems. Ambient temperatures are obviously not easily within the koi-keeper's control, although it is possible to influence the water temperature in the winter more than in the summer. Water heaters added to the system in winter can keep filters operational and the fish slightly more active.

The pH value of water

The pH scale is used to register the degree of acidity or alkalinity of a body of water. It ranges from 0 (extremely acid) to 14 (extremely alkaline) and is based inversely on the concentration of hydrogen ions (H^+) in the water in relation to hydroxyl ions (OH^-); the more hydrogen ions, the more acid the water and the lower the pH value. At the neutral point, pH7, the concentrations of hydrogen ions and hydroxyl ions are in balance. As hydroxyl ions outnumber hydrogen ions, the water becomes more alkaline and the pH value rises. It is extremely important to remember that the scale is logarithmic, i.e. each step represents a ten-fold change. Thus, pH6 is 10 times more acidic than pH7, and pH5 is 100 times more acidic than pH7. You can keep a check on pH values by using simple test kits (as shown on this page) or sophisticated electronic meters.

For koi, the ideal pH value is between 7 and 8, i.e. neutral to slightly alkaline. In the majority of koi ponds, the pH value rarely falls below 7 (i.e. becomes acidic), unless there has been some accidental

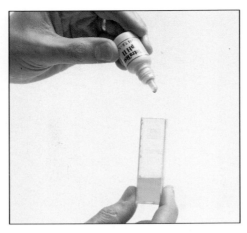

Left: *Using a test kit to check the pH value of the water is simply a matter of adding the required amount of a reagent to a measured sample of pond water in the container supplied with the kit. Shake the container gently to ensure complete mixing.*

Below: *Very quickly, the water sample changes colour and it is then an easy matter to compare the result with a pre-printed chart to read off the pH value. All test kits are based on the same basic principle. Be sure to keep the charts out of the sun to prevent colour fading that may give misleading results. Try to take tests at the same time of day and water temperature.*

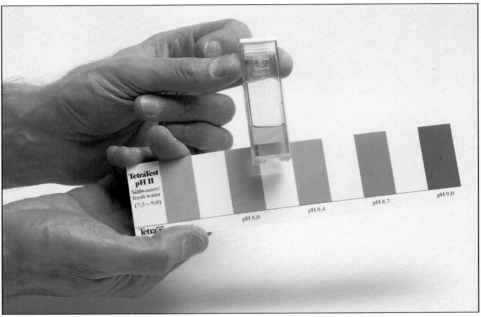

pollution of the pond. Slight fluctuations in pH value are quite normal and should not cause any problems. In ponds with green water (i.e. with an algal bloom), the pH value may fluctuate between 7 and 11 during a 24-hour period. Although this sounds drastic, these temporary fluctuations will not prove serious to fish that have acclimated to such conditions.

Water hardness

Natural fresh water carries a host of dissolved substances, including both inorganic and organic compounds that are picked up from the soil and rocks over which the water flows and that enter as run-off from the land along the banks of rivers and lakes. The mains water that you use to fill your koi pond is neither sterile nor distilled, and so retains this natural mix of dissolved compounds so essential for life (plus some others that the water supply company add, as we shall see later on). Many of these dissolved substances are present in extremely small amounts – literally 'trace' elements – while relatively few account

for over 95 percent of the total concentration. These major substances are chlorides, sulphates, carbonates, bicarbonates, calcium, magnesium, sodium and potassium. Among the characteristics they contribute to water are its hardness and salinity.

In fresh water, the salinity (i.e. the level of total dissolved salts) is relatively low (compared to sea water, for example), while the hardness varies quite considerably and depends mainly on the concentration of calcium and magnesium salts. In terms of hardness, koi can cope with a wide variation, although typically 'hard' water from chalky regions may be slightly beneficial simply because the calcium compounds it contains help to bind up toxic metals (such as lead) in the water.

Water hardness has two important influences on aquatic life and these are relevant to koi. First, it influences the osmoregulation system. In practice, hard water reduces the workload on the koi's osmoregulatory system, while koi living in soft water must have a more efficient osmoregulatory system to maintain their internal salt/water balance. In this connection, adding salt to the pond water benefits ailing or stressed koi by reducing their osmotic workload.

Secondly, water hardness influences alkalinity. In effect, a high degree of temporary hardness (caused by bicarbonate ions) increases the alkalinity of the water. Thus, it is important to view hardness and pH value as interrelated parameters when judging water quality in overall terms. Test kits, as well as electronic meters, are available for monitoring water hardness.

Oxygen content
The amount of oxygen dissolving in water is temperature dependent; as the water temperature increases, the maximum amount of oxygen that will dissolve into it decreases. As a koi-keeper, it is vital to understand this physical relationship between water and gas, and to be aware of the conditions that can cause oxygen deficiency and hence stress the koi in your pond.

Koi require at least 6mg/litre of oxygen in the water. In order to achieve this, the water should be pumped continuously in the pond 24 hours a day for 365 days a year. It is surprising how many people turn their pumps off at night or during the winter months (see *Seasonal care*, pages 78-79 for cold-weather strategy).

Since warm water can hold less oxygen than cold water, the summer months are the most vulnerable period for low oxygen levels, and the level at night is the most critical of all. During the day, water plants use carbon dioxide and release oxygen into the water during the process of photosynthesis. At night, the cycle is effectively reversed, with plant (and animal) respiration using up oxygen and producing carbon dioxide. It is not surprising, therefore, that warm summer nights can result in dangerously low levels of dissolved oxygen. This situation is often worsened during humid, thundery weather, when low pressure effectively reduces the amount of atmospheric oxygen available per unit surface area of water. Accumulated organic debris, either from uneaten food or faeces, will further reduce the oxygen content of the water and so it is vital to remove this from the pond and not allow it to form an organic silt.

During the summer months be sure to check the oxygen content of your pond water on a regular basis. You can use test kits or an electronic meter to obtain a reading. The ideal time for testing the water is between 6.0am and 7.0am, when the oxygen content will be at its lowest.

Below: *The principle of the venturi tube, a simple device for introducing air into the stream of water returning to the pond from the filter. The name arises from the Italian physicist who devised it.*

Above: *A venturi in full flow in a koi pond. The vertical tube (with cap) is clearly visible on the left and the oxygenating mass of air bubbles can be seen 'boiling' just beneath the surface of the water on the right.*

How a venturi works

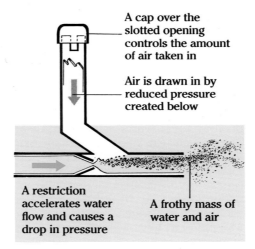

A cap over the slotted opening controls the amount of air taken in

Air is drawn in by reduced pressure created below

A restriction accelerates water flow and causes a drop in pressure

A frothy mass of water and air

Ammonia, nitrite and nitrate
The level of these three nitrogenous compounds in the water is a critical indicator of water quality conditions. Ammonia (NH_3) is a highly toxic gas produced from the decomposition of organic wastes and as a metabolic waste product by the koi, most of which is excreted from the gills. It is lethal in very low concentrations; depending on species and levels of other water conditions, 0.2-0.5mg/litre will kill fish fairly rapidly. Over long periods, a tenth of this concentration can cause increased susceptibility to disease and a hundredth can produce gill irritation. Other water quality conditions can affect the toxicity of ammonia; rising temperatures and pH values increase ammonia toxicity, while increasing salinity lowers it.

· To prevent koi mortalities, it is vital to monitor water quality for the build-up of ammonia. Various test kits are available that make this a straightforward task; most involve adding a measured amount of reagent to a small sample of pond water and comparing the intensity of the colour change against a graduated scale to read off the ammonia level as mg/litre nitrogen. If ammonia levels are too high, make partial water changes of up to 20 percent of the pond water to dilute the ammonia. Until the level subsides, you may need to make such water changes every day.

Nitrites (NO_2^-) are produced as a breakdown product of ammonia as part of a naturally occurring sequence of biochemical reactions that has become known universally as the 'nitrogen cycle'. (The 'motive force' for this cycle is provided by various kinds of bacteria, and we shall be considering their action more closely under *Biological filtration*.) Nitrite is highly poisonous; it disrupts the haemoglobin in red blood cells and produces listlessness and oxygen starvation. Raised nitrite levels can prove fatal to koi less than 15cm(6in) in length; larger koi become lethargic and may lie on their sides at the bottom of the pond, although they will still swim to the surface to feed. As we shall see later, nitrite commonly causes a problem in new

WATER QUALITY AND FILTRATION

Above: *This is the first stage in a three-step sequence for determining the level of nitrite in the water using a test kit. First add seven drops of reagent 1 to a 5ml water sample and shake the vial gently to mix them together. It is important to be accurate.*

Above: *Then add seven drops of a second reagent to the sample and allow up to five minutes for the colour change to develop fully. Using this kit, the colour produced at this stage will range from yellow through orange to deep red.*

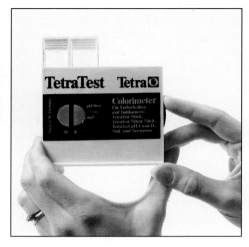

Above: *Place the vial into a comparator and turn the wheel until the 'window' colour matches that of the sample; the appropriate nitrite reading is displayed alongside. The colour gel is viewed through a 'control' of untreated water to improve accuracy.*

ponds, and so it is important to monitor the level using a suitable test kit. While the nitrite concentration is more than 0.15mg/litre, make regular partial water changes of 20 percent.

As with ammonia, increasing the level of dissolved salts in the water decreases the toxic effect of nitrite. Thus, adding 3gm/litre of cooking salt to the water (to make a 0.3 percent solution / approximately equivalent to 0.5oz per gallon) helps to counteract the effects of nitrite.

The third nitrogenous compound in this biochemical sequence is nitrate (NO_3^-), which is much less harmful to koi and other aquatic creatures than the preceding two compounds. In fact, koi can probably tolerate nitrate concentrations up to 500mg/litre, but these levels are very unlikely to occur in the average koi pond. Eggs and fry are more sensitive to nitrate than are adult koi, however. Since nitrate is used as a fertilizer by algae and other plants in the pond, high levels precipitate algal blooms ('green water'), particularly during the summer, when warmth spurs rapid plant growth.

Chlorine and chloramine

In addition to dissolved minerals and organic molecules, natural fresh waters also contain a wide range of microscopic living organisms, from tiny larvae and protozoans to bacteria and viruses. The majority of these are non-pathogenic, but some can cause disease in both humans and other animals. To render such waters fit for human consumption, water supply companies treat it with suitable disinfectants, the most widely used being chlorine. This is forced into the water as a gas and most combines chemically with water to form, among other compounds, hypochlorous acid, which acts as the disinfectant. A small part of the chlorine remains as 'free chlorine' and is relatively unstable in water and will readily diffuse into the air. Although the usual amounts of chlorine and chlorine compounds added to domestic water supplies are not harmful to humans, they can be highly toxic to koi and other fish, with respiratory distress being the most obvious sign. The degree of toxicity depends not only on the total amount of chlorine present, but also on the temperature, pH value, oxygen content and pollution/organic loading of the water in the pond.

With these facts in mind, it is obviously important to check the chlorine content of your local water supply using an appropriate test kit. And bear in mind that chlorine levels may rise in the summer, when water supply companies increase chlorination to cope with expected seasonal rises in pathogenic bacteria in the water. Adding domestic water directly to your pond can be particularly hazardous at this time of year.

Since free chlorine readily evaporates from water, it is relatively easy to drive this off during water changes by spraying the new water into the pond or splashing it from a reasonable height to maximize the mixing of air and water. When you are filling a new pond with water from the mains, it is best to fill it completely and allow the pond to run with maximum aeration for 7-10 days to dechlorinate the water before adding the koi.

A disturbing slant on the chlorination story is the use of chloramines for disinfection of domestic water supplies. Chloramines, complex organic derivatives of chlorine, are formed from the combina-tion of chlorine and ammonia, and are particularly effective because they are more stable than chlorine in water and release twice as much hypochlorous acid over a longer period. Chloramines can also form naturally when chlorinated water mixes with nitrogenous compounds such as nitrate fertilizers. The dilemma for the koi-keeper is that chloramines are even more difficult to eradicate. If you think your water may be affected in this way, fill your pond and run the water through the filters with maximum aeration for a period of 10-14 days before adding the koi.

Filtration

Like most animals, koi excrete urine and produce solid wastes (faeces), both of which are voided at the vent. The urine consists largely of water and a small amount of urea; the main nitrogenous waste product from the breakdown of proteins is ammonia, and this is excreted through the gill membranes. Faeces are largely the remnants of undigested food. In the wild, such waste products and the results of their decomposition are diluted and/or removed by the relatively large volumes of, usually, moving water in which the fishes live. In the enclosed environment of the pond, it is the job of the filtration system to perform this natural cleansing role.

Whatever form a filter system takes, the principal filtration processes involved can be divided into mechanical, biological and chemical. In practice, these processes often occur at the same time, but it does provide a convenient way of looking at what can be a complex and sometimes overlapping series of physical and biochemical reactions.

Mechanical filtration

Most filter media have a mechanical function. (See the photographic review of the most widely used filter media on pages 54-55.) In fact, the most basic forms of mechanical filters simply allow gravity to 'drag' solids out of suspension by taking the pace out of the incoming water flow. Such 'settlement chambers' invariably form the first part of a filter system and as such they prevent the second and any subsequent chambers of a filter from being clogged with solid particles, which would ultimately result in a build-up of sediment in the filter. This would eventually block the water flow and allow the pond water to become foul. If this happens, you will need to take the media out of the filter and remove the sediment from it before replacing it in the chamber. Some filters have a drain fitted at the bottom of each chamber so that you can draw off any sediment without needing to remove the media.

In addition to 'baffles' to slow down the incoming pond water, koi-keepers also use a variety of mechanical filter media to 'strain' the incoming water, including brushes, aquarium filter wool, matting, scouring pads (but not impregnated with soap or detergent) and even hair rollers.

Biological filtration

Biological filtration relies on the activity of specific bacteria cultured in the filter to break down toxic waste products into less harmful substances. These bacteria occur naturally and are used to break down domestic sewage in special treatment plants. Water treated at these plants is so clean that it is often recycled for domestic use. In effect, a biological filter on a koi pond is really a small sewage treatment unit, exploiting the natural sequence of biochemical reactions that occurs in the nitrogen cycle.

There are two stages in the breakdown of ammonia in a biological filter system, each stage involving different types of bacteria to 'power' the detoxification process. In the first stage, ammonia is broken down to nitrite by a number of different nitrifying bacteria, the most important of which is *Nitrosomonas*. A second group of nitrifying bacteria, principally *Nitrobacter*, converts the nitrite to nitrate. (These two stages, and how they relate to other steps in the nitrogen cycle, are clearly shown in the diagram on this page.)

Both these groups of bacteria are aerobic, i.e. they need oxygen to thrive and thus purify the water. The nitrifying bacteria require an oxygen level of at least 1mg/litre in the water continuously flowing through the medium. Sediment building up in the bottom of the filter can deplete oxygen levels in the water and encourage the growth of anaerobic bacteria (those that thrive in the absence of oxygen), rendering the filter ineffective. It is vital, therefore, to keep sediment to a minimum in the filter.

The second chamber in a filter system is usually the biological filter and contains a medium that will provide a large surface area on which the nitrifying bacteria can grow. Again, a variety of different, and equally effective, media is available. It really does not matter what type of filter medium you use, provided that the system is capable of breaking

The nitrogen cycle

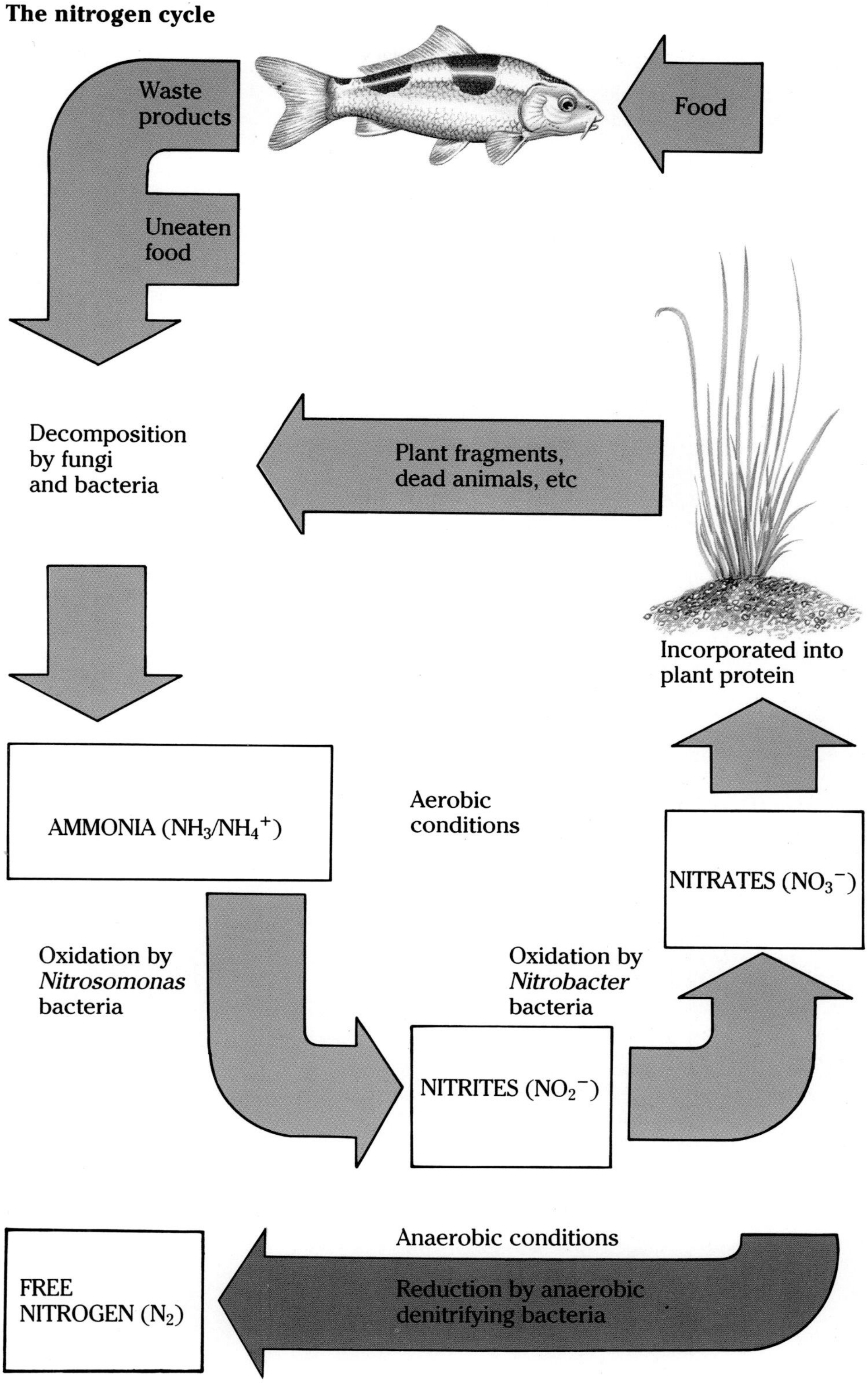

Waste products

Uneaten food

Food

Decomposition by fungi and bacteria

Plant fragments, dead animals, etc

Incorporated into plant protein

AMMONIA (NH_3/NH_4^+)

Aerobic conditions

Oxidation by *Nitrosomonas* bacteria

Oxidation by *Nitrobacter* bacteria

NITRATES (NO_3^-)

NITRITES (NO_2^-)

Anaerobic conditions

FREE NITROGEN (N_2)

Reduction by anaerobic denitrifying bacteria

Above: *These are the main steps in the nitrogen cycle – a naturally occurring sequence of biochemical reactions that keeps nitrogen circulating. The aerobic nitrifying bacteria play a crucial role.*

WATER QUALITY AND FILTRATION

down the poisonous waste products into harmless ones. (The biological value of certain filter media is explored further in the captions on these pages.)

Installing a biological filter system to a pond does not guarantee an immediate improvement to the water quality; ammonia and nitrite levels are likely to fluctuate in a new filter and it may take from six months to a year before the filter has finally matured. You may notice that the concentration of ammonia in the water increases dramatically, sometimes to dangerous levels, once you introduce koi into a new pond. These high levels of ammonia may take only a matter of days to subside in the summer, but up to several weeks during the winter months. This is because these filters are biologically active and thus their efficiency is affected by external parameters, such as the weather, water temperature and pH value, and the number and size of fish in the pond. The growth and reproduction of bacteria are inhibited by the cold, for example; both will cease at temperatures below 5°C(41°F). With these fluctuations

in mind, it is important to check pond water quality regularly, particularly after installing a new filter system. Get into the habit of taking ammonia and nitrite readings every week and recording these analyses on paper. If you run into difficulties with koi health, it is always useful to have a record of any preceding water quality problems.

Both freeze-dried and live cultures of nitrifying bacteria are available; adding one of these preparations to the biological filter on a new pond, or to an established pond in the spring, will boost the filtration process. Early evening is the best time to add these bacterial cultures to the pond, as water temperatures are then at their highest.

Chemical filtration

As the term implies, chemical filtration media remove impurities from the water flow by chemical means. In practice, chemical filtration media are often used in the second chamber of a non-biological filter system, the first one containing a purely mechanical medium to strain off

suspended particles. A typical combination would be filter wool as a mechanical medium and activated carbon as a chemical filter medium. Activated carbon removes ammonia and other organic waste products from the water by a process of adsorption. This means that the adsorbed substances became loosely linked to the surface of the filter medium.

The process of 'activating' the carbon granules – by heating them to a very high temperature – opens up millions of pores that present a large surface area for chemical adsorption. When the surface area becomes 'full up', you will need to replace the activated carbon. In fact, because of their limited lifespan, both filter wool and activated carbon are really only suitable for smaller ponds (i.e. with a capacity of not more than 500 litres/ approximately 110 gallons).

For larger ponds, it is more practical to use zeolite, a chemical filter medium that also removes ammonia and nitrite from the water. Zeolite consists of the hydrated silicates of calcium and alumi-

Filter media commonly used in koi pond systems

Filter brushes are ideal for removing sediment and large particles from the pond water. The individual brushes can be taken out of the filter and allowed to dry, then the dirt will come off easily.

Nylon pot scourers are also used as filter media, both in a mechanical and biological sense, because they also provide a large surface area for bacteria to colonize. They are durable and easy to clean.

Filter wool (usually manmade fibres, such as dacron floss, nylon floss, etc.) is ideal as a mechanical filter but only in smaller systems, as it eventually becomes blocked. Unfortunately, it is not easy to clean.

This commercial filter medium consists of pieces of plastic pipe, very similar to the hair rollers, although the latter have more perforations. Again, you will need to use a large amount of such medium in the filter.

Canterbury spar is prepared from natural flint pieces baked until they split into sharp-edged stones permeated with fissures. It acts as a mechanical filter and also offers a huge surface area for nitrifying bacteria.

These spherical granules of baked clay also provide crevices for bacteria to colonize but they are much lighter than the equivalent amount of Canterbury spar. The granules are also used to grow plants in water.

nium, sometimes with sodium and potassium. It looks like off-white or pale brown stone chippings and is available in various grades. As with most other filtration media, the larger the surface area of zeolite exposed to the pond water, the more effective it will be in removing

Above: *A commercial filter chamber with a venturi fitted on the water inlet, six rows of brushes in the main compartment and zeolite chippings in the final section. Such basic boxes are available in a range of sizes and configurations to suit most systems.*

waste products. While small grade chippings theoretically offer a relatively large surface area, in practice, they tend to compact down and become less efficient. The ideal grade to use is a particle size of about 10cm(4in). In any event, you will need a large quantity; filter systems that rely on zeolite alone need approximately 1kg per 5 litres (about 2.2lb per gallon) of pond water.

One of the advantages of using zeolite in preference to activated carbon is that it can be 'cleaned' and re-used. The chemical bond between zeolite and ammonia is very weak and can be broken by adding salt water to the 'tired' chippings. As the ammonia is released, the zeolite becomes effectively 'recharged' and ready for use again. To do this, remove the zeolite from the filter and replace it with new or 'recharged' zeolite. Put the used zeolite into a container and add a salt solution made up with 6gm of cooking salt per litre of water (approximately 1oz per gallon) for 24 hours. Wash the zeolite thoroughly in fresh water before using it in the filter again.

Unfortunately, using zeolite as the principal filter medium does have several disadvantages. For a start, considerable quantities are required, making it an expensive option for ponds with a capacity greater than 2500 litres (550 gallons). Also, recharging the zeolite can become an onerous and time-consuming task; in the summer months, when koi are most active, it will need recharging every week. Finally, using zeolite prevents you from using salt as a treatment, simply because ammonia and other toxins will be released from the zeolite back into the pond, creating detrimental water quality conditions that will only aggravate any prevailing health problems.

Many koi-keepers use zeolite in conjunction with a biological filter, adding the mineral rock to the final chamber of a multichamber filter. This is particularly beneficial in new pond systems and during the spring, when numbers of bacteria are low in the biological filter and using zeolite will help to keep the concentration of ammonia/ammonium compounds in the pond down to a minimum.

Filter matting consists of latex-coated fibres; it is easy to handle and clean and should not need replacing if regularly maintained. The coarse nature of the matting provides a large surface area for nitrifying bacteria.

Filter foam is usually placed in three layers in the filter chamber. The texture allows this medium to be cleaned easily and it is fairly durable in use. The foam tends to hold back particles and supports nitrifying bacteria.

Ordinary plastic hair rollers can make a very useful filter medium. They are easy to clean and provide a good surface area for nitrifying bacteria to colonize. Large numbers of hair rollers will be needed.

Use this freeze-dried preparation to seed the filter system with useful bacteria. Mix it with warm water and allow it to stand to 'reactivate' the bacteria. Some preparations contain live bacteria for immediate use.

Zeolite is an alumino-silicate mineral used to remove ammonia from the pond water. It is available in small, medium and large-grade chippings; the latter are best as they are easier to handle and do not pack down.

These granules of activated carbon soak up wastes by adsorbing the molecules on the extensive surface area. Activated carbon cannot be recharged once 'full' and must be replaced, making it rather expensive.

WATER QUALITY AND FILTRATION

Continuous flow filtration

In a continuous flow system the water is not recirculated, but passes through the pond to waste. The supply of water must therefore be spring fed, or a diversion of part of a small river system, which passes through the pond before returning once again to a natural water source. Although this type of system is favoured by trout farmers, it is not practical for the majority of koi-keepers. Firstly, a continuous flow system requires a great deal of land. Secondly, while spring-fed water will be fairly free of pathogens (disease-causing organisms), river water may well contain pathogens and/or parasites, such as fish leeches (*Piscicola geometra*) or snails acting as intermediate hosts for spiny-headed worms (*Acanthocephala*), that are detrimental to koi health. Finally, and most importantly, the majority of koi are imported and may be infected with diseases and/or carrying various parasites, which can be spread to wild fish in the untreated water returning to the river, with serious and even potentially devastating results for natural fish populations in these waters.

Sand filters

Some koi-keepers use a sand filter as a final stage in the filtration of pond water. The water is pressurized to 0.85-1.0kg/cm^2(12-14 lb/in^2) as it passes into the filter, where it is filtered through sand contained in a pressure cylinder. The sand filter removes fine solid particles from the water, so that on returning to the pond it is almost entirely free of solids. There is a great deal of evidence that bacterial activity takes place inside the sand filter to further the breakdown of toxic wastes produced by the koi. Without doubt, sand filters are a very beneficial addition to a pond's filter system.

On extremely rare occasions, however, a sand filter may draw in air with the pond water. When this happens, the air is forced by the pressure of the sand filter into solution in the water, leading to supersaturation. The supersaturated water builds up in the pond, giving the water a 'fizzy' appearance and coating the surface, plants and anything else in the pond with a fine layer of bubbles. This leads to a clinical disorder known as 'gas-bubble disease' (see *Health care*, page 111), in which gas bubbles form in the fins and beneath the fin bases, as well as in the blood and among internal organs.

Right: A sand pressure filter with its associated pipework. The whole affair looks complicated, but the large multiport valve is clearly visible on the left. This has various settings, including one for backwashing.

How a sand pressure filter works

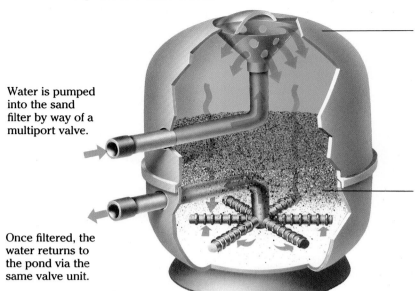

Water is pumped into the sand filter by way of a multiport valve.

Once filtered, the water returns to the pond via the same valve unit.

The sealed vessel is domed in shape to withstand the internal pressure.

The body of the filter contains a special grade of coarse silica sand that strains out any suspended solids as the water is forced through it.

Left: *This illustration clearly shows what goes on inside a typical sand pressure filter. It is important to select the correct size of filter and to match it with the appropriate pump to achieve an efficient flow rate.*

Should such a situation arise, by-pass the sand filter and seek immediate advice from the supplier. The excess air in the pond will 'gas off' over some hours as the water passes through the filters and aeration system. Koi suffering from gas-bubble disease may take several weeks to recover completely as they 'decompress'.

Controlling algae

Green water is caused by a bloom of microscopic algae that contain the green photosynthetic pigment, chlorophyll. Pond water containing these microscopic algae is usually free of both ammonia and nitrite, quite simply because these tiny organisms thrive on the final breakdown product of the nitrogen cycle, namely, nitrate. Nitrate is a powerful fertilizer for plants, and so as the filter unit becomes established and the quantity of nitrate in the pond increases, the algae thrive in the abundance of this nutrient.

Green water is not harmful to koi, but positively beneficial; koi feed on the tiny animals that eat the algae and in this way green water is one of the best colour enhancers of koi available. In Japan, many koi enthusiasts keep their koi at home in their ponds through the winter months but return them to the farms during the summer so that the koi can benefit from spending several months in green water. The disadvantage of green water, of course, is that you are unable to see the koi. Not only will this spoil your enjoyment, but koi that have injured themselves or are suffering from parasites, such as anchor worm, will remain hidden from your attention.

Green water can be very persistent and may take many months to clear from a newly established pond. The water may periodically go green in an established pond, depending on the aspect of the pond and the climatic conditions. During hot, sultry spells, algae will use essential oxygen during the hours of darkness and it is worth running an external pump, such as an aquarium pump, with an airline and airstones in the pond to ensure maximum aeration of the water.

Some koi-keepers have started to use ultraviolet (UV) light as a means of controlling algae. (UV light is very harmful; never remove the bulb from its protective casing while the light is switched on.) UV light damages the tiny algal cells internally, and thus kills them. The UV unit is usually placed at the end of the filter system, before the water is returned to the pond.

One of the major myths concerning this form of light is its ability to kill bacteria and render the pond sterile. Although this is true in part, the water passing through the unit would have to be almost motionless for the UV light to kill most of the bacteria. In practice, the flow of pond water through an UV light system is too fast to seriously reduce the number of bacteria present in the pond water. Be sure to replace the UV tube every six to nine months if you are using it continuously; after this period it ceases to be effective even though it appears undimmed.

It is also possible to control algae using ozone. Ozone (O_3) is a highly unstable form of oxygen (O_2), which has strong disinfectant properties. (It occurs naturally in the upper atmosphere, forming the so-called 'ozone layer'.) It is created for aquarium and pond use in a device known as an ozonizer, in which dried air is passed through an electrical discharge to 'weld' one extra oxygen atom onto each normal molecule. Since it is toxic to all life forms, it is vital to use it correctly and carefully. Ozone units are usually fitted in the return water plumbing, where the ozone gas effectively breaks down the algal cells. It is important that the ozone does not reach the fish and plants in the main pond. (Vigorous aeration or filtration over activated carbon will remove ozone from treated water.) The effective dosing rate of ozone is reduced by high levels of organic matter in the water.

Surprisingly, algal blooms can be controlled by magnetism; small electromagnets placed on the return water pipe will disrupt microscopic cells internally, either killing them outright or preventing their reproduction.

Many chemical products are available to clear algae from ponds. When using these algicides, be sure to follow the manufacturers' directions and never exceed the recommended dosage or frequency of treatments. There is always the possibility that, used incorrectly, such chemicals can harm the fish and aquatic plants. And remember that a sudden die-back of dense concentrations of algal cells can cause water quality problems. In such cases, consider using some mechanical method of removing the bulk of the algae, such as high-rate mechanical filters, before dosing the water.

Above: *Summer brings light and warmth to the pond, which, together with an abundance of nitrates, can cause algal blooms, especially in new ponds. If you need to control green water, do it with care.*

鯉の購入

BUYING KOI

Buying koi should be a pleasurable experience, but keeping them is a responsibility not to be undertaken lightly. Never buy a koi on a whim, and make sure that you have the capacity, without stretching the limits of your pond, to look after them properly. Having decided to buy, there are several things you will need to think about. When you buy will be dictated, in part, by the calendar of the koi-keeping industry – most dealers import koi in November and December and hobbyists generally stock their ponds in the spring. Think carefully, too, about where to buy your koi and, having found a reputable dealer, spend time watching any that interest you; the checklist on page 63 will remind you what to look for. In the second half of this section, we look at how to avoid stressing and damaging koi while transporting them and, finally, we examine the much-debated subject of quarantining newly purchased koi.

Choose koi carefully; your dealer will be happy to help you.

BUYING KOI

Sources of koi

The main countries that now export koi are Japan, Israel, Singapore, and the United States of America.

Japan is the home of the koi and those produced here are of top quality in terms of colour definition and availability of varieties in different sizes. If you are interested in showing your fish, then Japanese koi are the ones to buy, but they are generally more expensive than those from other countries.

Koi from America and Singapore tend to be of indeterminate variety, and colours are often indistinct. As they get older they seem to lose their body shape and may become fat and dumpy.

Israel tends to produce extremely pretty, small koi, which become more plain in appearance as they get older. Over the last two years, however, the number of koi imported from Israel has increased dramatically and it is expected that the quality will continue to improve.

When to buy

The best quality koi tend to be exported from Japan in November and December. There are two reasons for this; firstly, the growing-on ponds in Japan are harvested in October. Secondly, as the water temperatures are lower, water can contain higher levels of dissolved oxygen, and this, combined with the fact that the koi are less active and demanding on their environment at lower temperatures, makes the transportation of them less risky. Koi are also imported in March, April and May, but high-quality speci-

Above: *These fish are waiting to be sold by auction. In Japan, such events take place twice a month from April to October. Here,* many dealers buy young koi from breeders to grow on in their ponds over the winter before selling them the following year.

mens are not available for sale any later in the year as they are returned to growing-on ponds until October. 'Ordinary' quality koi are available throughout the year in most places, however.

Most enthusiasts buy koi to stock their ponds in the spring, when the water is beginning to warm up and the fish are becoming more active. Obviously, the majority of koi-keepers do not have indoor pools in which to house koi, recently arrived from Japan, throughout the winter, and you will find that most dealers will happily hold the koi until the spring. It is a good idea to buy your koi in time to allow them a generous settling in period before their first winter.

Where to buy

Having decided on when to buy, and from which country, the next decision you will need to make is where to buy. Try to visit a reputable dealer who has a sound knowledge of koi and their environment. It is best to avoid garden centres at busy times, such as the weekends, unless they have specialist staff. A good dealer will want to know that his koi are going to good homes and so will be happy to explain anything that is necessary to help you maintain your new koi in the best of health.

When you arrive at a dealer, the first thing to look for is the state of the pond

Left: *If you are setting up a pond for the first time, choose young koi such as these. Small fish in the size range 7.5-10cm(3-4in) are ideal for the new koi-keeper.*

water; it should be well filtered and clean, not only so that you can view the fish but, more importantly, because koi kept in poor water are prone to disease and infection. Bear in mind that clear water is not necessarily 'good' water – your nose will be as useful as your eyes in assessing its true condition. However, even the smell of the water may not be a guarantee of its cleanliness – the dealer may have just discharged his bottom drains – nevertheless, it should provide some indication. If there is a strong 'fishy' smell and the koi appear distressed, it may be worth bypassing that particular dealer.

Choosing your koi

Spend time watching a prospective koi; watch the way it swims – its movements should be fluid, not jerky – and see how interested it is in its surroundings. Pay particular attention to its gill movements, which should be slow and regular, using both gills. The gill plates of a healthy fish are close to the body, so avoid fish whose gill plates are proud of the head and that seem to be puffing hard or hanging near the surface of the water. Look out for a white bloom on the skin of the fish (similar in appearance to the bloom on grapes), which may indicate *Ichthyobodo* (previously known as *Costia*) or *Trichodina* parasites. Also look for raised scales or holes, as these, although common, can sometimes be difficult to treat. Avoid fish with cloudy eyes, fin rot, or bumps on either side of the gill plate or on the head. The cause of these bumps is not yet known, but they may burst, leaving holes in the gill plate that can take months, if not years, to heal. (See also *Health care*, starting on page 98.)

Once you have found a fish that appears to be healthy, ask the dealer to 'bowl' it for you so that you can examine it more closely. Watch the way that this is done – fish can be damaged if badly handled. The dealer should use a shallow pan net to catch the fish, and then encourage it to swim into the tilted bowl. Ideally, the dealer should not lift the koi out of the water.

Once the fish is in the bowl you can examine it for any redness on the body or fins. Such signs may suggest that the fish has been recently imported, but could indicate a developing internal problem. Watch out, too, for parasites on the fins, such as fish lice (*Argulus*), or anchor worms (*Lernaea*) around the dorsal and tail regions. Neither create serious problems but, even so, you should ask the dealer to remove any parasites. You should also treat your own pond, to prevent any further disturbances.

Ask the dealer to outline the good and

Above: *Always ask the dealer to 'bowl' a koi for you so that you can examine it carefully before you decide to buy. Note how the* dealer uses the edge of the net to dip the side of the bowl, so that the koi can swim in without leaving the water.

bad points of your selected fish and to tell you its variety name; this will give you a clearer understanding of what to look for in future purchases. Do not be influenced by merely snobbish considerations; look at the fish as a whole and respond to the impression it makes on you. Too many new hobbyists tend to spend hours evaluating all the bad points on an otherwise very impressive koi. Listen to the dealer's advice, of course, but don't be afraid to rely on your own judgement as far as personal preference is concerned.

Transporting koi

Once you have selected the fish and inspected it carefully, the dealer will bag it for you to take away. Be sure to tell the dealer if you have a particularly long journey home; he may be able to accommodate your special needs by providing extra bags or a special box in which to carry the fish, for example, or by packing ice around the bags in hot weather. Normally, fish are placed in a bag with one part water to two parts oxygen. There only needs to be enough water to cover the koi's gills; oxygen is much more important to the fish than water, especially on long journeys or if the water is warm. Unless you live locally, be sure to avoid dealers who do not oxygenate their fish bags.

When buying larger koi, make sure that the bags are long enough to contain the fish properly, without the risk of causing bent tails and broken fins. Koi are usually double bagged, or even triple bagged in the case of larger fish, to avoid accidents and leaks. In fact, it is a good idea to box larger fish, and to ensure that there is as little movement as possible between the box and the bag. Since moving a fish can be a very traumatic experience for it, it is vital to avoid undue stress during the process. As far as

BUYING KOI

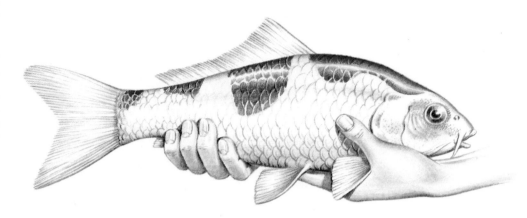

Above: *It is important that you handle koi correctly to avoid damage and undue stress. Hold the fish's head towards you with one hand underneath its jaw and the other behind the pelvic fins. This will give you a firm hold without inhibiting its movement.*

intact. It is less stressful for a fish to go from cold water to warm water than vice versa – imagine how you would feel diving into cold water on a hot day!

Quarantining

Newly imported fish are normally quarantined by the dealer, not because they are necessarily diseased on arrival, but to rest them. They will be stressed and will, therefore, be prone to disease and parasites in the same way that a person who is run down or has had a traumatic shock is prone to illness.

On their arrival in the country, the dealer will usually salt dip the koi and then rest them in a separate pond or quarantine tank, to which has been added a mild antiseptic solution to ward off infection while the fish are at their lowest ebb. Here they will be left for at least a week, without being disturbed. Koi that are highly stressed may be left longer; rest and recuperation are the best 'medicine' for the majority of fish. If, during this time, the dealer notices evidence of para-

possible, avoid sudden fluctuations in temperature, flashing lights, and loud noise, which may disturb the koi.

You will probably be transporting your koi home in the car. Avoid carrying the fish bag on your lap, as your body heat will increase the temperature of the water quite rapidly. For the same reason, do not place the bag in the front footwell of the car, where warm air from the heater will have the same effect. The best place to carry the fish bag is in the boot of the car. Tuck a blanket around it to prevent it rolling about or wedge it between objects that will not pierce it. If the car does not have a boot, place the bag in the footwells behind the front seats, preferably out of the way of anyone's feet. You can reduce stress to the fish by covering the bag with a blanket to cut out light. Drive steadily, trying to avoid bumps and holes in the road and remember not to take corners too quickly. This will help to prevent banged noses and split fins.

On arriving home, remove the bag from the car and float it on the surface of the pond or quarantine tank (see below) for an hour or two. If there is oxygen in the bag, this delay need not cause any problems. While the bag floats, the temperature of the water in the bag will gradually equalize with that of the pond or tank. (Check with the dealer the temperature of the water in his pond.) If the temperature of the bag water is very close to that of the pond water, you may remove one of the bags straight away. If the difference is more than a few degrees centigrade, leave both (or all three) bags

Below: *Once you have selected your koi, the dealer will bag it for you to take home. A double or triple layer of plastic bags are normally used and these should be filled with one part water – just enough to cover the koi's gills – to two parts oxygen.*

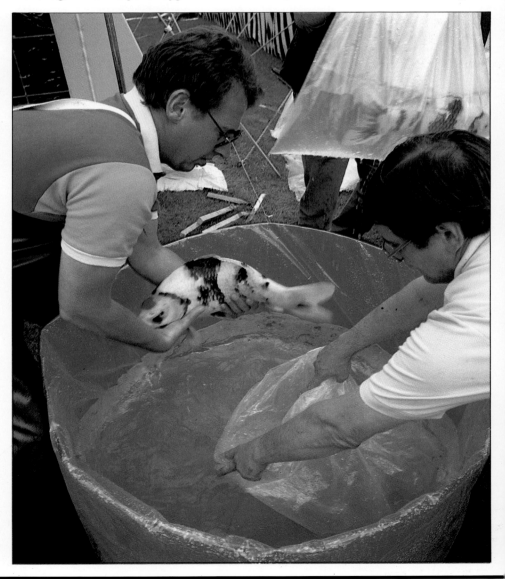

sites, such as anchor worm, he will be able to deal with the infestation before mixing these newly purchased koi with the rest of his stock.

Many koi-keepers are opposed to quarantining newly purchased fish themselves, however. Their arguments are that it increases, rather than diminishes, the stress because it involves moving the fish twice – to the treatment tank and then to the pond. Other possible causes of this increase of stress could be that koi are shoaling fish and do not like being kept on their own.

It is important to point out, at this stage, that the results of stress may take several weeks to become apparent and that the incubation period of some diseases can be as long as several months, or even years. Many fish diseases and problems can result from something that happened in the past; the symptoms of gill rot, for example, may appear approximately three weeks after the pump in the pond was turned off for a few days. Therefore, although some fish-keepers maintain that fish in quarantine develop the symptoms of any virus or bacterial infection they may have before they are mixed with other stock, this is not, in itself, an adequate reason to support additional quarantining of newly purchased koi.

If you do decide to quarantine new fish, make sure that the treatment tank or pond is large enough. Few hobbyists have adequate quarantine facilities and many people, to their cost, have quarantined fish in small, cramped ponds with inadequate filtration. When you consider all the stress-inducing factors involved, it is hardly surprising that the koi have died on being moved to the pond.

In the majority of cases, it is better to place the fish straight into your pond. You should, in any case, keep an eye on the progress of newly acquired koi for the first six weeks or so, particularly at, and just after, feeding times. Make sure that each fish actually swallows any food that it takes. Many fishkeepers find that fish 'sulk' after being introduced to a new pond; isolating themselves from other fish, seeming disinclined to feed and lying at the bottom of the pond. Do not panic – some fish respond better than others to being moved. Watch a particular fish carefully for a week to ten days, but do not touch it. If after this time it still takes no interest in its surroundings, you may need to administer a salt bath. This will kill parasites, such as *Ichthyobodo* and *Trichodina* (see *Health care*, page 102), which tend to multiply rapidly on stressed fish. Such a treatment will normally be sufficient to rouse the koi.

Bagging a koi

Koi will normally be bagged, and larger fish boxed, for you to carry home. It is important that these bags are large enough and that they are oxygenated; oxygen is more important to the fish than water.

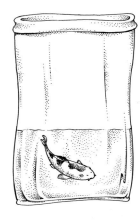

Place the koi in a bag with just enough water to cover the gills.

Holding the top, squeeze out any air trapped inside the bag.

Fill the bag with oxygen, holding the top firmly against the hose.

When there is enough oxygen in the bag, twist the top tightly.

Secure the top of the plastic bag with an elastic band.

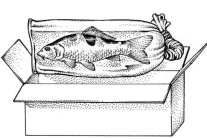

Larger koi should be boxed to prevent bumped noses and split fins.

What to look for when buying koi

Choosing your dealer
● How did you hear about the dealer?
● How far away is it from your home?
● What condition are the ponds in?
  Does the water appear well filtered and clean?
  Is there a strong 'fishy' smell?
  Do the koi appear distressed?
● How does the dealer handle and bowl the fish?
● Does the dealer oxygenate the bags?
● What sort of quarantine facilities are there?

Choosing your koi
● How does the fish swim? Are its movements fluid or jerky?
● How interested is it in its environment?
● How steady are its gill movements? (They should be slow and regular.)
● Is the koi using both gills?
● Do you *like* the fish? (Don't be persuaded by a pushy dealer!)

Koi to avoid
Avoid koi with any of the following:
● Parasites (such as fish lice on the fins or anchor worms around the dorsal or tail regions)
● Gill plates that stand proud of the head
● Bumps on the side of the gill plates or on the head
● Redness on the body or fins
● A white bloom on the skin
● Raised scales or holes
● Cloudy eyes
● Fin rot
● Also avoid any koi that seem to be puffing hard or that are hanging near the surface of the water.

鯉の餌

FEEDING KOI

Good body shape is the single most important feature that judges and breeders look for in koi. It should also be the priority of the fishkeeper, who should aim to provide a well-balanced diet that will build up the muscle, but not the fat, in the koi, and enhance their colour. The Japanese say that a healthy koi is a hungry koi, even after feeding. This is certainly true; koi will always accept more than they can comfortably eat, and often become too fat, with potentially fatal results. Overfeeding also leads to an increase in the volume of waste products excreted by the koi into the water and this, together with pollution resulting from decaying uneaten food, creates a new problem: poor water quality, that is, high ammonia and nitrite levels. 'Little and often' is a good rule to follow when feeding koi; in this way the koi, although receiving enough food, are kept hungry and will tend to feed from your hand.

Lettuce is a favourite treat for koi, and large fish, like these, will happily tear leaves from a whole one.

FEEDING KOI

Feeding and growth rate

The feeding pattern, and thus the growth rate, of koi depends on many factors, such as water temperature, water quality, stocking density and genetic background. Koi feed most actively at temperatures in excess of 15°C(59°F), thus sexually immature fish can grow rapidly during the summer months when the temperature is warmer (see below). Once koi are mature, their growth rate slows considerably; in sexually mature fish, most of the food eaten is utilized in producing eggs or sperm in preparation for breeding. However, unlike many other vertebrates, fish continue to grow throughout their lives and it is easy for pampered koi to reproduce and continue to grow because of their artificially high feeding rates. The cycle of rapid growth in summer and retarded growth in winter produces rings on the fish's scales (much like the growth rings of a tree) and a koi's age can be determined by counting these rings. Some koi-keepers, however, who heat their pools in the winter, continue to feed their koi throughout the year. If a koi has continued to feed during winter its rings will not be clearly defined and it will therefore be difficult to age.

Water quality affects the rate of growth because koi lose their appetites and may even stop eating if their environment is poor. Poor water quality can also affect the fish's metabolism, thus hindering digestion of food.

The stocking density of the pond can

Below: Koi can become quite tame. Encourage hand feeding with prepared foodstuffs or give your koi a treat with prawns, brown bread or lettuce.

also have marked effects on koi growth rate. In a lightly stocked pond, koi will become sexually mature while still of a relatively small size (25-30cm/10-12in) and once mature, growth is retarded (see above). Although koi in a densely stocked pond will mature at a much larger size (50-60cm/20-24in), competition for food will slow the growth rate, food will be scarcer and the 'battle' for it can stress some koi. You will have to decide on optimum stocking levels for your own koi pond bearing this in mind. In fact, these considerations are really most important for koi farmers.

The genetic background, too, influences the size to which koi will grow; as the children of tall parents tend to be tall, and short parents produce small children, so the same is true of koi. This is obviously a simplified view of gene action, however, because of the significant role the environment plays in influencing size.

Water temperature affects fish more than any other single factor. Fish are ectothermic – their body temperature fluctuates in accordance with the temperature of their environment, usually remaining 1°C higher (see page 72). As the temperature drops, the ability of the koi to digest and assimilate food decreases. In the winter months, therefore, at temperatures below 10°C(50°F), it is a good idea to feed cereal diets that the koi can digest quickly and easily and that do not stay in the gut too long. High-protein diets linger in the gut and can cause severe problems; the bacteria found in the fish's gut, which play a role in breaking down some less readily digestible substances, such as cellulose,

may become pathogenic if food is retained in the gut too long. As the water temperature rises, however, the koi need protein for growth, repair of damaged tissue and injuries, and for reproduction. In the summer, koi will benefit from a high-protein diet containing 35 to 40 percent of fishmeal-based protein. (See also *Seasonal care*, pages 70-79.)

Nutritional content of food

Food contains various elements, such as proteins, fats, carbohydrates, vitamins and minerals, which are essential for all animals to maintain healthy bodies, grow and reproduce. Here we explain what these elements are and why they are important components of food.

Proteins are made up of amino acids. Thirteen essential amino acids should be included in any fish diet, although there are about 20 found in natural proteins. An adequate diet contains sufficient quantities of both essential and non-essential amino acids to allow the koi to grow, repair damaged tissue and produce either eggs or sperm. Deficiency of protein or any of the essential amino acids causes koi to grow more slowly and, if this dietary problem continues, can result in a deformation of the spine. (Spine deformities may have a number of other causes, such as disease, however).

Fats provide a source of energy to koi; their important role is in providing fatty acids (see below), such as triglyceride and phospholipids; vital components of membranes surrounding all cell walls. Koi can make almost all of the fatty acids they need with the exceptions of linoleic and linolenic acids, which are essential and must be provided in the food. Linolenic acids are required for growth.

All fats are made up in a similar way to proteins, but of fatty acids, rather than amino acids, bonded together with glycerol. If essential fatty acids are omitted from the diet, symptoms of fin erosion and heart and liver problems may result. Fats have a low melting point and are thus more easily digested by koi. They are found in fish, soya and corn oils and in high concentrations of wheatgerm. Fatty acids become rancid on exposure to air - a chemical process known as oxidation. In koi, the liver is the chief organ for storing fats and if stale food is fed to them it can result in disease and death. Unfortunately, rancid food has no outward appearance of having 'gone bad'. It is, therefore, worth buying smaller packs of food, rather than a large quantity which is utilized slowly, and never keep food from one year to the next.

The function of some vitamins in the koi diet

Vitamin	Source	Function	Consequences of deficiency	Notes
Fat-soluble vitamins				
Vitamin A (Retinol)	Greenfood	Important for skin and sight	Poor growth; haemorrhaging; blindness	An excess of Vitamin A can lead to liver, spleen and skeletal problems
Vitamin E (Tocopherol)	Wheatgerm	Anti-oxidizing agent in food to stop fats turning rancid	Skeletal disorders; fatty degeneration of the liver (the latter probably caused by fats turning rancid)	An excess of Vitamin E may lead to clinical disorders
Vitamin K	Green plants	Aids blood-clotting	Internal haemorrhaging in the muscle and gut; excessively long blood-clotting time; anaemia	
Water-soluble vitamins				
Vitamin B complex				
Thiamin (B1)	Yeast and wheatgerm	Nerve function; digestion; reproduction	Disturbed swimming behaviour (skittishness); poor coloration; haemorrhaging at fin bases; paralysis of the fins	Koi have an enzyme that can destroy this vitamin but, fortunately, some is absorbed. It is not clear whether koi can make thiamin themselves
Riboflavin (B2)	Liver, kidney, heart of various animals; milk	Assists the absorption of oxygen in muscle and tissues that have a poor blood supply	Formation of blood vessels in the cornea; cataracts; bleeding inside the eyes; sensitivity to light; bleeding from the nostrils and gills; loss of appetite; retarded growth; anaemia	
Nicotinic acid	Mainly meats	Aids growth (particularly important in fry and young koi)	Stunted growth	
Choline	Meats, egg yolk, cereals, legumes	Aids metabolism of fat	Fatty liver degeneration	
Pantothenic acid	Liver, kidney, egg yolk	Aids metabolism of fat and carbohydrate	Loss of appetite; abnormal mucus production; gill problems	The gill filaments become clubbed and fused, leading to respiratory distress
Pyridoxine (B6)	Meats, wheat, yeast	Aids metabolism of protein	Can be fatal; rapid ventilation of the gills; skittishness; retarded growth; internal haemorrhaging; pop-eye disease	Absence of pyridoxine has caused high mortalities in koi
Inositol		Function in metabolism unknown	Ulceration and haemorrhaging in juvenile koi; anorexia; reduced growth and anaemia	
Folic acid	Some leafy plants; liver and kidney	Important for cell formation	Anaemia	
Cyanocobalamin (B12)	Animal meats, especially liver and kidney	Aids blood cell formation	Possible reduced appetite, otherwise none	
Vitamin C (Ascorbic acid)	Leafy vegetables; fruits	Development of cartilage and collagen	Deformed spine and gills; internal haemorrhaging	Particularly important in the diet of young koi

FEEDING KOI

Carbohydrates also form a source of energy for koi but fish metabolize them less readily than omnivorous birds or mammals. Too much carbohydrate is very bad for koi health, resulting in either degeneration of the liver or an excessive storage of these substances as glycogen, leading ultimately to heart failure.

Vitamins are essential for the normal metabolism and growth of koi, and requirements of some are increased during spawning. Vitamins are complex-structured substances, needed in only small amounts in the diet, but deficiencies can cause clinical disorders.

Vitamins are divided into two categories: fat soluble and water soluble. Fat-soluble vitamins are found in a variety of forms, all of which are metabolized slowly and can be stored in the body fat. An excess of fat-soluble vitamins can lead to a condition known as hypervitaminosis, which, depending on the vitamin, can lead to clinical disorders.

Water-soluble vitamins are easily absorbed and are not usually excreted.

All essential vitamins are supplied in more than adequate quantities in proprietary koi foods and it would be unusual for the hobbyist to meet clinical symptoms associated with deficiency.

Minerals, too, aid basic metabolic functions, as well as performing their own duties, which include building skeletal structures, osmoregulation, building of nerves, and maintaining the efficiency of gaseous exchange in the blood system. Little is known about mineral deficiencies in fish, probably because most minerals are absorbed from the surrounding water. Normally 12 percent of the diet is made up of minerals, being contained in fish food in the form of ash.

Nutritional requirement of koi
The type of food you give your koi and the quantity you offer them will vary according to their size. The majority of

proprietary koi foods have a cereal base (see table) with different ingredients added either to enhance colour or aid digestion. Choose a food size that is small enough to be eaten by the smallest fish in the pond, otherwise they may die of starvation. If you keep very small koi with larger ones, offer a mixture of large and small foodstuffs, but always make sure that young fish are adequately fed.

Most koi food comes in two forms: floating and sinking. Koi are bottom-feeding fish and are, therefore, better suited to sinking food. This is made by compressing the meal through a die at high pressure. The meal is held together with fats and, again, takes a long time to be dissolved by cold water. The disadvantage with relying on this type of food is that you will be deprived of seeing your koi feeding. Fortunately, koi will take food from the surface – indeed, you can even tame your koi to feed from your hand – and special expanded (hollow) foods have been formulated for this pur-

A selection of foods suitable for koi

Koi sticks
Koi sticks contain all the essential nutrients for a balanced diet, together with additives to enhance colour.

Colour enhancer pellets
Feed these pellets in the summer to enhance colour. Choose the size of pellet to suit the smallest fish in the pond.

Wheatgerm pellets
Wheatgerm, which has a high cereal content, should form an essential part of the koi's diet in the spring and autumn.

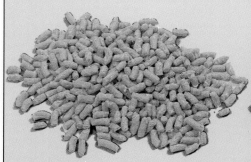

Pond sticks
Often mixed with koi sticks to add variety, pond sticks are ideal when the water temperature exceeds 10°C(50°F).

High-protein pellets
High-protein pellets promote maximum growth during the summer. Feed when the water temperature exceeds 20°C(68°F).

Staple pellets
Many koi-keepers like to mix staple with colour enhancer pellets to provide variety in the diet, particularly in the summer.

pose. These are steam cooked to create an outer shell, which protects the food particle from saturation for a while. (Once the pond water has dissolved the shell, the food will sink.) Another advantage with floating food is that it is easy to see when the koi have eaten enough. Take care when feeding sinking types – uneaten food can easily pass unobserved, particularly in murky water.

Provide just enough food so that after five minutes it has all been eaten. On koi farms in summer, smaller koi (i.e. below 15-20cm/6-8in in length) are fed five percent of their body weight per day, whereas large mature koi (i.e. over 20cm/8in long) are only fed two percent. The nutritional value of koi food is calculated by weight and not by volume. Normally, 1kg(2.2lb) of fish food will increase koi growth by 500gm (1.1lb) or even 700gm (1.5lb) in favourable conditions.

In the winter, provide wheatgerm-based diets on a maintenance basis, in order to keep the body functions ticking over, since it is too cold for the koi to grow. Wheatgerm is also a good source of Vitamin E (see table).

Feeding to enhance colour

Koi are highly valued for their colour and certain additives can be included in the diet to maintain and enhance the fish's natural coloration. Carotene affects the red pigmentation, but if used at too high a concentration, even the white pigment on the koi will turn pink. *Spirulina platensis* also enhances and fixes the red pigment, but does not turn the white to pink to the same extent. It is a type of algae found and cultured in Mexico and eaten by the people, since it contains a high level of protein. Initially, it was fed to koi on account of its nutritional value and not because of its colour-enhancing characteristics. Now that these have been established, it is fed to koi for only one month each year, usually during September, but can be given at any time, even during colder periods, at temperatures of 10°C(50°F), but no lower. Some koi farmers feed it for the month before the fish go to market to bring out the best colours in the koi.

Good coloration is not only enhanced by good feeding, however. Healthy fish tend to have much brighter colours than diseased ones. To bring out the colour in koi, particularly the white, you must provide good living conditions. Strong red and yellow pigments develop well in waters rich in green phytoplankton (single-celled plants). Because koi are difficult to see in green water, it helps to feed a diet that will enhance the red pigmentation. Black pigment is enriched in hard water with a pH level of 7.5-8.5. Remember, however, that changing the pH and hardness of the water can affect the toxicity of ammonia and nitrite.

Livefoods

Koi will relish a variety of livefoods, including cockles, worms and prawns. Earthworms can be fed to the fish all year round and, like prawns and cockles, are high in protein and soon become a favourite treat – a sure way to gain the affection of your koi. Tadpoles from frogs are another great treat in spring and, in summer, silkworm pupae, imported from Japan, are an excellent source of protein. Feed these pupae only as an occasional treat, however, as they have been shown to cause a diabetes-like disease in koi. Chironomid larva (bloodworms) and mosquito larva are a popular diet for small fish, though not easily available. Daphnia ('water fleas'), plentiful in earth ponds, are one of the first foods for koi fry but tend to be too small for adult koi. Maggots are not recommended as they can carry harmful bacteria from the decaying flesh. Do not rely on livefoods to form the staple diet for koi, however, but offer them as a supplement to the regular diet. If koi are fed on these titbits alone, there is a risk that nutritional diseases will set in as the result of a lack of vitamins or amino acids.

Other foods

Koi will accept many foods thrown to them in their pond, but many of these are of little or no nutritional value and may even harm the fish. Brown bread is acceptable, but white bread contains a mild form of bleach, which does the koi no good at all. Do not offer beans, peas or corn, since koi are unable to digest the hard outer casing of these foods.

Koi will take lettuce leaves and may also eat duckweed and other plants around their pond (with the exception of blanketweed, which is too coarse for them to pull off the sides).

Flake food
Ideal for small koi (less than 15cm/6in long), each colour flake represents a different nutritional ingredient.

Brown bread
Brown bread is another good treat for koi. Roll the soft dough into pellets of a size suitable for the smallest fish.

Prawns
Prawns are an ideal, if expensive, treat. Whole prawns are best; the red pigment in the shells is a very good colour enhancer.

Lettuce
Lettuce is a favourite with koi; large fish will tear pieces off a whole lettuce, but smaller koi will require individual leaves.

SEASONAL CARE

Unlike most other pets you may choose to keep, koi are generally kept outside. Although some koi-keepers have an additional pond built into a garage or conservatory for overwintering their fish, the majority have only a single pond in their gardens. Here, koi are subject to the whims of the changing seasons, which may include wide fluctuations in temperature, flower fall (from flowering cherry trees, for instance) and leaf fall. Caring for koi and maintaining them in a healthy condition therefore requires certain adjustments to pumps, filters and routine pond maintenance, as well as changes to the koi's diet, at various times of the year. In this section we chart the progress of the year from spring through summer and autumn to winter, outlining the steps you should take to ensure that your koi enjoy the best possible water quality and remain in peak condition throughout the year. Checklists provide a quick reminder of tasks for each season.

The red foliage of a Japanese maple provides a colourful focal point to this koi pond in autumn.

SEASONAL CARE

Spring

Spring marks the beginning of an active time for the koi-keeper. The air temperature gradually rises but may be subject to wide variations, with warm, sunny days followed by cold, even frosty, nights in many parts of the world. Water takes much longer than air or land to warm up and, consistent with this, tends to maintain slightly more constant temperatures than air.

Spring is probably the most hazardous season of the year for koi. Like most fish, koi are ectothermic, that is they have little ability to physiologically maintain a constant body temperature. Their body temperature is usually fractionally higher than the water in which they live due to muscle activity and metabolic functions, both of which generate a small amount of heat. The koi's immune system is more or less inoperative at temperatures below 10°C(50°F) and becomes effective quite slowly as the temperature rises. However, with the advent of warmer days, many species of bacteria and protozoa quickly become very active and, as the temperature approaches 10°C(50°F), begin to reproduce rapidly. It is therefore imperative that you pay close attention to routine maintenance work, such as cleaning the pond and adding proprietary brands of bacteria to the pond filter system to give the koi every opportunity of surviving the hazards that spring brings with it.

Feeding

As the pond water gradually warms up, koi start to look around for food. When the water temperature first reaches 10°C(50°F), feed the koi very sparingly, in the mornings only. The reason for this cautious approach is that the fish's metabolism (i.e. their entire bodily function) is governed by the surrounding water temperature. Overnight frosts in early spring can chill the water, and food in the digestive tract moves very slowly when the water is cold. As a result, undigested food decomposes inside the gut, leading to internal bacterial problems (see *Health care,* particularly pages 108-110). To minimize this risk, avoid high-protein foods in early spring and instead offer a readily digestible laxative food, such as wheatgerm pellets.

Once water temperatures stabilize at around 10°C(50°F) and above, start to introduce a balanced diet of carbohydrate wheatgerm, protein and trace elements, often marketed as 'staple' food. Once temperatures stabilize above 15°C(59°F), you can begin to offer them a higher protein food.

Resist the temptation to rush for last

year's leftover food, as any opened pack may have oxidized and deteriorated or, worse still, grown microscopic moulds that are highly toxic to koi.

Pond management

If you have not installed bottom drains in the pond (see page 32), it will benefit from a thorough clean with a good vacuum pump to remove all the detritus and debris that have accumulated over the winter months. The filters will also benefit from a good backwash; since the growth of bacteria is retarded in cold and cooler weather, there is no risk of seriously damaging the activity of the filter. However, always try to avoid using tapwater to clean your filters, particularly during late spring and summer, as it contains chlorine to control bacteria that are pathogenic to humans. The chlorine can have an equally destructive effect on the bacteria specifically cultivated in the filter media to break down fish waste.

Above: A small koi pond in spring, with petals from a cherry tree settling on the water's surface, but these few should not cause any real problems for the fish.

Use pond water to wash through the filter, and then top up the pond with mains water using a mist spray to 'gas-off' the chlorine added by the water authorities. The chlorine evaporates readily, so by spraying water into the pond, the chemical will have effectively 'gassed off' by the time it reaches the 'friendly' bacteria in the biological filter.

As the koi become more active, you should take steps to increase the flow rate of the pond water. Cooler, dirtier water at the bottom of the pond is thus filtered more positively and more water is exposed to the warming atmosphere and to the aeration system. The near-freezing water will have retarded the growth of the bacteria in the filter chambers. Now that the flow of waste products from the

Above: *As the water warms up, so algal blooms are likely to turn the water green. Here, small koi gasp at the surface in the competition for oxygen.*

koi is increasing, the biological filter must be restored to full activity. Freeze-dried or live-cultured bacteria are particularly beneficial in the spring to colonize new filters and to reactivate an established system. Subject to temperatures, freeze-dried or live bacteria can help to make the filter more efficient. If water temperatures, oxygen levels and nutrients are favourable for bacteria to flourish, they will multiply at a prodigious rate.

Controlling algae

In spring, microscopic algae often flourish, giving rise to green water. Green water offends the pride and spoils the enjoyment of many fishkeepers, who may turn to biological filter starters to clear the algae. However, by far the largest constituent of algae is chlorophyll, which oxygenates the water in the presence of light but de-oxygenates it in the dark, sometimes leaving insufficient oxygen for the filter bacteria before dawn. Presumably for this reason, some manufacturers warn that their filter starters are ineffective in green water. Nevertheless, experience has shown that a reduced dosage of either the freeze-dried or live bacteria preparations applied to the filter system every morning when dissolved oxygen levels are rising can clear a pond in 10-14 days. By continually replacing the bacteria after a few hours of warmth during daylight hours, they will gradually become established.

Interestingly, however, green water is usually indicative that the filters are functioning perfectly, the algal bloom being caused by the presence of a large quantity of nitrate, the final product of nitrifi-

cation (see below and page 53). Green water can be very beneficial to koi, enhancing the colour patterns of small koi and providing essential nutrients to newly hatched fry. On Japanese koi farms, green water is positively encouraged in the fry ponds with the addition of large quantities of manure!

Nitrogen cycle

Remember that the nitrification process that recycles fish waste in the biological filters is a two-stage transaction. Koi produce ammonia as waste, and *Nitrosomonas* and other bacteria increase in response to the increasing ammonia concentration to convert it to nitrite. This in turn encourages other bacteria, principally *Nitrobacter,* to multiply and change this lethal byproduct to nitrate. All biological filters undergo these unavoidable stages in their early development and even a mature filter will do so during the spring.

Nitrite poisoning is probably responsible for more mysterious disease and deaths than any other disturbance. Symptoms are often observed about three weeks after the koi have been subjected to this toxin; large koi may respond to excess nitrite in the water by lying on their sides and are generally lethargic, although they will continue to feed; small koi usually die.

Testing water conditions regularly while new filters are becoming established, after the winter when mature filters are becoming fully operational once again, or following some other disruption, will enable you to monitor any potentially dangerous increase in nitrite levels. Reducing, or even withholding food from koi in order to limit the ammonia production is one way of minimizing potential damage, while adding zeolite to the filtration system will extract surplus ammonia.

In the case of high nitrite levels you may need to change as much as 30-40 percent of the water daily. If the nitrite level is extremely high, you can neutralize it to some extent by adding cooking salt to the water at the rate of 3-6gm/litre (0.5-1oz per Imp. gallon) of pond water. This will discourage many parasites and inhibit bacterial growth, while gently encouraging the production of protective mucus on the fish's skin. (Do not add salt to the pond if you have zeolite in the filter, since this will release ammonia back into the water.) Many koi-keepers like to treat the pond against bacterial and parasitic problems in the late spring. (See the table on pages 112-113 for advice on suitable chemicals; always follow the supplier's directions for use.)

Seasonal checklist:
SPRING

POND MANAGEMENT

- Clean the pond thoroughly with a vacuum pump if you have not installed bottom drains.
- Top up the pond with mains water, using a mist spray to 'gas off' any chlorine in the water.
- Increase the flow rate of the pond water as koi become more active.
- Give filters a good backwash (but avoid using tap water).

WATER QUALITY

- Restore biological filters to full activity and add proprietary freeze-dried or live-cultured bacteria to reactivate them.
- Test water conditions regularly to monitor ammonia and nitrite levels.
- If nitrite levels are high, carry out daily water changes of up to 30-40 percent of the pond water.

FEEDING KOI

- Feed koi sparingly once the water temperature reaches 6°C(43°F).
- Feed readily digestible laxative foods, such as wheatgerm, while temperatures are low.
- As temperatures stabilize at 10°C(50°F) and above, start to add 'staple' food to the diet.
- Offer higher protein foods only once temperatures consistently reach 15°C(59°F).
- Avoid using up food remaining from last year; it may have oxidized or, worse, become mouldy during storage.

HEALTH CARE

- Treat the pond against bacterial and parasitic problems in the late spring. Use treatments according to the manufacturer's instructions.

SEASONAL CARE

Summer

Summer is the zenith of the koi-keeper's year, when koi are active and may breed. This is also the time of year when koi develop formidable appetites. As summer progresses, offer the koi larger amounts of food, but stick to the general principle of giving them only as much as they will consume in five or ten minutes, feeding them little and often. Always remember that while you are feeding your fish, you are also feeding the filter; be careful not to feed beyond its limitations or you will poison your koi.

Water changes

The question posed most often in summer by the fishkeeper with a newly established pond and filter system is 'how much and how often should I change the water?' It does seem that the longer a pond has been established, the less water changing goes on. This is not just because the koi-keeper gets lazier, but because the water quality improves as a filter matures. Where a new filter is still allowing high concentrations of ammonia and nitrite in the pond water, a water change will not necessarily dilute these contaminants, but may incur the risk of introducing other toxic substances, principally chlorine, and will probably reduce the pond temperature at the same time. A good compromise is to run off just enough water to flush the bottom drains, or to vacuum pump the detritus off the bottom and occasionally service the filter system. (Remember to keep the hose pipe away from your biological filters at all times.)

Water flow and aeration

While you should take care not to pump water too fast through the filter, it is essential to keep the water continuously well aerated, particularly during hot, thundery weather and overnight, and especially so if you have plants, blanketweed or green algae in the pond. Before becoming dedicated fishkeepers, many water gardeners enjoy an array of fountains, waterfalls and gushers, and turn pumps off at night, believing them to be unnecessary. Unfortunately, when they put koi into their ponds, they continue to turn off the pumps nightly and are distressed when fish that were perfectly healthy one evening are dead the next morning. This immediate evidence of a problem is followed a few weeks later by outbreaks of fungus, fin rot, gill rot and all manner of parasitic infestations that take advantage of fish stressed by living in oxygen-deficient water with, perhaps, an excess of carbon dioxide.

Chlorophyll – the substance that

Summer set-up for water circulation

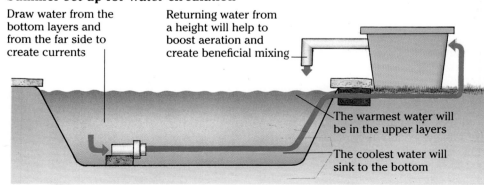

Draw water from the bottom layers and from the far side to create currents

Returning water from a height will help to boost aeration and create beneficial mixing

The warmest water will be in the upper layers

The coolest water will sink to the bottom

makes plants green – is responsible for photosynthesis, a process by which carbon dioxide and oxygen are chemically converted to sugars used for plant growth or storage. This formation of sugars is a two-stage process; the first stage takes place in daylight and the biochemical process causes oxygen to be released and carbon dioxide absorbed. When the light fades, carbon dioxide is

released and oxygen absorbed, increasing the amount of carbon dioxide in the water. The plants are thus competing with fish for oxygen at night. The more greenery there is in the water, the greater the oxygen consumption and carbon dioxide production, which will in turn lead to overnight asphyxiation of the koi.

In addition to these processes, we must also consider that the capacity of solves into the water. However, this process can be inhibited by any surface film, such as undigested oily products or dust.

Most experienced koi-keepers have some sort of device to skim off this film from the surface of the pond. Ideally, such a device might consist of a floating weir falling into a basket to catch leaves and large pieces of debris, before feeding a pump to a high-pressure sand filter, which runs continuously. If you are not fortunate enough to have a skimmer, it is worth fitting an overflow onto the pond and using this occasionally, even though it will necessitate running precious mature water to waste.

One further piece of summertime advice: if your pump is submerged in the pond, check it regularly and unblock the inlet, which often sucks in pieces of debris or detritus. Throughout the summer and autumn months, the filter can be supplied with water pumped from near the bottom of the pond.

Spawning

In late spring and early summer, koi measuring 38cm(15in) or more may spawn. This usually takes place early in the morning following warm days but cold nights. A 'naturalized' pond, with shallow edges and marginal plants, is an ideal area for koi to spawn. In the summer, be sure to walk around such a pond every morning in case any females have been driven out of the water by energetic males, as spawning is extremely frantic. Stranded fish can often survive out of water for a considerable time and it is well worth returning them to the water even though they may appear to be dead.

Koi are very bad parents; as soon as they have finished spawning, they will return to the eggs and eat them! If you intend to rear the fry from the koi eggs, it is vital that you remove the spawning ropes from the pond as soon as the koi have finished spawning. Even if you do not want to rear the fry, it is advisable to remove the eggs from the pond, as the adults often damage themselves raking through the weeds and gravel to eat the eggs. The dead eggs may grow fungus and the spores can infect any of the females damaged during spawning.

After koi have spawned, it is worth checking ammonia and nitrite levels in the pond for a week or so, as these are often higher at this time. During spawning, the excited koi produce more urine, and this, together with the decomposition of dead or unfertilized eggs, causes the ammonia level to increase quite dramatically and the population of nitrifying bacteria in the filter may be unable to degrade it into less harmful substances.

Above: *The brilliant light and warmth of summer herald the most productive period for the koi pond. Properly planted, these water lilies provide welcome shade against the harsh rays of the sun.*

Left: *It is very important to maximize the water flow and aeration during the summer months. This simple configuration of submersible pump and external filter shows how bottom water should be cycled.*

the water to absorb dissolved oxygen decreases as the temperature rises. Furthermore, warm water induces greater activity in many animals, including fish, thus placing even greater pressure on the dissolved gas content of the water. Clearly, any disturbance and rippling effect created as water returns from the filter will also increase the surface area in contact with the atmosphere. The surface of the pond is where the greatest gaseous exchange takes place, i.e. it is here that carbon dioxide and other volatile toxins evaporate and oxygen dis-

Seasonal checklist:

SUMMER

POND MANAGEMENT

- If a new filter is still allowing high concentrations of ammonia and nitrite in the pond, run off just enough water to flush the bottom drains, or vacuum pump the detritus off the bottom.
- Remove debris from the surface of the pond with a skimmer, or fit an overflow and use it occasionally.
- If your pump is submerged, check it regularly for blockages.
- Place spawning ropes in the pond during late spring and early summer, check them regularly and remove them as soon as the koi have spawned, to prevent egg-eating.
- Walk around the pond every morning to ensure that no females have been driven out of the water during spawning.

WATER QUALITY

- Service the filter system occasionally to ensure that ammonia and nitrite levels are minimal.
- Take care to avoid over-pumping filters, but ensure that the pond water is continuously well aerated.
- Keep a check on ammonia and nitrite levels for a week or so after koi have spawned; they are likely to be higher at this time.

FEEDING KOI

- Offer the koi more food in summer but give them only as much as they can consume in five or ten minutes.
- Feed little and often; any uneaten surplus will only cause pollution.

HEALTH CARE

- Check for infections and parasites; they develop faster in warm water.

SEASONAL CARE

Autumn

Autumn can be a very unpredictable season in many temperate parts of the world, with temperatures occasionally soaring above those recorded for the preceding summer months, followed by increasingly cooler days. With regard to water temperature, autumn is the reverse of spring; the water remains warmer for longer than the air and cools more slowly. For the koi, this is the last opportunity to fatten up in anticipation of the onset of winter and, for you, the time to make preparations to help your koi overwinter as healthy fish.

Feeding

During early autumn, koi will continue to feed as energetically as during the summer, in preparation for the winter. As the water cools, koi become less active and their appetites decrease. Start to introduce a little wheatgerm to their diet and gradually increase this element until early winter, simultaneously phasing out the dietary pellets, which contain high proportions of protein. Wheatgerm pellets, which have a high cereal content, are readily available from most koi dealers or aquarist shops.

Pond management

Throughout the summer, the management and maintenance requirements of your pond will change very little. However, with the advent of autumn, falling leaves may become a problem and, if you have not fitted an adequate skimmer to the pond, you should put nets in place to catch falling leaves. Once they sink to the bottom, leaves readily decompose, aided by bacteria. The bacteria that cause decompostion of organic debris, such as leaves, are 'opportunist' organisms, feeding from dead or damaged tissue. If koi have any damaged scales or dead anchor worm on their bodies, these bacteria will start to feed on them, gradually eating their way into the living tissue and giving rise to ulcerous lesions or septicaemia (blood poisoning). Allowing dead leaves to decompose on the bottom of the pond causes the numbers of these bacteria to increase and form a potential problem to the koi. Some trees even produce natural insecticides that become activated as the leaves are damaged or decay and these can make koi very ill. A net over the pond might also usefully serve to deter herons, cats, foxes and other potential predators.

Right: *The shorter days of autumn bring a cooling influence to the koi pond. Be sure to keep the water clear of leaves and check your koi for parasites and disease.*

Autumn is also a good time to clean out the filters. If you have a multichamber system, clean out one chamber at a time, waiting a week or so before cleaning the next. This will give the nitrifying bacteria an opportunity to re-colonize the chamber and minimize any adverse effect on water quality (see page 53). Remember to keep the hosepipe away from filters at all times and *never* scrub filters clean with detergent or disinfectant, which will kill the bacteria in the filter and endanger the koi by causing the water quality to degenerate.

Health care

The autumn is a good time to ensure that the koi are free from parasites, such as fish lice and anchor worms (see page 104), particularly if you have added new stock during the summer. Anchor worms and fish lice can cause lesions to develop on the skin of the koi, which if left can become ulcerous. Wounds on koi heal very slowly, if at all, below 12°C(54°F). As the autumn temperatures cool the water, the koi's immune system starts to become less effective, and at temperatures of 10°C(50°F) and below, ceases to work altogether, while most bacteria are active down to 2°C(36°F). It is vital that koi with any wounds or lesions recover during the autumn period and it is worth setting up a treatment pond for any koi with unhealed wounds. Ideally, you should prepare this treatment pond in advance and use healthy fish to start up the filter and overcome the problems of intitially high ammonia/nitrite levels that occur with any new filter system (see page 51). Sick fish cannot tolerate the fluctuations in water quality of a newly installed filter system and will die. Once the treatment pond is ready, place the sick koi into it with some healthy fish to keep them company. ('Ordinary' hardy goldfish are generally much more resilient to disease than koi, being less highly inbred!) The water in the treatment pond should be maintained at a minimum temperature of 16°C(61°F).

There are many preparations on the market that will kill fish lice and the free-swimming stages of anchor worms. (You will need to remove adult female anchor worms with a pair of tweezers.) However, although they are safe for use with koi, many of the preparations on the market designed to kill these parasites are highly dangerous to some other fish species. (It takes about seven days for the chemicals in these preparations for killing fish lice and anchor worm larvae to degrade into an innocuous form.) If you keep species such as orfe, tench or rudd, you must remove them from the pond before treating it. Place them in a suitable container, ideally another pond, and remember to aerate the water. If the container does not have a filtration unit, then test the water at least daily for ammonia. If the ammonia content in the water starts to rise, either add zeolite to the final chamber of your filter or, alternatively, carry out 20 percent water changes daily until the fish can be returned to the pond. If you are treating the pond for fish lice, remember to check the other coldwater species to ensure they are not harbouring any of these parasites before returning them to the koi pond.

Below: *This simple holding tank is ideal for treating koi with unhealed wounds or any health problems before the winter 'recess'.*

Seasonal checklist:

AUTUMN

POND MANAGEMENT

- Use a skimmer, or a net over the pond, to catch falling leaves. A net will also discourage herons from raiding your pond to build up their own fat reserves for the winter.
- Give the filters a thorough clean. Leave a gap of a week or so between cleaning each chamber of a multichamber filter and, of course, never use detergents or disinfectants in the process.

WATER QUALITY

- Use a thermostatically controlled heater (in the filter) to stabilize erratic water temperatures.

FEEDING KOI

- Continue to feed koi little and often during early autumn.
- As water temperatures decrease and koi become less active, start to introduce a little wheatgerm to the diet and gradually increase amounts until early winter, simultaneously phasing out high-protein foods, such as most dietary pellets.

HEALTH CARE

- Keep the pond clear of fallen leaves; any that decompose on the bottom of the pond may cause harmful bacteria to proliferate.
- Check koi thoroughly for parasites, such as fish lice and anchor worms, particularly if you have added new stock during the summer.
- Set up a treatment tank for any koi with unhealed wounds. Maintain a minimum temperature of 16°C(61°F).
- Remember that fish such as orfe, tench and rudd can be killed by some remedies used in the pond.

SEASONAL CARE

Winter

As temperatures drop, koi move into the deeper parts of the pond and become more reluctant to feed, and below temperatures of 6°C(43°F) cease feeding altogether. As the water continues to cool, the koi tend to lie huddled together on the bottom of the pond with all fins except the tail fin clamped tightly against their bodies. This conserves some body heat, as each fin is supplied with a tiny network of blood vessels through which heat escapes if the fish lie with their fins outspread. One of the major areas of cooling of a fish's body is through the gills, where the warm blood is cooled by the water passing over the gill filaments. You may have noticed that koi seem to breathe more slowly in winter – this is a method of conserving body heat. At temperatures between 2°C and 6°C (36-43°F) koi are described as being in a 'torpid state'. Their senses such as smell and taste are inoperative but they can still see and respond to some external stimulation, such as touch, or water movement below the surface.

Temperatures below 2°C(36°F) are critical to koi, as there is an increasing risk of ice crystals forming in the delicate gill membranes. Because water expands when it freezes, these crystals break the tiny cells in the gills and the koi die.

Winter filtration and aeration

Like many other materials, water expands when it warms and contracts as it cools. Because water is a liquid, warm water is light and therefore rises. (If you feel your hot water storage tank, you will notice that it is hotter at the top than at the bottom.) Logically, you might expect, therefore, that freezing water (ice) should lie at the bottom of exposed water but, as we all know, this is not the case. In fact, a reversal of this principle occurs at temperatures just below 4°C(39°F), when colder water rises to the surface and warm water sinks. This is the salvation of most underwater life. Water is a poor conductor of heat, so the cold water and ice form an insulating layer that retains the heat of the warmer water below it. As we have seen in the section on pond and filter construction, the pond should be at least 1.5m(5ft) deep; depth will aid the temperature stability of the warmer water below the ice and the water will also absorb heat from the ground.

Keep all biological filters running throughout the winter. It is important that the water continues to ventilate so that oxygen can diffuse into the water and harmful carbon dioxide (the byproduct of respiration) does not become sealed in by total ice cover. If the pump is

Winter set-up for water circulation

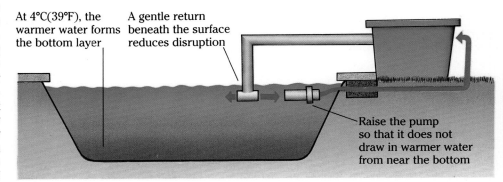

At 4°C(39°F), the warmer water forms the bottom layer

A gentle return beneath the surface reduces disruption

Raise the pump so that it does not draw in warmer water from near the bottom

turned off, the fish will suffer and the plumbing will corrode or freeze if the pump is then left in the water. If a variable flow pump is fitted in the pond, turn it down to its minimum output. If your system enjoys the versatility of two or more pumps, then using one should be sufficient at this time of year in all but the very largest ponds. This will give you the opportunity to service any pumps not in use. (Most pumps are now sealed units and you need only clean them and check the strainers, cables and switches.)

You may have a submersible pump in the pond or a variable level gravity feed pipe, if so, you can vary the level from which the filter is fed. As the water temperature drops towards the critical 4°C(39°F), raise the pump or filter feed to 15-23cm(6-9in) below the surface. This will avoid disturbance and chilling of bot-

Above: *This is how the simple set-up shown in the summer section on page 74 should be rigged for winter. The vital change here is that circulation is reduced and the bottom water is thus left undisturbed.*

tom water and allow the koi to rest, while preventing the pond from completely icing over.

You may decide to moderate the water return to the pond. Restrict the air flow on your venturi, bypass waterfalls and turn off fountains, since all these means of aeration are no longer necessary, as cold water is usually rich in oxygen, and, if left on, will excessively chill the water. If your water return is via a straight pipe from a filter above pond level, terminate it with a 'T' piece or elbow pipework to prevent disturbing the lower water.

It is not a good idea to use rubber balls,

Above: *Beneath the crisp whiteness of this winter scene, the koi are in a state of torpor. It is vital that you keep one area of the pond free of ice and maintain a continuous but gentle circulation to ventilate the water.*

Right: *Yes, this smart koi pond is in the foyer of a public building, but it does show what can be done for koi indoors. You may wish to consider this strategy during the colder months of the year.*

hammers or kettles of boiling water to prevent or break up ice formations. Although the koi are torpid (see above), they can sense any water movement, and breaking ice sends violent shock waves through the water, which can severely stress, and even kill, koi. (It is a sensation probably similar to someone suddenly crashing a loud drum close to your ear while you are sleeping and waking you with a start!)

Heating outdoor ponds

A growing number of enthusiasts are installing heating systems in their outside pond to keep their koi active and feeding, and thus growing, throughout the year. Avoid placing heaters in the bottom of the pond, however, as they can set up convectional currents that lift the warmer water, which chills as it rises towards the surface or towards a layer of ice, thus returning cold water to the koi. (You should also remove any airstones from the bottom of the pond in winter for the same reasons.) Instead, place small heaters in the filter system, preferably in the settling chamber or transfer ports. Any heating unit should be thermostatically controlled and capable of maintaining the water temperature at a minimum of 10°C(50°F), even through the severest of winters. Rapidly fluctuating temperatures are highly undesirable and temperatures sufficiently high to activate the fish but too low for safe feeding can

have a debilitating effect. Furthermore, between 0°C and 10°C(32-50°F) the koi's immune system does not operate, but bacteria in the water are still active. If your heater cannot maintain an adequate temperature throughout the winter, use it only to help stabilize autumn and spring temperatures.

Indoor ponds

An alternative to heating outdoor ponds that is favoured by some koi-keepers is the installation of pond systems in the garage, greenhouse or conservatory, and some enthusiasts even have permanent fish houses. Such pond systems are usually smaller and may be used at certain times of the year, for quarantine purposes or for raising baby koi, or they may be rested throughout the summer and used only during the colder months, to protect koi from the chill of winter.

Use mature water from the existing pond rather than tapwater to fill the inside pond. In this way, you avoid subjecting the koi to a change in temperature and water quality when you move them inside. In addition, you could move a small portable filter to the inside pond when you transfer the fish, having matured it with established pond water. Alternatively, by transferring some of the media from the active outdoor filter, you can overcome the ammonia/nitrite problems associated with new filters and pond systems (see also page 54).

Seasonal checklist:

WINTER

POND MANAGEMENT

- If you have a variable flow pump fitted in the pond, turn it down to its minimum output. One pump should be sufficient in all but very large ponds at this time of year.
- Check strainers, cables and switches of any pumps not in use.
- Restrict the air flow on venturis, bypass waterfalls and turn off fountains in the pond.
- Raise the filter feed to 15-23cm(6-9in) below the water surface as the water temperature drops. This will prevent disrupting the warmer water at the bottom.
- Remove any airstones from the bottom of the pond.
- If you have an indoor pool, transfer the koi here, using mature water from the pond to fill it.

WATER QUALITY

- Keep all biological filters running throughout the winter.
- Place small, thermostatically controlled heaters in the filter system (ideally, fitted in the settling chamber or transfer ports) to prevent water temperatures dropping below 4°C(39°F).

FEEDING KOI

- Gradually decrease the amount of food as the water temperature drops. Cease feeding koi altogether below a temperature of 6°C(43°F).

HEALTH CARE

- Ensure that temperatures do not drop below 4°C(39°F). Temperatures below 2°C(36°F) are critical to koi, as ice can form in the gill membranes, causing fatal disruption.

LANDSCAPING AND WATER GARDENS

Your pond should, of course, be planned to provide an ideal environment for your koi, but water is also an excellent design element and, with a little forethought and flair, will greatly enhance the layout and general impact of your garden. Its movement and light-reflecting properties can play interesting visual tricks, producing the illusion of space in a small area, for example, rather like a mirror indoors, while streams and watercourses and the shape and position of ponds can appear to lengthen and widen the plot. Modern materials offer more scope for creativity with shape and design and enable you to produce a formal or informal focal point, or a complete water garden complex employing a wide range of water-based effects. The pond's primary role will be to show off your koi to best advantage, and so it is important that you plan it in relation to your total garden design. You should consider not only its position and setting, but also your choice of surrounding features and plants. This way your water garden will look completely natural and you can successfully capture exactly the atmosphere you want – whether that be Oriental minimalism or the lusher, more colourful Western style of landscaping. For it to look good and work well, you should consider the style of a pond as carefully as its construction details.

Here, the combination of water, plants and rockwork demonstrates what can be achieved in a water garden.

LANDSCAPING AND WATER GARDENS

Siting the pond

There are several points you will need to consider when deciding on the position of a pond (see also page 24). It should always be sited away from deciduous trees or large shrubs, where dropping leaves, and sometimes fruits, seeds and insects, quickly pollute the water or make regular dredging a difficult but necessary chore. A sunny spot is important for healthy water and fish and flourishing plants, although a little shade should be provided for your koi in summer. The position should not be too shady, but it must be well sheltered, both for your comfort and for that of your fish. An evergreen hedge, fencing or screening between the pond and prevailing winds should be sufficient and their filtering effect is far more efficient than a solid barrier, such as a wall. Bamboo screening or brushwood is equally effective and gives the area a distinctly Oriental atmosphere.

It makes good practical and financial sense to be close to services such as electricity and drainage, and a site near to the house is often ideal. A koi pond, large or small, can make the perfect patio feature, offering plenty of opportunity to enjoy the koi at close quarters. Proximity to the house is also convenient for feed-

Above: *A small, stone-slab retaining wall around a koi pond is suitably informal and yet adds an essential safety feature.*

ing and general maintenance. In Japan, koi ponds are traditionally installed near the house, and in some cases the pool even runs under the foundations and re-appears indoors. You can imitate this effect in various ways without embarking on major constructional alterations: a timber-decked patio running from the

house to overlap a pond will give the impression that the water runs right beneath it and you may wish to emphasize this effect by setting a smaller pool in the decking itself. Alternatively, butt the pond up to the house and install a corresponding small pool inside the living room, conservatory or sun room extension. Patio doors across the width of the wall, or a large floor-to-ceiling window will provide plenty of light for your indoor pond and will enable you to see both indoor and outdoor ponds, making them appear undivided.

If a position close to the house is impractical, you will have to consider other likely spots in the garden. Incidentally, your pond need not be at the rear of the house; sometimes converting the whole of the front garden into a large formal pond with a bridge across to the front door looks stunning and makes a spectacular approach to the house. Elsewhere, any low spot or hollow is ideal for a pond. Following the natural contours of the garden will give the best effect and avoid any feeling of incongruity, so do walk around it at leisure and get an idea of the lie of the land. This will also help you get an impression of how your water garden will look from every vantage point – from nearby paths and corners

Below: *Informal ponds are easier to blend into the natural contours of your garden site. A corner position (left) affords an*

excellent backdrop and screening using the garden boundaries. Often a site nearer the house is more convenient, however (centre

and right). Remember to check the shape and position of the proposed pond site from inside the house as well as in the garden.

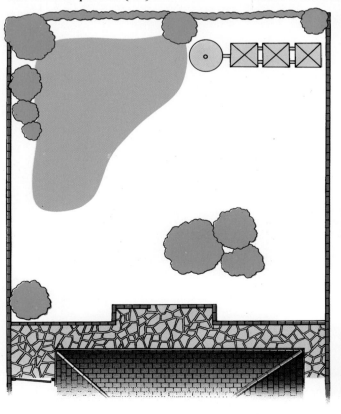
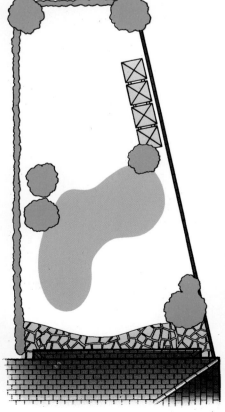

and from the opposite end of the site as well as from the house. Remember, you enjoy the garden all around you, not just as a stage from the back door. You may find it helpful to sketch out the rough shape and position of the pond in the garden, using a hosepipe or stakes and string. This will enable you to view it not just from every angle, but also, if appropriate, from the upstairs windows of your house, to see how it fits the general layout of your garden.

While a formal pond can be excellently integrated into a patio design, an informal style makes a fine focal point in the lawn or landscaped into a break of slope where you can make the most of a sunny aspect. Bear in mind that your pond's position should facilitate easy and comfortable observation of your koi, so access must be good and remain dry underfoot in wet weather. Ideally, you should be able to sit and laze at the waterside in fine weather. If you have a summerhouse at the opposite end of the garden, a water feature within sight of the verandah may be the ideal spot.

Other practical points to consider when planning the position and layout of your water garden include proximity to boundary hedging or fencing, which might inconvenience neighbours and make construction and maintenance difficult (see page 28). It is also worth digging down a little way with your spade within your proposed site; if solid rock is only inches below the subsoil or you have a particularly high water table, you may have to opt for building a raised pond. Consider, too, who will be using the garden. Young children under five years will be at risk unless you can arrange for the pond area to be fenced or gated off until they are older (something grandparents may forget). Where there is an elderly or disabled member of the household, a raised pond may again be the best option, with seats or wheelchair bays integrated into the design so that the water and its occupants can be more easily appreciated.

Size and shape
The size and shape of your pond must be kept in scale with the rest of the garden, although it is usually better to err on the large side, especially if you are hoping to create an eye-catching focal point. Large areas of water, if carefully planned and well integrated with good background landscaping, look stunning even in small gardens and provide plenty of room for fish. A pond that is too small will look cramped and insignificant.

Shape and style will depend on your own preference and the general scope

Left: *A formal square or rectangle butted up to the house is a popular Oriental koi pond design, here reinforced by background planting of dwarf conifers and interesting foliage plants among stone and rock.*

Below: *Twin ponds with a path between offer plenty of opportunity to wander through the garden and observe your fish at close quarters. The central position of these ponds has been softened by their irregular shape and varied foliage planting.*

and atmosphere of your garden or pond area. If you wish to maintain an Oriental feel, the Japanese prefer an informal-style water garden, but with the right materials and surroundings it is possible to create a similar atmosphere around a more formal koi pond, particularly a simple square or rectangular shape within a small courtyard or patio complex. Generally, simple shapes are best, even for formal ponds, where a combination of squares, rectangles and hexagons produce the best effects. This style lends itself to a series of ponds, maybe on different levels and linked by timber or paving, and offers the opportunity to display different varieties of koi in separate ponds. Most popular, particularly for a simple Japanese-style patio or back yard, is a formal L shape which emphasizes the sense of seclusion and enclosure away from the hurly-burly of life outside the

garden; essential to the Oriental philosophy of gardening.

More informal ponds, usually edged with stones or boulders, should also be restricted to simple shapes, such as ovals, irregular circles and kidney shapes. A pond whose shape is too intricate – with narrow necks, for example – will be difficult to construct, will inhibit adequate water flow and cause maintenance problems later (see page 25). It is particularly important to get a feel for the natural contours of the land if you want an informal pond, so that it looks as natural as possible when completed.

When considering a liner for your pond (see page 30), remember that the preformed type will limit you to a particular shape and size and that, while the choice is reasonably large, some koi-keepers prefer to use butyl or concrete for the greater creative scope they offer.

LANDSCAPING AND WATER GARDENS

General landscaping

To tackle your pond or water garden as a complete landscaping project, you will have to plan in detail the background area and surrounding plants and materials. The best way to do this after you have mapped out your prospective features on the ground with stakes and string, is to draw it up roughly to scale on a piece of graph paper. Now you can start adding the other elements, aiming for a good blend of hard landscaping – boulders, stones and paving; and soft – plant material and maybe timber. You will also want to achieve a good variety of shapes and colours and plan for something of interest right through the year for all-seasons appeal. This is where you can re-inforce your desired style, restricting your hard landscaping to natural stone or gravel and choosing plants with bold architectural shape and form (rather than bright flower colour) to create an authentic Japanese feel.

Ponds need a good backdrop to set them off, preferably something with a bit of height; use carefully selected trees or shrubs guaranteed not to drop too much plant matter into the water – maybe a bamboo or rhododendron, or carefully contour the plot, making use of the sub-soil and rubble saved from excavating the pond. You need not attempt anything too exaggerated; a gentle slope, planted with alpines between the boulders or with a small waterfall installed, can make all the difference, providing not just shelter and dappled shade, but also interesting reflections in the water's surface. If more shelter is required, plant trees or shrubs, but not too close so that they won't shade too much of the pond. Those species that love a damp location and that have light foliage, producing only a dappled shade, look the most natural; the sort of trees you see growing beside streams and ponds in the wild are ideal (but avoid invasive weeping willows!). For smaller gardens or patio ponds you may need to resort to screening. Build it no higher than you need to for privacy and shelter and choose a sympathetic material, such as timber, wattle hurdles or bamboo. Plants in containers can be used to soften their outline. (This is a useful planting device around ponds where you need to keep soil and other vegetable matter out of the water.) Hedging, screening, shrubs and trees will make your water garden seem more secluded, the foliage plants adding a sense of coolness and lushness; vital to both Oriental and Western schemes.

While your plans are still in this experimental stage, consider extending your water garden with other features, such as

Above: *Hard and soft landscaping around the pond will help it blend with the rest of the garden, particularly if you choose a more formal style like this simple square.*

a wide shallow stream to link one pond to another or to other parts of the garden; you could even incorporate a simple bridge or stepping stones. A waterfall makes interesting use of a rocky outcrop and, like the stream, adds the delightful sound of moving water to your garden. Both streams and waterfalls require a pump to recycle the water and this must be carefully chosen to suit the volume of water you wish to move (see page 37). You can achieve a similar effect with watercourses and cascades; both are constructed in a similar manner to ponds and can be finished with brick, stone or timber to match the style of the main pond. They are a popular device in the Japanese-style water garden where an informal, natural effect is preferred. The Japanese have also developed a form of water gardening without water: the dry stream, complete with weirs at every break of level, following the general course and shape of a natural stream and crossed by low timber bridges or large flat stepping stones, but filled only with rocks and stones. With water-loving, streamside plants along the dry banks, the effect can be remarkably realistic, without all the effort and expense involved in lining and pumping an elaborate moving water feature.

Water garden style

Before you begin choosing specific plants and hard landscaping materials and plotting them in on your plan, you should have a clear idea in your mind of the kind of atmosphere and the style of water garden you are trying to create.

A Japanese or Oriental flavour is often popular with koi-keepers, not only because koi are traditionally associated with Japan, but because the architectural, more spartan style of an Oriental pond, which uses shapes rather than colours, serves to show up the koi to best advantage. A subtle setting will enhance, rather than distract the eye from, their shape, colour and movement. It is a structured but essentially informal style, ideally suited to small town gardens or a secluded corner of a larger site. The Japanese garden is a peaceful retreat from the stress and hubbub of everyday life, and uses natural forms, such as water, rock and sand, to imitate mountains, lakes and seas. This gentle feeling of harmony is created with subtle foliage effects rather than bright flowers; a pattern of greens and greys relying on leaf shape and size for variety. There are usually a lot of evergreens for year-round interest and a mixture of informal wood-land plants, such as rhododendrons, along with more formal clipped shapes. There may be mounds of box or azalea, simulating the rolling countryside, contrasted with strong shapes, such as bamboo and *Enkianthus.*

The Japanese water garden looks good all year round, but is particularly striking in spring and autumn, when it blazes into colour and provides special dazzling reflections in the water's surface. Japanese varieties of small trees, such as *Acer* (maple) and *Prunus* (plum and cherry) are often grown for their beautiful blossom in spring and glorious foliage colour in autumn, and a single tree is often placed strategically to provide a special focal point in the pond setting.

The surrounding area of your pond (or ponds, stream or waterfall) is an essential element of the total design of the Japanese water garden, a resting place where the lazy perambulations of the fish can be observed at leisure, either from the comfort of a waterside stone slab or seat, or from a low bridge or stepping stones just skimming the surface of the water. The pond itself is likely to be surrounded with stones or boulders, or, for a formal pond, bricks or stained timber decking (see *Surrounding surfaces,* page 86). These, combined with a few Japanese-style plants, such as bamboo or a small *Acer palmatum,* (plant them in pots or Chinese 'ginger jars' for small patio gardens) will instantly create an

Oriental atmosphere. This type of water garden could be adapted to either a small patio pool or a large informal pond landscaped in the lawn.

Since the starker, rather controlled style of Oriental water gardening isn't to everyone's taste, there is nothing to stop you adapting the basic principles of Japanese design and softening or extending your plans to suit a more Western ideal of the perfect water garden. This type of garden will contain more plants and brighter colours, particularly around the pond itself – something hardly ever seen in Japanese water gardens. Hard landscaping – usually of stone or brick – tends to be semi-concealed by foliage and a lush combination of flowering plants chosen to create a dense display of colour. It is a good idea to enforce some kind of discipline on your choice of plants or the effect can look too garish – thriving moisture lovers and pond plants can range from pinks and purples to bright yellows and blues. You will create a more interesting and pleasing water garden if you devise a basic framework of interesting foliage shapes and colours (the choice here is wide) and then add more colourful elements sparingly, in clumps of maybe one or two shades only. Thus East can meet West harmoniously.

If you intend to grow marginal plants - species that will grow with their roots in the boggy or waterlogged soil at a pond's

edge – you should incorporate a shallow shelf (see *Pond and filter construction,* page 42) and contain the plants in tubs or with a stone or brick retaining wall for protection. Koi delight in uprooting these marginal plants, which is one of the reasons why you do not see them very often in strictly styled Japanese koi ponds. This is also a problem should you wish to plant aquatic species (those that float on or in the water) in your pond, as these, too, will usually be eaten or scattered by the koi. Aquatic plants also tend to reduce the oxygen levels in the water. You must be content, therefore, with more interesting and varied marginal planting and, if you must have plants or flowers on the water's surface, try one or two of the more vigorous forms of water lilies. They will naturally have to be of a deep-water variety and supported so that their leaves and flowers are just level with the surface of the water.

Your choice of surrounding surfaces and features such as ornaments, pots and containers, even garden furniture and screening materials, will also influence the look of your pond, as well as your planting scheme. If the water garden is quite large and ambitious, you could maybe create an Oriental corner with a few large boulders and tub of bamboo or grasses, and develop a lusher, more Western-style planting further round the pond.

Above: *In a larger garden, you can afford to be more ambitious, making your pond a* *major feature. Here, a change of level allows for an informal waterfall linking two ponds.* *The design also incorporates a rustic bridge and small viewing platform.*

LANDSCAPING AND WATER GARDENS

Surrounding surfaces

It would be foolish to try to economize on pond construction materials, but for the surrounding surfaces, the less expensive options are often the most exciting and successful. Local stone, for example, costs far less than good manufactured paving or something carrying heavy transportation charges, and will look far more natural and in keeping with most pond styles. Similarly, second-hand timber gives an instantly mature look, while cheap timber treated to a coloured stain or varnish offers all kinds of exciting creative possibilities you wouldn't think of with a more expensive pre-treated type. For formal ponds, second-hand bricks are worth looking out for. To soften or age the effect of new brick or stone, chop moss stems in yoghurt or buttermilk and spread over the surface, keeping well watered until established. A special 'antiquing fluid' is also available to prematurely age stone should your pond look rather raw and new. (Of course, if you are going to use it on stone that comes in contact with the pond water, do check first whether it is toxic to fish and plants.)

You will need some form of flat paving or timber effect such as this to hide your pond construction, but you may also want large, sculptural pieces of rock and stone, to disguise the pool edges, to form a backdrop, or maybe an artificial beach, or to position in the water as a decorative

Above: *A pebble 'beach' makes a beautiful informal edging if allowed to run right down into the pond shallows. Contrast with larger boulders and some spiky plants.*

feature. This is particularly important in Japanese-style water gardens where large boulders – sometimes weighing several tonnes – are used to represent mountain ranges or surrounding hills. Ideally, the boulders should be water-worn, with smooth facets or natural, craggy outlines. You can buy these from a specialist supplier or quarry, but remember: large pieces are going to be expensive and difficult to transport and

position, so make sure you know exactly what you need beforehand. It helps to make a rough model of the pond area or water garden and experiment with stones and pebbles to see the kind of effect you want and how many rocks and of what size you need. It is important to keep these larger elements to scale and, again, local stone will look most natural.

Rock varies considerably in colour, form and performance according to type.

Above: *This delightful pond complex divides up an otherwise boring suburban strip. A timber-decked platform follows the shape of the pond and leads naturally across a small bridge to create circular walks of the garden and good views of the water.*

Pebbles are frequently used in Oriental-style water gardens, to make shingle 'beaches', to mix with boulders at the edge of the pond or to construct dry streams. They are ideal for creating contrasting effects among other surfaces. Use them to cover the bare soil below plants to conserve moisture – an excellent plan beneath trees where nothing will grow in the shade – or below plants in tubs and containers to reinforce an Oriental look in the garden.

Sand and gravel are also popular in Japanese-style water gardens, for paths and seating areas, beneath trees and shrubs to maximize the impact of foliage and flowers, or to create special effects, such as dry streams or ponds, maybe mirroring the real thing. The Japanese use a special type of sand that comes in a wide choice of colours and large grains, up to 2mm(0.08in) in diameter. These may be raked into swirls and ripples to imitate water, and surrounded by boulders and dwarfed trees and bushes to simulate mountains and forests. Areas of sand or gravel are worth incorporating around your pond as they make an interesting change of texture and, like many other Japanese features, require little maintenance.

Timber is equally useful in the water garden providing it is well treated and maintained. A hardwood, such as redwood or red cedar, is costly but long lasting; relatively inexpensive softwoods, such as larch or spruce, will need annual treatment against rot. The beauty of timber is its soft mellow appearance – a welcome change of surface from stone or paving – and its flexibility – it can be built around any shape or size, or formed into integrated seating or planting areas. Its big advantage over paving is that it is less expensive and easier to install over large areas, especially on a sloping site. You can lay it in all manner of decorative patterns, from vertical and horizontal planking to diagonal herringbone and elaborate weave patterns.

Decking can be used to create an excellent patio area, overlapping the pond like a jetty and making the perfect spot from which to observe or feed your fish. Secure a platform from the house using steel or timber ledger strips and strong bolts, or support freestanding decking on joists and beams set in concrete footings high up or only just off the ground, according to your needs. You could use timber walkways instead of paths to link your decked area to other parts of the garden, or to build low bridges over streams and ponds. Position these almost level with the water's surface so that you can observe the koi at close

Above: *Blending a variety of materials around the pond can be very effective. This informal koi pond is balanced between a* curving planting bed edged with boulders and a timber-decked viewing platform to provide a change of level and textures.

Above: *Raked sand or gravel and rough stone provide a traditionally Oriental setting for a koi pond. Keep plants to a minimum;* here a collection of miniature Bonsai trees are the perfect companions. Stepping stones allow access to the pond across the gravel.

quarters. Decking is ideal for concealing filters and service areas; a hinged hatch will allow access.

Planting areas can be incorporated in decking surrounding a pond to accommodate bamboos, lush foliage plants or simply areas of pebbles, with no risk of polluting the water. Alternatively, use tubs and containers for your plants. The Japanese are equally fond of timber's design potential and low maintenance benefits. In Japan, timber is simply treated and varnished, or stained a dramatic black walnut or deep red for extra impact. Stains and coloured varnishes are readily available for outdoor use:

white and grey produce an attractive weathered look, while blue looks surprisingly good in both Western and Oriental settings. The more coats you apply, the deeper the colour.

Don't be afraid to mix materials – turf with boulders, timber abutting paving, or areas of larger and smaller stones – for variety within your scheme. (Never mix rock types though, as this tends to look confusing and incongruous if the contrast is too striking.) Remember, too, to incorporate a built-in seating area or flat slab for sitting right at the water's edge – koi can be trained to come to a certain point and feed from your fingers.

LANDSCAPING AND WATER GARDENS

Planting

As we have seen, planting can affect the whole shape, nature and theme of your water garden. Certain types, such as bamboo and *Acer*, produce an instant Oriental atmosphere, while rampant *Lysimachia*, ferns and primulas can be used to create a woodland effect. Moisture-loving plants tend to grow quickly, so don't plant too many different types; it is better to aim for a good variety of foliage shapes rather than to concentrate on flowers. You can blend giant-leaved marginal plants, such as *Gunnera manicata* or *Petasites japonicus*, with spiky bamboos and grasses, the thick, deeply veined leaves of hostas, the arrow-shaped *Saggitaria* or feathery ferns and *Astilbe*. Marginal plants tend to have strong dramatic shapes, so choose them carefully to ensure that they blend well. Japanese water gardens prefer a strong framework of evergreens and a mixture of architectural shapes balanced with the more formal domes of clipped box or mosses: mix these with plenty of rocks and boulders and you should achieve the right effect around your pond.

Acers, particularly *A. palmatum*, the Japanese maple, make a beautiful focal point close to water with their lovely

Below: *These illustrations show a variety of marginal and water-loving plants that will flourish in and around the koi pond.*

Above: *Dwarf conifers and heathers are ideal pondside plants. They offer endless combinations of shape and colour, and here effectively disguise filter pipework.*

shaped foliage and superb autumn colour. Some forms have interesting bark for winter interest, too – *A. griseum*, the paperbark maple, has a bright orange-coloured trunk. They are a popular element of Japanese gardens, particularly the smaller cultivars.

Azaleas are grown mainly for their beautiful spring flowers but the Japanese have also developed evergreen forms, which they clip into formal shapes. They are all lime haters, i.e. need acid soils.

Bamboos are dramatic evergreen grasses with a decided Oriental appearance. They like a rich soil and plenty of sunshine, forming dense groves of ornamental stems topped with fluttering foliage in the right conditions. Stems may be bright green, yellow or striped with black. *Sasa palmata* is a useful hardy form; *S. veitchii* grows only to about 1m(3.3ft) and tolerates shade.

Ferns love cool, damp shady spots and are the perfect companions for pond or stream edges. Their bright green feathery foliage is familiar enough and makes a welcome contrast to large-leaved or spiky marginal plants. There is an interesting choice of different shapes and forms including the glorious Royal Fern, *Osmunda regalis*, which is hardy and has good autumn colour; and the Hart's Tongue Fern, *Phyllitis scolopendrium*, which has more crinkly, less divided fronds than the Royal Fern.

Iris are among the few flowering plants you might see in the Japanese water garden. They are prized for their sword-like foliage and delicate, exotic-looking blooms. Most species are hardy and flower in summer.

Mosses enjoy shady, moist areas and produce a dense mat or mound of tiny foliage that is popular ground cover in Japanese gardens. You can collect them from the wild or encourage them to grow on rocks and boulders as described earlier on page 86.

Rhododendrons (the family group includes Azaleas) come in a very wide choice of sizes and varieties, grown primarily for their evergreen foliage and breathtaking spring blooms. Their exotic shape and colour make them a popular shrub for Japanese gardens, where their relatively brief burst of glory in spring and dependable glossy green foliage all year round are valuable in background planting for a garden pond.

Right: *Many lush marginal plants will thrive in pots arranged at the water's edge, making them easier to maintain and ideal for enclosed formal ponds.*

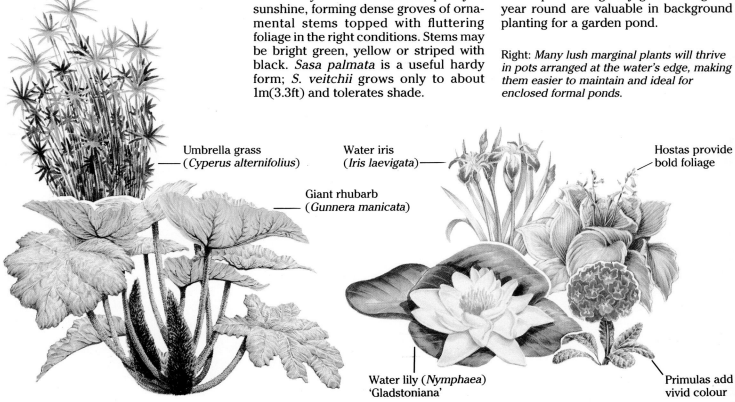

Umbrella grass
(*Cyperus alternifolius*)

Giant rhubarb
(*Gunnera manicata*)

Water iris
(*Iris laevigata*)

Hostas provide bold foliage

Water lily (*Nymphaea*)
'Gladstoniana'

Primulas add vivid colour

LANDSCAPING AND WATER GARDENS

Above left and right: An Oriental-style bridge looks best in larger gardens where it can span a large pond and be softened with foliage and surrounding shrubs. The strong red colour is traditional but you will need to choose nearby leaves and flowers carefully to avoid a garish effect. Here, soft lilacs and strong greens complement the bridges without competing with them for attention.

Water lilies in the koi pond are restricted to vigorous, deep-water types, such as most forms of *Nymphaea.* These include the white-flowered Gladstoniana, pink *N. tuberosa rosea,* or yellow *N. marliacea chromatella,* which can be planted with up to 120cm (48in) of water above the crown. Planting the tubers in solid containers, rather than mesh baskets, and topping the rich loam soil with coarse gravel, will help discourage the koi from disturbing the soil.

Other features

Other, more ornamental, features will also set the tone and style of your pond and you can choose these to reflect an Oriental or more Western theme. It is important not to overdo the effect with too many ornaments or too large a bridge, for example. Keep any additions in scale and take care they do not detract from the pond itself. Most of these features tend to serve a practical as well as an ornamental purpose.

Bridges create an obvious crossing place but are also a means of enjoying the water mid-pond, as it were. Large, oriental, arched bridges, usually painted red, are for large gardens only; smaller water gardens are better equipped with a small, simple timber-planked design, preferably just skimming the water's surface, and which will lose no points on style if you are trying to recreate a Japanese atmosphere. Alternatively, install a series of staggered timber walkways straight across, or changing direction to zigzag over, a wide stretch of water for equal Oriental panache.

Stepping stones are another popular Japanese device for getting from A to B at a leisurely pace. These large, flat, water-washed stones or slabs of timber were originally used to lead across grass, moss or gravel, through the garden to the tea house for a formal tea ceremony. They impose a careful, relaxed pace and wider stones encourage a rest and the chance to appreciate a particular focal point or feature. Securely positioned, they make an informal crossing and rest-

Above: Simple bridges are often the most effective and the closer they are to the water, the better you will be able to observe your koi. This shingle path is contained by rustic logs, travelling across the koi pond and around the garden.

ing place in the larger water garden.

Other features from the traditional Japanese tea garden have survived as ornamental features: the little stone lanterns, once a means of lighting the garden so that it could be enjoyed at night; the stone buddha enshrined on a stone slab among ferns or leafy evergreens, and the charming *shishi odoshi* – a length of hollow bamboo on a pivot. As water drips through this bamboo tube, the stem is forced downwards to pour its contents into a small stone trough or basin before springing back to hit a strategically placed rock with a distinct 'dock' noise. Frequently employed as a small ornamental water feature, the *shishi odoshi* was once as important as the scarecrow – its purpose to frighten deer away from tasty foliage plants.

If you are hoping to create a water garden with a more Western influence, you should be keeping your eye open for interesting statuary or sculpture to make a special focal point or extra feature. Even plant tubs and containers on the deck or patio should be chosen with a certain

Below: *The* shishi odoshi *is an ornamental Japanese water feature, originally designed to scare animals away from foliage. As the bamboo drains, it springs back with a noise.*

Above: *Used with restraint, Oriental ornaments can look effective beside a koi pond. These stone lanterns are best arranged singly among rocks and foliage.*

emphasis in mind: Versailles tubs for elegance; cut down barrels for rustic charm; terracotta for a Mediterranean feel, or glazed Oriental pots for your bamboos and small *Acers*.

Lighting the water garden

When installing electricity for filters and pumps, don't forget to make provision for lighting, too. Subtle use of outdoor lamps will make a stunning feature of your water garden by night as well as day, to be viewed from the house or enjoyed from the patio when entertaining or indulging in an al fresco dinner. Forget all those garish underwater coloured lights and instead use outdoor spotlights and lamps to highlight trees, shrubs or bold marginal planting whose reflected form in the water's surface will be far more effective. Lamps used to light paths, walkways and bridges are not only functional but also look quite charming beside a reflective pond. Alternatively, string lanterns or fairy lights in the trees, or above a bridge, for party nights. Special features, such as waterfalls, a piece of sculpture, or a particularly fine rock or boulder, can all benefit from being highlighted with a spotlight. You may find some lights are supplied with optional coloured filters; white light is best in most instances, although a blue or green cast is sometimes effective when highlighting foliage plants, for a softer, more subtle effect. Avoid red and yellow filters, however, which add a garish grotto atmosphere to the night scene.

BREEDING KOI

Whether you are an experienced koi-keeper, keen to understand and implement efficient methods of breeding and rearing koi, or simply enjoy watching these beautiful fish in your garden pond, seeing the results of your koi spawning will bring a sense of pride and excitement. Left to themselves, koi will naturally spawn in summertime, and if any of the resulting eggs are to hatch and fry survive, you will need to know what to do. In this section, we look at how to differentiate between the sexes, collect koi eggs without damaging them and successfully incubate them, and how to raise the fry. Later in the section, we examine various methods used in farm culture of koi, including those where man interferes with the koi's biochemistry to dictate where and when the fish releases its eggs.

In these mud ponds in Japan, koi are farmed in huge numbers for an international market.

BREEDING KOI

Sexing koi

It is impossible to sex koi smaller than about 25cm(10in) in length, because they are sexually immature. Once the koi exceed this size, the testes (in males) and ovaries (in females) begin to develop. The ovaries are much larger organs than the testes (see *Koi anatomy*, page 20). Females are usually easier to spot, as the belly of a mature female koi is generally plump, whereas males remain streamlined and more 'torpedo' shaped.

When males are ready for spawning, they develop breeding tubercles on the head and pectoral fins, principally along the bones of the fin rays. These breeding tubercles appear as fine raised spots and could be mistaken for white spot (*Ichthyophthirius*, see *Health Care*, page 102). The tubercles are most profuse on the pectoral fins, where they are quite rough to the touch and arranged in fairly regular rows. They are used during breeding, when the male nudges the female with his head and fins to induce her to spawn.

Spawning

Koi will naturally spawn in the hobbyist pond in the early summer. A water temperature of 20°C (68°F) is ideal, although koi will occasionally spawn at a temperature of 17°C (63°F). As the water in the pond warms, the koi will try to spawn 'en masse'. This is known as flock spawning and, although it can produce very healthy offspring, the quality of the patterns and colour are generally poor.

The female koi deposits her eggs – approximately 100,000 per kilogram of her body weight – over the pond walls, floor and on any plants. Unfortunately, it is very difficult to collect eggs deposited in this random manner in order to incubate them in an environment where they will not be eaten by their parents or attacked by parasites. If left to their own devices, a few of the eggs will hatch and you can then collect the offspring and raise them in an aquarium.

You can, however, ensure the survival of a greater number of eggs by placing artificial spawning ropes in the pond. The koi will deposit their eggs on these in preference to using the hard pond wall. To make these spawning ropes, cut 10cm(4in) lengths of 10-15mm (0.4-0.6in) thick nylon-fibre rope and thread these between the strands of a 120cm(4ft)-piece of the same sort of rope.

As the koi prepare to spawn, you will notice males chasing a female, nudging her side with their mouths. The female will occasionally stop and suck at the sides of the pond in an attempt to clean an area on which she can deposit her

Mature female koi

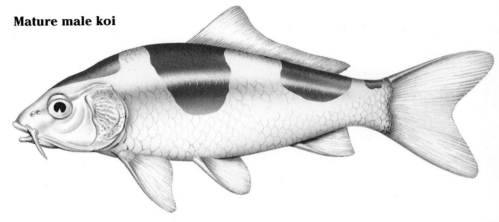

Above: *The pectoral fins of a female koi tend to be smaller than those of a male. During the months of April and May in the second year of life, a female koi develops* ripe ovaries and begins to show secondary sexual characteristics. Her abdomen swells with the egg-filled ovaries, and her vent reddens, becoming slightly swollen.

Mature male koi

Above: *Secondary sexual characteristics also appear in the male in the second year of life, with the development of long pectoral fins and a rough texture to the gill* covers. (It is vital to distinguish these 'spots' from the signs of white spot disease.) However, there are no outward signs of the testes developing within the fish.

eggs. This is the time to gently lower the spawning ropes into the pond. Spread out the coils of rope into a fanlike shape and anchor them to the side of the pond.

Try to avoid disturbing the fish before and during spawning, but keep a careful eye on them, as the males may bully some females. If this happens, remove the female and place her in a separate pond. Koi may prefer to spawn around dawn but they may also spawn throughout the day. When they have finished spawning, the females hang head down, respiring heavily, and the other fish will become less excited. Gently remove the spawning ropes and carefully place them in a vat for incubation. Koi are not good parents and unless you remove the eggs from the pond quickly, they will begin to eat them. Immature koi may also eat the eggs, so if you want to rear them, you should separate the spawning koi from others in the pond.

Incubating koi eggs

The incubator should have a reasonable capacity – a household water storage

Above: *Spawning ropes are easy to make using a 120cm(4ft) long, stranded nylon rope and several 10cm(4in) lengths. Untwist the strands of the longer piece and thread the shorter lengths through the loops, fraying out the fibres to give as large a surface area as possible on which the thousands of eggs can attach themselves.*

tank (about 450 litres/100 gallons) is ideal – and should, of course, be made of nontoxic materials. It will need a valve-operated water inlet point, and an outlet with as large a surface area as possible, screened with a fine (0.3-0.5mm) stainless steel or plastic mesh. Fine nylon stockings may provide an adequate alternative, although they are less robust.

Lay the ropes out in the vat with 0.2mg/litre malachite green solution to stop fungus (*Saprolegnia*) from attacking dead eggs and spreading infection to living eggs. Place three lengths of string across the vat to keep the ropes 5cm(2in) below water level. Do not add any more water at this stage, but place an airstone on the floor of the vat to gently and continuously aerate the water, as developing eggs need plenty of oxygen. When you begin to see the growing koi's eyes in the egg – after one or two days – run a fine trickle of water into the incubation vat. The day before the koi hatches, the eyes in the egg will have a shine to them. Soon afterwards, the young koi will begin to wriggle then, gradually, over the next few hours, it will break out of its 'shell'. It will take three to four days for the koi eggs to develop and the fry to hatch at temperatures of 20-22°C(68-71°F). Koi fry can develop at temperatures as low as 17°C(63°F), in which case their incubation will take five or six days, or as high as 25°C(77°F), which will decrease their hatching time. However, there is a greater chance of the fry being deformed at such extreme temperatures.

An incubator for koi eggs

Below: *A household water storage tank (with a capacity of approximately 450 litres/100 gallons) is easily converted into a suitable incubator for koi eggs. Transfer the spawning ropes, on which the eggs will have attached themselves, into this tank as soon as spawning has taken place, as adult koi are prone to eating their own eggs.*

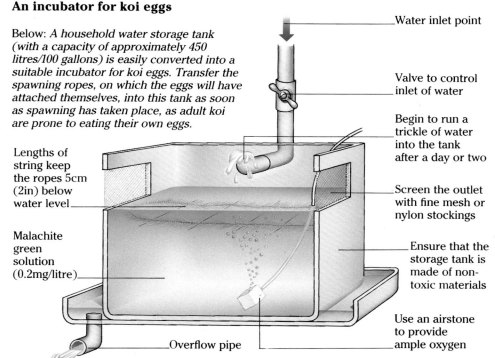

Water inlet point

Valve to control inlet of water

Begin to run a trickle of water into the tank after a day or two

Screen the outlet with fine mesh or nylon stockings

Ensure that the storage tank is made of nontoxic materials

Use an airstone to provide ample oxygen

Lengths of string keep the ropes 5cm (2in) below water level

Malachite green solution (0.2mg/litre)

Overflow pipe

Development and growth of fry

When the fry have hatched, they will instinctively seek shelter and hide in any cover they can find. The spawning ropes are ideal for this. Using a special sticky pad on their heads, the fry attach themselves to the ropes' fronds, or to the vat wall. At this stage in their development, the young koi have no swimbladder, mouth or vent. They breathe by absorbing oxygen through the fine blood capillaries that surround the yolk sac, which is still attached to the gut. It is essential that there is plenty of oxygen entering the water at this stage, as a reduction in the quantity of dissolved oxygen in the incubator could lead to mass mortality.

The koi fry have only one fin, which encircles the posterior end of the body. As the koi grow, feeding on their yolk sacs until all the yolk is utilized, they develop paired fins, a mouth and other organs. After two or three days, the young koi swim up to the surface and take two or three gulps of air, which they force into their swimbladder. They then start to swim freely in mid water, usually congregating around the airstones – a sign that they are ready to be fed.

First feeding

Koi fry at the 'swim up' stage do not have any developed taste buds and so must detect their food by sight. Therefore, they need to have food all around them. Hard-boiled egg yolk is an ideal food for the first day or so – this has very little dietary value, but will increase the size of

Left: *This sequence shows the stages of development of the koi egg and young fry, from the newly laid egg to the three- or four-week-old fry, ready for release into growing-on facilities. The eyes first become apparent after one or two days (5) and a day or so later will develop a shine (6). Shortly after this, the fry will break out of its 'shell' and attach itself to the spawning rope, using a sticky pad on its head.*

The development of the koi egg and fry

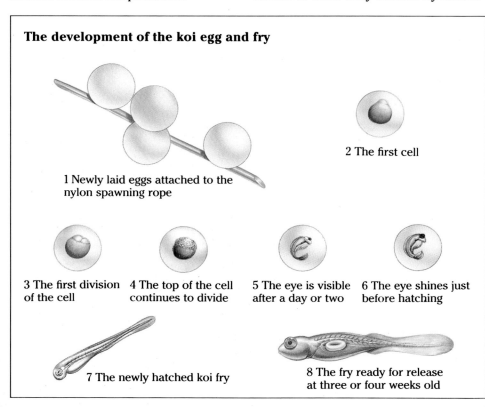

1 Newly laid eggs attached to the nylon spawning rope

2 The first cell

3 The first division of the cell

4 The top of the cell continues to divide

5 The eye is visible after a day or two

6 The eye shines just before hatching

7 The newly hatched koi fry

8 The fry ready for release at three or four weeks old

BREEDING KOI

the stomach. Newly hatched brineshrimp (*Artemia salina*) larvae are also a good food source for young koi fry. Start feeding the brineshrimp when the koi are about one week old. After another week or so, the koi will be ready for a mash diet (the powder dust that is left after the manufacturing process of fish food). From this time onwards, feed the koi food of a size that can be taken by the smallest fish in the vat.

You will need to remove accumulated debris and waste frequently during this first feeding stage. A siphon made from aeration tubing is ideal for removing settled and suspended waste from the incubator, and an old toothbrush is useful to clean the outlet screen. You should also add fresh water regularly to the vat to remove nitrates and ammonia. Tap water, which contains high concentrations of chlorine, should be aerated before it is added to the vat, to allow the chlorine to evaporate. After three or four weeks, the fry will have grown to 5-10mm(0.2-0.4in) in length and will be starting to take larger quantities of more generously sized foods.

Growing on

At this stage, move the koi to a growing-on facility, such as an aquarium, tank or pond. Watch the young koi carefully, as cannibalism is not uncommon. If you suspect this, remove any larger fry to another tank. You can heat this to 20-25°C(68-77°F) to provide faster growth rates, but be careful; if koi grow too fast, they lose their colour. One-month-old koi need about five percent of their body weight in food and should be fed little and often. As they grow, koi need less food – about two percent of body weight at 15cm(6in) or larger. The size of pelleted food is critical; not all fish grow at the same rate and it is too easy to look at the larger koi and select the pellet size to suit them, forgetting the smaller fish. Unfortunately, koi that are nearer to the common carp in appearance grow faster than the prettier koi. This is because nishikigoi are highly inbred – that is, they are mated with other koi to which they are closely related, such as either parents or siblings – and, as with any highly inbred animals, nishikigoi are not as hardy as their wild counterparts.

Right: Although not generally favoured in Japan, these ponds are commonly used for breeding koi elsewhere in the world. Both the Dubisch and Hofer types rely on the cultivation of grass as a spawning medium on the elevated section of the pond. The koi are introduced to the pond when the water is 45cm (18in) deep and the level is then raised to induce the koi to spawn.

Farm culture of koi carp

Koi have been grown for food for over 2000 years in China, where they were cultivated in earth ponds and became a vital source of protein in the leaner winter months. Interestingly, similar breeding techniques have developed in Asia and Europe (the native home of carp) and, indeed, wherever koi have been artificially reared. Over the last century, culture methods have progressed remarkably with the discovery and use of hormones and induced spawning. In the rest of this section, we look at methods of breeding koi that are used by professional koi-breeders throughout the world. Some of these methods are only practical where large numbers of koi are being spawned. Other methods rely on the use of hormones, and such techniques are best left to experts, as the drugs used will interfere with the metabolism of the treated fish and misuse may result in the death of the parent, or malformed offspring.

Dubisch and Hofer ponds

These small ponds, about 100m^2 and 0.3m deep (1076ft^2 x 1ft) were devised in the 19th century for spawning and rearing carp. The original design by Dubisch was later modified by another fish farmer, Hofer. Around the edge of the Dubisch pond is a ditch, 15cm(6in) deeper than the rest of the pond, which allows the fish swimming space. The Hofer type has a ditch only along one side, and the elevated section slopes gently towards the ditch. Both types of

pond use the same drainage system, known as a 'monk' after the monastic people who invented it centuries ago. This is a three-sided box, open at one end and with a pipe at the lowest point of the middle wall. A series of boards, placed in the open end, regulate the water level, and vertical metal bars in front of the boards prevent the fish from swimming out of the pond.

Both systems rely on the cultivation of grass, used by the fish as a spawning medium, on the elevated section of the ponds. Before flooding, the drained ditch is cleaned of all debris. The pond water, which is checked for purity, is continuously aerated to saturate it with oxygen. Koi are very sensitive to rapid changes in temperature, so the time at which the pond is filled and the adult koi introduced is critical to reduce the possibility of such fluctuations. The adult fish are placed in the pond when the water has reached a depth of 45cm(18in) and a temperature of between 18°C and 22°C(64-72°F). The water level is then raised gradually in an attempt to induce the koi to spawn. The water level should be maintained at a height just covering the grasses, with a constant trickle of water flowing through the pond.

After a few days, the koi will be triggered to spawn, and the parents are removed from the pond a day later to prevent egg-eating or spreading of disease to the fry. Under favourable conditions, about 50 percent of the eggs will hatch. At temperatures of 18-20°C(64-68°F), the eggs take two to three days to 'eye up'

Dubisch breeding pond

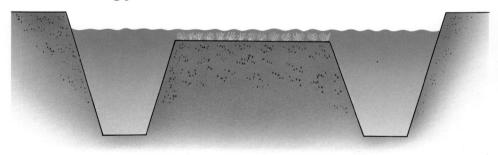

Hofer breeding pond

and four to six days to hatch, and at 21-25°C(70-77°F), about one to two days and three to four days respectively. After another two to four days, the fry are ready to be moved to growing-on facilities. The water level is slowly lowered so that the fry gather around the ditch. Here, the farmers can collect them easily using a fine net. Rough handling at this stage can cause damage, which may deform the koi or even kill them.

Dubisch and Hofer ponds are not generally favoured by koi farmers in Japan, probably because of the higher water temperatures there.

Using spawning ropes

This method has been used for many years and is the main technique employed by the Japanese for the propagation of koi. Spawning nets are suspended in the pond, which is usually 30m^2(330ft^2) and 90cm(3ft) deep, is filled with water to a depth of 25-30cm(10-12in). Airstones are used to provide maximum saturation of oxygen. The female koi and then two males are placed in the pond, together with 10 spawning ropes (or 15 for a large fish), placed evenly over the pond.

Usually the fish begin spawning at about four o'clock in the morning and they may spawn again at the same time the following day. The female will suck at the ropes to prepare them for laying her eggs and the males will nudge her abdomen, inducing her to release the eggs. She will then rush through the pond, with the males in pursuit, leaving a green cloud of eggs, which the males will fertilize with a white cloud of sperm.

When the fish have finished spawning, the ropes are removed and placed in a pond of water containing a 0.2mg/litre malachite green solution. The parents are then removed from the pond, malachite green is added at 0.2mg/litre, and the spawning ropes are replaced. The aeration is kept on, but the water supply is turned off. As soon as the eggs start to 'eye up', a gentle trickle of water is added to remove the ammonia and nitrates, which will be produced as a byproduct of the developing eggs.

The eggs hatch after three to five days and the fry gather around the spawning ropes. Once all the fry have filled their swimbladders – two or three days after hatching – they will crowd around the airstones. They are then placed into growing-on facilities.

Using pituitary hormone injections

This modern method is not recommended for use by the inexperienced hobbyist as it interferes with the fish's

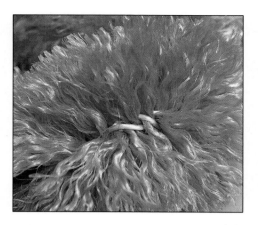

Above: *Spawning ropes are used by amateur and professional koi-breeders. This is a commercial one, but they are easy to make.*

natural hormone levels. Spawning is induced with an injection of a hormone called gonadotropin, which is extracted from the pituitary gland of a donor fish's brain. The pituitary gland stores the gonadotropin hormone and this acts as a messenger between the gonads (ovaries in females and testes in males) and the brain. Release of the hormone is triggered by increasing day length and rise in temperature. In females, the hormone will only stimulate the ovulation and release of the eggs if they are in a ripe condition. In the wild state, a koi is able to regulate its own level of hormone and release it at the right time. Unfortunately, it is hard for the koi-breeder to regulate the precise time of spawning, and the usual time – about four o'clock in the morning – is not ideal for the hobbyist. With hormone-induced spawning, it is possible to determine both the time of year and the hour at which the eggs are released. However, the koi farmer will have to 'strip' the koi of eggs and milt

(sperm), as explained below.

The koi are removed from the pond and placed in a tank containing water at the same temperature. The temperature is then raised 1°C every day until it reaches 22-25°C(71-77°F). The fish are then kept in water at that temperature for 1000°C days, that is, at 25°C(74°F) for 40 days. The male and female are then injected with a solution of pituitary hormones, each fish receiving 0.3mg of acetone-dried pituitary per kilogram of body weight. (Each whole pituitary weighs on average 2.5-3mg.) Twenty four hours later, the female only is given a decisive dose of 3mg per kilogram of body weight, and ten hours after this the koi are ready to be stripped.

It is advisable to have the fish anaesthetized before hand stripping; this relaxes the koi and helps the eggs to flow. The fish is wrapped in a slightly damp towel, leaving the vent clear. Holding the anal fin against a clean dry bowl, a gentle pressure is then applied to the abdomen to release the eggs from the vent. No excess pressure should be applied to force the eggs out. Sperm from the male fish is collected in the same way, and spread over the eggs. A fertilization solution made up of urea and sodium chloride dissolved in distilled water is then added to the bowl and the eggs are gently agitated, either by stirring the solution with a feather or by aerating it gently for three to five minutes. About 40-45 minutes after the koi have been stripped, milk is added to the solution to prevent the eggs from sticking together and the eggs are placed in a glass jar, where they hatch in water at 23°C(74°F). The jar is then emptied into a tank. When the fry have filled their swimbladders with air, they are ready for release into growing-on ponds.

Above: *Netting koi from a growing-on lake after the summer season has*

finished. The best fish selected from these are destined for dealers' ponds.

HEALTH CARE

During the course of its life, a koi may receive an injury, act as host to any one of a number of parasites, or fall ill. With a basic understanding of koi anatomy and some knowledge of health care, you will be equipped to treat some of the misfortunes that may occasionally befall your fish. In this section, we consider the subject of health care in five areas: first-aid and injuries, anaesthetics, parasites, diseases, and environmentally related disorders – including stress in general.

Before starting to consider health care practices, however, we should offer a few words of caution. Although there are no hard and fast rules governing when to treat koi or when to leave them alone, it does far more harm than good to keep netting koi to check them over for possible problems. Sometimes, however, they do require medical attention. If in doubt, consult someone with experience in fish health to come and see the koi in your pond; it is often more beneficial to see the afflicted fish in its own environment rather than trying to determine whether a highly stressed fish in a plastic bag is ailing. Like any other animal, a sick fish is best treated at home if possible; moving it around will only stress it further and reduce its ability to fight off illness. Finally, before rushing off to consult someone about a sick fish, check the water quality in the pond; it is always possible that ammonia or nitrite levels are too high.

A koi losing buoyancy in a treatment salt dip; it should recover quickly on being returned to the pond.

HEALTH CARE

First-aid and injuries

A first-aid kit is essential to treat any injuries that koi are likely to incur. Ideally, this should include a sharp pair of scissors, a pair of tweezers with rounded tips, cotton buds, an antiseptic cream or lotion, and a towel in which to wrap the koi when treating it. You should be able to treat koi up to 30cm(12in) long without resorting to the use of anaesthetics; larger fishes are difficult to hold and treat and so usually need to be anaesthetized (see below). Always wrap koi under treatment securely in a towel dampened in pond water. Make sure that your hands, too, are wet before handling koi – dry hands stick to the scales, pulling them out and leaving ugly scars until new scales grow.

Many brands of antiseptic cream are available, all equally effective in the treatment of wounds, but it is best to select one with an oil base since this will not dissolve so easily when the koi is returned to the pond. Several antiseptic lotions are also used in treating wounds. These include malachite green, povidone iodine, potassium permanganate, methylene blue and mercurochrome. Koi-keepers usually have their own preference, but it is worth noting that mercurochrome, which has a mercury base, is highly toxic to humans. Wear protective gloves when using this treatment and wash off any splashes immediately with plenty of water.

As a caring koi-keeper, you should go to great lengths to ensure that there are no sharp projections or obstructions in the pond on which your fishes could damage themselves. Despite these precautions, some fishes will still sustain injuries. Koi use the lateral line organ (see page 17) to detect any projection or obstruction in the pond, but they will periodically rub themselves against submerged objects, an action known as 'flicking'. This behaviour is frequently seen after feeding and is probably associated with cleaning their bodies. It may also be seen when the fish has some skin irritation, such as that caused by a parasite. As you might imagine, flicking can easily lead to a superficial cut on the body. Similarly, koi will jump from time to time, either from sheer 'joie de vivre' or from irritation caused by a parasite. Such blind leaps can end in disaster, since the koi may leap into a projection above the pond, or even out of the water and onto the surrounding area.

Damage is usually superficial, but it is better to take some simple first-aid precautions to prevent the koi suffering a secondary bacterial infection. If the wound is on the body, clean the area with a cotton bud and apply antiseptic cream or lotion. Lotions are best applied by dipping a cotton bud into the solution and painting it, neat, onto the affected area. If the wound is in the region of the head or gills, use cream; antiseptic lotions are more likely to run into, and damage, sensitive areas such as the gills, eyes and nostrils.

If the koi only bruises itself, this is seen as blood beneath a number of scales, which may also be raised. If the bleeding has been slight and the scales are not raised, it is best to leave the injury to heal on its own. Should the bleeding be heavy enough to raise the scales, be sure to treat the fish, since such bruising can become a focus of infection, resulting in a hole developing. Express the blood by carefully raising the scale with a needle and, keeping it in close contact with the scale, gently puncture the skin of each one that is affected. Using slight pressure on the affected area, squeeze the congealed blood through the perforation made by the needle. Finally, treat the whole area with an antiseptic lotion. Bruising may also occur if koi are badly netted or handled. If the bruising is severe, treat it as described above. Take great care not to worsen existing injuries or create new damage when catching koi and removing them from the pond.

Occasionally, koi will jump right out of the pond onto the surrounding area. If the fish has recently jumped out and is still actively thrashing, simply return it to the pond. If it is still breathing but slightly laboured, it is worth treating it to a 10-minute, well-aerated salt bath before returning it to the pond. Make up the salt bath by dissolving 20gm of cooking salt per litre of pond water in a separate container. This makes a 2 percent solution. (On a larger scale you can dissolve 1kg of salt in 50 litres of water, or approximately 2.2lb in 11 gallons). As a result of stress, and a prolonged exposure to an alien environment (i.e. being out of the water), the fish will be susceptible to secondary fungal and/or bacterial infections. The salt bath should help to prevent any fungal spores or bacteria from colonizing the koi's protective mucus.

These photographs show basic first-aid and treatment techniques. Do not attempt any of these procedures unless you are qualified or experienced. The top row from the left shows an anaesthetized koi about to be wrapped up in a wet towel, cleaning the damaged area with a cotton bud and then applying mercurochrome lotion. Always use mercurochrome with care and, ideally, wear gloves. The bottom row shows the application of a waterproof ointment to protect and further sterilize the area, and then attending to another lesion.

Above: *Salt baths can be a very effective way of controlling parasites such as* Ichthyobodo *and* Trichodina. *(See the table on pages 112-113 for concentrations). Note the use of an airstone to aerate the water.*

Koi can often be successfully resuscitated, even when they appear to be dead. Before casting the 'corpse' away, take a close look at it. Look for the slightest movement of the skin surrounding the operculum, or gill cover, turn the fish upside down and watch the eye closely to see if it rolls, and check the mouth – it may gape in a last desperate attempt to breathe. The koi is literally suffocating when it is out of water. In the water, the delicate gill filaments are able to absorb oxygen because they are separated as they literally 'float' in the respiratory current. Out of the water, the gill filaments stick together, immediately reducing the respiratory surface, and as they start to dry out, the mucus on them congeals. This damage to the gills is a problem which may need to be resolved after the fish has been resuscitated.

The heart continues to beat even for some hours after a koi stops showing any sign of life. To resuscitate the fish, take hold of the section of the body between the caudal fin and the dorsal and anal fins – known as the caudal peduncle – and pull the koi firmly but gently backwards not more than about 30cm(12in). This action forces water under the opercula, over the gills and out through the mouth. Then push the fish forwards so that the water forces the opercula closed. Ideally, resuscitate the koi where air is being pumped into the pond, such as alongside a venturi. Continue this action until the fish can breathe regularly on its own.

This could take two or more hours, depending on the size of the fish.

Once the fish is able to breathe on its own, place it in a floating basket or bowl containing pond water, with an air supply from an aquarium pump and leave it. At this stage, the koi will be on its side. When the koi is upright, which may take several hours, release it into the pond. Over the next few days, pay particular attention to this koi. The fish may still succumb to a fungal infection but, hopefully, will make a complete recovery.

Anaesthetics

Anaesthetics are drugs whose effect is to produce insensibility to touch and pain. The only purposes for anaesthetizing a koi should be to inject it, treat it or to perform surgery. Anaesthetics have also been used to subdue koi when transporting them, but this is an inadvisable and risky practice, since the fishes are likely to become comatose and die. If all possible preparations and precautions are taken (see *Buying koi*, page 61), there should be no need to anaesthetize koi when transporting them.

The range and availability of anaesthetics varies from country to country, as do the regulations about their use. The chemicals used as fish anaesthetics include benzocaine, quinaldine and ethyl-m-aminobenzoate (MS 222). If you are not qualified and/or experienced in using anaesthetics, always consult a veterinarian or qualified expert. The following notes are offered for general guidance only and must be interpreted in the light of your local situation and regulations, plus your own qualification and/or experience of dealing with fish.

While the use of anaesthetics is some-times necessary, none of them is completely safe; even at the recommended doses, it is extremely easy to over anaesthetize a koi, from which recovery is rare. Occasionally, you may find a koi that is allergic to the chosen anaesthetic. Unfortunately, there is no way of knowing before immersing the fish whether it will be sensitive to the drug. A sensitive koi will respond instantly by losing all mobility, and this can have fatal results unless you remove it immediately.

Before mixing the anaesthetic with the pond water (in a separate container), ensure that you are prepared for treating the koi; have the first-aid kit immediately to hand and the wet towel ready to receive the fish. If you have never anaesthetized a fish before, it is a good idea to watch over the shoulder of someone experienced with the technique before trying it for yourself. If the fish is very large (over 45cm/18in long), use a large, floating bowl. Place it in the pond, fill it to the required level with pond water and add the necessary amount of anaesthetic. Once the koi has been netted, 'swim' it towards the bowl and tip it to receive the fish. You will probably need to lift the koi over the inclined edge of the bowl, to avoid tipping any of the anaesthetic into the pond. You can net smaller fishes into a floating basket and then lift them (with wet hands) into the receptacle containing the anaesthetic. You can also anaesthetize a koi in a plastic bag, but it is difficult to get it out quickly if it reacts adversely to the anaesthetic.

Having placed the koi into the anaesthetic, watch it all the time. At first, it will open and close its mouth rapidly, as though it has swallowed something distasteful, and may well thrash about for a minute or so before becoming subdued. Gently push the fish over onto its side and hold it there; if it struggles, leave it in the anaesthetic until it stops pushing against your hand, then lift it out of the anaesthetic and wrap it in the wet towel.

Above: *Koi being anaesthetized. Once on its side, remove each koi and wrap it in a towel moistened with pond water. Do not attempt this if you are not experienced and never leave fish unattended in an anaesthetic.*

HEALTH CARE

Once the fish is anaesthetized, the opercular movements are greatly reduced although still discernible. A lightly anaesthetized or sedated koi will still be slightly responsive; wrapping it in the towel will help to hold it still and also prevent any further injuries should it struggle while it is out of the water.

Once you have completed the treatment, bring the koi round by placing it in a floating basket in the pond. Usually, the anaesthetic-free water is sufficient to revive the fish, but sometimes you may need to place it in the air flow from the venturi to aid its recovery. Not all fishes react in the same way to anaesthetics – some will 'go down' very rapidly, while others take an exceptionally long time to react and then recover more slowly.

Parasites

A parasite is an organism that lives on or inside another organism, termed the host, and benefits from the association, usually by feeding off the host. The host does not benefit and, indeed, the presence of a parasite is usually harmful. Koi can be host to a wide variety of parasites, ranging from tiny single-celled organisms (protozoans) to large, visible ones, such as fish lice, leeches and 'worms'. As there are so many different parasites to consider, we examine them here according to their biological category, starting with protozoans.

Protozoan parasites

Protozoans are tiny, single-celled organisms, the very largest of which is less than 1mm(0.04in) across and just visible to the naked eye. There are many different types of protozoans, most of which are free living in damp and watery environments, where they feed on dissolved nutrients or tiny particles, including bacteria. The parasitic protozoans infect a variety of hosts, including fishes, where they can reproduce rapidly and form large populations, either remaining in or on an individiual fish or spreading to the remainder of the stock. Of the many protozoans detrimental to fish health, some affect a wide range of fish species while others are host specific, i.e. they occur only on one type of fish. Here, we look at a number of conditions caused by protozoans that can affect koi.

Sliminess of the skin

The common name of this condition aptly describes the chief sign of infection, a greyish white film of excess mucus on the body. This is the skin's reaction to the presence of a range of irritating protozoan parasites, notably *Ichthyobodo*, *Trichodina* and *Chilodonella*.

Above: *A tancho koi suffering from an infestation with* Ichthyobodo. *These flagellate protozoans feed on skin cells and cause a whitish grey film as the fish produces excess mucus as a response. The skin also becomes slightly inflamed.*

Ichthyobodo (formerly known as *Costia*) is a very small, bean-shaped protozoan parasite that moves around using long whiplike threads called flagella. It moves around the body and gills of the fish, feeding on the skin cells. In the early stages of infection, *Ichthyobodo* invades the pockets of skin at the bases of the scales. As their numbers increase, the parasites move onto all parts of the body, including the gills. In addition to the whitish film on the body, the signs shown by koi infected with *Ichthyobodo* include scratching and leaping, followed by failure to feed and lethargy. *Ichthyobodo* has a wide temperature tolerance of at least 2-29°C(36-84°F), although recent reports show that it has a much higher temperature tolerance than this, being able to reproduce at 38°C(100°F). Like other protozoans, *Ichthyobodo* is particularly active in the early spring, increasing in numbers while koi are still recovering from the winter. Because it infects the scale pockets, it is difficult for the koi to eradicate. The main problems associated with an infection by this organism are the secondary bacterial and fungal infections that invariably occur as a result of the damage caused.

Trichodina and other trichodinid parasites are probably among the most familiar protozoans to the koi-keeper. These saucer-shaped organisms have distinctive rings of tiny hairs (cilia) around the body which enable the cell organism to move. (These cilia are clearly visible at a magnification of x100-200 through a microscope.) Koi infected by *Trichodina* develop the familiar grey film over the body in response to the infestation. This excess mucus simply encourages the *Trichodina* to reproduce at a faster rate. Trichodinids are found on even the most healthy koi, but if the fish is diseased or in poor condition, they reproduce unchecked and allow secondary baterial infections to occur. Trichodinids can also

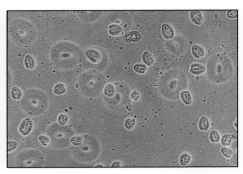

Above: *A microscope view of* Chilodonella, *a common cause of sliminess of the skin. It is particularly common on injured or weakened fish. Each of these ciliate protozoans is about 50 microns across. (A micron is a thousandth of a millimetre).*

infect the gills, where damage to the delicate filaments makes the gills susceptible to bacterial infection. In the early stages of infection, koi repeatedly scratch themselves and leap out of the water. As the infection progresses, the fish stop feeding and hang at the surface, usually where air enters the pond. They may be seen to gasp and frequently gulp air at the surface. At this stage, there is very little chance that an infected koi will survive, even with treatment.

The protozoan *Chilodonella* looks rather like a tiny gooseberry and is found on the fins, body and gills, where it feeds on skin cells. *Chilodonella* reproduces very rapidly in the early spring, when the koi are still rather lethargic, allowing the infestation to become well-established before the fish can groom them off. Koi affected by *Chilodonella* have the usual signs of a grey-white film on the body, plus the typical behaviour pattern of scratching, leaping, followed by lethargy. Left untreated, affected koi will die. *Chilodonella* is usually associated with fish that are already weakened by stress or disease and is often found together with bacterial and fungal infections.

White spot (Ich)

White spot is familiar to everyone who keeps fish. It is caused by a protozoan with the scientific name of *Ichthyophthirius multifiliis*, hence the alternative common name of 'ich'. White spot has a very complicated life cycle and spreads rapidly through a fish population. The white spots on the skin, fins and gills are individual protozoan cells that become enclosed between the epidermal cells of the fish and feed on the body fluids and cells. They 'mature' at about 1mm(0.04in) across and 'punch' out of the skin and fall away from the fish. Within a few hours, they settle in the pond, form into a cyst and inside begin dividing to produce a thousand or more

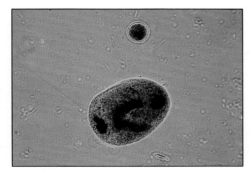

Above: *A single mature cell of the protozoan parasite* Ichthyophthirius multifiliis *that causes white spot disease in koi and a wide range of other fish. Special staining clearly reveals the characteristically curved nucleus. Each cell matures at 1mm (0.04in).*

Right: *1 Individual cells beneath the skin. 2 Mature parasites 'punch' out and swim away. 3 Parasites become enclosed in a gelatinous capsule. 4 Each cell divides to form 1000 or more infective stages. 5 'Swarmers' must find a host in 24 hours.*

White spot disease cycle

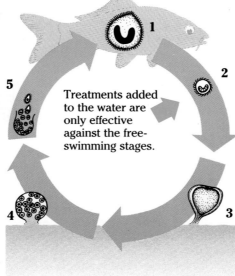

Treatments added to the water are only effective against the free-swimming stages.

tiny infective stages. When these free-swimming 'swarmers' break out of the cysts, they must find a fish host within about 24 hours in order to survive. They are well equipped to penetrate the skin or gills of any fishes on which they settle and quickly establish themselves to start the infection cycle again.

As well as showing the typical white spots, infected koi tend to scratch and swim into the water inlet. As the infection progresses, they stop feeding, become lethargic and often discoloured. Left untreated, white spot is fatal. Fortunately, effective commercial white spot remedies are widely available.

Nodular disease
The last strictly parasitic protozoan included here is *Myxobolus*, the most important feature of which is that it produces spores, which are very resistant to chemical treatment. *Myxobolus* infects

Above: Myxobolus *spores collected from an infected fish and photographed at a magnification of x200. These spores are released from nodules that form within the tissues. The infection can spread between fish in a number of different ways.*

koi internally, where the parasites invade the gut or muscle. Thousands of tiny spores form inside cysts and, once released into the water (in a number of ways, including from the decomposed bodies of dead fish), it is these that spread the parasites to other koi, although the precise details of the life cycles of these parasites are poorly understood. Koi suffering from nodular disease (named from the 'nodules' that the cysts produce) lose weight and become lethargic, showing symptoms very similar to those produced by the bacterium causing tuberculosis (see page 109). There is no cure for infected koi and those fish known to be suffering from heavy infestations of this parasite are best disposed of humanely before the infection spreads throughout the remaining fish.

Opportunistic protozoan infections
A number of protozoans colonize koi without being strictly parasitic. Notable among these are the so-called 'bell animalcules', scientifically known as the Peritrichida (literally meaning 'hairy mouthed'). Around the mouth there is a fringe of tiny hairs that waft microscopic food particles into the hungry bell animalcule. The food particles are usually bacteria or tiny pieces of organic debris, so these protozoans are very common in biological filters. When affecting koi, the bell animalcules are found near ulcers or damage on the body, where they feed on bacteria infecting the wound. Alternatively, they may also be found on the fins, busily feeding on the bacteria responsible for causing finrot (see page 109).

Protozoans of this type include *Vorticella*, *Epistylis*, *Carchesium* and *Apiosoma*. *Vorticella* has a bell-shaped 'body' on a long spiral stalk. When feeding, the stalk is very long as the organism 'stretches out' to reach food particles. It is a solitary organism but occurs in large groups of individuals. *Epistylis* and *Carchesium* are both colonial organisms. Their bell-shaped bodies are able to lengthen or shorten and are located at the tips of branched, twiglike stalks. *Apiosoma* is rather more funnel-shaped and sits on a short, fat stalk. Like *Vorticella*, it is solitary but occurs in groups of large numbers. In addition to bacteria, *Apiosoma* also feeds on other protozoans smaller than itself.

Thus, these bell animalcules are not truly parasitic but opportunistic, appearing as whitish patches (often tinged green with algae) on koi that are already damaged or infected by bacteria.

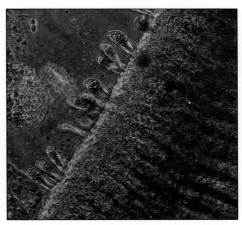

Above: *Groups of* Apiosoma *protozoans clinging to a gill filament. Each cell reaches about 100 microns (thousandths of a millimetre) long. In large numbers, these opportunistic ciliates can block the gills and cause respiratory distress.*

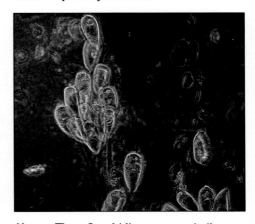

Above: *These* Scyphidia *are very similar protozoans to* Apiosoma. *This microscope view clearly shows the typical flask shape of these cells, each with a terminal ciliated 'mouth' that strains out organic debris and microorganisms from the water.*

HEALTH CARE

Crustacean parasites

Crustaceans are jointed-limbed invertebrates that encompass a huge range of creatures, from crabs to 'water fleas' (*Daphnia*). Many are free-living aquatic species that pass through several larval stages during their reproductive life cycles. The majority are harmless to koi and other fish, but some species have developed a specialized parasitic way of life and can pose serious health problems if they occur in large numbers. Here, we look at the most common of these crustacean parasites.

Anchor worm

One of the most notorious crustacean parasites that infest fish is the anchor worm, *Lernaea*. There are several species of anchor worm, all of which are parasitic on fish. The complete life cycle of the anchor worm takes 17-33 days, depending on the temperature. At 20°C(68°F), for example, the cycle takes 25 days; below 15°C(59°F) it may not complete at all. The newly hatched anchor worm, or nauplius, is elliptical in shape and free swimming in the pond water. The nauplius moults into a second stage (the metanauplius), which is also free swimming. Subsequent juvenile stages are parasitic and must find a fish host, where they settle on the gills. When these juveniles mature into adults, the males mate with the females and then become nonparasitic and leave the host.

The fertilized females leave the gills and settle on the body of the koi, where they continue to grow, gradually losing their crustacean features and becoming

Anchor worm life cycle

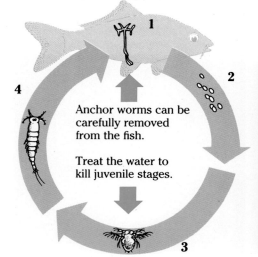

Anchor worms can be carefully removed from the fish.

Treat the water to kill juvenile stages.

Above: *1 Adult female anchor worm embedded in skin. 2 Eggs released into the water from mature egg sacs. 3 First free-living juvenile stage. 4 Later juvenile stages are parasitic. When mature, the adults mate and the female develops a wormlike shape.*

elongated and 'wormlike' in shape. At the same time, they burrow deep into the skin and underlying tissues, developing anchorlike processes that hold them firmly in place. At this point, the mature anchor worms are clearly visible attached to the fish, being up to 20mm(0.8in) long, depending on species. Digestive juices secreted by the anchor worms enable them to draw in and feed on dissolved body tissues. The nutrients received from feeding on the koi are used to produce eggs, visible as twin white egg sacs at the posterior end of the mature female. A single female can produce several thousand eggs in her lifespan. As these eggs are released into the water, so the life cycle starts again.

Anchor worms are usually seen on koi when they have been feeding for some time, producing characteristic bloody spots that are highly prone to secondary infection by bacteria or fungi. And if an anchor worm dies while still attached to the koi, bacteria and/or fungi will readily invade the dead parasite's tissues and then spread to the koi. In fact, anchor worms are probably one of the biggest culprits in causing holes on the body.

Fish lice and gill maggots

The fish louse, *Argulus*, is yet another type of parasitic crustacean familiar to fishkeepers. Both male and female fish lice are parasitic on the body and gills of koi. Up to 10mm(0.4in) across, the fish louse has a distinct round shape, with two prominent, disc-shaped suckers on the underside. (Looking at microscope views of fish lice, these suckers appear at first glance like two eyes, but the eyes are smaller black dots located further forward on the head.) Each sucker is hard, being made of a substance very similar to the exoskeleton of insects. They allow

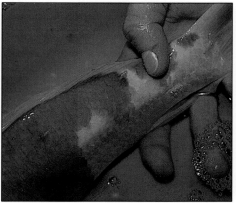

Above: *An anchor worm is clearly visible clinging to the tail region of this koi. These crustacean parasites can be quite deeply embedded in the body wall and underlying tissues, causing wounds that often become secondarily infected with fungi and bacteria.*

Fish lice life cycle

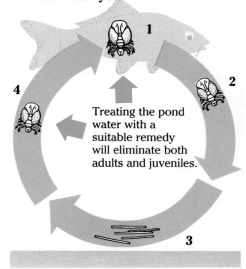

Treating the pond water with a suitable remedy will eliminate both adults and juveniles.

Above: *1 Adult lice clinging to skin by means of suckers. 2 Mature females leave fish to lay eggs. 3 Eggs are laid in long gelatinous capsules. 4 Juveniles pass through several stages before becoming adult.*

Above: *This close view of the underside of a fish lice* (Argulus) *clearly shows the feathery crustacean legs and the two prominent suckers, with the smaller, darker eyes further forward. These parasites grow to a maximum size of about 10mm(0.4in).*

the fish louse to stick onto the koi's body and help it to glide around on the layer of mucus. Fish lice are very adept swimmers; when brushed off the surface of a koi, they simply swim around until they find another fish. Between the suckers are needlelike mouthparts that the fish louse inserts through the koi's skin. Glands produce a toxin that flows down the hollow 'needles' and the louse breaks up the affected tissue using a sawing action of the mouthparts. Where a fish louse has been feeding, a prominent red welt develops on the koi's body.

Not surpisingly, fish lice cause intense irritation to koi, and they may show outward signs similar to those resulting from infestation with protozoan parasites, i.e. scratching followed by jumping. Affected koi may also show weight loss, since they

Gill maggot life cycle

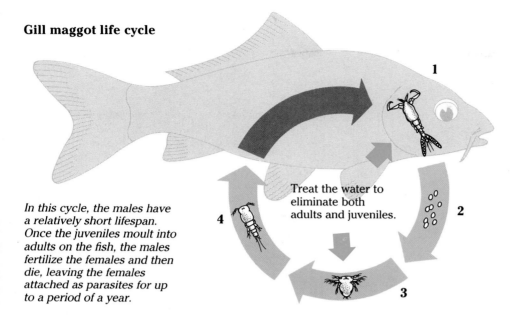

In this cycle, the males have a relatively short lifespan. Once the juveniles moult into adults on the fish, the males fertilize the females and then die, leaving the females attached as parasites for up to a period of a year.

Treat the water to eliminate both adults and juveniles.

1

2

3

4

are distracted from feeding by the fish lice and, left untreated, the presence of these parasites will retard the growth of the fish. The damage caused by fish lice is often a prime target for secondary infection by bacteria or fungi. If they infect the gills, the damage they cause is very severe, resulting in respiratory distress and often leading to secondary infection by bacteria. Fish lice can also transmit disease from fish to fish in a population, including protozoan parasites, various bacterial infections and spring viraemia of carp (see page 108).

The term 'gill maggots' refers to the mature females of the parasitic crustacean *Ergasilus*, with their distinctive maggotlike, white egg sacs. (The males are not parasitic, dying very soon after mating.) The females are found on the body and fins, but principally on the gills of affected fish. The first pair of legs are modified into grasping organs, with prominent hooks that enable the parasites to grasp the gill filaments and feed on the tissues. Heavy infestations can cause severe damage by eroding the filaments and allowing secondary infections with bacteria and fungi to develop. Although not a very common problem with koi, it is advisable to check new fish, since it is only on affected fish that such parasites can be introduced into the pond.

Insect pests
A wide range of flying insects pass through larval stages in an aquatic environment. Some of these insect larvae are predatory and can pose a hazard to baby fish. Dragonflies, for example, lay their eggs in or close to water, either on the water surface or inside the tissues of water plants. The nymphs that emerge from these eggs have large, pincerlike jaws which they use to catch and eat

Above: *1 Parasitic females attached to the gills. 2 Eggs are released into the water from the prominent white egg sacs. 3 Eggs hatch into free-living juveniles. 4 Later juveniles must find a host fish to survive.*

Above: *These gills are clearly infested with gill maggots* (Ergasilus). *The term 'maggots' aptly describes the appearance of the long, white egg sacs produced by the mature female parasites, first during the spring. Heavy infestations can damage the gills.*

small fish up to about 3cm(1.2in) long. Similarly, the larvae of great diving beetles, *Dytiscus*, are armed with a formidable pair of jaws and can easily devour baby koi up to their own size of about 5cm(2in). Both these and dragonfly larvae are harmless to fish larger than about 10cm(4in).

Skin and gill flukes
Most koi-keepers are aware that koi are host to flukes. They are just about visible to the naked eye, but being translucent are difficult to see without the aid of a microscope. There are two kinds usually found parasitizing koi: *Dactylogyrus*, which is usually known as the gill fluke (and has two pairs of eyes); and *Gyrodactylus*, the skin fluke (which does not have any eyes). Despite these common

names, both may be found on the body and the gills, feeding on the koi's mucus. *Dactylogyrus* lays eggs that hatch to produce free-swimming larvae, while the young of *Gyrodactylus* develop within the body of the parent, which 'gives birth' to live flukes. Both types of fluke have an array of hooks by which they grasp the surface of the koi. It appears that the irritation they cause stems from the use of these hooks as grapples to move around on the gills and skin.

Flukes are present on all koi; they are the fish equivalent of fleas on cats, dogs and wild mammals. Healthy fish can keep the numbers of flukes to a minimum, by scratching them off and expelling water with force through the gills to wash them away – an action that looks as though koi are yawning. Koi that are stressed or

Above: *A portion of dissected gill tissue with several gill flukes* (Dactylogyrus) *attached to the filaments. Each fluke may grow up to 2mm(0.08in) long. The life cycle of such flukes involves the release of eggs that hatch into free-swimming larvae.*

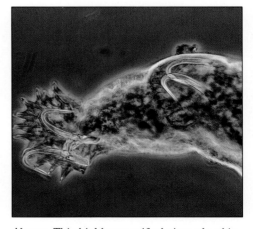

Above: *This highly magnified view of a skin fluke* (Gyrodactylus) *shows the 'grappling hooks' of the adult and also those of an unborn juvenile within its body. Such flukes are the fish equivalent of fleas.*

HEALTH CARE

diseased, however, are less able to cope with these grooming activities and the flukes may increase to large numbers. Sometimes, sick or stressed fish may have literally hundreds of flukes on the gill filaments. In the spring, flukes can be a nuisance, as they respond to rising temperatures more quickly than the koi. This is an evolutionary adaptation that enables parasites to increase their numbers before their unwilling hosts can effectively remove them. It is not known whether flukes can transmit viral or other disease agents.

Parasitic worms
It is very uncommon for koi to be infested with worms, but if they do occur, they are usually parasitic in the gut, feeding on the koi's food as it passes through the intestine. The worms that parasitize fish are either flatworms, tapeworms or threadworms. Koi infested with worms tend to be thin and rather sickly, but show no other outward signs. In most cases, worms in the intestines of newly imported or wild fish will die and reinfection will be unlikely because of the absence of the intermediate hosts in their complex life cycles.

Leeches
The leech most commonly found parasitizing koi is the fish leech, *Piscicola geo-*

Fish leech life cycle

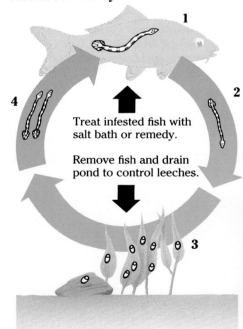

Treat infested fish with salt bath or remedy.

Remove fish and drain pond to control leeches.

Above: *1 Adult leeches feed on fish blood for 2-3 days at a time. 2 They leave the fish to digest their meal or to lay eggs. 3 Leech eggs laid in oval cocoons attached to rocks and plants. 4 Newly hatched leeches must find a fish to feed upon.*

metra. It is slender and up to about 5cm(2in) in length, with prominent ridges and pale yellow hoops at regular intervals around the body. It moves by a characteristic looping action and, when not feeding on a fish, is found among the pond plants or substrate. A hungry fish leech stretches out from the plant or substrate and waits for a passing koi to brush against it, when it will grasp the fish. Once on the fish, it moves around with a looping action until it finds a suitable place to feed.

Once attached to the koi, fish leeches can pierce the skin to feed on the fish's blood. They will attach anywhere on the body, but particularly where the skin is soft, such as around the fin bases, vent, mouth and gills. The amount of blood each leech takes from the fish is very small, but heavy infestations can reduce the health of a koi, causing it to become anaemic and laying it open to other infections. Leeches can transmit some protozoan parasites and spring viraemia of carp to koi, and there is some evidence that they can also transmit certain bacterial infections.

The leeches that parasitize koi produce eggs in a cocoon with a hard, leathery coating that is resistant to most chemicals with the exception of lime (calcium hydroxide). Where leeches are a problem in a pond, the only remedy is to remove those on the koi and place the fish in another pond while you drain down the affected pond and then treat it with lime. This will kill the adult leeches in the plants and substrate and also destroy the egg-filled cocoons. When setting up the pond again, be sure to wash everything well and use new plants.

Leeches are usually introduced on wild fish or plants – so it is worth checking any aquatic plants carefully before putting them in the pond. Few retail outlets would have access to plants infected with leeches or their cocoons, but beware of taking plants from the wild!

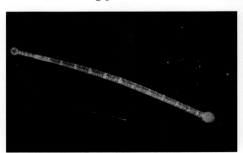

Above: *A single fish leech,* Piscicola geometra, *full of blood after feeding. The suckers at both ends of the elongated body are powerful attachment organs. The 'head' end has sharp cutting mouthparts and the slightly smaller of the two suckers.*

Fungal diseases
Fungi are plants that lack the pigment chlorophyll, which enables green plants to harness the sun's energy to form essential nutrients in the process of photosynthesis. Fungi obtain nutrients from organic sources, either from dead plants or animals, or, in the case of entirely parasitic fungi, from living tissues. The most familiar types of fungi consist of long, branched threadlike filaments (hyphae), that tangle together to form a matted structure called the mycelium. Since fungi need to live in damp or wet conditions, they are always present in the koi pond. Dead fish are an ideal growth medium for fungus, so be sure to remove them immediately from the pond. Fungus also infects koi eggs, which are rich in nutrients and an ideal target for attack. Always remove contaminated eggs and dispose of them as soon as you discover them. Both eggs and koi infected with this type of fungus show grey, woolly patches. Here, we consider two fungal infections that fall into this category, *Saprolegnia* and *Branchiomyces*.

Saprolegnia
One of the most common fungal infections of koi is caused by *Saprolegnia*. As part of its complicated life cycle, *Saprolegnia* forms fruiting bodies that release spores into the water. These are the 'infective agents' that germinate on koi tissue already damaged by pests, parasites, other disease organisms, accidental damage (such as caused by careless netting), water quality problems or stress. The fungal spores will grow anywhere on the body, including the gills, initially ger-

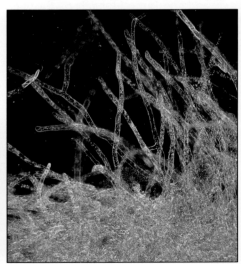

Above: *The individual strands, or hyphae, of* Saprolegnia *fungus intertwine to form a white fluffy mass, or mycelium, that can be seen on the surface of severely affected fishes. Each of these strands is 20 microns (thousandths of a millimetre) across.*

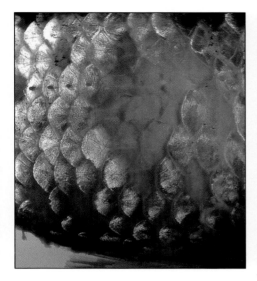

Above: *Whitish tufts of fungus erupting from between the scales show that these threadlike growths have become established in the underlying tissues. Such outbreaks often start from spores germinating on dead tissue around wounds or other damage.*

Above: *A particularly severe case of* Saprolegnia *fungus allied with scale erosion on a young koi. The fungal growths are tinged green with algae. Prompt treatment with a suitable remedy is essential to contain such infections.*

minating on areas of dead tissue. The threadlike hyphae produced by the spores invade the dead tissue, releasing juices that dissolve the tissue and create a nutrient-rich 'soup' on which the fungus feeds. As the fungus grows, these digestive juices start breaking down living cells, thus enabling the hyphae to invade other areas of the body, until the fungal growth becomes easily visible on the surface. Infected gills are not so easy to see, but if your koi become lethargic, cease feeding and show signs of respiratory distress – hanging at the water surface, breathing hard and often gulping air – examination of the gills may show them to have the characteristic grey cotton-wool-like growths of *Saprolegnia* fungus. (Take care, however: these signs are not exclusive to fungal infection.)

Branchiomyces
Branchiomyces is a fungus that contaminates the gills. It is spread through the water and thrives in areas where the water is slightly acidic (pH 5.8-6.8). It has a life cycle similar to *Saprolegnia*. Spores released into the water either remain in suspension or sink to the bottom of the pond, where they are sucked in by koi grubbing around for food. On contact with the gill filaments, the spores germinate and begin to form hyphae that invade and kill the gill tissues. This dead gill tissue is still infective and under laboratory conditions will produce fungus very quickly. Because of the close proximity of the blood supply to the gill tissue, some spores may enter the bloodstream, and *Branchiomyces* has been found in the liver and spleen of infected fish.

The disease caused by this fungus is called branchiomycosis. Koi suffering from the infection initially become lethargic, cease to feed and hang at the surface of the pond, usually near the water inlet, respiring heavily and showing signs of respiratory distress. (Unfortunately, these symptoms are common to many other diseases.) Examination of the gills will show the characteristic cotton-wool-like growths. Before panicking that all the koi in your pond will succumb to branchiomycosis, it is worth remembering that this fungus must be introduced into the pond; it is not part of the natural flora of the water. If there is a history of *Branchiomyces* in your pond then it is likely that your koi may become infected, otherwise it is more likely to be the fungus *Saprolegnia* causing the problem.

Viral diseases
Viruses are probably among the most successful organisms ever to have evolved and, apart from other viruses, can infect all other living organisms, including bacteria. Their structure is one of elegant simplicity, consisting essentially of a protein coat surrounding a core of genetic material. The life cycle might also be described as simple compared with other organisms that must recreate whole cells or whole bodies in the process. The infecting virus literally 'injects' its own genetic material into a single cell of the host. Once inside the cell, the viral genetic material takes command of the cell's genetic material and causes it to produce more viruses. Very simply, it may proceed in one of two ways. The virus may cause the host cell to mass produce other virus particles that are released when the host cell ruptures, allowing the virus particles to infect other cells and organisms. Alternatively, the virus can incorporate itself into the host cell's genetic material and may have an initial infective stage causing more virus particles to be produced. The virus then enters a non-infectious state during which the particle remains in the host cell's genetic material but is inactive. Stress or other diseases can then cause this type of virus to become infective again. A classic example of this type of viral infection is the herpes virus which causes cold sores in man.

One of the sinister aspects of any virus is that its genetic material is not very stable; it mutates very easily, giving rise to 'new' viral strains. The perfect example of this are the viruses that cause influenza, with different types appearing apparently each winter to plague us!

There is no treatment or cure for any viral disease. Prevention of viral disease using vaccination is the only method currently available. With respect to viral fish diseases, there are a few vaccines that have been shown to be effective, but most of these are used by commercial fish farmers with stock destined for food. The study of viruses that infect fish is still in its infancy. Many scientists are investigating this area of fisheries science but it will be many years before they can establish all the diseases caused by viruses.

Here, we look at two viral diseases known to occur in koi.

Carp pox
Carp pox produces solid waxy lumps, usually on the fins but also on the body, and is caused by the type of virus that incorporates its own genetic material into the host cells (i.e. the second of the two strategies outlined above). Carp pox will

Above: *The typical waxy growths of the viral infection carp pox are clearly visible near the head of this koi. These are often seen on infected fish during the spring as the water warms up. They are quite firm and may change colour with age.*

HEALTH CARE

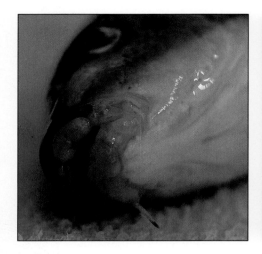

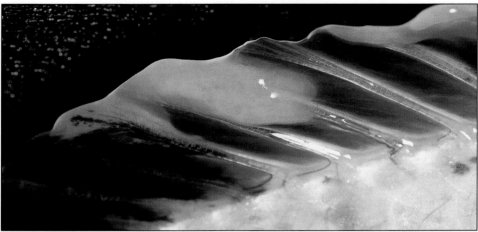

Above: *Here, carp pox has produced unsightly growths on the 'lips'. These may not necessarily interfere with the fish's ability to feed and live normally, and such symptoms may fade away on their own.*

Above: *Smooth growths of carp pox on fin rays. This viral infection cannot be treated in any reliable way, but it does not usually pose a serious threat. It seems to be spread by contact, but is not highly infectious.*

not kill koi, but in severe cases the lumps it produces can look very unsightly. It is not clear how the virus is transmitted, although it is clear that koi develop carp pox by contact with other koi already infected with the virus. Koi-keepers may notice that koi often develop the characteristic waxy lumps during the spring, when rising temperatures 'warm up' the virus before the fish's immune system becomes fully effective. Koi infected with the carp pox virus also develop the signs when they are stressed.

Spring viraemia of carp

As the name implies, spring viraemia of carp (svc) commonly occurs in the spring, when the water temperature starts to increase. (Studies of outbreaks have shown maximum mortalities at 13.5-15.5°C/56-60°F.) The typical signs of infection are a bloated body (as in dropsy, see page 110), pale gills and sometimes bleeding under the skin on the body and around the vent. Internally, the body fills with a either clear or brown fluid. The blood vessels around the swimbladder are often ruptured and the liver and spleen become enlarged.

Young koi are highly susceptible to this virus and few survive it. Those that do survive will have developed immunity to the disease but are potential carriers of the virus. The virus is released into the water with the faeces of an infected koi. It appears to infect a new host via the gills and from there enters the bloodstream. The virus can also be transmitted between koi by direct contact with infected fish, through mucus, contaminated equipment and water, and by the fish louse, *Argulus*, and the fish leech, *Piscicola geometra* (see pages 104 and 106).

There is no cure for svc. The best preventative measures are to buy fish from reputable sources, quarantine new introductions, disinfect equipment, maintain your koi in the best possible water conditions and check them regularly for any signs of ill-health.

Bacterial diseases

There are many different types of bacteria, the majority are not harmful and may even be useful – such as nitrifying bacteria in biological filters – but that still leaves a large number that are potentially harmful, or pathogenic. Most pathogenic bacteria will cause disease in many different species of fish, including koi, while some are more discriminating and infect just a few species.

So what are bacteria? They are single-celled microorganisms, with an average size of 0.5-1.0 microns (thousandths of a millimetre). There are three basic shapes of bacteria: spherical (cocci), rodlike (bacilli), and spiral (spirillum), and these can be arranged singly, in chains or in clusters. Some bacteria have tiny threadlike flagella which they use to move themselves around with surprising speed and agility.

Bacteria absorb food materials through their rigid outer cell wall and can be grouped according to whether or not they require oxygen for growth. Thus, aerobic bacteria can only grow in the presence of oxygen, while anaerobic bacteria will grow only in the absence of oxygen, since this gas is toxic to them. (Just to confuse matters, there is a third group of bacteria that will grow in the absence of oxygen but, if oxygen is present, will utilize it readily.) Bacteria usually reproduce by simply splitting into two (binary fission) and, in ideal conditions, some bacteria may divide every 15-30 minutes. Bacteria also have a form of sexual reproduction, during which genetic material is exchanged between two cells.

The size, shape and colour of the colonies that bacteria form are useful pointers to their type, although accurate identification involves a complex procedure of taking swabs and incubating the bacteria on plates of nutritive gel. Further incubation on different gels may be necessary and then treatment with stains, such as those that classify bacteria into Gram-positive or Gram-negative types. These procedures are carried out at specialist laboratories and are not within the scope of hobbyists.

Here, we consider briefly the most common bacterial infections known to affect koi, starting with fish TB.

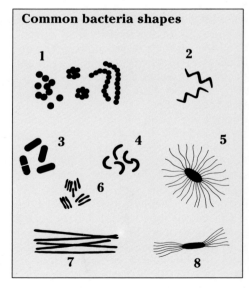

Common bacteria shapes

Above: **1** Cocci *(spheres) singly, clusters or chains.* **2** Spirillum *(spiral).* **3** Bacilli *(rods). Variations on this theme are:* **4** Vibrio *(comma shaped)* **5** Peritrichous *(flagella all round)* **6** Mycobacterium *(very small rods)* **7** Flexibacter *(long thin rods)* **8** Lophotrichous *(flagella at each end).*

Fish tuberculosis

Fish TB is caused by bacteria such as *Mycobacterium.* (A very similar disease is caused by *Nocardia* bacteria.) Infected koi become progressively thinner and hollow bellied, the eyes bulge, the skin is inflamed and often open wounds develop on the body. Tiny tubercular nodules also usually appear within the internal organs. To prevent the infection of other koi in the pond, it is vital to separate affected fish and humanely dispose of them if they do not improve. Although certain antibacterial drugs are available from veterinarians, successful treatment is far from guaranteed. In short, when the fish develop full-blown signs of fish TB, the condition is invariably fatal. Accurate diagnosis relies on identifying the clinical symptoms of the disease and subsequently confirming the presence of the bacteria by examining prepared and stained sections of tissue under a microscope, and also by culturing bacteriological samples (as outlined above).

These bacteria are transmitted from fish to fish by way of contaminated food or debris. The bacteria are voided with the faeces and can also be picked up from skin tubercles and from dead fish. Thus, it is important to remove dead or dying fish from the water to prevent the spread of infection.

Finrot, ulcers and septicaemia

A number of bacteria, notably *Aeromonas* and *Pseudomonas*, are associated with finrot, skin lesions and internal haemorrhaging. The bacteria are common in fresh water and may cause disease at temperatures as low as 10°C(50°F) and so they can be particularly problematical in spring and autumn. They often cause infections in fish weakened by stress, physical damage or poor water conditions, and so providing the best possible environment in the pond goes a long way towards preventing these problems arising in the first place.

Carp erythrodermatitis, a skin disease caused by one species of *Aeromonas*, results in ulcerous lesions developing in the skin of affected koi. (In salmon and trout, this disease is often termed 'furunculosis'.) The condition usually starts at the site of an injury, and the damage caused by this aeromonad infection often suffers secondary fungal infections. Left untreated, aeromonad infections will invade the body, leading to internal lesions and septicaemia (blood poisoning). If diagnosed in time, this condition should respond to antibiotic treatment, although there may be some problems of antibiotic resistance where these drugs have been misused (see below).

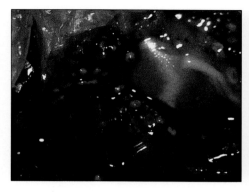

Above: *These whitish nodules among the internal organs are typical of a severe TB infection. At this stage, treatment (difficult at the best of times) is not likely to be effective. Remove dying or dead fish to block the spread of infection.*

'Hole disease' is probably the term used by many koi-keepers to describe the ulcerous lesions that may appear on the body surface as a result of bacterial infection. Such holes invariably lead to osmoregulatory problems. In a healthy fish, there is a balance between the amount of water entering the body (mainly by osmosis through the gills) and that excreted as urine by the kidneys. In koi that have holes in the body, water enters freely through the damaged skin and creates an extra burden on the kidneys, which can lead to their failure. In these circumstances, it is worth adding salt to the water at a concentration of 3gm per litre (approximately 0.5oz per gallon). This 0.3 percent solution helps to restore the osmotic balance at the site of the wound and reduces the workload placed on the kidneys.

Salt treatment is often used to help stressed koi recover their equilibrium, since stressed koi are more prone to bacterial infection. Salt is a powerful antiseptic and will often kill any pathogenic bacteria before they have a chance to cause any problems. On receiving shipments of koi from Japan, for example, the majority of dealers allow a period of time for the fish to recover by leaving them in a pond that may contain up to twice the above concentration in the water! It is in the koi-keeper's interest to have a large bag of salt constantly available and at the first sign of a problem add some to the pond water. (The salt concentrations recommended in this book for use with koi are generally lower than those usually quoted. In effect, we are being cautious; using too much salt and/or not diluting it with water before adding it to the pond can easily produce 'salt burns', as shown in the photo on page 111. If you are experienced in keeping koi, then you may already be using slightly more salt than we recommend.)

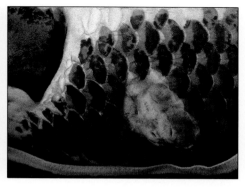

Above: *Abscesses can arise very quickly in fish and cause extensive swelling. Sometimes, an abscess may burst, as shown above. It is best to seek expert advice immediately in such cases. Treatment may involve antibiotics or other antibacterial.*

Above: *Chronic finrot can lead to the total erosion of the affected fish. In this case, almost the entire dorsal fin has rotted away, making effective treatment very difficult. Good environmental conditions should forestall such bacterial infections.*

Above: *Ulcers of the belly region can lead to further complications, as shown above, where the gut is protruding through the infected muscle wall. Such cases are usually fatal. Adding salt to the water can provide some help in less severe examples.*

Cotton-wool disease

This is another bacterial infection that is most likely to strike when koi are kept in poor conditions or when a sudden change in water quality stresses the fish. The common name originates from the whitish tufts that typically develop first around the mouth (hence the alternative, but misleading, name of 'mouth fungus')

HEALTH CARE

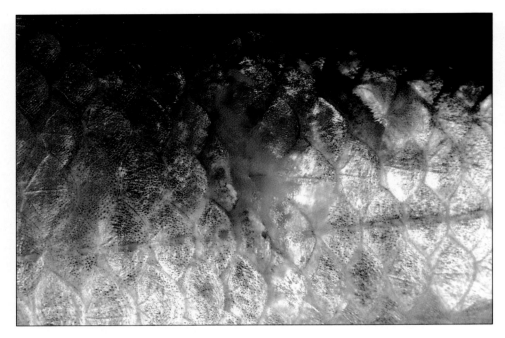

Above: *These are the characteristic growths of cotton-wool disease caused by the* Flexibacter *bacterium. At first sight, they can be confused with a fungal infection. In fact, the term 'mouth fungus' is often used.*

and then spread to the body and fins, often leading to ulcers and an overall thin appearance. The bacterium involved is *Fexibacter*, which has a characteristic appearance under the microscope, a colony consisting of relatively long, thin rods that move with a smooth flexing motion. *Flexibacter* is especially common in warm, organically rich water, and will spread rapidly from fish to fish in these conditions. Treatment with antibacterial drugs is usually effective.

Bacterial gill diseases

The gills are open to invasion by many different types of bacteria, the signs varying according to the kind and severity of the infection. In many cases, microscopic examination of the gills shows the tips of the filaments to be clubbed or, in severe cases, fused together. Alternatively, the filaments may become eroded, leaving only the central cartilage rod. It is important to note that bacteria are not always responsible for producing these signs, and many diseases of the gills remain undocumented.

Bacterial diseases of the gills are not easy to treat; if diagnosed in the early stages of infection, the koi may recover, but all too often, by the time the signs are noticed the damage is irreversible.

Dropsy

The signs of 'dropsy' are unmistakable; the eyes bulge out from the head (often referred to as exophthalmia, or 'pop-eye') and the scales are raised and stand out from the body rather like a pine cone. It is very important to note that dropsy is a sign of a number of possible health problems; it can be caused by kidney failure or congestive heart failure, for example, but may also be caused by bacterial invasion of the body. In fact, it is extremely difficult to differentiate between the possible causes of dropsy; ultimately, infection by bacteria may only be confirmed by the development of the signs in more than one koi. Bacterial dropsy is infectious and so it is best to isolate affected individuals. Treating the pond water with a suitable antibacterial may help to stop the disease spreading to other koi, while those koi that have developed the symptoms of bacterial dropsy are best treated in isolation with a broad-spectrum antibiotic or similar drug (see the table on pages 112-113).

Bacteria and antibiotics

Without doubt, the discovery of antibiotics is the most important medical and veterinary advance this century. Within the last 30 years, more and more drugs with antibiotic properties have been discovered (including synthetic antimicrobials) and this has led us to become very complacent about their use. Antibiotics are powerful drugs, and should only be used under strict veterinary supervision. Using antibiotics where they are unnecessary or as a prophylactic (i.e. to prevent a disease occurring) is misuse and leads to bacterial resistance.

Bacteria are rather unusual in that their genetic material is free inside the cell rather than contained in a nucleus. This enables bacteria to freely exchange genetic material with each other, including species that are totally unrelated or even dead individuals! By adding antibiotics to the pond water, resistance can be induced in the 'beneficial' bacteria that break down fish waste in the biological filter and then these bacteria can pass on resistance to pathogenic bacteria. This not only causes problems for koi-keepers, but also has wider implications, since some of these bacteria are pathogenic to humans and it is quite feasible for us to become infected with drug-resistant strains.

Another dilemma for koi-keepers is that few veterinarians are willing to prescribe drugs for fish, usually because many lack experience in this field. Many koi dealers, however, work in close conjunction with the few veterinarians that

Below: *Exophthalmia, or pop-eye, is one of the symptoms that may be associated with dropsy. The causes of dropsy may be many and varied, but the result is usually an excess of body fluid that causes swelling.*

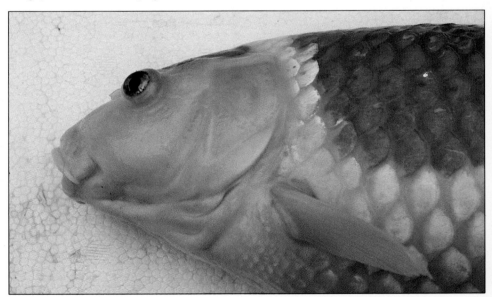

are experienced in fish disease and are willing to obtain the necessary information about antibiotic treatment of fish.

Environmentally related disorders

Like other fishkeepers, koi-keepers are under an obligation to ensure that the water quality in their ponds is as near perfect as possible. If the water quality is poor, the fish become stressed and are more likely to become diseased. As we have seen on pages 48-57, water quality embraces a number of different (and often interacting) physical, chemical and biochemical parameters. Here, we consider these briefly in terms of their impact on koi health.

Temperature In addition to the close correlation between temperature and oxygen content (see page 51), the main health problems involving temperature concern the activity of parasites, spawning, and the immune response.

In the spring and autumn, many parasites are actively reproducing and the koi may be too drowsy to cope with their large numbers. Usually, treating the pond water with a suitable remedy can solve this problem.

In temperate regions, the increasing hours of daylight from early spring onwards induces the maturation of eggs inside the female koi. Spawning is triggered by temperatures in excess of 20°C(68°F). If these temperatures are not realized, female koi can become highly stressed by their inability to spawn, and fall prey to disease. Temperature can also affect the development of eggs and baby koi. Sudden temperature fluctuations, for example, can cause various abnormalities, usually of the skeleton and particularly of the spinal column.

Temperature has a great influence on the immune system of koi. Below 12°C(54°F), koi do not produce antibodies (the special cells that seek out and destroy pathogens), but many bacteria and viruses are still active at this temperature. Similarly, koi subjected to a substantial increase in temperature of, say, 10°C(18°F), will take a week for their immune system to become more active. For bacteria, on the other hand, a temperature rise of half that amount is sufficient to stimulate their growth rate, bearing in mind that a single bacterium can produce a colony in excess of 25 million in 24 hours in ideal conditions. So, it is vitally important that any temperature changes are undertaken gradually. In normal circumstances, koi are protected from rapid temperature changes simply by the physical characteristics of the watery medium in which they live. On a

hot day, for example, while air temperatures soar rapidly, it takes many hours for the water to increase in temperature significantly.

pH value Slight daily fluctuations in pH value around the usual range of pH7-8 should not cause any health problems. As we have mentioned on page 50, in ponds with green water, the pH value may fluctuate between 7 and 11. Although these higher (more alkaline) peaks may cause some stress, the resident fish will be acclimated to these variations and should be able to cope. But do not introduce new fish to such conditions; they will surely succumb. Of course, it makes sense to check the pH value of your pond water on a regular basis to avoid any health problems related to this aspect of water quality. A continual reading above pH9, for example, demands swift investigation and a suitable response.

Oxygen content Insufficient oxygen in the water causes koi to stop feeding and become lethargic, with stressed fish often seen at the surface, respiring heavily. Such stress not only has direct physical effects but also makes the fish more susceptible to 'opportunistic' parasites and disease organisms. In a pond with low oxygen levels, the morning after a humid summer night may see the largest fish floating lifelessly on the surface. (The largest individuals always die first in these circumstances because their oxygen needs are greater than those of small fish.) To redress the oxygen balance in vulnerable ponds, it is vital to keep plant life down to a minimum and to add a second or larger pump to the system to boost the aeration of the water entering the pond.

Ironically, too much aeration can supersaturate the water with gases and possibly cause so-called 'gas-bubble

disease', with bubbles of gas appearing in the skin and fins. It is not necessarily dissolved oxygen that causes this problem; it is the total dissolved gases that create gas-bubble disease, and as 80 percent of air is nitrogen, the result of saturating water with air can produce behavioural signs equivalent to those of 'the bends' in human divers. Unless this supersaturation is remedied, koi can die from gas bubbles forming in the blood vessels and in delicate tissues such as the gills and eyes. Supersaturation with oxygen can arise in well-planted ponds (through excessive photosynthesis) or from the over use of venturis.

Ammonia and nitrite Even the most well-maintained ponds and filter systems may be subject to fluctuations in ammonia and nitrite levels. Some pond treatments, for example, can disrupt the action of biological filters by killing the nitrifying bacteria they support. The result is that ammonia excreted by the koi as a toxic waste product (mainly through the gills) is not broken down into nitrites and, in turn, these highly poisonous nitrites are not converted into less harmful nitrates. Raised levels of ammonia and nitrite can have devastating effects on koi health, including severe gill irritation and malfunction, reduced oxygen uptake by the blood, destruction of mucous membranes of the skin and intestine, external and internal bleeding, and damage to the nervous system and organs such as the liver, spleen and kidney. Following pond treatments, therefore, it is vital to monitor the levels of these two chemicals once a day for 7-10 days (see page 52 for test kits).

Chlorine As we have seen on page 52, excessive amounts of chlorine and chloramines in treated tap water can cause respiratory distress as the chlorine

Above: *During the warm summer months, large numbers of aquatic plants, together with insufficient aeration in the pond, can cause major tragedies, as the largest fish die from lack of oxygen. These koi are victims of just such an episode in their pond.*

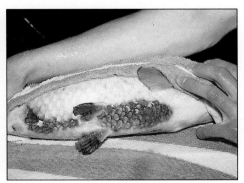

Above: *While common salt is a very useful medication and supportive treatment, it is vital to ensure that the required amount is completely dissolved before adding fish to strong dips. Otherwise, the belly and fins may be severely damaged, as here.*

HEALTH CARE

attacks the gill membranes. The level of chlorine needed to have lethal effects varies with a number of water quality parameters, including the dissolved oxygen content, the presence of pollutants, the pH value and temperature. In general, 0.2-0.3mg/litre of so-called 'residual chlorine' will kill most fish species fairly rapidly, while concentrations 100 times lower can cause chronic toxic effects. Fortunately, clearing chlorine from tap water is not difficult, by aeration for several days. It is worth asking your local water supply company if it adds chloramines to the water, however, since these take a little more effort to eradicate successfully.

Algae Microscopic algae are responsible for a phenomenon termed 'green water'. In most cases, green water is not harmful to koi, but the fluctuations in pH caused by the algae can stress fish that have not become gradually acclimated to such conditions (see page 111). Some koi may suffer respiratory distress caused by clogging of the gills by the algal cells, but this is very rare. Like other plants, algae deplete oxygen at night and this may cause a problem in the summer months, when dissolved oxygen levels are relatively low. At such times, it is worth checking the dissolved oxygen content of the pond water regularly.

Pollutants In most ponds, the only likely source of pollution is from treatment applied to nearby lawns and gardens. It is difficult to advise on the course of action to take if the pond becomes polluted. The most sensible first step is to make a water change and then contact the manufacturers of the product to ask for their advice on the best course of action.

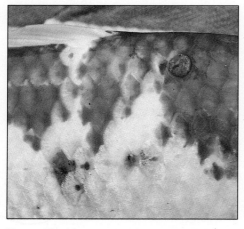

Above: *The damaged scales on this koi could have been caused by accidental injury and will be a prime site for fungal and bacterial attack. The small tumour could be caused by environmental pollution, but may not necessarily cause any lasting problem.*

Guidelines for using chemicals

Chemical	Concentration mg/litre (ppm)	Dosage range per 100 litres
Benzalkonium chloride	Bath: 1-4	0.2-0.8ml
Chloramine T	Bath: 2.2 Pool: 0.5	0.2gm 0.05gm
Ethyl-m-aminobenzoate (MS 222) Anaesthetic	Bath: 25-100	2.5-10gm
Formalin (A solution containing approx. 37% formaldehyde)	Bath: 24 Pool: 13.5	2.4ml 1.3ml
Formalin and malachite green mixture	Pool: Formalin 15 and malachite green 0.05	1.5ml of mixture
Levamisole	Bath: 10	1gm
Malachite green	Bath: 0.4 (*1) Pool: 0.2 (*1)	2ml 1ml
Methylene blue	Bath: 2(*2)	8ml
Nifurpirinol	Bath: 1-4 Pool: 0.25	0.1-0.4gm 0.025gm
Nitrofurazone	Bath: 1-3	0.1-0.3gm
Oxolinic acid	5gm per kg of treated food	Give treated food at rate of 1% of fish body weight per day
Oxytetracycline	Bath: 13-120 In food: 50mg per kg of fish	1.3-12gm
Para-chloro-phenoxyethanol	Bath: 20	1.8ml
Phenoxyethanol	Bath: 100 Food: Soak in 1% solution (10gm/litre)	9.1ml
Sodium chloride (Common salt)	Bath: 30,000 (3%)	3kg
	Bath/Pool: 10,000 (1%)	1kg
	Pool: 3,000 (0.3%)	300gm
Trichlorphon (Dimethyltrichloro-hydroxyethyl-phosphonate)	Bath: 22 Pool: 0.3	2.2gm 0.03gm

(*1) Parts per million (ppm) based on solid. Dosages based on 2% solution in water.
(*2) ppm based on solid. Dosages based on 2.5% solution in water. To convert dosages for 100 Imperial gallons and 100 US gallons, multiply figures in 'Dosage range' column by 4.55 and 3.79

Treatment time	Other details	Effective against
60 mins	Dosage based on liquid formulation containing 50% active ingredient	Cotton-wool disease, finrot, tailrot and other external bacterial diseases
60 mins Continuous until cured. Repeat after 3 days	Available as powder. Maximum of 3 consecutive treatments	Slime disease, white spot, skin flukes, myxobacterial gill disease, external bacterial diseases
1-3 mins, depending on pH, temperature, size and condition of fish	Requires care. Consult veterinarian or other skilled person. Ensure preparation is suitable for fish anaesthesia	Used as anaesthetic. MS 222 is a water-soluble form of benzocaine
30 mins Continuous until cured. Repeat after 7 days	Rarely used alone. Normally used with malachite green, see below. Aerate water	Combined with malachite green: fungus, slime disease, white spot, skin and gill flukes
Continuous until cured	Use 3.3gm of malachite green solid in one litre of formalin	Fungus, slime disease, white spot, and skin and gill flukes
12-24 hours		Intestinal worms
30 mins Continuous until cured. Repeat after 7 days	Use with formalin or sodium chloride	Fungus, slime disease, white spot, other parasites, such as skin flukes
Continuous until cured	Do not use with biological filters; it will disrupt their action	Traditional treatment for fungus, protozoan parasites. Commercial remedies better
60 mins Continuous until cured	If difficult to obtain, consider using para-chloro-phenoxyethanol	Cotton-wool disease, finrot, tailrot, plus other bacterial and fungal diseases
60 mins	If difficult to obtain, consider using para-chloro-phenoxyethanol	Cotton-wool disease, finrot, tailrot, plus other bacterial and fungal diseases
Use for 10 days	Available ready mixed with food; take advice from veterinarian	Dropsy, ulcer disease, plus other bacterial diseases
Continuous until cured. Use for 7 days	Antibiotic. Use lower concentration unless hard water reduces effect	Bacterial diseases
Continuous until cured	Take care to dissolve and disperse thoroughly	Fungus, finrot, tailrot, and other bacterial diseases
Continuous until cured. Use for 7 days	Supplied as oily liquid. Take care to dissolve and disperse thoroughly	Fungus, cotton-wool disease, finrot, tailrot. Use soaked food against nematode worms
Up to 10 mins	Remove fish immediately if it shows distress	Cloudy eye and parasites. (Increases mucus flow)
1-2 weeks	Use with malachite green or phenoxyethanol	Supportive for various diseases and wounds/ulcers
Continuous until cured		General protection, e.g. against nitrite toxicity
60 mins Continuous until cured. In hard water repeat after 7 days	Maximum 3 consecutive treatments. Take great care with bath treatments. Kills tench, orfe and rudd	Fish lice, anchor worms and other parasites, such as skin and gill flukes

respectively. Internationally accepted chemical names used where possible. Local regulations affect the availability of drugs. Seek veterinary advice.

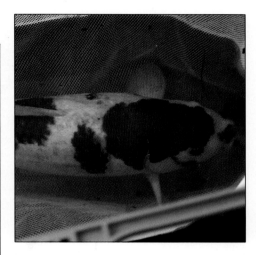

Above: *The reddening of the white areas on this koi are caused by stress. Netting a koi too frequently can cause stress, as can unsuitable changes in a wide range of environmental parameters, including temperature, pH value, oxygen content and levels of ammonia and nitrite. A stressed fish is more likely to succumb to disease.*

Stress

One word that appears repeatedly in this section on health care is 'stress', but what does this word really mean? For the majority of people, stress implies a psychological or emotional disturbance. Indeed, stress can be induced by an emotional disturbance but it is not just our minds that react to the situation; changes also occur in our body chemistry. Some of these changes help to prepare the body to cope with the situation, such as the release of hormones that break down fat reserves and mobilize them for energy production, while others effectively close down some of the body systems, such as the immune and digestive systems (hence feeling 'sick with worry'), to focus the body's resources. The result of these changes is that when the crisis has subsided, our bodies are weaker than before and our immune system is not able to fend off any opportunistic infection. Similarly, if we are physically stressed by heat, cold, over exertion, injury or tiredness the same physiological responses occur in our bodies.

While it is difficult to measure emotional stress in koi, it is certainly true that physical stress produces the same reactions as it does in us. Thus, in stressed koi the immune system is less effective, digestion is interrupted and important hormonal changes take place. In short, it is easy to see why stressed koi are more vulnerable to disease than are those kept in ideal conditions. Which brings us neatly to the constant realization that good health stems from preventing problems rather than simply curing them.

品評会

SHOWING KOI

Showing koi is a popular, if somewhat controversial, subject among koi-keepers. Although some may disapprove of the stress of transporting koi to shows and the sometimes unsatisfactory conditions under which they are kept throughout the period of the show, few would deny the virtue of koi shows in increasing the hobbyist's knowledge and appreciation of koi. Certainly, a well-run koi show is an exciting day out for all koi enthusiasts, whether they are competitors, or just spectators, and everyone enjoys the opportunity of seeing so many top-quality koi at such close hand.

Koi shows are organized on many levels, from huge extravaganzas, such as the All Japan Show (see page 119), held annually in Tokyo, at the top end of the scale, to small local events. Competitive spirit runs high in shows of all sizes, and show organizers, dealers and hobbyists spend a great deal of time in preparation. The beautiful koi you see at a show will be the result of much hard work on the part of their owners.

Large national shows, such as this Western-style one, are the climax of the koi-keeping year for many hobbyists.

SHOWING KOI

Koi shows and societies

Most hobbyists interested in showing their koi start at local shows organized by koi societies. In some countries, national koi societies have local sections where hobbyists meet periodically for talks, visits to members' ponds and to discuss various koi-keeping issues.

Koi societies usually hold shows, and these may be either closed or open. Only members may enter their koi in a closed show. At such events, benching, judging, and public viewing tend to take place on a single day. Open shows, on the other hand, are accessible to any member of the public who wishes to enter their koi in the competition. When run by local sections, these shows may be either one or two day events, depending on the projected attendance and the venue. Larger open shows are often organized by national societies. Professional shows, run by and for koi dealers, are open to the public for viewing.

Koi shows are usually advertised in koi magazines, national fishkeeping magazines and by dealers, and local koi societies generally have information on events taking place in their area.

Preparing for a show

An unhealthy koi is not going to look at its best no matter how good its pattern or body shape. In the same way that dogs have wet noses and a shiny coat when they are well, a koi that is in good condition will have a healthy looking shine on the skin, which enhances its pattern and general appearance. A koi whose skin lacks this healthy lustre will not be considered by judges. You should therefore do everything in your power to ensure the best possible conditions in the pond so that your koi will be in peak condition ready for showing.

As well as taking all the usual precautions and carrying out regular checks to ensure that ammonia and nitrite levels are acceptable, and that the level of debris in the pond is low, you can improve the mineral content of the water by adding a special supplement (ask your dealer for advice). This will help improve general health and vitality, as well as enhancing colours on the koi and aiding digestion. The fine, claylike powder gives the pond a muddy appearance for approximately 48 hours. During this time, the koi swim through it and it

passes through their bodies, binding up their waste and causing it to sink to the bottom of the pond along with any other suspended debris, leaving the water sparkling clear.

A healthy diet is also of paramount importance, particularly in the build-up to a show. Feed the koi a well-balanced diet, incorporating colour-enhancers with other foodstuffs to help improve the depth of colour and sharpness of pattern and to guard against shimis (black flecks) on the skin. It is a good idea to stop feeding koi a few days before the show so that they produce a minimum amount of waste while travelling to and from the show and while they are in the show vats. This will help to protect your koi by preventing poor water quality.

Below: *Benching in progress at a koi show. This is the first critical stage in the day's proceedings. Here, show officials are sorting the koi according to their size and variety. To keep track of each individual fish, all the koi that pass this initial stage are photographed. The main reason for rejection at this stage is on health grounds; any koi that show signs of disease or parasite infestation are withdrawn from the show.*

Shade is important, especially during the summer months, as koi can suffer from sunburn if their pond is exposed to direct sunlight. This normally exhibits itself as a reddening of the skin along the dorsal and will make the koi unshowable.

Disturb your koi as little as possible in the months preceding a show. The more the koi are disturbed, the more nervous they become and the more prone to parasites or infection caused by knocks and bumps. In the week preceding the show, examine the koi for any knocks or abrasions, split fins, fading colours or any sign of disease.

In Japan, koi are kept in 'mud' ponds in the months preceding a show. These natural ponds are full of green algae and minerals, providing a perfect food source for koi and promoting their growth and colour. Japanese dealers generally have their own mud ponds and keen hobbyists often pay to keep their koi outside in these mud ponds for the summer, when maximum growth can be achieved. The koi are taken from the mud pond a month or so before the show and any parasites and abrasions are dealt with so that the koi are in peak condition. This facility for growing on koi in mud ponds is currently rare outside Japan. Elsewhere in the world, hobbyists would be reluctant, on the whole, to part from their precious koi; many are more interested in their koi as pets than as potential show winners.

Benching koi

On the morning of the show you will need to catch and bag your koi ready to transport them to the show. Take great care not to damage the koi at this late stage or they will be unshowable. The way in which you transport the koi is important, not only to reduce stress, but also to avoid bumped noses and split fins.

On arrival at the show ground, show officials will 'bench' your koi, that is, they will sort them into the appropriate variety and size ready for judging. Normally, koi are exhibited in large blue vats, which have airlines running into them to supply oxygen. Show officials carry out regular water tests on each of the vats and attach small filters to the airlines in vats containing larger koi, which obviously create more waste.

In Japanese-style shows, koi of the same size and variety are exhibited in the same vat, irrespective of owner. This makes life simpler from the judges' point of view because it enables them to directly compare koi competing against one another. However, many hobbyists are concerned about the risk of infection or parasites if their koi are mixed with others. In some shows, therefore, all the

koi owned by one person are exhibited in the same vat. The risk of transmission of disease is thus reduced, provided that nets, bowls and hands are sterilized and equipment is not transferred between vats. Judging, however, is made more difficult as direct comparison between koi of the same variety is not possible.

Fourteen different variety classifications are currently recognized in most of the koi-keeping world. These are:

| Kohaku |
| Taisho Sanke |
| Showa Sanshoku |
| Bekko |
| Utsurimono |
| Asagi |
| Shusui |
| Koromo |
| Kawarimono |
| Hikarimono (Ogon) |
| Hikari-Utsurimono |
| Hikarimoyo-mono |
| Tancho |
| Kinginrin |

These classifications are explained on pages 122-201, where the various varieties included in each are illustrated, listed and described.

The koi are then separated into different sizes. The number of size groups will depend on the extent of the show.

Above: *An early stage in the first round of judging. Here, the judges vote on the merits of an individual koi 'bowled' into a plastic floating basket to allow closer inspection. The judges work as teams, each team being responsible for judging different size groups throughout the day. At this point, decisions are arrived at by open majority with a show of hands; from the second round, voting is carried out by secret ballot.*

Outside Japan, koi are generally divided into six size groups for judging purposes. These are:

| Size one – up to 15cm(6in) |
| Size two – 15-25cm(6-10in) |
| Size three – 25-35cm(10-14in) |
| Size four – 35-45cm(14-18in) |
| Size five – 45-55cm(18-22in) |
| Size six – over 55cm(22in) |

After its classification and size has been established, each koi is carefully scrutinized for any form of disease, such as fin-rot, anchor worm, fish lice, carp pox, white spot, bacterial infections or any evidence of damage or deformity. Any koi found to have such faults is automatically withdrawn from the contest.

Each koi is then photographed in colour and its variety, size and owner's name are recorded before it is moved to the appropriate variety and size show vat ready for judging.

SHOWING KOI

Judging koi

Koi shows have gradually changed their format over the years. Since 1987, shows in most parts of the koi-keeping world have followed the Japanese style (see page 119). The judges – there may be as many as 24 – group into teams and draw lots to decide which sizes each will judge. The teams then select first and second place koi in each of the 14 classifications and six sizes and these koi are moved into the best in size vats. From these koi the judges select a first, second and third in each of the six sizes, irrespective of variety. This second stage of judging determines the best 18 koi from which the three supreme champions are singled out. The supreme champion baby koi is chosen from sizes one and two, the supreme champion adult koi from sizes three and four, and the supreme champion mature koi from sizes five and six. The grand champion of the show is chosen from these three winners. All decisions from the second stage onwards are by secret ballot.

Awards are then presented for 'tategoi' – the koi that shows most potential for the future, whether or not it has already won a prize. The judges decide on first, second and third place tategoi in group discussion. Decisions on awards for the best home-bred koi, the best koi in the dealers' section and the best jumbo koi (awarded to the largest koi in the show) are also made on majority open ballot.

Right: *A typical scene from a national koi show, with a vat of koi awaiting the judges' attention once they have finished their deliberations around the vat in the background. Judging the koi is a serious business and nothing must be allowed to interfere with this day-long process.*

Below: *This diagram shows the logistic sequence of judging and prize giving at a typical national koi show (but not the All Japan Show). The circles represent vats, with the arrows reflecting physical movement of koi as well as status attained after judging. The cup and rosette are used merely as symbols to highlight some of the major prizes awarded at a show.*

The judging sequence at a typical koi show

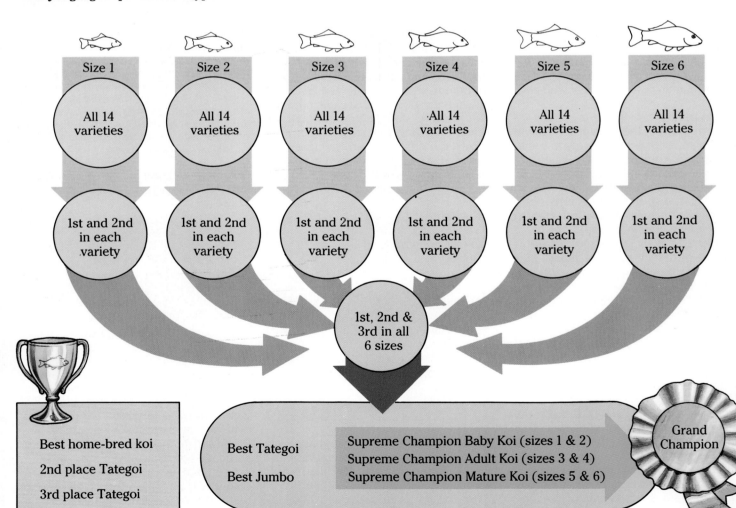

The All Japan Show

The All Japan show, which takes place each January in the capital city of Tokyo, Japan, is the climax of the koi-keeping year for dealers, breeders and hobbyists all over the world, and in many respects is, therefore, the 'blueprint' for the many koi shows, which are held throughout the world.

The show is organized by the All Japan Nishikigoi Dealers Association with the help of the Zen Nippon Airinkai (the koi-keeper society with a worldwide membership). The show is open to both professional and amateur koi-keepers (although all the koi must be entered by dealers). The show takes place over five days; the koi are benched on the first day, judged on the second, and on general view to the public for the rest of the period of the show.

Each dealer collects koi from his customers and keeps them in his own ponds to rest before beginning what is, for many, a long journey to Tokyo. On the morning of travel, the dealer measures each koi and takes four photographs of it, which he attaches to the paperwork required for benching and entry to the show. (See *Benching koi*, page 117).

On arrival at the show, which is held indoors in a very large hall about 5km(3 miles) south of Tokyo city centre, the dealers are met by the show officials and directed to the various benching areas. Over 1200 vats will be ready to receive the 5000 or so koi that are entered each year from all parts of Japan, with entries, too, from the USA, Taiwan, Korea, Thailand and the UK. Each vat has its own air supply line coming down from the roof and many of the vats containing larger koi have their own filter systems. (These are necessary since the koi will be swimming in the vats for up to five days.) There are also reservoir vats where koi can be deposited before being transferred to the main exhibition vats.

Officials check each koi with its paperwork and photographs and examine it for any damage that may have been caused during the journey to the show. Benching, that is, sorting the koi into the appropriate variety and size groups, is the responsibility of the dealers, but in the event of a dispute, officials will adjudicate.

The koi are currently divided into 16 variety groups for judging purposes. These include the 14 listed on page 117, along with a further two groups – Goshiki (see page 166) and Doitsu (see page 125) – which have been judged independently only since 1988. Although, at present, these two classifications are recognized only in Japan, it seems probable that eventually they will be adopted internationally.

Because of the huge numbers of koi entered in this and other Japanese shows, each variety is divided into 15 size groups. Male and female koi of sizes 10 to 15 inclusive are judged separately and so there are 21 groups in all. These are as follows:

Size 1 – under 15cm(6in)
Size 2 – 15-20cm(6-8in)
Size 3 – 20-25cm(8-10in)
Size 4 – 25-30cm(10-12in)
Size 5 – 30-35cm(12-14in)
Size 6 – 35-40cm(14-16in)
Size 7 – 40-45cm(16-18in)
Size 8 – 45-50cm(18-20in)
Size 9 – 50-55cm(20-22in)
Size 10 – 55-60cm(22-24in) males
Size 10 – 55-60cm(22-24in) females
Size 11 – 60-65cm(24-26in) males
Size 11 – 60-65cm(24-26in) females
Size 12 – 65-70cm(26-28in) males
Size 12 – 65-70cm(26-28in) females
Size 13 – 70-75cm(28-30in) males
Size 13 – 70-75cm(28-30in) females
Size 14 – 75-80cm(30-32in) males
Size 14 – 75-80cm(30-32in) females
Size 15 – over 80cm(32in) males
Size 15 – over 80cm(32in) females

The organization room is split into two sections; on one side are the 150 or so helpers, and on the other the judges, press, and important guests. There are around 100 judges, about 90 percent of whom are members of the All Japan Nishikigoi Dealers Association.

Before judging begins, the show chairman calls all the judges to a meeting, where they are divided up into small groups. They then draw lots to determine which three or four sections each group will judge. Each group of judges nominates a leader who will have the casting vote in the event of a tie.

The judges look at one, two, or three vats (depending on the size of the show) of a particular variety of a given size and ask the helper to lift any that warrant a better look into a fibreglass vat on a trolley nearby. They choose the best koi by a show of hands count and it is then moved to a separate vat. The second best koi is also chosen and the award pinned onto its photograph above the vat. If two koi of a particular variety and size impress the judges equally, they may decide to nominate one as a winner and award a special prize (between the first and second place awards) to the other koi they have chosen.

After each variety winner has been selected in a particular size, it is taken to join the other winners of that size in a separate vat. The judges then move on to the next size group they are judging, and the same process takes place. Finally, after all the size groups have been assessed, the judges select the winner of each size, independent of variety, known as the 'Kokugyo'. All judges then reunite to group these Kokugyo into classes to select the following size group champions. This is done by secret ballot and the count takes place under strict supervision.

Grand prize in the Yogyo section (Baby koi) sizes 1-3Bu*

Grand prize in the Wakagoi section (Young koi) sizes 4-6Bu*

Grand prize in the Sogyo section (Adult koi) sizes 7-9Bu*

Grand prize in the Seigyo section (Mature koi) sizes 10-12Bu*

Grand prize in the Kyogoi section (Jumbo koi) sizes 13-15Bu*

These winning koi are all transferred to one vat and the judges then select the Grand Champion of the All Japan Show. It is interesting to note that, although breeders, dealers and hobbyists all compete against one another, this highest award is almost invariably won by a private hobbyist. Of course, the breeder of the winning koi and the dealer will also be important figures on the day.

*Bu is the Japanese abbreviation for 'size'. This term is frequently used in shows throughout the world.

SHOWING KOI

Judging criteria

To lay down criteria for the perfect koi is no easy matter; beauty, as we all know, is in the eye of the beholder. Until recently, there have been hard and fast rules about what constitutes a 'good' koi, but over the past few years, this attitude has softened as new varieties have been introduced and many beautiful and unique koi have been produced.

What is important is the overall impression that a koi makes on the eye – how imposing is it? Its shape, balance of colour and pattern and the lustre of its skin are all qualities that the judge has to consider critically, concentrating as much, if not more, on a koi's positive attributes as on its negative aspects.

In this section, we look at the qualities a judge will be looking for in a show-winning koi of any variety. (In Part Two of the book, we examine in more detail the particular colours and patterns that are considered ideal in the many different varieties.) There are approximately four main aspects that a judge will be considering in examining your koi. These are: shape, colour, pattern and overall quality, lustre and shape.

Shape The koi's body shape is of primary importance; even a koi with good coloration and a perfect pattern will lose points if its shape is poor. The body should be symmetrical on either side and the backbone straight. Although koi are bred to be viewed from above, the shape of the body seen from the side is also important; the abdomen should be more rounded than the dorsal line.

The judge will also be looking at the way a koi moves in the water; it should swim straight through the water without twisting its body. A koi that swims awkwardly will be disqualified.

Volume and imposing appearance are important attributes to be assessed. A striking aspect may compensate for a lack of strong colour and pattern, and a large impressive koi will always be selected in preference to an equally outstanding smaller one. Apart from the fact that a large koi of high quality is very majestic, it is far more difficult to maintain good body shape and skin quality in a large mature koi than it is to produce a baby koi, or a relatively young one, with the same qualities. This is the reason why the Grand Champion of a show is nearly always a jumbo koi.

The koi's fins should be in proportion to the rest of its body and should enhance the overall movement and elegance of the koi. A female's pectoral fins are often slightly smaller and more rounded than the males'. Ideally, the dis-

Above: *Obviously, this particular koi is causing quite a stir among the judges. It is important that they take their time and arrive at a well-considered opinion, especially in the final stages of the show. The judges will be looking at the shape of each koi and assessing its colour, its pattern and its overall quality. They will give more credit to a larger koi with the same good points exhibited by an equivalent small fish, since it is much harder to retain good quality in more mature koi.*

tance between the dorsal fin and the tail should be one third of the distance between the first ray of the dorsal fin and the head region. A koi whose dorsal fin is too close to the tail – a common fault – will appear unbalanced.

The elegant beauty of the head is much easier to appreciate in a mature koi. The head should be in proportion to the rest of the body and should not be too rounded or pointed. There should be no pit marks or indentations on the head and, on jumbo koi especially (sizes 5 and 6), the cheeks should be solid and round. The round black or red marks often found just under the skin on young koi are not, in fact, colour pigmentation, but the internal organs showing through the skull of the koi. As the koi grows, its skull will skin over and these marks will eventually cease to be visible. Minute bubbles may also be apparent on the head of a small koi. These are a sign of good skin quality but tend to disappear when the koi is two years old.

Colour The clarity and depth of the koi's coloration is of obvious importance in judging. All colours should be of an even hue over the koi's body and unblemished by any other pigmentation, unless these markings form part of the pattern.

The white should be snow white, without flecks – known as 'shimis' – of red ('hi') or black ('sumi'). Unfortunately, the head, in particular, can appear yellowish in colour on some koi.

The hi (red) markings should be of a uniform shade, well defined and free of sumi (black) shimis. Bright hi of an orange-brown hue is preferred to purplish hi (see *Kohaku*, pages 128-135).

As a general guide, round sumi markings are favoured in preference to uneven, angular ones, but this depends on the particular koi concerned. Sumi should be ebony in colour, and shiny, like chinese lacquer.

Pattern No two koi are alike and, although each variety has its own pattern characteristics, unique patterns are now often preferred to standard traditional ones. All the markings must be well balanced, however, and the pattern should normally be consistent over the body of the koi to give a pleasing aesthetic effect. For example, hi markings on a Kohaku should normally be balanced along the length and breadth of the koi. The edges of a marking ('kiwa'), such as the border between hi and white markings on a Kohaku, for example, should be crisp and well defined.

Overall quality

The quality of the skin is an important factor in the koi's overall appearance. The skin should have lustre, that is a shiny finish, so that the koi looks as though it has been lacquered with a clear varnish and may appear to be slightly metallic. Such skin quality is quite common in young koi, but jumbo koi that retain this lustre are much admired. Judging quality in koi is a skill that is mastered only after years of experience. Essentially, the quality of a koi can be defined as the sum of its shape, pattern, colour and overall elegance.

Right: *This five-year-old Taisho Sanke has a near perfect body shape, balanced beautifully by superbly shaped fins. The skin quality is excellent, being snow white with no yellowing, flaws or discoloration. The hi is intense and even in colour and creates an interesting pattern, with a breaking design over the shoulder and dorsal area complemented by smaller hi markings near the tail. The sumi is very strong and clean edged, with two small, but attractive, markings on the shoulder. A fine example.*

PART TWO

KOI VARIETIES

All koi belong to one species, Cyprinus carpio, of which about one hundred colour varieties have been developed. However, these are not genetically fixed, which means that spawning one variety produces offspring of other varieties. Those currently in existence are the result of much cross-breeding (i.e. breeding together closely related types) to produce stable varieties, and new ones are appearing all the time.

On pages 124-5, we show how the many (and, at the outset, confusing) variety names are made up of Japanese words that describe the colour, pattern, lustre or scalation of a particular koi. Learning to recognize the different varieties is made simpler when you understand the various classifications into which they are grouped. Some of these, such as Kohaku, feature only one variety, while others embrace several varieties; Hikarimono, for example, includes all single-coloured, metallic koi. On pages 126-7, we explain and review the classifications, with illustrations of some of the more popular varieties or those most typical of their group. Appreciating the different patterns and becoming familiar with the Japanese names will come with practice. Meanwhile, most dealers will be happy to help you by telling you the correct names of any koi that take your eye.

The broad sweep of Part Two (pages 128-201), looks in detail at over one hundred different koi varieties, including all the classic 'favourites' as well as many of the more unusual ones. The wealth and range of patterns involved are shown in the form of symbol-like illustrations of a large number of the varieties. Of course, every koi is unique and, although certain criteria will have to be satisfied on a prize-winning koi, a diversity of different patterns are acceptable in most varieties. Therefore, these illustrations are representative as well as stylized. The photographs show real koi and here the captions point out any shortcomings as well as celebrating their finer qualities.

The variety of colour and pattern on these graceful koi justifies their universal popularity.

KOI VARIETIES

The ever-increasing number of koi varieties and their seemingly arbitrary classifications are apt to confuse the new koi-keeper, and the abundance of Japanese names, too, can be bewildering. Unfortunately for the new koi-keeper, no 'Westernized' names and groupings have been devised and so we have adhered to the traditionally accepted Japanese variety names and classifications.

Over the next few pages, we will try to unravel some of the mystery that surrounds these variety names. Most, in fact, are made up of Japanese words that describe a single aspect of a koi. If you understand the meaning of some of these words, you will find it easier to learn the different variety names.

We have chosen to look at these terms under the four headings of colour, pattern, scalation and lustre. As we saw in the section on *Showing koi* (pages 114-21), these are all aspects that a judge will be looking at during the evaluation of a koi in a show. There is a more comprehensive glossary of Japanese and other 'koi' words on page 202.

Colour

There are several Japanese words associated with colour that are used to describe koi. For example, red markings are usually called 'hi' markings, but there are also other words for red, such as 'aka' and 'beni', which are generally used to describe an overall red colour. The same is true of black; sumi is the word for black markings, while 'karasu' (literally, 'crow') is the name given to a totally black koi. The list of colour-associated words below will help you to begin to understand how koi names are built up.

Ai	blue
Aka	red (as a base colour over the body)
Beni	orange-red (usually as a base colour over the body)
Cha	brown
Gin	silver (metallic)
Hi	red (markings on the body of the koi)
Karasu	black (as a base colour. Literally, 'crow')
Ki	yellow
Kin	gold (metallic)
Midori	green
Nezu/nezumi	grey (literally, 'mouse')
Orenji	orange
Shiro	white
Sumi	black (markings on the body of the koi)
Yamabuki	yellow (literally, a Japonica bush with pale yellow flowers)

Above: **Sumi-goromo**
The dark edges to the red scales are clearly visible on the body of this koromo koi. On Sumi-goromo the 'robed' pattern is combined with solid sumi markings.

Pattern

Many variety names incorporate a Japanese word that describes the pattern. An understanding of some of the more common ones will help you to appreciate the patterns and learn the variety names of your koi.

Budo Literally, 'grape'. In fact, this word refers as much to the colour as to the pattern of the koi, being used to describe the purple, grapelike cluster pattern on Budo Goromo and Budo Sanke, both from the Koromo classification (see pages 158-9).

Kage Literally, 'shadow' or 'phantom'. The word kage refers to the blurred, reticulated sumi, or black, pattern that appears on certain Utsuri and Showa. These koi are classed as Kawarimono rather than Utsurimono and Showa.

Kanoko Literally, 'fawn'. This word is used to describe the dappled 'hi', or red, markings found on certain Kohaku, Sanke and Showa. These Kanoko koi are judged in Kawarimono (see pages 166-9).

Koromo Literally, 'robed'. Koi in the Koromo classification have a hi pattern that is outlined (or 'robed') in a darker colour (see pages 156-9).

Inazuma Literally, 'lightning strike'. Used particularly with reference to the hi pattern on some Kohaku, where 'inazuma' describes a zig-zag marking stretching from head to tail.

Matsuba This word describes a black pattern in the centre of the scales, commonly described as a 'pine-cone' pattern. Non-metallic Matsuba koi are classed in Kawarimono, metallic ones in Hikarimono (see pages 163 and 178-9).

Tancho Literally, 'red spot on the head'. Tancho koi have only one hi marking, which is on the head. These Tancho Kohaku, Sanke and Showa are judged in a separate Tancho class in shows.

Utsuri Literally, 'reflections'. Actually, the name of a group of koi (the full classification name is Utsurimono), utsuri describes the pattern on these koi, where the sumi markings are often mirrored by the second colour (white, red or yellow, depending on the variety) on the opposite side of the dorsal.

Above: **Tancho Sanke**
Tancho koi, with their striking red head marking, are understandably popular with koi-keepers all over the world.

Above: **Gin Matsuba**
The matsuba pattern in the scales, which creates a latticelike effect, shows up particularly well against the metallic white skin of this impressive variety.

Scalation

Most koi are fully scaled over the body. Such normally scaled koi are called '*wagoi*', but this term is rarely used. Other Japanese words used to describe the scalation of koi include:

Doitsu Koi that are only partially scaled are known as doitsu koi (see page 12 for their history). If a koi has doitsu scalation, the word doitsu is used as a prefix to its variety; for example, Doitsu Hariwake, Doitsu Purachina. There are a few exceptions to this when a doitsu koi becomes a separate variety; for example, a doitsu Asagi is a Shusui. Although variations are not generally differentiated in shows, there are, in fact, three separate types of doitsu scalation:

Leather koi have no scales along the lateral line and only very small scales along the dorsal line. This is the normal type of doitsu scalation.

Mirror doitsu koi have large scales along both the lateral and dorsal lines.

Yoroi or Ishigaki doitsu koi are partially scaled koi that have scales other than along the lateral and dorsal lines, in jumbled patterns. ('Yoroi' means 'armour', and 'ishigaki' means stone wall scales.) These koi are not considered to be of high enough quality to be worth entering in competitive shows.

Kinginrin This term, often abbreviated to ginrin, refers not to the extent of scalation but to a certain type; kinginrin scales are highly reflective, sparkling when they catch the light. Although any koi may have some kinginrin scales, only a koi with about 20 or more would be classed as Kinginrin. Until 1988, all Kinginrin koi were judged independently from normally scaled koi of the same variety. Now only Kinginrin Kohaku, Sanke and Showa are judged in a separate Kinginrin class (see pages 198-201).

Fucarin A term adopted only in the late 1980s, fucarin describes the area of skin between the scales rather than the scales themselves. Fucarin is usually associated with good metallic koi. It is generally considered that the smaller the scales, the better the lustre on the koi. The diagrams below show the difference between fucarin and normal scalation.

Normal scalation

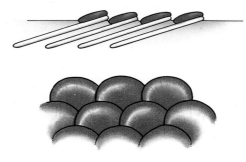

Fucarin scalation

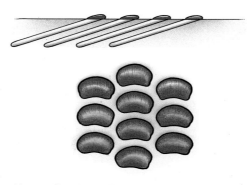

Above: *Good metallic koi have smaller scales that allow the skin to show between them (bottom). Such scalation is known as fucarin and the effect is to improve the quality of lustre, or shine, on the koi.*

Above: **Kinginrin Showa**
The sparkling deposit on nearly all the body scales of this beautiful koi differ from the all-over metallic lustre of, for example, the Gin Matsuba shown in the opposite photo.

Lustre

Lustre is a word sometimes used to describe the shine that should be present on the skin of a healthy koi. However, it can also be used to differentiate between metallic and non-metallic koi. The two principal words that are used to describe the lustre on a koi are:

Hikari Used as a prefix to a classification name, hikari indicates that all the koi in that group are metallic. Hence, Hikarimono denotes single-coloured metallic koi, for example. Of the fourteen classifications, the three containing truly metallic koi are all prefixed 'Hikari': Hikarimono, Hikari-Utsurimono and Hikarimoyo-mono. (Kinginrin koi have a number of sparkling scales rather than being truly metallic, see above).

Kawari This word, normally used as a prefix, means non-metallic. It is used primarily in Kawarimono, which is probably the largest group of koi. This classification contains all non-metallic koi not included in any other group.

KOI VARIETIES

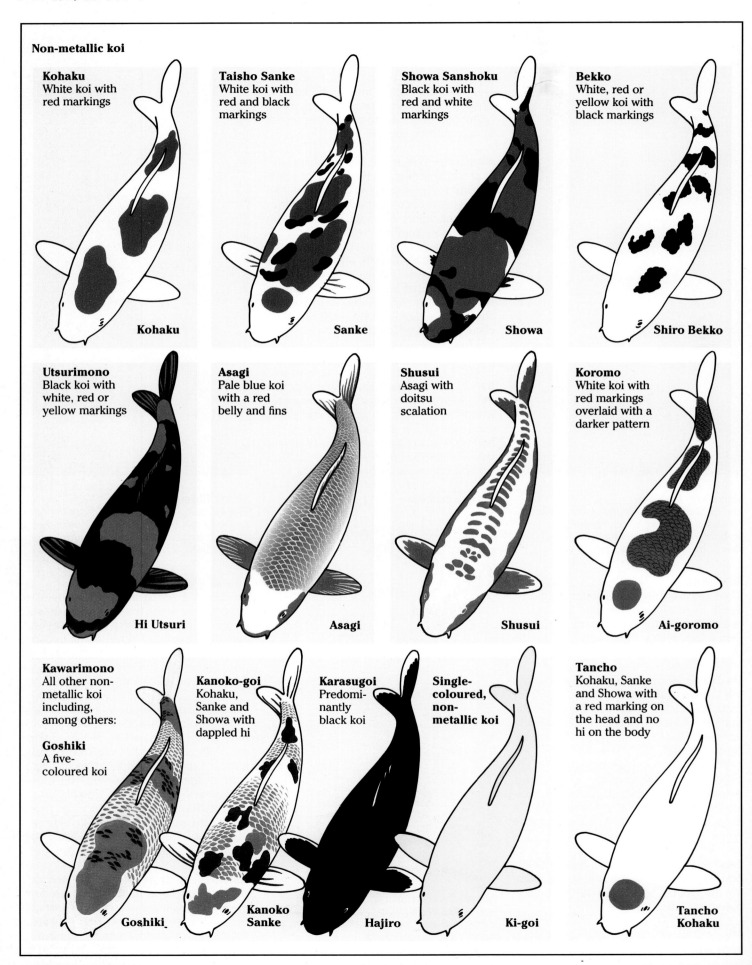

Non-metallic koi

Kohaku
White koi with red markings

Kohaku

Taisho Sanke
White koi with red and black markings

Sanke

Showa Sanshoku
Black koi with red and white markings

Showa

Bekko
White, red or yellow koi with black markings

Shiro Bekko

Utsurimono
Black koi with white, red or yellow markings

Hi Utsuri

Asagi
Pale blue koi with a red belly and fins

Asagi

Shusui
Asagi with doitsu scalation

Shusui

Koromo
White koi with red markings overlaid with a darker pattern

Ai-goromo

Kawarimono
All other non-metallic koi including, among others:

Goshiki
A five-coloured koi

Goshiki

Kanoko-goi
Kohaku, Sanke and Showa with dappled hi

Kanoko Sanke

Karasugoi
Predominantly black koi

Hajiro

Single-coloured, non-metallic koi

Ki-goi

Tancho
Kohaku, Sanke and Showa with a red marking on the head and no hi on the body

Tancho Kohaku

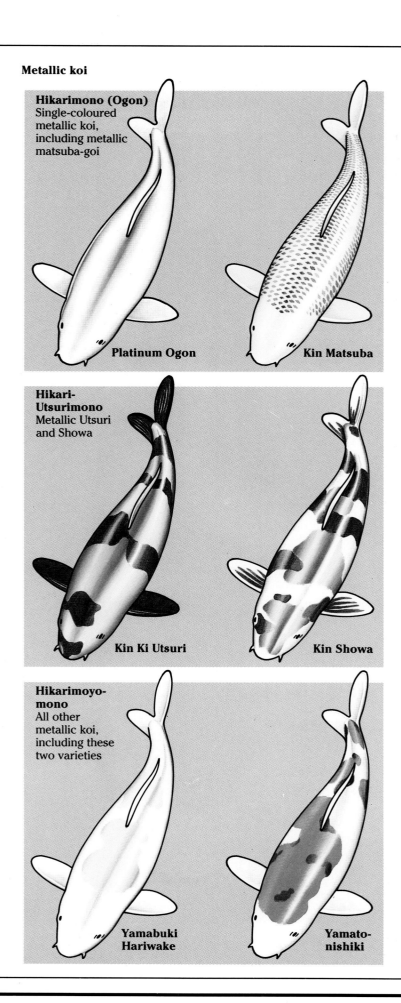

Metallic koi

Hikarimono (Ogon)
Single-coloured metallic koi, including metallic matsuba-goi

Platinum Ogon

Kin Matsuba

Hikari-Utsurimono
Metallic Utsuri and Showa

Kin Ki Utsuri

Kin Showa

Hikarimoyo-mono
All other metallic koi, including these two varieties

Yamabuki Hariwake

Yamato-nishiki

As you might imagine, many koi are produced that do not fit easily in the confines of a specific variety. The Japanese, in particular, are adept at accepting new and interesting koi (and thinking up new names) and their classifications for showing purposes reflect this. So, although your koi may not have a specific variety name, you should be able to place it, however tenuously, in one of the classifications that we review briefly here and consider in more detail in the following pages. These are:

1 Kohaku
2 Taisho Sanke
3 Showa Sanshoku
4 Bekko
5 Utsurimono
6 Asagi
7 Shusui
8 Koromo
9 Kawarimono
10 Hikarimono (Ogon)
11 Hikari-Utsurimono
12 Hikarimoyo-mono
13 Tancho
14 Kinginrin

The Japanese system of classification is designed to accommodate not only the specific variety groups (1-8 and 10 above), but also the following, more flexible, classifications:

Kawarimono This group includes all non-metallic koi that do not appear in a more specific variety.

Hikari-Utsurimono. These are metallic Utsuri and Showa.

Hikarimoyo-mono All metallic koi that do not fall in any other classification are included in this group.

The remaining two classifications, Tancho and Kinginrin, both include Kohaku, Sanke and Showa with, respectively, specific markings or type of scales. (Kinginrin koi are not illustrated here because their markings are the same as those of Kohaku, Sanke and Showa; they differ only in their scalation.)

Two other classifications have been recognized in Japanese shows since 1988:

Goshiki This five-coloured koi is still judged in the Kawarimono classification elsewhere in the world.

Doitsu koi Doitsu koi of any variety (except Shusui, which is a variety in its own right) are now judged in a separate classification in Japan.

KOHAKU

One of the most quoted phrases in koi-keeping is that the hobbyist begins with the Kohaku and ends with the Kohaku. In fact, many new hobbyists overlook the Kohaku in preference for the brightly coloured Ogon (see pages 174-9) and other metallic koi because they feel that Kohaku 'look too much like goldfish'! However, as they begin to appreciate the colours and patterns of koi, hobbyists often turn to Kohaku because of their simplicity and elegance.

Not only do Kohaku share the red and white colours of both the Japanese flag and the symbol of that country, the Tancho crane (a white bird with a red head), but it is much more difficult to find a prize Kohaku than a show winner of any other variety. In Japan, to own a good Kohaku is the ambition of every koi-keeper.

The history of Kohaku

Red and white koi first appeared in Japan between 1804 and 1829, when the off-spring of a black carp was found to have red cheeks. She was called Hookazuki and her white offspring were bred with a Higoi, a red fish, to produce koi with red stomachs. By 1829, a koi with red gill plates called Hoo Aka had been produced, and between 1830 and 1849 several different patterns appeared, including Zukinkaburi (red forehead), Menkaburi (red head), Kuchibeni (red lips) and Sarasa (red spots on the back).

The breeding of Kohaku continued and varieties were improved, especially in the Niigata region, now considered the birthplace of koi-keeping. In about 1888, a gentleman called Gosuke bought a Hachi Hi, a red-headed female, and bred it with his Sukura Kana, a cherry blossom patterned male. It is believed that the modern Kohaku was developed from the offspring of these koi.

Between 1949 and 1952, Gosuke's koi were inherited by Tomoin and at least two distinct lineages resulted from these fish. Two of Tomoin's koi were sold to Buketa, who developed Kohaku with a very fine skin of transparent white, occasionally prone to yellowing, and with a purplish hi (red marking). This lineage has a particularly good body shape.

The second line evolved in about 1944, when a Tomoin female was bred with a Monjiro male, and between 1950 and 1960 the Yagozen line was created. These Kohaku also have good shapes but the hi is of a vermillion hue, which tends to splatter. However, markings are usually well defined and the white opaque.

These are the two principal lines that have been developed; there are others, but most hobbyists would find individual lineages difficult to identify.

Above: Kohaku
This impressive female Kohaku displays a voluminous, well-shaped body. Excellent colour and definition add precision to the well-balanced pattern, which extends from the head to the tail of this particular koi.

Maruten Kohaku

Left: **Maruten Kohaku**
*This a well-shaped male. Note the hi
marking on the head, known as the maruten
spot, which is distinct from the pattern on
the rest of the body. Definition between the
colours is good on the whole, although the
pattern is slightly smudged on the shoulder.*

KOHAKU

Kohaku colours

Kohaku are white koi with red, or hi (pronounced 'he') markings. Ideally, the hi should have a good depth of colour but, more importantly, the colour should be of a uniform shade and the edges of the hi pattern should be well defined. This definition between hi and white markings is known as 'kiwa'. There appear to be two types of hi coloration. The purplish red hi is dark but does not fade easily. This colour is considered to lack elegance and tends to splatter over the koi. Brownish red hi can produce a very fine, almost translucent, colour but tends to fade easily. The Japanese tend to prefer this colour hi, which they consider more elegant than the purplish hi.

The white should be the colour of pure snow and free from blemishes. A poor white, which can be dirty yellow in appearance, will spoil an otherwise good Kohaku because the hi pattern does not stand out well against it. Small black specks can sometimes appear on Kohaku. These are known as 'shimis' and are detrimental to the koi's appearance. They may be caused by poor nutrition or water quality and will often disappear if the koi is kept under better conditions.

The unity and balance of colour and pattern on a Kohaku are of utmost importance. As a general guideline, the hi should cover between 50 and 70 percent of the koi and the white between 30 and 50 percent. If there is more than 50 percent of white on a Kohaku, the koi may be bland in appearance. It is the hi, complemented and emphasized by the white, that creates the impression on the eye.

Kohaku patterns

Because Kohaku appear such simple koi in terms of coloration, the criteria by which they are judged are severe. The pattern on a Kohaku is the last factor to be considered when the koi is being judged but is probably the most discussed. Balance over the whole of the koi's body is the key to any pattern.

Head

On any Kohaku the hi pattern begins on the head. Kohaku without hi on the head are considered worthless in terms of competition. The traditional head pattern for the hi is a large U shape, which should reach down as far as the eyes. Hi that extends over the eyes is considered a defect, however. If the hi does not reach the eyes, the pattern may be compensated for, or balanced by, 'kuchibeni' or lipstick-like markings. In Japan this throwback to the original carp is frowned upon, but elsewhere it is considered charming and is greatly admired by hob-

Below: **Kohaku head patterns**
A variety of hi patterns are acceptable on the head of a Kohaku. The traditional pattern is the U shape. The menkaburi pattern, which extends over the head and face of the koi, is generally unpopular.

Kuchibeni

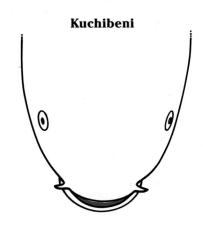

Hanatsuki

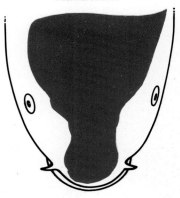

Traditional U shape

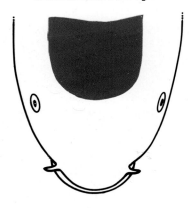

Menkaburi

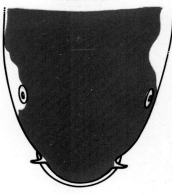

byists. A hi marking that reaches the mouth is known as 'hanatsuki', and a pattern that spreads over the face is called 'menkaburi'. Both these patterns are generally unpopular as they are considered to lack refinement or elegance.

Recently, however, koi-keepers have begun to appreciate Kohaku with interesting or irregular-shaped markings on the head; for example, Tancho Kohaku with a diamond-shaped mark (see page 194). Such markings can add character to the fish and their aesthetic appeal may override any preconceived ideas as to what constitutes 'good' markings. A koi whose hi reaches the nose may, therefore, be redeemed by other markings, such as a blush on the cheek.

There are two varieties of Kohaku that are named in connection with their head markings. These are:

Tancho Kohaku This is a white koi with a red spot on the head. In a show, Tancho Kohaku would be judged in the Tancho classification (see pages 194-7), rather than with other Kohaku.

Maruten Kohaku This koi has a separate red spot on the head along with other hi markings on the body.

Body

Large hi markings, known as 'omoyo', are preferred to small hi markings (komoyo) on Kohaku as they create a stronger impression against the white. This is especially true of markings behind the head since this is the part of the Kohaku pattern that most attracts the eye. A break in the hi pattern is preferred between the back of the head and the shoulder. Variation is also important, however; an interestingly patterned koi is more highly prized than a Kohaku with a straight hi pattern. A continuous pattern without variation from head to tail is known as 'ippon hi' (see page 132) and is a valueless pattern in terms of showing.

Koi grow from the abdomen, so when selecting young Kohaku, look for patterns with large hi markings as they will stretch and may even break up. The small hi markings on a young Kohaku will also stretch but will rarely cover the body

Inazuma Kohaku

Right: Inazuma Kohaku
This cigar-shaped male koi shows good, even coloration and excellent definition of pattern. Unfortunately, the hi pattern is rather heavy and the final hi marking extends into the tail. The slightly yellow coloration on the head is also a flaw.

KOHAKU

sufficiently to make a good impression.

Smaller hi markings, resembling splatters of paint, are known as 'tobihi' (which literally means hi that has 'jumped away') and are considered detrimental to appearance. If such markings appear on the lower half of a large koi they do not represent a serious defect as they are not too conspicuous. If, however, they appear on the shoulder they break up the homogeneity of the pattern and are considered a more serious flaw.

Another thing to look for when choosing Kohaku is secondary hi, known as 'nibani', which suggests the koi is of a poor quality. This hi will appear and disappear depending on such factors as the amount of colour enhancer that is incorporated in the koi's diet.

Balance of pattern over the body of the koi is most important. A Kohaku that has most of its hi pattern at the front of its body, for example, lacks balance and elegance and is of no value for showing. Patterns should begin at the head and end at the tail. On larger koi, the hi pattern should, ideally, wrap around the body below the lateral line to add elegance. This type of pattern is called 'makibara'. On smaller koi, the hi should extend only to the lateral line.

Kohaku patterns can be divided roughly into two categories:

1 Continuous patterns that extend from the head to the tail are known as 'moyo'.

Inazuma Kohaku This is a continuous pattern, extending from the head to the tail, but with variation. Inazuma literally means 'lightning strike'.

2 Stepped patterns are known as 'dangara' or 'danmoyo' and are much more highly valued by the Japanese than continuous patterns because they are more obviously balanced. Dangara patterns are described by the number of markings down the body of the koi.

Nidan Kohaku Nidan means two and a Nidan Kohaku has two hi markings.

Sandan Kohaku This is a Kohaku with three hi markings.

Yondan Kohaku This is a Kohaku with four hi body markings.

The hi pattern on either the continuous or dangara-patterned Kohaku should be balanced not only down the length of the koi, but also on either side of the dorsal fin. A pattern on only one side of a koi's body is called 'kata moyo'.

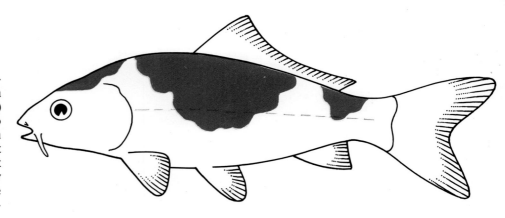

Above: *A hi pattern that wraps around the body below the lateral line on the koi is especially important on a large Kohaku. This pattern is called 'makibara'.*

Below: *On this Kohaku, the hi pattern does not extend below the lateral line. Judges generally prefer this pattern to the makibara pattern on smaller koi.*

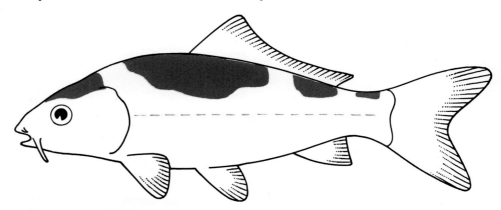

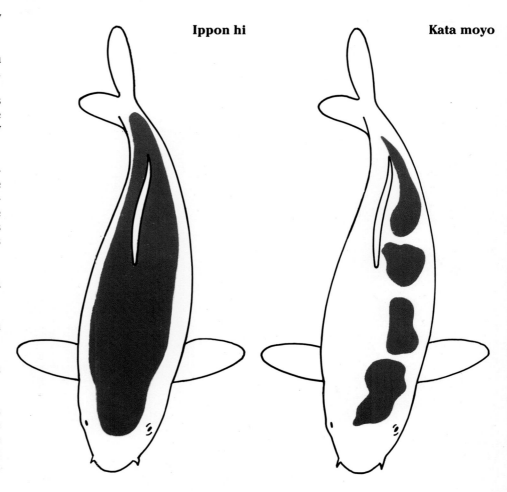

Ippon hi

Kata moyo

Nidan Kohaku

Left: **Nidan Kohaku**
This male Kohaku has a good balanced shape, although it lacks volume. The pattern and colour are excellent; note in particular the break in the hi near the front of the dorsal fin. A weakness is the head hi pattern, which moves into the eye.

Other varieties of Kohaku include:

Goten-zakura Kohaku This koi has a pattern more commonly known as a cherry-blossom pattern. The hi is dappled and looks like clusters of grapes.

Kanoko Kohaku
    See *Kawarimono* (pages 166 and 168).

Tail
The end of the pattern is as important as its beginning and continuation along the body. On a perfectly marked Kohaku, the hi pattern ends just before the tail joint. A hi marking that spreads into the joint of the tail gives the pattern a heavy and unfinished appearance and is considered a defect. Likewise, if there is no hi marking near the joint of the tail, there will be an area without pattern, known as 'bongiri', which will also be considered a flaw if the koi is entered in a show.

Fins
Snow white fins are the perfect accompaniment to the red on white pattern of a

KOHAKU

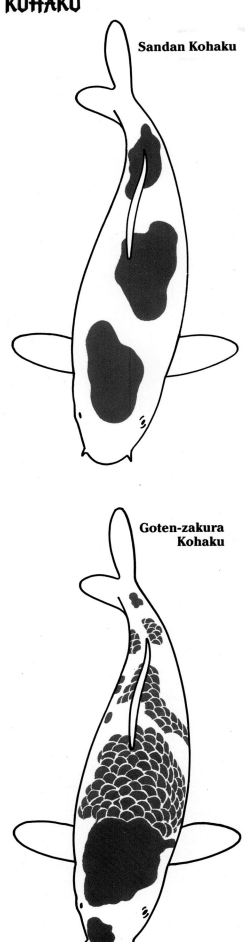

Sandan Kohaku

Goten-zakura Kohaku

Yondan Kohaku

Left: **Sandan Kohaku**
The white fins show off the deep even hi of this koi. The head pattern is the traditional U shape but, unfortunately, the hi marking moves slightly into one eye.

Right: **Yondan Kohaku**
This is a young koi, probably male, with a long, thin, but symmetrical, body shape. The hi pattern on the body is good, but the head marking is messy and unfinished.

large Kohaku. As a general rule, hi extending into the fins is considered detrimental to the koi's markings. Hi in the pelvic fins is not a problem because it cannot be seen when a koi is judged, while hi in the pectoral and caudal fins devalues the koi. If the hi wraps round the body of the koi, hi in the joints of the pectoral fins may be permissible. Kohaku occasionally have black in the fins and this is obviously unacceptable.

Scalation

Scalation should be even all over the body of the koi. The Japanese prefer hi that is strong enough to disguise the individual scales. Scales that are visible because the hi is thin are known as 'kokesuki'. Scales with 'shadows' under the skin are known as 'madoaki'. A Kohaku of any pattern with scales only along the dorsal and lateral lines is known as a Doitsu Kohaku (see *Scalation*, page 125).

TAISHO SANKE

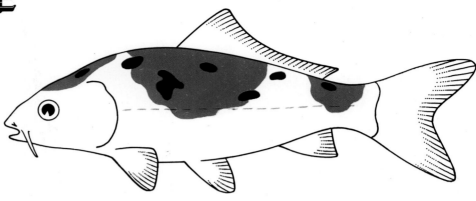

Sanke are extremely popular with hobbyists in all countries and, along with Kohaku and Showa, are among the major prize winners in competitions. Their wide variety of patterns can give them a more individual appearance than Kohaku at first glance.

The word Sanke literally means tri-colour, the three colours being red, white and black. In Japanese characters the word Sanke is also read as Sanshoku, the term used in early works on koi.

The history of Sanke

The word Taisho refers to the period in Japanese history when the Sanke was first recorded, that is, between 1912 and 1926. Sanke were among the first koi ever exhibited. A male Sanke, owned by a man called Gonzo Hiroi from Shoiya, was shown at the Tokyo Exhibition in 1914, where the Emperor's son saw koi for the first time. The names of the first breeders of Sanke were not recorded, but, as this koi was approximately 15 years of age at that time, the first Sanke were probably produced at the end of the nineteenth century (or between 1868 and 1912 – the Meiji era of Japanese history).

Among the first Sanke recorded were those from Ojiya City, in Niigata, where Heitaro Sato found them among Kohaku fry in 1915. These were bought by Eizab-ura Hoshino from Takezawa who then crossed one with a male Shiro Bekko (see pages 144-5), so forming one of the first distinct Taisho Sanke lines.

Over the past 60 years the markings of the Sanke have changed quite dramatically. The first Sanke were very striped in appearance but today's show-winning Sanke is a beautifully balanced koi whose sumi, although deeper in shade, is more delicate in appearance than that of its ancestors. Many distinct lineages have been developed. Among the better known is the Sadazo Sanke bred by Sadazo Kawakami, which has bright hi markings with small sumi markings that do not overlap the hi. This koi differs greatly from a Sanke from the Jimbei lineage, where both the hi and the sumi are dark in colour, but whose large, shiny sumi markings resemble those of Showa.

Sanke colours

The Sanke is a three-coloured koi with hi (red) and sumi (black) markings on a white base. As with the Kohaku, the depth of these colours is very important. The white should be the colour of snow – a yellowish white does not give a good background for the pattern to stand out against, gives the koi a dull appearance, and generally lacks the visual impact of a pure, opaque white.

The hi should be of the same quality as on a good Kohaku, that is, it should be of a deep hue and of uniform shade. The proportion of red to white should, again, be the same as on a good Kohaku. The base of any good Sanke pattern is a good Kohaku pattern; Sanke are basically Kohaku with Bekko markings.

The sumi (black) of a Sanke, like all other koi colours, should be fine, uniform in shade, and with a good depth of colour. It should be shiny in appearance, like Japanese lacquer. As sumi should overlay the Kohaku-style pattern, the markings need to be clearly defined in order to stand out. They should also appear in a balanced pattern.

Sumi can appear and disappear over the lifetime of a koi, and sumi of a poor quality may be affected by water quality, temperature and change of environment. A koi with poor sumi will obviously never make a good show koi because the pattern may fade when it is bowled, giving it the appearance of only a second-rate Kohaku. Sumi that is apparent in fry and remains in the adult koi is known as 'moto', or original sumi, and that which appears later is called 'ato', or late sumi. It is as well to bear in mind, when buying young Sanke, the fact that a Sanke's sumi can change in quality throughout its life. Good sumi in baby koi, for example, can deteriorate as the fish grows; it is rare for a Sanke with good sumi markings as a baby to keep in that condition above size 4 (see *Showing koi*, page 117). A Sanke that has underlying sumi markings – known as 'sashi' – as a baby, on the other hand, becomes more stable with age.

Sumi markings on Sanke are also described by their position on the pattern of the koi, so sumi that appears on the white skin is known as 'tsubo' sumi, while sumi that appears on the hi is known as 'kasane' sumi. Tsubo sumi is believed to be more stable than kasane sumi, but appreciation depends on the quality and position of the sumi as a whole. (Note the solid, deep kasane sumi on the Aka Sanke on page 139.)

Above: *The basis of a good Sanke pattern is a Kohaku pattern. Hi may extend below the lateral line but sumi rarely does so.*

Right: **Taisho Sanke**
A stunning aspect of this impressive Sanke is its skin quality; the translucent appearance of its skin enhances the clear coloration and interesting pattern. Note the break in the hi behind the head.

Sanke patterns

Although Sanke differ from Kohaku in that they have three colours, the criteria by which the two varieties are judged are very similar. As we have mentioned, the balance of colour and pattern is of the greatest importance on koi. Very simply, if the sumi were removed from a well-marked Sanke it would be a good Kohaku, whereas if the hi were removed, it would make a good Shiro Bekko.

Head

There should be no sumi on the head of a Sanke. The head pattern required is the same as on a Kohaku; that is, a large U-shaped hi marking, which should not extend down over the eyes, the face, or as far as the mouth. Unusually shaped head markings are not so easily tolerated as on Kohaku, possibly because there is an extra colour on the fish and a 'busy' pattern lacks elegance and visual impact. This does not mean that a blush on the cheek or 'kuchibeni' lips are necessarily detrimental to a Sanke, however; it all depends on the particular fish.

Body

Large hi markings are preferred down the length of the Sanke's body, complemented by sumi markings, which should also extend the length of the body. Sumi markings should start on the shoulder, along with a hi marking, giving a balanced pattern down the body.

Sumi markings should be small in number – an excessive amount of smaller sumi markings gives the koi an untidy appearance – and should not extend below the lateral line of the koi.

TAISHO SANKE

Hi markings should be similar in pattern to those of Kohaku and balanced on either side of the koi. These may be stepped or there may be one large hi marking down the body of the koi. If the hi markings are concentrated at the front of the body, the koi will lack balance.

Aka Sanke This is a Sanke whose hi marking extends the length of the body.

Maruten Sanke This is a Sanke with a separate hi marking on the head.

Fuji Sanke Not a variety as such, this is the name given to a Sanke with a highly metallic lustre on the head, visible as minute bubbles. Such markings tend to disappear when the koi grows.

Tail
Sanke tend to suffer with too much sumi towards the tail, and this can be detrimental to the fish's appearance. As with Kohaku, the pattern over the body of the koi – of both sumi and, even more importantly, hi – should end cleanly just before the tail joint.

Maruten Sanke

Above: **Maruten Sanke**
This is a young adult koi, probably male. The head spot is symmetrical and well placed and the hi pattern on the body is traditional, though rather heavy. The sumi is not yet fully developed.

Aka Sanke

Above: Aka Sanke
The hi extends from the nose to the tail on this young koi and the small, deep sumi markings are well balanced along the body. Note the charming, clownish head marking, which ends with a dot on the nose.

Right: *Traditional sumi stripes in the pectoral fins of the Sanke complement the sumi pattern on the body. Alternatively, the fins may be white (see page 137).*

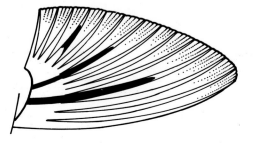

Fins

Striped sumi is preferred in all the fins, but especially in the caudal and pectoral fins of the koi. Sumi in the fins is a sign of stability in the sumi over the body of the koi. Too large a number of sumi stripes can lead to a loss of gracefulness in appearance, however. Solid sumi in the joint of the pectoral fins, and hi in any of the fins, is also considered detrimental. Sanke may have no colour in their fins. This is not frowned upon; again, it depends on the overall balance of pattern on the koi. Such Sanke have normally derived from Kohaku lineage.

The following Sanke appear in other classifications:

Koromo Sanke
  See *Koromo* (page 159).
Kanoko Sanke
  See *Kawarimono* (pages 166 and 169).
Sanke Shusui
  See *Kawarimono* (page 169).
Yamato-nishiki
  See *Hikarimoyo-mono* (pages 184-5).
Tancho Sanke
  See *Tancho* (page 194).

SHOWA SANSHOKU

Here we look at Showa, the last of the big three. Like Sanke and Kohaku, this variety is very popular. Showa have much more sumi in their pattern than Sanke and are very imposing.

The history of Showa
This is a relatively new variety, first produced by Jukichi Hoshino in 1927, when he crossed a Ki Utsuri (a black koi with yellow markings, see pages 146 and 149) with a Kohaku. On the original Showa the hi was yellowish brown in colour, but this has been improved by crossing with Kohaku until the Showa we know today was produced, in about 1964.

Showa colours
Although Showa, like Sanke, are three-coloured koi, they differ from Sanke in that they are predominantly black koi with red and white markings, while Sanke are white koi with black and red markings. As with both Sanke and Kohaku, the depth and uniformity of colour are very important, and the white should be the colour of snow. A traditional Showa should generally have about 20 percent of white over its body, but this is not always the case (see Kindai Showa). The large sumi markings should be ebony in colour and the hi blood red. All colours should be clean and well defined.

Showa patterns
Not only do Showa have more sumi than Sanke, but on a Sanke the sumi markings are roundish and appear above the lateral line, while on a Showa they are larger, encompassing the body of the koi. The most obvious difference between the two varieties, however, is the sumi head marking on a Showa, which a Sanke lacks. Sumi should also appear in the joints of the pectoral fins of a Showa.

Head
The hi on the head of a Showa should be similar in pattern to that on a Kohaku except that it may extend much further down the head, over the nose, cheeks and jaws on the former.

The sumi head marking of Showa is one of the most important features of the pattern of this variety. The two most common head patterns occur where either the sumi divides the hi on the head in two (this is the traditional pattern and is known as 'menware'), or the sumi draws a V shape behind the head, with another sumi marking on the nose. This V-shaped marking is a modern pattern, which is very impressive because it so beautifully defines the head.

Body
A bright, well-defined pattern over the body of the Showa is very important. The sumi often appears as a lightning strike - 'inazuma' – over the body of the koi (see Kohaku, page 131), or may be highly patterned and distinct, producing a 'flowery' effect. Sumi markings tend to be large and can often produce asymmetrical patterns very similar to those found in Utsuri (see pages 146-9). The white and hi of a Showa emphasize the delicate or elegant pattern of the sumi by producing a distinct contrast. The hi pattern on the body of the Showa should be similar to that on a Kohaku; that is, balanced down the entire length of the koi on both sides of its body, being complemented by the white. Balance in colour is again the key factor in the pattern of a Showa.

Hi Showa This is a predominantly red Showa, that is, with a straight hi marking from nose to tail. The hi tends to be more orange in colour than on other Showa varieties (see page 142).

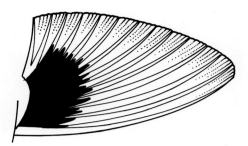

Above: Traditionally, Showa have sumi in the base of their pectoral fins. Markings should be even in both fins and of a symmetrical shape in the base.

Kindai Showa This modern Showa has a predominantly white pattern, with significantly more white on its body, therefore, than the 20 to 30 percent found on most traditional Showa.

Boke Showa The sumi on this Showa is blurred and indistinct, more grey than black in appearance. This variety is becoming very popular.

Tail
Although the requirements for tail patterning in Showa are not as clearly defined as for Kohaku and Sanke, the pattern, nevertheless, should be balanced and should not extend into the tail. A white tail gives a clean finish.

Fins
The markings in the pectoral fins on Showa are very important to balance and offset the pattern of the koi. Sumi should be found in the base of the pectoral fin and should be the same on both sides.

Other varieties of Showa appear in other classifications:

Koromo Showa
   See *Koromo* (page 159).
Kage Showa
   See *Kawarimono* (page 164).
Kanoko Showa
   See *Kawarimono* (pages 166 and 167).
Kin Showa
   See *Hikari-Utsurimono* (page 180).
Tancho Showa
   See *Tancho* (pages 194 and 197).

Right: **Showa**
The solid sumi in the base of the pectoral fins sets off the markings on the body of this beautiful koi. The sumi pattern on the head is heavy and deep in colour but balances with the hi, which is even and extends along the length of the koi. The body shape is symmetrical and elegant.

Below: **Menware head marking**
This traditional Showa head pattern is called 'menware'. Here the sumi divides the hi marking on the head, often with an 'inazuma', or 'lightning strike', pattern.

Below: **V-shaped head marking**
On this modern Showa pattern the head is defined by a sumi marking on the back of the head. This may be balanced with a sumi marking on the nose or jaw.

SHOWA SANSHOKU

Right: Hi Showa
The superb body shape and colour of this koi are balanced by large pectoral fins with solid, even sumi in the base. The sumi markings are deep and evenly spaced along the length of the body and are complemented by the hi. The colour and pattern on the head are particularly good and the skin quality is excellent.

Hi Showa

Kindai Showa

Boke Showa

Above: Kindai Showa
This interesting young koi has a large proportion of white on its body. The sumi overlaps the hi marking and is well spaced down the body. Unlike most Showa, this koi has clear, white pectoral fins.

BEKKO

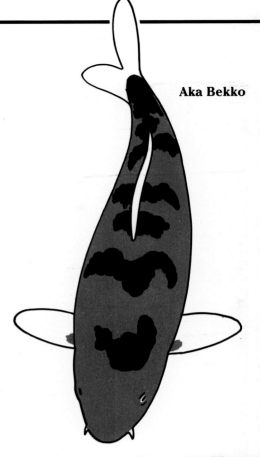

Aka Bekko

Bekko are mat (that is, non-metallic) white, red or yellow koi that have a distinctive set of sumi markings over their body. They are often mistaken for Utsuri, which are similar but are predominantly black koi with white, red or yellow markings. Their simple coloration and pattern ensure that the criteria by which they are judged are severe.

Bekko are a derivative of the Taisho Sanke family. In simple terms, a Shiro Bekko, for example, is a Sanke with no hi pattern on its body. These koi are not produced in great numbers and good Bekko under size 4 are very hard to find.

Bekko colours

The Bekko's sumi markings should be jet black and solid in appearance.

Shiro Bekko This is a white koi with sumi markings. The white should be pure and the colour of snow. A yellowish head is detrimental as it lacks elegance and gives the fish a dirty appearance. The colour should be even over the body of the koi. Doitsu Shiro Bekko can also be very attractive, particularly when the markings are clearly defined. Large doitsu scales, however, can complicate the elegant simplicity of the pattern.

Aka Bekko This is a red koi with sumi markings. (Aka is another word for red). Often the red is of an orange hue; Aka Bekko with a deep red coloration are rarely seen, especially as the colour seems to fade as the koi grows in size.

Ki Bekko This koi has a yellow base colour with sumi markings. The yellow should be of the same hue over the whole body of the koi. Like Aka Bekko, this is a very rare variety.

Bekko patterns

The pattern on Bekko is very simple and elegant, with small sumi markings spread evenly over the body.

Head

The head of a Bekko should be free of any sumi markings and the same shade of colour as the rest of the koi. It is difficult to find a Bekko that is 'bald' of any pattern on the head; any blemishes are obvious through the skin on the scalp. However, a small sumi marking on the head, for example, may be acceptable if it complements the pattern on the body. A black tancho marking is sometimes considered attractive on a Bekko, although a koi with this type of marking would not be classed as a traditional Tancho because Tancho markings have to be red (see *Tancho*, pages 194-7).

Body

A large sumi marking on each shoulder of the Bekko is desirable, as are small clusters of sumi balanced along the length of the koi's body (as on the Aka Bekko, below). Small, isolated spots of sumi, resembling freckles, are not favoured, however, although they often appear, to the detriment of Ki Bekko, in particular.

Tail

The pattern of sumi markings should finish just before the tail in the way that the pattern on a Sanke ends.

Fins

A Bekko's fins may be either white or have sumi stripes in them, similar to those of the Sanke.

Below: **Aka Bekko**
The colour of the hi is even over the body of this young koi. The deep sumi markings are relatively evenly spaced. The pectoral fins are unusual in that instead of striped sumi there is hi in the joints of the fins.

Shiro Bekko

Ki Bekko

Above: Shiro Bekko
The sumi pattern over the body of this Shiro Bekko is good and there are very few sumi stripes in the fins. The white, however, is rather too soft and slightly pink – probably a sign that the koi is stressed.

UTSURIMONO

Koi in the Utsurimono group are often confused with those in the Bekko classification (see pages 144-5) because of their similar coloration. The main difference between the two is that Utsuri are black koi with white, red or yellow markings, whereas Bekko are white, red or yellow koi with black markings. A further distinction can be made in the head markings of these two groups - unlike Bekko, Utsuri have a sumi marking on the head that reaches down to the nose.

In Japanese, 'utsuri' means reflections. This refers to the sumi pattern on the koi, which is often mirrored by the second colour on the opposite side of the dorsal.

The history of Utsurimono
The history of this variety is unclear. It is believed that Shiro Utsuri are of Magoi lineage and were first produced in around 1925 by a gentleman called Kazuo Minemura. However, it is known that Ki Utsuri appeared quite early in the history of koi, possibly at the beginning of the Meiji era (in about 1875), and were originally known as Kuro-Ki-Han, which literally translated means black with yellow markings. They were renamed Ki Utsuri in 1920 by Eizaburo Hoshino.

Utsurimono colours
Utsuri have striking, heavy sumi, which should be jet black in colour and of uniform shade. The second, and contrasting, colour of any Utsuri should emphasize the sumi pattern.

Shiro Utsuri This is a black koi with white markings. The white should be pure and unblemished by a yellow tinge or small black specks or 'shimis'. The cleaner the white, the more the black pattern stands out on the koi.

Hi Utsuri This is a black koi with red markings. The hi should be uniform in shade, which is difficult to achieve in this variety. Often the hi on the head is much darker than that on the body, and this divides the pattern on the fish and detracts from the sumi pattern. It is hard to produce a good Hi Utsuri because these koi are not as stable in coloration as many of the other varieties. Black specks in the hi, which detract from the basic symmetry and simple elegance of the koi, often mar this beautiful variety.

Ki Utsuri This is a black koi with yellow markings. Ki Utsuri are rarely found but can be quite exquisite and delicate. Unfortunately, they often suffer from the same problem as Hi Utsuri, that is, black specks in the markings.

Utsurimono patterns
The Utsuri pattern owes much to the Showa Sanshoku with regards the sumi, which is the most striking aspect of this koi. In the same way that the sumi pattern on a Bekko resembles that of a Sanke, the Utsuri pattern can be described as that of Showa without the extra colour.

Head
The sumi pattern required on the head of an Utsuri is the same as that on a Showa; that is, a lightning strike sumi that divides the face, or a V shape. Whereas in Showa the modern V shape is more popular, on the Utsuri the sumi marking that divides the face is favoured.

Body
The sumi pattern required on the body is, again, similar to that of the Showa. Large, imposing sumi markings in a reflective pattern (black reflecting white) are preferred to a smaller chequered pattern. If the pattern is highly reflective, it is often described as 'flowery'.

The sumi on an Utsuri should wrap around the body below the lateral line, (while on a Bekko the sumi pattern remains above the lateral line). The sumi markings should extend from the nose to the tail and be balanced down the length of the body and on both sides of the dorsal line of the Utsuri.

Shiro Utsuri

Fins
The fins should have sumi in the pectoral joints. The striped fins of Bekko are not favoured on Utsuri, however.

Below: *The traditional pectoral fin pattern of Utsuri resembles that of Showa, but on the former stripes shoot out from the solid sumi in the base of each fin.*

Left: *The Utsuri is a black koi with red, white or yellow markings. The sumi wraps itself around the body, extending the pattern below the lateral line.*

Right: **Shiro Utsuri**
This modern Utsuri has a larger proportion of white on its body than is usual on Utsuri. The solid sumi pattern is even down the body and less 'flowery' than many patterns. Unfortunately, the head is slightly pointed and the body rather thin.

UTSURIMONO

Above: Kinginrin Hi Utsuri
The bright colours and distinct pattern of this Hi Utsuri are complemented by kinginrin scales (see page 125), which lighten the colours of the body. The solid sumi of the fins beautifully highlights the koi's predominantly orange body. The pattern is of a modern type, that is, with less sumi than the traditional Utsuri.

Hi Utsuri

Ki Utsuri

Above: Ki Utsuri
This is a very rare koi, so slight inconsistencies in the eveness of the ki *(yellow) pattern are forgivable. Note the hi spots on the left side of the body and the irregularity of colour in the fins.*

ASAGI

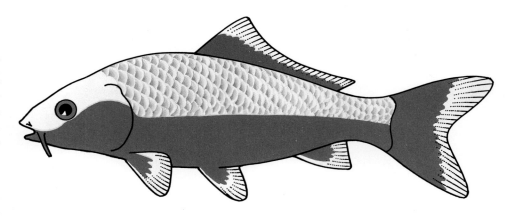

Asagi are plain koi compared with other varieties; they are non-metallic and lack the bright coloration of many koi, being grey-blue in colour with hi along the sides, cheeks and in the fins. However, a first-class Asagi is a quiet, elegant fish, with a delicate pattern of scalation and fine colour.

It is as well to remember that koi are usually viewed in a group and their value to the hobbyist depends as much on the impression they make juxtaposed with other koi in the pond as on their individual appeal. A pond full of bright metallic koi, for example, would be less striking than one of different varieties, including 'lowlights', such as Asagi.

The history of Asagi
Asagi are one of the original types of nishikigoi and their history has been documented for 160 years. These koi were developed from one of the three types of Magoi – the black carp, which is the ancestor of all modern nishikigoi varieties. One of these fish, the Asagi Magoi, has a blue back with a light blue or white pattern definition around the scales, and hi on the cheeks, sides and pectoral fins. Two types of Asagi have developed from the Asagi Magoi. The first is the Konjo Asagi, which is dark blue and very similar to the Magoi. This is a valueless form in terms of showing. The second variety, and the one from which modern Asagi are developed, is the Narumi Asagi. This koi is lighter in colour, and its scales have a dark blue centre, paling towards their edges. Its name comes from a similarly patterned tie-dyed fabric made in Narumi, Japan.

Asagi colours
The blue coloration of the Asagi varies in shade but a lighter blue is preferred. The pattern of the scalation is distinct; darker blue in the centre, lighter blue at the edges. The hi on the head, sides and pectoral fins should be strong in colour, but often tends to be orange. In colder waters, Asagi tend to become very dark, even black, in colour. This is undesirable and makes the koi worthless with regard to showing. Black specks often appear over the head and body of the koi and these are also detrimental to the appearance of this variety.

Asagi patterns
The head should be light blue-grey in colour with no inference of black or speckling. There should be hi marking along the cheeks, reaching the eyes, and the markings should be symmetrical on both sides of the face.

The markings on the body of the Asagi

Above: *The hi marking on an Asagi normally extends from the belly up to the lateral line. There should also be hi on the jaw and in the base of all the fins.*

Below: *A good Asagi will have a deep orange (hi) marking in the base of its light grey-blue pectorals, similar in pattern to the sumi on a Showa's fins.*

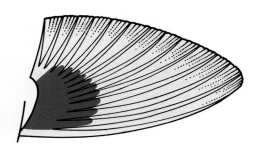

should also be symmetrical, hi should extend beneath the lateral line, and the belly should be white. The pattern on the back of the Asagi should be even over its entire length and the scales should be outlined clearly. The contrast between the centre of the scale and its edge should also be clearly defined.

Hi should extend into the base of the fins, particularly the pectorals.

Scalation
Regularity of scalation is of paramount importance. The scales should evenly cover the whole body from head to tail and the light edges of the scales should be of equal length on all scales.

Above: *The deep blue centre of each scale should be juxtaposed with a light blue edge. The eveness of the scalation over the body of an Asagi is of paramount importance.*

Narumi Asagi This is the typical light-blue patterned Asagi.

Konjo Asagi This very dark Asagi is almost black in colour.

Mizu Asagi This is a very light Asagi.

Asagi Sanke This Asagi has a pale blue back, red head and sides.

Taki Sanke The blue body of this Asagi is divided from its red sides by a white line.

Hi Asagi The hi marking of this Asagi extends over the lateral line – sometimes up to the dorsal.

Narumi Asagi

Above: Asagi
This large koi is an impressive example of an Asagi. Note the evenness of the hi markings along the jaw line and on either side of the head, which is a perfect blue-grey in colour, with no hint of black. The fins, too, are even in coloration. However, it is the uniform scalation over the body of this koi that is its most striking feature.

SHUSUI

Their unusual coloration and doitsu scalation have made Shusui firm favourites with koi-keepers, particularly those new to the hobby. They are basically doitsu Asagi and, like Asagi, have a tendency to go very dark in colder waters. As dark Shusui are worthless in terms of competition, it is not advisable to keep too many of this variety. Unlike the majority of other varieties, good Shusui are more common at size 1 than at size 4 and above, because of their tendency to darken with age. The coloration of bright young Shusui can, however, be quite startlingly beautiful.

Shusui were first produced in 1910 when Yoshigoro Akiyama crossed an Asagi Sanke with a doitsu mirror carp. Until 1986, both Asagi and Shusui were judged in the same classification but, because the lack of scale pattern on Shusui changes its appearance so dramatically, they are now regarded as separate classifications.

Shusui colours
The colour of the Shusui is basically the same as that of the Asagi. The head is blue-grey with hi on the jaws and the scales along the lateral and dorsal lines of the koi are darker blue than the rest of the koi. Because the scale pattern of Asagi is lacking, the skin on the back of the Shusui is an unusual pale sky blue, more delicate in shade than on Asagi.

Shusui patterns
The pattern on the pale blue-grey head of Shusui is the same as that on the Asagi, namely a hi marking on the jaw. The head should be free from any other markings.

Below: *The striking blue and red colours of Shusui contrast beautifully with other koi. This group includes two Shusui with Kohaku, Utsuri, Yamato-nishiki and Sanke.*

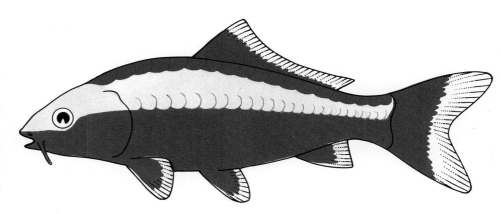

Above: *As on Asagi, the hi on Shusui should extend from the belly up to the lateral line. The evenness of the doitsu scalation is particularly important on this variety.*

The blue of the Shusui's body should be of an even shade over the length of the koi, extending from just below the lateral line up to the dorsal line on either side of the body. There should be two parallel stripes of hi reaching from behind the gills to the tail on either side of the dorsal.

Hi should extend into the base of the fins, particularly the pectorals.

Scalation
Scalation is an important aspect of the pattern of Shusui, as it is on Asagi. The scales along the dorsal line (and lateral line, if present here) should be neatly aligned. Rogue scales on the body will devalue this koi in terms of competition.

Hana Shusui This koi, also known as a flowery Shusui, has hi markings between the abdomen and the lateral line and between the lateral and dorsal lines.

Hi Shusui The hi on this Shusui spreads up from the belly and covers the back.

Ki Shusui This very rare Shusui is yellow with a greenish dorsal.

Pearl Shusui This is a Shusui with silver scales. It is very rarely seen.

Other varieties of Shusui appear in other classifications:

Sanke Shusui
See Kawarimono (page 169).
Showa Shusui
See Kawarimono (page 169).
Goshiki Shusui
See Kawarimono (page 169).
Kinsui/Ginsui
See Hikarimoyo-mono (page 190).

Right: **Shusui**
This is not a perfect example of a Shusui, although the blue coloration is good. Note the irregular scalation along the dorsal, the thin, rather poor, body shape, and the uneven hi markings in the fins.

Shusui

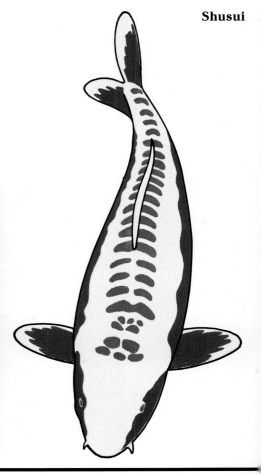

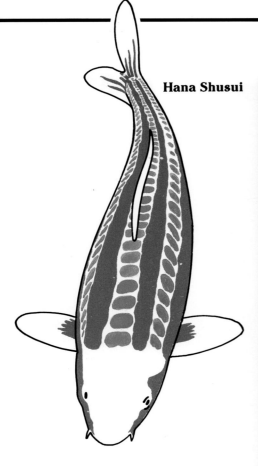

Hana Shusui

Left: **Hana Shusui**
The coloration is particularly striking on this voluminous koi; note the way the hi covers the blue to give a deeper colour. The head and fins are particularly impressive.

Hi Shusui

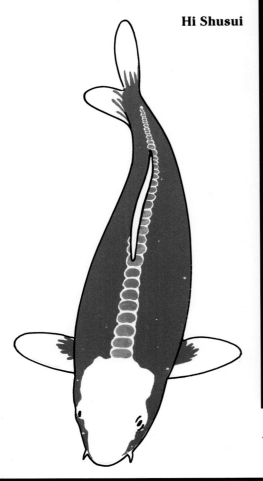

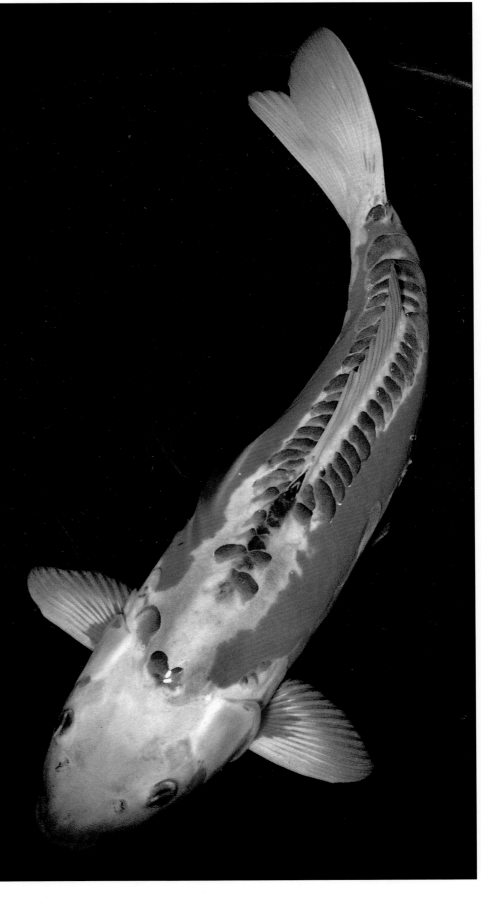

Above: **Hi Shusui**
The hi on this Shusui is strong and even but, unfortunately, the blue is nearer to grey in colour and suggests that the koi may eventually turn black. The scalation along the dorsal line is rather uneven.

KOROMO

Koi found in the Koromo group are much admired by collectors. Koromo literally means 'robed'. This describes the hi pattern, outlined in a darker colour, which varies with the particular variety. Although they tend to be insignificant as young koi, large specimens are very impressive, with an elegance to match that of Kohaku. A Koromo very rarely appears 'finished' as a young koi. If the patterns are complete when the fish is still small in size, the sumi is likely to overdevelop and become unbalanced as the koi grows. The chances of achieving a good Koromo are small compared with most other koi varieties.

Koromo koi are bred from Kohaku crossed with Narumi Asagi (see page 150). All the koi in this group have been in existence only since about 1950.

Koromo colours
The most important aspect of the Koromo is the basic Kohaku pattern with a very deep hi. This depth of colour is

Right: **Ai-goromo**
One of the most impressive features of this male Ai-goromo is the even scalation. Note the lack of sumi (or any darker markings) on the head and the interesting shape of the hi marking – a traditional Kohaku pattern.

Ai-goromo

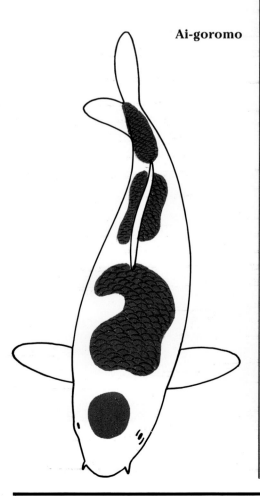

even more important than in Kohaku because a pale orange will appear 'washed out' with the overlay of Koromo.

The white should be the colour of snow and the same quality all over the koi. The white is very important in Koromo as it should offset the lace or 'robed' pattern on the hi. The colour of the lace pattern depends on the variety.

Ai-goromo This is the most common of the Koromo group. The literal translation of Ai-goromo is 'blue robed' ('Ai' means blue) and the Ai-goromo is basically a Kohaku whose hi scales have blue semicircular borders, giving the koi a reticulated pattern.

Below: *The blue-edged hi scales, shown here in close-up, are responsible for the elegant pattern of Ai-goromo. The reticulated scales should appear regularly on the hi markings over the body.*

Sumi Goromo

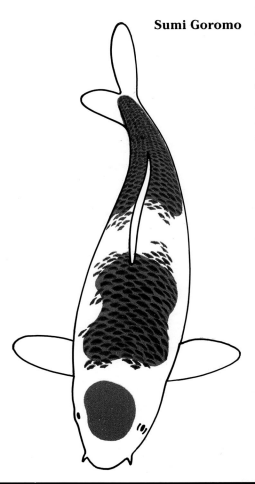

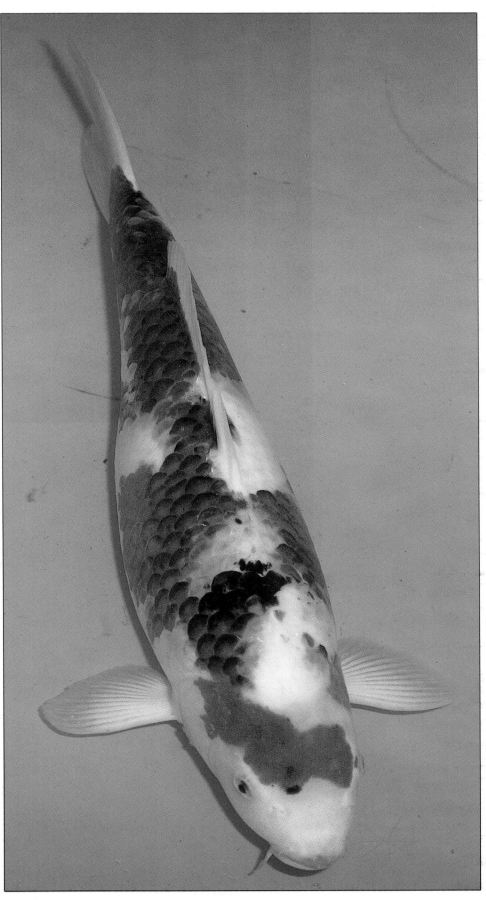

Above: **Sumi Goromo**
The basic koromo pattern on this koi is excellent and the interesting hi marking has plenty of movement. The solid sumi markings in front of the dorsal and near the tail complement the rest of the pattern.

KOROMO

The head pattern on the Ai-goromo should be the same as that on a Kohaku. A U-shaped head marking is preferred, but more unusual head markings are more easily tolerated than on Kohaku, as perfectly marked Ai-goromo are rare. The body of the Ai-goromo should have the same hi pattern as that of the Kohaku, with the Koromo blue reticulated overlay pattern. This should be evenly spread over the hi, and should not extend to the edge of the hi or into the white. On young Ai-goromo, the blue overlay is rarely fully defined, but develops with maturity. If the blue is clearly defined on a young koi, it tends to deteriorate as the koi grows.

Male Ai-goromo tend to mature younger than female koi, whose pattern does not generally develop until size 4 or 5, so what is thought to be a baby Kohaku can sometimes develop into an Ai-goromo.

The fins of an Ai-goromo are either white, or have hi in the pectoral fins. There should be no sumi.

Sumi-goromo These koi, as the name implies, have sumi on the hi pattern, which creates an impression of dark elegance. This sumi is solid (unlike the overlaid blue on the Ai-goromo), but does not overshadow the hi pattern, which is the same as that on Kohaku.

Above: **Budo Goromo**
The snow-white base colour and elegant white fins of this well-shaped koi highlight the deep maroon pattern over its body. Note that the sumi does not extend into the white base, but is confined to the hi.

Sumi-goromo lack the neat reticulated patterns of Ai-goromo and the sumi, which is present only on the hi pattern, appears irregularly in the scales. Unfortunately, Sumi-goromo are prone to over-large sumi spots, which spoil their otherwise elegant appearance. The fins, as on an Ai-goromo, should either be white, or have hi in the base.

Budo Goromo

Budo Goromo These koi were, until about 1986, extremely rare, but now seem to be appearing in larger numbers. Good specimens of this variety are still exceptional, however.

The word 'budo' is literally translated as grape. This refers to both the pattern and the colour of the koi. The snow white quality of the base colour is very important as a background to the purple grape-like cluster of colour which constitutes the pattern over the body of this koi. The sumi overlays the hi, giving a purple appearance to the markings, and the delicate pattern is similar in its position to the hi pattern on a Kohaku. The clarity of the pattern on a good Budo Goromo can be startling; often it is as though the very light sumi has slipped slightly on the deep hi to show red at the front of the scale and deep purple at its base.

There may be no head markings on a Budo Goromo (that is, the head may be clear white with no markings beneath the skin), or the koi may have a head pattern similar to that of a normal Sanke or Kohaku (see pages 130 and 136 respectively). Ideally, the fins should be white and clear of any colour.

Budo Sanke The Budo Sanke is called a Sanke because both the pattern and colours of the Sanke are evident but in a different form. That is, it has sumi overlaying the hi to give a purplish effect, like the Budo Goromo, combined with solid sumi markings, placed as on a normal Sanke. A good specimen is highly prized.

Koromo Sanke The Koromo Sanke is bred from an Ai-goromo and a Taisho Sanke. It has the Koromo reticulated pattern over the hi markings along with the sumi markings of a traditional Sanke. The Sanke sumi is called the 'hon' sumi, which means 'genuine', and the overlay on the hi is called the Koromo sumi.

This variety is extremely rare and is considered a connoisseur's koi because of its sometimes complicated pattern, which is not always appreciated by newcomers to the koi-keeping hobby.

Koromo Showa This koi is the result of crossing Ai-goromo and Showa. As on the Koromo Sanke, the hi pattern of the Koromo Showa is overlaid with the reticulated Koromo pattern. This koi is sometimes referred to as Ai-Showa.

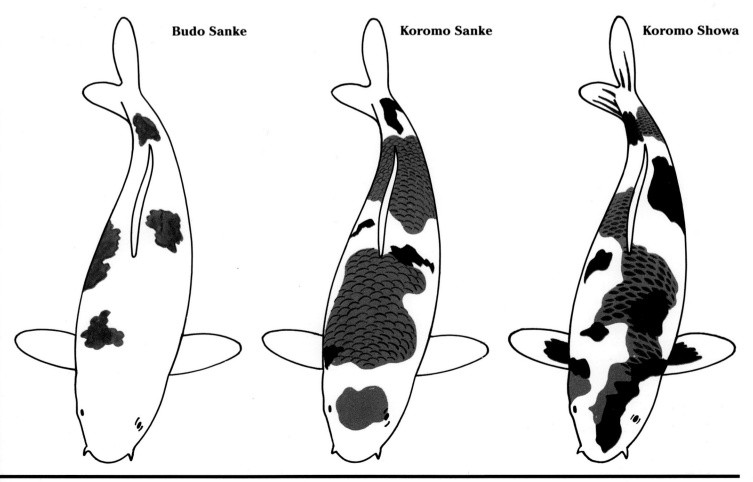

Budo Sanke   **Koromo Sanke**   **Koromo Showa**

KAWARIMONO

The Kawarimono classification accommodates all non-metallic koi that do not fall into the other varieties and is, therefore, a constantly expanding group. It includes koi that are the result of a cross between different varieties and others whose exact lineage is uncertain. Some, such as Kage Shiro Utsuri (see page 164), have been developed beyond the confines of their original classification, although their lineage is certain.

Although the Kawarimono group includes many different types of koi, the criteria by which they are judged is no less vigorous than for other varieties. All should have definite, clear-cut patterns and colours, and should be aesthetically pleasing. Larger Kawarimono can rival Kohaku, Sanke and Showa for major prizes in shows because of their subtle coloration and understated elegance.

Buying baby Kawarimono can be difficult because small Kawarimono are rare and can be singularly unimpressive. Judging how a pattern will develop with age comes only with experience, as does the confidence to appreciate 'different' varieties. Distinctive koi often appear in this classification because Kawarimono are not limited to the same variety specifications as Kohaku, for example.

Here we examine Kawarimono koi from various lineages: Karasugoi, Matsuba-goi, Kage Utsuri and Showa, Goshiki, Kanoko-goi and those of Shusui lineage, as well as other varieties whose lineages are less clearly defined. Some Kawarimono, such as Hajiro and Kumonryu, are very popular, but many are quite rare and some have not been seen, as yet, outside Japan.

Karasugoi

Some of the most sought-after koi in the Kawarimono group come from the Karasu lineage. Karasugoi are black koi with white or orange bellies. (Karasugoi literally means 'crow' fish.) The Karasugoi sumi, which is ebony in colour and darker than that of a Magoi (see pages 12 and 150), should be of the same dark hue all over the body or the koi will be worthless. Most Karasugoi are not generally admired by hobbyists because their black bodies do not show up well in the pond. However, some people like to keep one black koi in a pond because of the startling impression it makes as it suddenly breaks the surface to feed.

Right: **Kumonryu**
Note the striking contrast between the black and white markings over the body and head of this koi. The pattern on this variety is complemented by large doitsu scales along the lateral and dorsal lines.

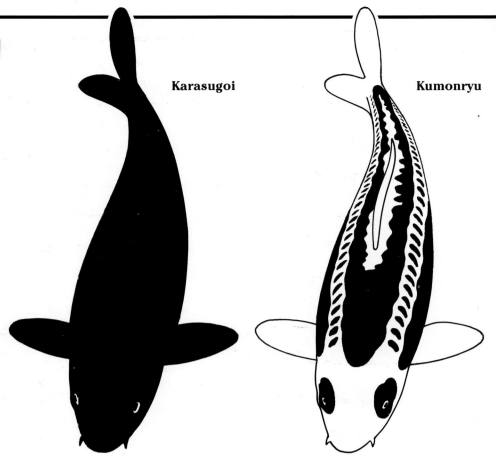

Karasugoi

Kumonryu

Sumi-nagashi

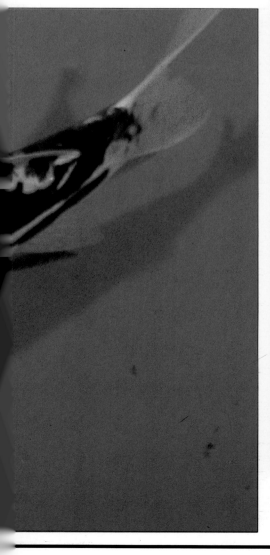

Above: **Sumi-nagashi**
The delicate pattern of black scales outlined in white is surprisingly complicated on this elegant koi. Patterns vary considerably in this variety; compare this koi with the illustration shown at above right.

KAWARIMONO

Hajiro This is a black koi with white tips to its caudal and pectoral fins. It is greatly admired by hobbyists because of the way that its white fins define its black body and make the koi visible in the pond.

Hageshiro This koi has not only white tips to its caudal and pectoral fins, but also a white head and nose.

Yotsushiro (Literally, 'five whites'.) This relatively rare koi has a white head and white pectoral and caudal fins.

Matsukawa-bake The pattern of this black and white koi changes with the time of year and water temperature.

Kumonryu Its black and white pattern, complemented by large doitsu scales, has given this koi its name, which literally means 'dragon fish'. Kumonryu is a doitsu koi with white markings on the head and fins and additional white on its body. Unfortunately, this variety has a tendency to go either completely white or black. However, the clarity of contrast between the white and black on the body of a good koi of this variety can be very beautiful. Kumonryu have become very popular since the mid 1980s and are appearing in increasing numbers.

Sumi-nagashi This is a very subtle koi whose black scales are outlined in white, creating an effect very similar to an Asagi pattern. In Japan it is sometimes known as Asagi Sumi-nagashi.

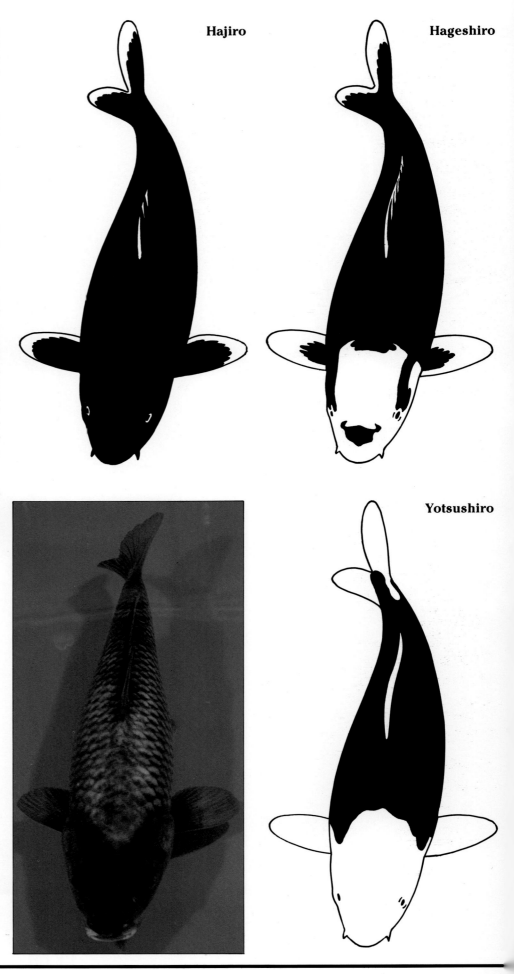

Hajiro

Hageshiro

Yotsushiro

Right: Matsukawa-bake
The patterns and coloration of this unusual koi change quite dramatically depending on such factors as water temperature and level of stress. In other conditions, the scales may be white with black centres.

Matsuba-goi

Matsuba-goi that are included in the Kawarimono classification are single-coloured, non-metallic koi with a matsuba (or 'pine-cone') pattern in the scales along the back.

Aka Matsuba This is a red koi ('aka' means red) with black markings in the centre of the scales. The red head of the Aka Matsuba should have no black markings or speckling. Although not as rare as Ki or Shiro Matsuba, this koi has become less common in recent years.

Ki Matsuba This is the yellow-based equivalent of the Aka Matsuba and is an extremely rare koi.

Shiro Matsuba This white koi has a black pine-cone patterning in the scales. Like Ki Matsuba, it is a very rare variety.

Aka, Ki and Shiro Matsuba also appear with doitsu scalation. These rare koi have black matsuba scales along the dorsal and lateral lines, which contrast with the single-coloured, non-metallic skin of the rest of the koi.

Ki Matsuba

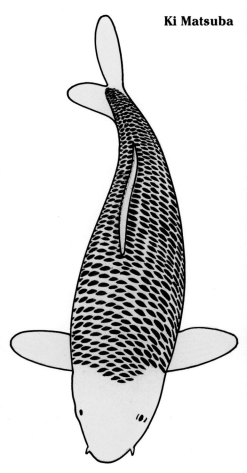

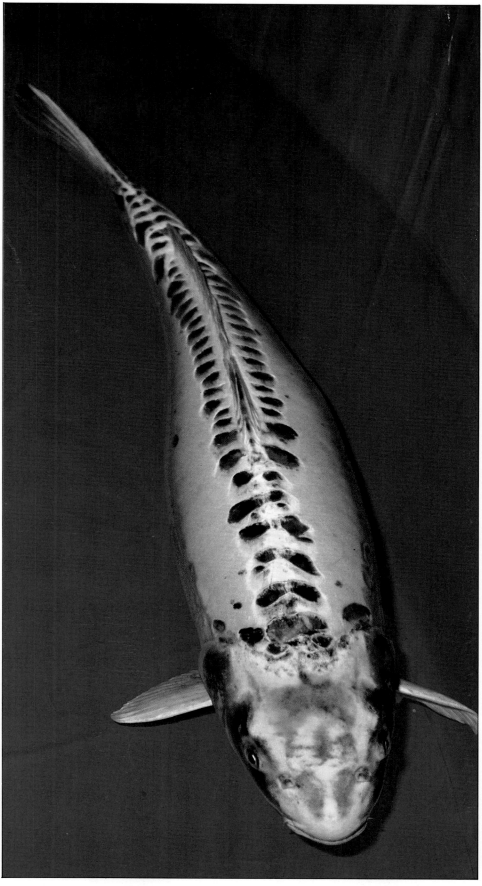

Above: **Doitsu Ki Matsuba**
The impressive scalation, body shape and yellow skin are responsible for the commanding appearance of this koi. The rarity of this variety vindicates the hint of black coloration on its head.

KAWARIMONO

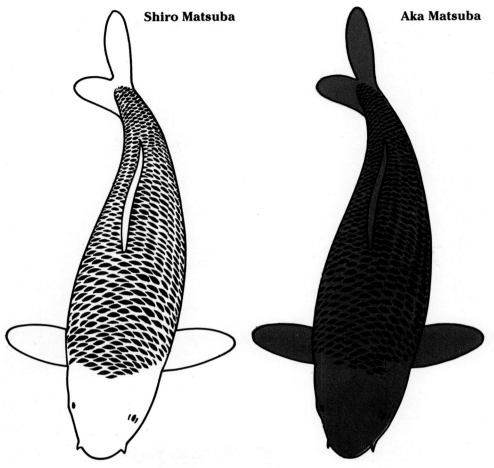

Shiro Matsuba

Aka Matsuba

Kage Utsuri and Showa

Kage varieties of koi include both Utsuri and Showa that have a blurred, reticulated black pattern over the white or hi of the koi. (The word kage literally means 'shadow' or 'phantom'.) These koi should also have a solid sumi pattern, complementing this 'shadowy' Kage pattern.

Although they are still comparatively rare, Kage koi are beginning to appear in greater numbers. Their quiet, elegant pattern is greatly admired, particularly by 'connoisseur' koi-keepers.

Kage Shiro Utsuri This variety has the basic black and white utsuri pattern with the Kage, shadowy, reticulated pattern over the white of the body.

Kage Hi Utsuri This koi has the red and black pattern of the Hi Utsuri (see pages 146 and 148) with a Kage pattern over the hi. It is especially important that the sumi pattern should be solid on this variety.

Kage Showa The Kage Showa has the basic showa markings with the Kage pattern over the white of the koi.

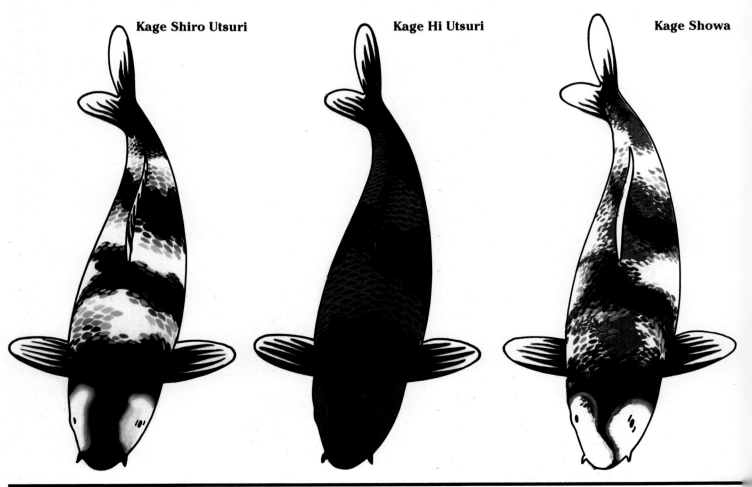

Kage Shiro Utsuri

Kage Hi Utsuri

Kage Showa

Above: Kage Showa
This koi needs a little more volume to be truly impressive. The sumi pattern is especially interesting on the head but is also balanced down the length of the body. The hi markings, also well placed, are even in hue. The 'kage', or 'phantom', sumi does not extend over all the white on this koi, but, where it is present, it is even.

KAWARIMONO

Goshiki

Goshiki means five colours. These colours are white, red, black, blue and dark blue, but since they are mixed together on the body of the koi, they often give a purplish appearance.

Goshiki were originally bred from a cross between an Asagi and a Sanke and are popular with hobbyists because of their flowery patterns. They should be kept in warm water as cool water makes the colours darken and, indeed, may cause the koi to turn almost black.

Kanoko-goi

Kanoko means 'fawn' and refers to the dappled pattern of hi found on some koi. Koi with this type of marking are classified with Kawarimono rather than in their original variety groups.

Kanoko Kohaku The hi markings on this Kohaku should be Kanoko (or dappled) but the hi marking on the head almost always remains solid.

Kanoko Sanke This is a Sanke whose hi markings are dappled rather than solid.

Kanoko Showa It is rare indeed to find good dappled hi markings on this Showa.

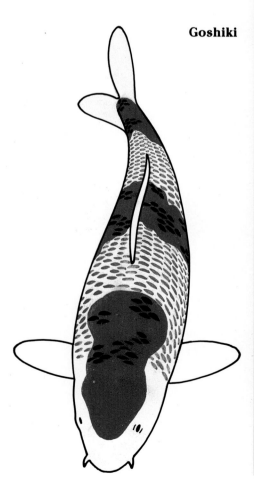

Goshiki

Kanoko Showa

Left: Goshiki
This young adult koi shows stunning coloration and pattern. The deep, clear hi shines through the grey-black pattern on the body with surprising brightness and is well balanced down the length of the koi. The rest of the pattern is reticulated, each scale having a lighter edge.

Right: Kanoko Showa
The good, strong sumi pattern on this Showa is particularly apparent in the menware stripe across the face. The white is clear and the hi is of a good even hue. The kanoko, or dappled, pattern is not fully developed but its clear definition shows promise for the future.

KAWARIMONO

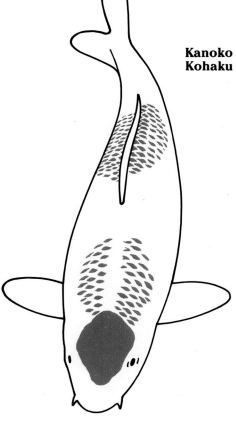

**Kanoko
Kohaku**

Ki-goi

Left: **Akame Ki-goi**
This beautiful bright yellow male Ki-goi has remarkably even coloration and lacks the hi spots that spoil so many koi of this variety. Note the red eyes ('akame'), which many hobbyists find very attractive.

Kanoko Sanke

Shusui hybrids

Other Kawarimono are derived from other crosses. One important group includes the following varieties, which have Shusui lineage, that is, they all have the basic blue coloration of the Shusui on the body, on which the markings of another variety are superimposed.

Sanke Shusui The pattern on this doitsu Sanke is underlaid with the blue back of the traditional Shusui.

Bunka Sanke This is a blue Sanke with shiny pectoral fins. These koi are only seen as babies because they lose this sheen in maturity.

Showa Shusui This koi should have the strong sumi and pattern of a Showa but with the underlying blue of a Shusui.

Goshiki Shusui As its name suggests, this is a doitsu non-metallic blue Goshiki.

Single-coloured koi

The following varieties are single-coloured, mat (non-metallic) koi. They tend to acquire volume in body shape more easily than other varieties and larger specimens can be quite beautiful.

Ki-goi This is a non-metallic single-coloured, bright yellow koi, whose colour should be of an even hue all over. Large Ki-goi are very impressive. A Ki-goi with pink eyes (albino) is called Akame Ki-goi (see far left).

Cha-goi (Cha means brown.) This is a single-coloured, non-metallic koi of a light brown or saffron colour. (The young Cha-goi is brownish green in colour.) It is also one of the most easily tamed of all koi, and exceedingly fast growing. Although Cha-goi appears quite plain at first glance, its faintly reticulated scalation is very attractive and this koi gains in appeal with association.

Cha-goi

Right: **Cha-goi**
This non-metallic, coffee-brown variety is not to everyone's taste and often suffers from black pigmentation spots. The elegance of Cha-goi lies in its simplicity, however, and, in this particular case, in its beautiful body shape.

KAWARIMONO

Sora-goi

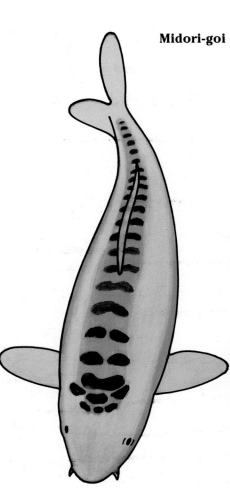

Midori-goi

Sora-goi This is a single-coloured, non-metallic, grey-blue koi. Like Cha-goi, it is a very fast growing variety.

Midori-goi (Midori means green.) This variety is so rare that it has an almost mythological reputation. A doitsu Midori-goi was produced by Tacho Yoshioka in 1963 – the result of a cross between a female Shusui and a male Yamabuki Ogon. This bright green koi with black or silvery scales has a tendency to go black, because of its Shusui lineage, or a very light green. It is unlikely that

Below: **Midori-goi**
This is a very young Midori-goi, which is not yet fully developed. The illustration, at below left, shows the bright green coloration that this extremely rare variety should obtain when it is mature.

anyone would try to specialize in breeding these koi, as in a spawning of 50 or 60 thousand young, probably only five or six Midori-goi would result.

Shiro-muji This non-metallic white koi is derived from Kohaku. Such koi are normally culled out or discarded, but large unstained Shiro-muji can be surprisingly impressive.

Aka-muji This is a non-metallic red koi. (The name derives from 'aka' meaning red, and 'muji' meaning skin.)

Beni-goi This attractive koi resembles Aka-muji but is deeper red in colour.

Aka Hajiro This is an Aka-muji with white tips to its pectoral and caudal fins.

Beni-goi

Aka Hajiro

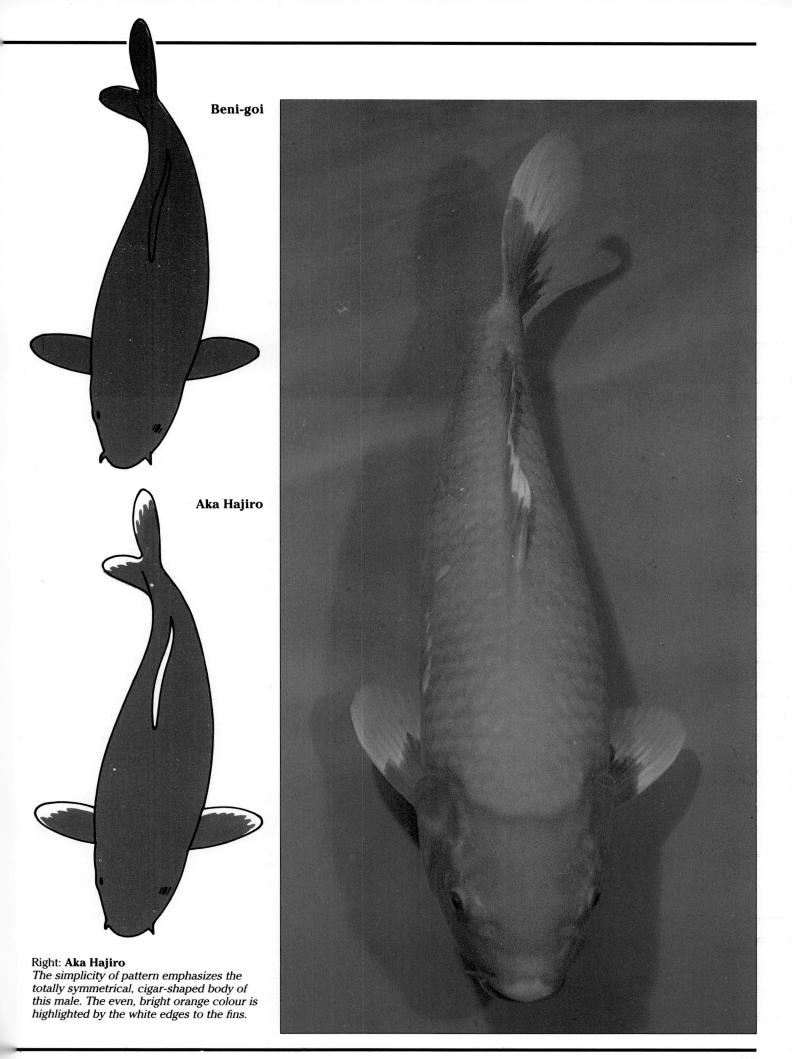

Right: Aka Hajiro
The simplicity of pattern emphasizes the totally symmetrical, cigar-shaped body of this male. The even, bright orange colour is highlighted by the white edges to the fins.

KAWARIMONO

Other Kawarimono include:

Hi-botan This koi is derived from Utsuri lineage and has a pattern that resembles Bekko. There are no sumi markings on the head but those on the body are much larger than on a Bekko.

Ochiba-shigure This koi is blue-grey in colour, with a brown pattern. The literal translation of Ochiba-shigure is 'autumn leaves on the water'. This is another variety for the connoisseur.

Right: **Ochiba-shigure**
This is another unusual variety, whose patterns and shades of colour vary considerably from one koi to another. Many patterns are more delicate than those of the fish shown here. Note the way that each scale on this koi is defined, as though it had been drawn with a pencil.

Ochiba-shigure

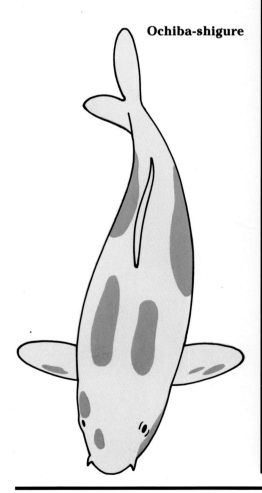

Above: Asagi (patterned)
Although this koi has the basic pattern and coloration of an Asagi, it would be classified in Kawarimono (the group containing all non-metallic koi not belonging to any other classification) rather than with other, traditionally marked, Asagi because of the way that the hi is highly patterned and irregularly placed over the body.

HIKARIMONO (OGON)

The category Hikarimono ('hikari' meaning metallic, 'mono', single colour) includes one of the most popular varieties of koi, particularly with new koi-keepers – the Ogon. Ogon are highly metallic koi, normally silver or golden yellow in colour, and contrast beautifully with other koi varieties. Indeed, it is generally agreed that the hobbyist should keep at least one Ogon in a pond for this reason. However, since they are such simple koi, the more experienced koi-keeper and breeder may miss the challenge of developing such patterns as are possible in Sanke, for example.

Because of their popularity, Ogon are bred in huge numbers, but the competition in shows is fierce. As with Kohaku, the deceptive simplicity of these single-coloured koi means that the criteria by which they are judged are severe.

Also included in this variety are Gin and Kin Matsuba; the metallic, and more common, counterparts of Shiro and Ki Matsuba (see Kawarimono, page 163).

The history of Hikarimono
The history of the true, gold Ogon began in 1921 when a gentleman called Sawata

Aoki took a koi with gold stripes along its back and selectively bred from it and its offspring, choosing those with the most gold coloration on their bodies. After about five generations, the koi known as Kin Kabuto, Gin Kabuto, Kinbo and Ginbo were developed.

Kin Kabuto and Gin Kabuto These koi, now considered rejects of the Ogon variety, are black koi whose scales have gold or silver edges. Their heads are gold or silver with a black marking, sometimes described as a helmet.

Kinbo and Ginbo These koi, which are black with either a gold (kin) or a silver (gin) metallic sheen, are also considered by modern koi-keepers to be valueless.

The Ogon lineage was stabilized in about 1946 when two entirely gold Ogon were produced. The development of Ogon has done much for the development of koi generally; Ogon have been cross-bred with other varieties to produce many fine koi in the Hikari-Utsurimono and Hikari-moyo-mono varieties, for example (see pages 180-3 and 184-93 respectively).

Originally Ogon were rare, and therefore expensive, koi, but due to very successful breeding they are now more common and have, consequently, decreased in value. As with all koi, a good Ogon can still command a high price, but these koi rarely win top prizes in shows.

Colour
Although Ogon are traditionally gold koi, colours vary depending on the variety. Whatever the colour, it should be of the same hue all over, from head to tail and down to the tips of the fins.

Pattern
Ogon are single-coloured metallic koi and should have no markings. Be particularly careful when buying young koi to avoid any with marks underneath the skin or on the head; these are likely to become more noticeable with age.

Right: **Platinum Ogon**
This beautifully shaped female koi has even coloration, although there are a few red stress marks on the head and a slight black tinge in the scales. Normally, Ogon have more metallic lustre than this.

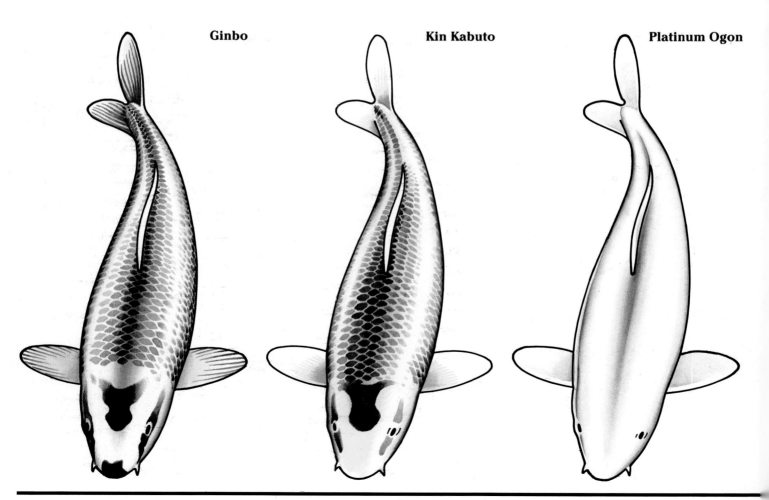

Ginbo   Kin Kabuto   Platinum Ogon

HIKARIMONO (OGON)

Lustre

The lustre (or metallic quality) is the most important factor of Hikarimono koi and should extend all over the body, head and fins. The head should be bright and the fins highly metallic. Ogon are frequently spoilt by fins that are unbalanced or that are small in comparison with body size. Large fins are highly desirable on Ogon to offset the plain body.

Scalation

The scalation of these koi is very important; the scales should, ideally, spread into the abdominal region, and their edges should be trimmed with gold. An Ogon that has lost scales (through damage or disease) is valueless because it lacks regularity of scalation.

Matsuba koi (see below) have black centres to each of their scales, giving an attractive pine-cone effect to the body.

Platinum Ogon This is a metallic white Ogon. The first Platinum Ogon was bred in 1963 by Mr Tadao Yoshioko as a result of pairing a Ki-goi (see page 169) with a Nezu Ogon (see below). This variety was originally called Shirogane, which means white gold. Another commonly used name is Purachina. As with the traditional gold Ogon, the head should be bald of all markings, and the lustre and scalation should be even over the whole koi.

Nezu Ogon This Ogon is silver grey in colour. The word 'nezu' is an abbreviation of 'nezumi', meaning 'mouse' or grey. This koi has a dull metallic lustre, clear head and even scalation.

Yamabuki Ogon This yellow-gold Ogon ('yamabuki' means yellow in Japanese) is now one of the most common of all Ogon. It was produced in 1957 from the cross between a Ki-goi and an Ogon.

Orenji Ogon As its name implies, this Ogon is a deep metallic orange in colour. First produced in about 1953, it is becoming very popular with hobbyists because of its brilliant coloration.

Fuji Ogon This is the name given to any Ogon with a highly metallic head.

Left: **Yamabuki Ogon**
The even scalation, bright colour and clear lustre of this voluminous female koi would cause her to stand out in any pond.

Right: **Orenji Ogon**
This is another Ogon with impressive scalation and coloration, lacking black shimis on the head or in the scales. Ideally, the body should be plumper and the head a little less pointed, however.

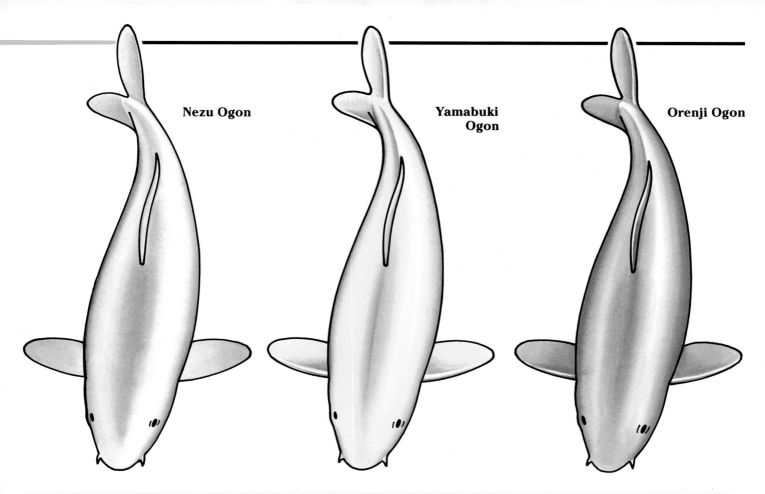

Nezu Ogon

Yamabuki Ogon

Orenji Ogon

HIKARIMONO (OGON)

Kin Matsuba (Matsuba Ogon) Each scale of this metallic gold or yellow koi has a black centre, giving the body a 'pine-cone' pattern. The head is clear of any hint of black on a good koi.

Kin Matsuba was first produced in 1960 by Eizaburo Mano, when an Ogon and a Matsuba were bred together.

Gin Matsuba This is the silver version of the Kin Matsuba.

Right: **Kin Matsuba**
A stunning, full-bodied koi. Note the evenness of the deep metallic orange of the body and fins and the regularity of the matsuba pattern in each scale. Particularly commendable is the lack of black markings on the head – a clear head is unusual in a Kin Matsuba of this size.

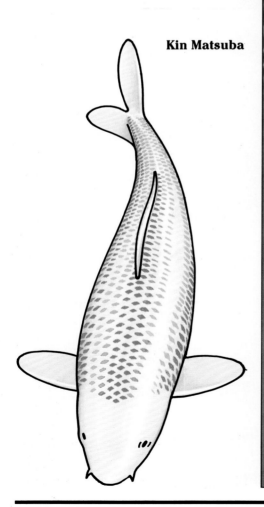

Kin Matsuba

Right: Gin Matsuba
This is the silver counterpart of the koi on the opposite page. The matsuba pattern is less clearly defined on this koi, although it is of an even hue all over the koi, as is the base colour. Unfortunately, there is a slight trace of yellow around the nose and eyes.

Gin Matsuba

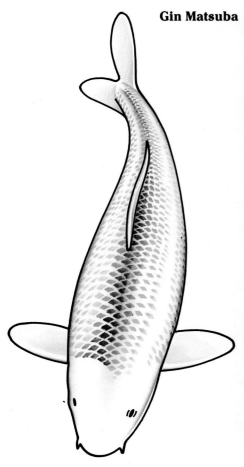

HIKARI-UTSURIMONO

Hikari-Utsurimono, like Hikarimoyo-mono, have arisen from an Ogon cross, in this case with Utsuri or Showa. Koi in the Hikari-Utsurimono group are basically metallic Showa and Utsuri and the same criteria for appreciation apply, for example head pattern and pectoral fin markings (see pages 140 and 146).

These very beautiful koi are living proof of the far-reaching effect that the Ogon has had in the breeding and classification of nishikigoi over the past 25 years. The one drawback with these elegant koi is that the strong metallic lustre can make the colours appear to fade, so that the hi becomes brownish and the sumi grey and blurred. However, this is not always the case and fine-quality koi in this classification are imposing, attractive and elegant in appearance.

Kin Showa and Gin Showa
Kin Showa and Gin Showa are both the result of Showa and Ogon crosses. Kin Showa have a golden lustre while Gin Showa are predominately silver. The name Kin Showa now tends to be used for both varieties, however.

Gin Shiro
This koi is a metallic Shiro Utsuri (see page 146); the sumi markings on its silver body should form the same patterns as on a Shiro Utsuri. This variety was, until

Kin Showa

recently, quite rare and, although it is now appearing in greater numbers, larger Gin Shiro are still uncommon.

Kin Ki Utsuri
This variety occurs from the cross between the Ki Utsuri and the Ogon. These are beautiful koi with bright colours, clear sumi and a metallic gold lustre. Again, they can be appreciated in the same way as Utsuri.

Kin Hi Utsuri
This is a metallic Hi Utsuri, the result of a cross between a Hi Utsuri and an Ogon.

Right: **Kage Gin Shiro**
The rather faint sumi and underlying hi on the nose and body are vindicated by the very even and balanced pattern over the head and body of this koi. The slight shadow of sumi over the silver – described as 'kage' (see page 164) – would group any such non-metallic koi with Kawarimono, but there is no such group for metallic koi.

Below: **Kin Showa**
This is a highly metallic koi with a good lustre. The fins are beautifully matched, with sumi stripes down to the base. Often, as here, the sumi on a metallic koi loses depth, and the pattern of both the sumi and hi could be more evenly spaced down the body of this koi. Nevertheless, this Kin Showa is an attractive fish.

Gin Shiro

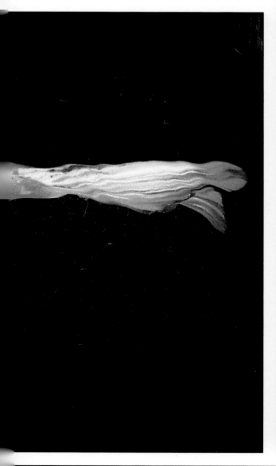

HIKARI-UTSURIMONO

Gin Showa

Kin Ki Utsuri

Left: Kin Ki Utsuri
The beautiful Utsuri pattern over the body of this stunning metallic koi is enhanced by its warm gold coloration, which is even in hue from nose to tail. Note that the sumi is paler than it would be on a non-metallic koi.

Below: **Kin Hi Utsuri**
The metallic red counterpart of the Kin Ki Utsuri opposite, this koi, too, has superb colour and lustre and a good Utsuri pattern, although there are a few black marks along the dorsal fin and on the head.

HIKARIMOYO-MONO

Metallic koi that have more than one colour but are not of Utsuri lineage generally fall into the class of Hikari-moyo-mono. (Note, however, that Gin and Kin Matsuba belong to the Ogon category, see page 178.) The koi in this classification are extremely popular because they are highly metallic, appear in many colours and are immediately attractive to the eye. Koi-keepers, especially those new to the hobby, are very attracted to baby koi in this classification because they are so bright. However, when buying one of these young koi, make sure that its head is clear of a black helmet-like marking. Although this is not unattractive on a young koi, it becomes more noticeable as the koi grows and will be a serious defect if you wish to show your koi. In fact, such a koi would be ruled out immediately by the judges.

The koi varieties in the Hikarimoyo-mono classification have arisen from two sources. The first group includes koi that have resulted from crossing a Platinum Ogon with any other variety except Utsuri. These crosses have produced such varieties as Yamato-nishiki (also known as a metallic Sanke), Gin Bekko and Kujaku. These koi all have a metallic base overlaid with coloured patterns.

The second group consists of varieties known collectively as Hariwake, and includes Orenji Hariwake, Hariwake Matsuba etc. These koi all have two colours; platinum, and metallic orange or gold.

Yamato-nishiki

This variety is the result of the cross between a Taisho Sanke and a Platinum Ogon and was first bred in 1965 by a gentleman called Seikichi Hoshino. In fact, there were originally two distinct varieties; Yamato, which was the direct result of a cross between a Sanke and a Fuji Ogon (see page 176), and Koshi-nishiki, which was the result of a cross between a Sanke and an Ogon. However, the differences between the two were so minimal that Yamato-nishiki became the accepted name for both varieties.

The very attractive Yamato-nishiki is basically a metallic Sanke, with a platinum (metallic white) or silver skin with hi and sumi markings. The sumi markings on Yamato-nishiki are often pale and blur into a metallic grey, while the hi tends, more often than not, to be pale orange in hue instead of the blood red normally associated with Sanke. This is because the red pigment is transparent and the silver lightens the red, like the sun shining through a stained glass window. Yamato-nishiki with good hi and sumi do exist however, and can be very startlingly beautiful in appearance.

Above: **Yamato-nishiki**
A male koi with the excellent lustre of a good Hikarimoyo-mono. Both hi and platinum are strong and although the sumi is slightly blurred, it is well balanced and deeper than on many metallic koi.

Yamato-nishiki

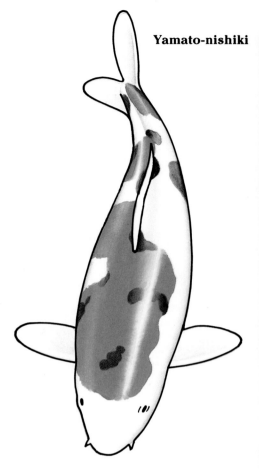

Kujaku

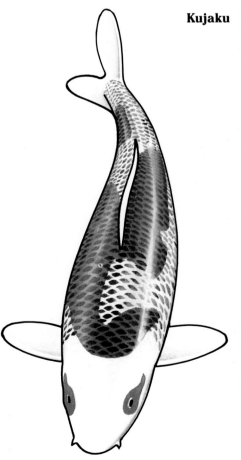

Above: **Kujaku**
Excellent body shape and large fins are responsible for the impressive quality of this koi. The regular matsuba pattern in the scales complements the metallic gold coloration. Note the unusual head marking.

HIKARIMOYO-MONO

Platinum Kohaku

Kujaku

(Also known as Kujaku Ogon) Kujaku are platinum koi with hi markings that normally cover a large proportion of the body. The scales are overlaid with a matsuba (or black pine-cone) pattern, which is said to resemble peacock feathers. The most prized Kujaku have heads that are red with no black markings. These koi look especially impressive in a pond of non-metallic varieties, and good specimens, which are appearing in larger numbers, are highly sought after.

Kujaku were first produced in 1960 by Toshio Hirasawa from Ojiya and are derived from Shusui, Matsuba and Hariwake. Many of the original offspring were doitsu, but fully scaled Kujaku are generally considered to be more impressive and are now produced in greater numbers than their doitsu counterparts.

Beni Kujaku This is a Kujaku with hi markings all over the body. It is a rare, but beautiful variety.

Doitsu Kujaku This is a platinum koi with hi markings over its body and sumi markings only in the scales along the dorsal and lateral lines.

Platinum Kohaku (Kin-Fuji)

This koi, which is quite rare, is derived from the Kohaku and the Platinum Ogon. The skin is platinum with an overlaying hi pattern that tends to be of a brownish orange hue rather than scarlet. There should, ideally, be no hi on the head and the fins should be glossy platinum in colour and lustre.

Kikisui

(Literally, 'water chrysanthemum'.) This doitsu platinum Kohaku is highly sought after by hobbyists. The Kikisui has a deep gold or orange wavy line along the length of the body on either side of the pattern. Its head should be platinum.

Gin Bekko

This koi is the result of a cross between the Shiro Bekko and Platinum Ogon. It should have platinum skin with sumi markings as those on a Shiro Bekko. Good sumi is rare on a Gin Bekko.

Right: **Doitsu Kujaku**
The lustre on this koi's body is good and the hi pattern is well defined. Unfortunately, the thin body shape makes the head appear disproportionately large and there are traces of black coloration on the head.

Kikisui   **Gin Bekko**   **Doitsu Kujaku**

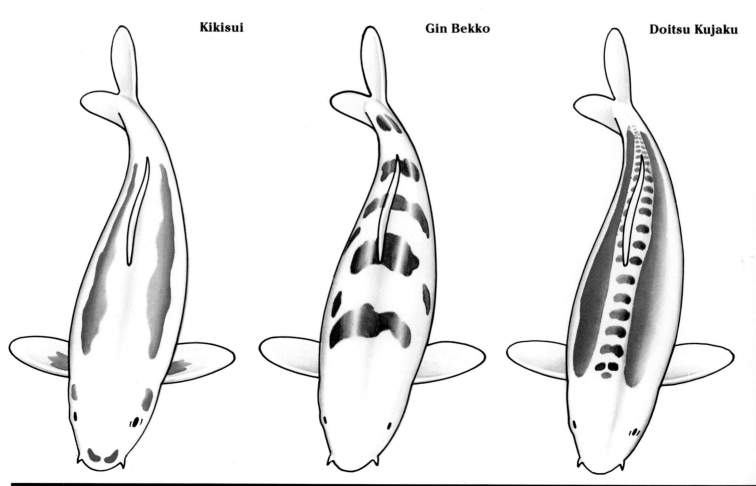

HIKARIMOYO-MONO

Above: **Kinginrin Sakura Ogon**
This young koi is an excellent example of its variety with a good body shape. The pattern is varied and interesting; note particularly the markings on the head and the 'inazuma' pattern on the body. The coloration, too, is impressive; it is unusual to find such a deep red on a metallic koi. The kinginrin scales cover most of the body.

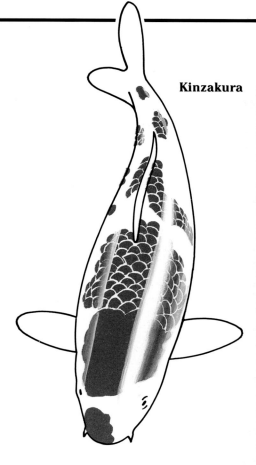

Kinzakura

Right: **Shochikubai**
*This metallic Ai-goromo is a very rare
variety. The pattern down the body is
evenly spaced and well defined on this koi.
Because of the good metallic lustre, the hi
appears slightly brown in colour.*

Sakura Ogon

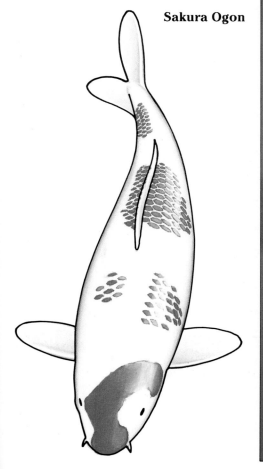

HIKARIMOYO-MONO

Sakura Ogon
In simple terms, a Sakura Ogon can be described as a metallic Kanoko Kohaku (see pages 166 and 168). It is often mistaken for the Orenji Hariwake because of its similar coloration. Unlike the markings of the Orenji Hariwake, however, those of the Sakura Ogon are dappled.

Kinzakura
This is a metallic Goten-zakura (see *Kohaku*, pages 133 and 134) and the name Kinzakura is seldom used. It is an extremely rare variety.

Shochikubai
This is a metallic Ai-goromo and should have a metallic lustre all over the body. It is a rare and very highly prized variety.

Kinsui and Ginsui
Both these koi varieties are metallic Shusui. The lustre of both varieties is good on young koi but tends to grow dull with age. Kinsui have a greater number of hi markings than Ginsui.

Tora Ogon
(Tora means tiger.) This Ogon with black markings is basically a metallic Ki Bekko. Good specimens in large sizes are rare.

Hariwake
Hariwake have two metallic colours; platinum and either orange or gold. They fall roughly into four categories:
1 Fully scaled   3 Matsuba
2 Doitsu   4 Doitsu Matsuba

Doitsu Hariwake tend to be the most popular because of the beautiful metallic lustre of their skin.

Yamabuki Hariwake (Yamabuki means bright yellow.) Yamabuki Hariwake is a silver koi with metallic yellow markings, which should be balanced over its body. On a fully scaled Yamabuki Hariwake the edges of the scales should be visible in relief. The head should, ideally, be free from colour (that is, it should be silver). However, a yellow pattern on the head is usual and is not a severe defect. These attractive koi are very popular.

Orenji Hariwake This variety is the orange equivalent of the Yamabuki Hariwake. The orange markings on the platinum body should be deep and metallic.

Hariwake Matsuba This is a silver and yellow metallic koi with a matsuba pattern of sumi in each of its scales.

Right: Yamabuki Hariwake
Although it is young, this koi has a good body shape. Both the yellow and platinum are clear and of even hue over the body, and the lustre is excellent. The head pattern and fins are also commendable. The rather uninteresting pattern of the yellow will probably break into a more appealing one as the koi grows in size.

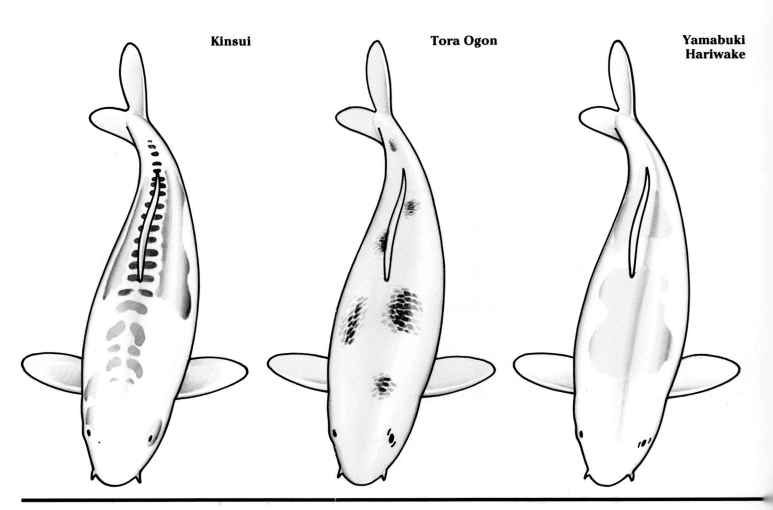

Kinsui   Tora Ogon   Yamabuki Hariwake

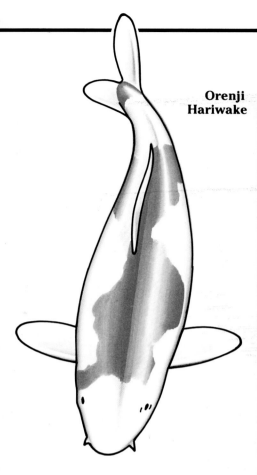

**Orenji
Hariwake**

Left: Orenji Hariwake
*An engaging aspect of this koi is its white
nose, which has an excellent lustre. The
platinum on the fins enhances the fish's
deep orange colour. More pattern and
volume would be desirable, however.*

**Matsuba
Hariwake**

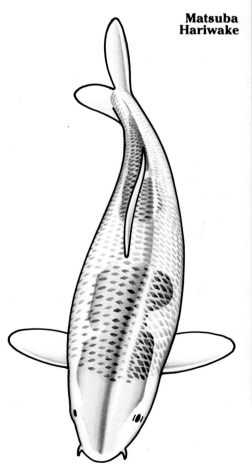

Above: **Matsuba Hariwake**
*This is a beautifully coloured koi with
interesting markings. The matsuba pattern
is faint but evenly distributed in the scales.
The pectorals are particularly attractive,
with yellow in the base of each fin.*

TANCHO

Tancho koi are among the most popular of all koi varieties and it is quite common for hobbyists to have more than one Tancho in a pond. Tancho Kohaku, in particular, are simple koi and yet it is obvious that a great deal of effort has taken place in their development.

The name Tancho is derived from the national bird of Japan, the Tancho crane (*Grus japonensis*), which has one round red marking on its head, and the word tancho literally means 'red spot on the head'. These koi are highly prized in Japan because of their similarity with the Japanese flag. The Tancho classification differs from others in that it contains koi from different varieties – namely, Kohaku, Sanke and Showa – that have one distinguishing feature – a red mark, or tancho, on the head.

Tancho colours
The hi marking should be of a deep, even red. The white on any Tancho is very important because it provides the background for a very startling pattern. (This is particularly true of the Tancho Kohaku.) Sumi markings on both the Tancho Sanke and Tancho Showa should be deep ebony in colour.

Tancho patterns
The distinguishing factor about the Tancho's pattern is the hi marking on the head, combined with a lack of hi elsewhere on the body.

Head
The hi marking should be on the centre of the head and should not cover the eyes, or extend back onto the body of the koi. The edges of the marking should be clearly defined. There are variously shaped tancho markings. In terms of judging, the most highly prized are the perfectly round spots, but hobbyists enjoy collecting other markings, such as oval, heart shaped and diamond, which add an element of uniqueness to the koi.

Body
The body pattern varies depending on the variety concerned.

Tancho Kohaku The hi marking on the head is the only marking that should be visible on this Tancho. Its body should be snow white from head to tail and there should be no hi in the fins.

Tancho Sanke The only hi marking allowed on a Tancho Sanke is on the head; the rest of the body is black and white. Many koi-keepers are confused as to why this variety is classed as a Sanke and not as a Tancho Bekko, as it is basically a Bekko with a red spot on its head. (Sumi markings on a Sanke are similar to those on a Bekko.) There are two things to remember that will help to clear up this confusion. Firstly, a Tancho of any variety lacks any other hi on the body and, secondly, it is not possible to have a Tancho Bekko because there is no hi on a Bekko. (However, a Bekko may have a black tancho marking, see page 140.)

Tancho Showa This koi combines the black and white pattern of a Shiro Utsuri over its body and head with the tancho hi marking on its head.

Fins
Fins should be as for the different varieties; that is, on a Tancho Kohaku the fins should be pure white, on a Tancho Sanke they should be white or have black stripes in them, and on a Tancho Showa there should be a sumi at the base of the pectoral fins (see pages 139 and 140).

Left: **Tancho head markings**
The tancho should be central on the head. The round marking is the traditional one, but other shapes are also popular.

Right: **Tancho Sanke**
This is a beautiful, large koi with a strong tancho marking placed squarely on the centre of the head. The sumi markings down the body are accompanied by very impressive sumi stripes in the fins.

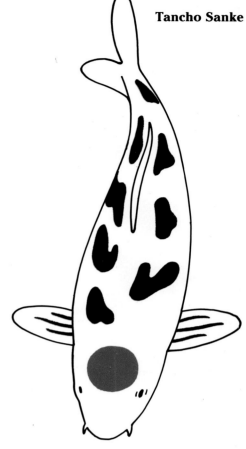

Tancho Sanke

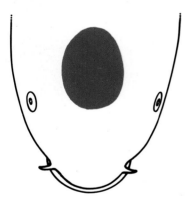

Oval tancho

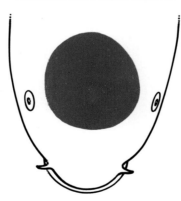

Traditional round tancho

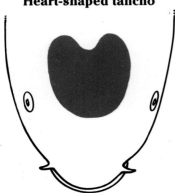

Heart-shaped tancho

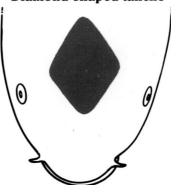

Diamond-shaped tancho

TANCHO

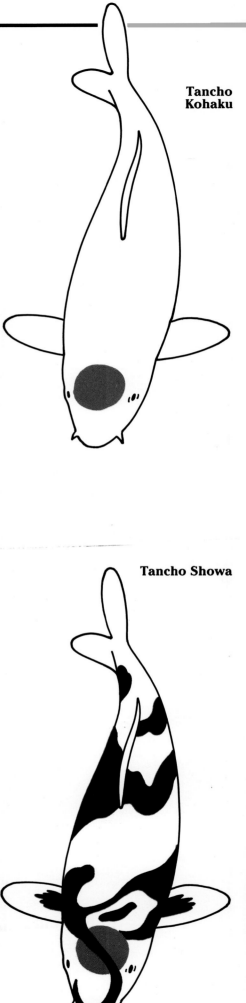

Tancho Kohaku

Tancho Showa

Above: Tancho Kohaku
The traditionally shaped oval tancho of this koi is generally good although it moves slightly over one eye. Pure white fins complement the clear coloration and elegant body shape of this male.

Above: Tancho Showa
This koi has an unusual pattern; the tancho is well placed but unsymmetrical in shape and the sumi markings on the head and body are less extensive than on some other Tancho Showa. The pectoral fins are the most striking feature of this koi, with solid sumi over the entire fin except for a thin white stripe along the front edge.

KINGINRIN

Kinginrin literally means 'golden silvery scales' and refers to the sparkling effect of the scales, which appears golden over hi and silver over white and sumi. The impression is of an iridescence in individual scales rather than the overall metallic lustre of koi in the Hikari-mono group, for example. A koi may have any number of such scales on its body but if there are less than about 20, the koi will not be described as Kinginrin.

These koi, which first appeared in 1929, are highly prized by hobbyists because of the way they shimmer in the sunshine and stand out from other koi. Kinginrin has sometimes been considered a weak point as it can blur the edge of sumi and so spoil the pattern, but this is now not always the case, and kinginrin scales can add an impressive dimension to the colour and pattern.

Until recently, Kinginrin of all varieties were entered and judged as a separate group. This changed in Japan in 1988 and it is expected that the rest of the world

Pearl Ginrin

Diamond Ginrin

Beta-gin

Kado-gin

Above: **Types of kinginrin**
These illustrations show the various forms that the shiny deposit, or kinginrin, can take on a koi's scales. In reality, these types are rarely differentiated in koi shows.

will follow Japan's example. Now only Kinginrin Kohaku, Sanke and Showa are judged in this separate, Kinginrin group. Kinginrin koi from other varieties are entered in their normal variety groups.

Kinginrin scale forms

Kinginrin appears in different forms and affects different parts of the scales. These types, which do not alter the koi's classification, can be divided into two groups:

Pearl Ginrin (also known as 'tsubu-gin' or 'tama-gin'). On this type of Kinginrin there is a solid sparkling area on each scale, giving the koi the appearance of being covered with tiny pearls, as the name suggests. Its iridescent centre makes the scale stand out in relief. Although Pearl Ginrin koi are very attractive when young, they become more dull as they grow larger and it is rare to find good Pearl Ginrin koi larger than size 2.

The second type of Kinginrin has three variants. In all these forms, the effected scales have a flat appearance, lacking the solidity, or lumpy appearance, of the Pearl Ginrin scales.

Beta-gin Here, the whole of the surface of the scale sparkles. Beta-gin is considered the finest type of Kinginrin. However, these shimmering scales are often uneven over the body, being most prominent on the sides of the koi.

Left: *This Kohaku displays exquisite kinginrin in its scales. However, the white is rather pink in tone and the hi pattern is fragmented and badly defined. The hi markings at the tail joint and on the eyelids would also be considered defects.*

Diamond Ginrin This koi was first produced in Hiroshima in 1969. The brilliant scales, which sparkle like diamonds, are greatly admired outside Japan but are generally unpopular among Japanese koi-keepers, who consider that their brilliance lacks elegance.

Kado-gin Here, only the edges of the scales are iridescent ('kado' means edge). Kado-gin koi are not generally admired in Japan because the amount of shiny deposit on each scale can be variable and uneven and, as on the Diamond Ginrin, is often missing from the scales along the dorsal line of the koi.

Although these different types of Kinginrin exist, koi with kinginrin scales are generally divided only into Pearl Ginrin and other Ginrin types. Most hobbyists would neither need, nor be able, to distinguish further between them but would agree, nevertheless, that these koi are the living jewels of nishikigoi.

Right: **Kinginrin Kohaku**
A stunning example of a Kinginrin Kohaku. The kinginrin is especially noticeable along the dorsal of the koi, particularly on the white, where it shows up as a silvery 'mother-of-pearl' deposit on each scale. The colour on this koi is superb; the depth of the hi is normally lightened by kinginrin scalation but this is not the case on this koi and the vivid hi pattern is well balanced along the length of the koi's body.

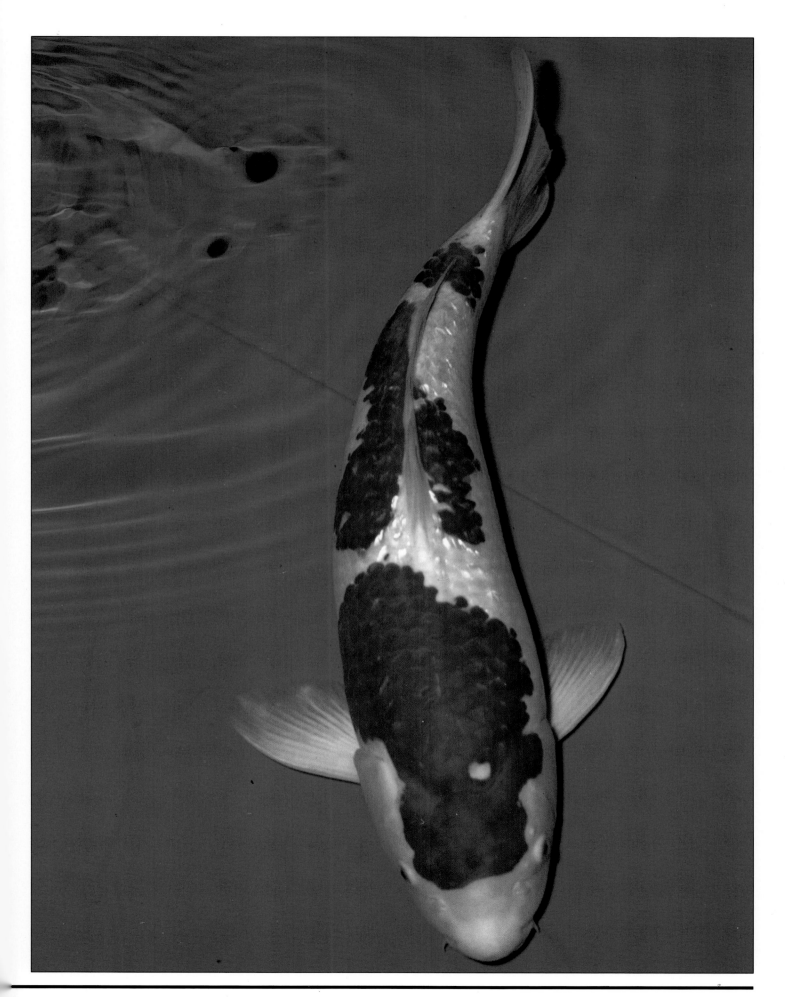

KINGINRIN

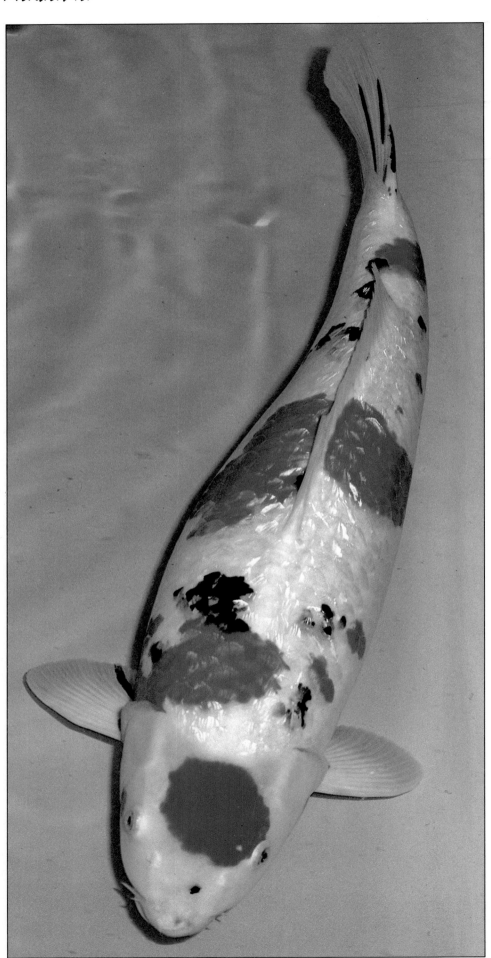

Left: Kinginrin Sanke
This koi shows excellent, even kinginrin scalation along the dorsal. The lightening effect of the kinginrin scales is clearly visible on both the sumi and the hi markings over the body of the koi. The pattern is interesting, with a particularly charming maruten marking to one side of the head.

Right: Kinginrin Showa
This koi is probably one of the most famous of its variety ever, having won many major competitions in Japan. The excellent silver lights in the white, and gold lights in the hi, markings are the perfect accompaniment to the balanced pattern, both on the head and, more particularly, on the four hi markings, which are evenly spaced along the body.

用語解説
GLOSSARY

A

Ai-goromo Basically a *Kohaku* whose red scales have blue semicircular borders, giving the koi a reticulated pattern. *(Koromo)*

Ai-showa See *Koromo Showa*. *(Koromo)*

Aka Red (usually as a base colour over the body of a koi).

Aka Bekko A red koi with black markings. *(Bekko)*

Aka Hajiro A red koi with white tips to the pectoral and caudal fins. *(Kawarimono)*

Aka Matsuba A red koi with a black 'pine-cone' *(matsuba)* pattern in the scales along the back. *(Kawarimono)*

Aka Sanke A *Sanke* whose red marking extends the length of the body. *(Sanke)*

Aka-muji A non-metallic red koi. *(Kawarimono)*

Akame An eye with a red iris. Most often seen in *Ki-goi*.

Asagi A grey-blue koi with red along the sides, cheeks and in the fins.

Asagi Magoi An early ancestor of the modern *Asagi*.

Asagi Sumi-nagashi A koi whose black scales are outlined in white. More commonly known as *Sumi-nagashi*. *(Kawarimono)*

B

Bekko Mat white, red or yellow koi with black markings.

Beni Red (usually as a base colour over the body of a koi).

Beni Kujaku An orange-red *Kujaku* with red markings all over the body. *(Hikarimoyo-mono)*

Beni-goi A non-metallic red koi, resembling *Aka-muji* but with a deeper red coloration. *(Kawarimono)*

Beta-gin Probably the finest type of *Kinginrin*, where the whole surface of each scale sparkles.

Boke Showa A popular form of *Showa*, with blurred, greyish *sumi*. *(Showa)*

Bongiri An area without pattern near the tail joint, considered a flaw.

Budo Literally 'grape'.

Budo Goromo A koi with a purplish, grape-like pattern on its white body. *(Koromo)*

Budo Sanke A koi with a pattern resembling that of *Budo Goromo* combined with solid black markings. *(Koromo)*

Bunka Sanke A blue *Sanke* with shiny pectoral fins. Seen only as a baby koi. *(Kawarimono)*

C

Cha Brown.

Cha-goi A non-metallic light brown koi. *(Kawarimono)*

D

Dangara A stepped pattern on the body of a koi, also known as *Danmoyo*.

Danmoyo A stepped pattern on the body of a koi, also known as *Dangara*.

Diamond Ginrin A form of *Kinginrin* where the scales sparkle like diamonds.

Doitsu A koi with scales along the dorsal and lateral lines only.

Doitsu Kujaku A platinum koi with red markings over its body and black markings in the scales along the dorsal and lateral lines only. *(Hikarimoyo-mono)*

F

Fucarin The area of skin around the smaller scales of good metallic koi. The smaller the scales, the greater the lustre.

Fuji A highly metallic lustre on the head of a young koi, visible as minute bubbles. Most often seen in good young *Sanke* and, occasionally, *Ogon* and *Kohaku*.

G

Gin Bekko Basically a metallic *Shiro Bekko*. *(Hikarimoyo-mono)*

Gin Kabuto A black koi whose scales have silver edges. Now rejected as a poor *Ogon*.

Gin Matsuba A metallic silver koi with a black 'pine-cone' *(matsuba)* pattern in the scales. *(Hikarimono)*

Gin Shiro A metallic *Shiro Utsuri*. *(Hikari-Utsurimono)*

Gin Showa A metallic *Showa* with a silver lustre. *(Hikari-Utsurimono)*

Ginbo A black koi with a silver metallic sheen. Now considered valueless.

Ginrin The more commonly used term for *Kinginrin*, referring to sparkling scale types.

Ginsui A metallic *Shusui* with a silver lustre. *(Hikarimoyo-mono)*

Goi Fish.

Goshiki A five-colour koi, on which white, red, black, and light and dark blue are mixed to give a purplish appearance. *(Kawarimono)*

Goshiki Shusui A *doitsu*, non-metallic blue *Goshiki*. *(Kawarimono)*

Goten-zakura Kohaku A cherry blossom patterned *Kohaku*. *(Kohaku)*

H

Hachi Hi An early ancestor of the modern *Kohaku*.

Hageshiro A black, non-metallic koi with white tips to its pectoral fins and a white head and nose. *(Kawarimono)*

Hajiro A black koi with white tips to its pectoral fins. *(Kawarimono)*

Hana Shusui A form of *Shusui*, also known as a flowery *Shusui*. *(Shusui)*

Hanatsuki A hi pattern that reaches the mouth.

Hariwake Koi with two colours, one of which is platinum, the other metallic orange or yellow. *(Hikarimoyo-mono)*

Hariwake Matsuba A silver and yellow metallic koi with a black pattern in each of its scales. *(Hikarimoyo-mono)*

Hi Red (markings).

Hi Asagi An *Asagi* whose red marking extends over the lateral line. *(Asagi)*

Hi Showa A predominantly red *Showa*. *(Showa)*

Hi Shusui A *Shusui* whose red pattern spreads up from the belly and covers the back. *(Shusui)*

Hi Utsuri A black koi with red markings. *(Utsurimono)*

Hi-botan A koi resembling *Bekko*, derived from *Utsuri* lineage. *(Kawarimono)*

Higoi A red koi, an early ancestor of the modern *Kohaku*.

Hikari Metallic.

Hikari-Utsurimono Metallic *Utsuri* and *Showa*.

Hikarimono The classification for single-coloured metallic koi.

Hikarimoyo-mono A classification including all metallic koi with two or more colours, except metallic *Utsuri* and *Showa*.

Hon sumi Literally, 'genuine *sumi*', referring to the black *Sanke* markings on a *Koromo Sanke*.

Hoo Aka A koi with red gill plates. An early ancestor of the modern *Kohaku*.

Hookazuki A black carp with red cheeks. An early ancestor of the modern *Kohaku*.

I

Inazuma A zig-zag pattern.

Ippon hi A continuous pattern, without variation.

Iromono The collective name for all metallic koi.

K

Kabuto A cap or helmet, referring to koi with a head colour different from that on the body.

Kado Edge.

Kado-gin A form of *Kinginrin* where only the edges of the scales are iridescent.

Kage Literally, 'shadow' or 'phantom', referring to koi with a blurred, reticulated black pattern over the white or red.

Kage Hi Utsuri A koi whose red and black *utsuri* pattern is complemented by a *kage* pattern over the red. *(Kawarimono)*

Kage Shiro Utsuri A koi with the basic black and white *utsuri* pattern and *kage* pattern over the white. *(Kawarimono)*

Kage Showa A koi with the basic *showa* pattern and *kage* pattern over the white. *(Kawarimono)*

Kanoko Literally, 'fawn', referring to the dappled red pattern found on some koi. *(Kawarimono)*

Kanoko Kohaku A *Kohaku* with dappled red markings.

Kanoko Sanke A *Sanke* with dappled red markings.

Kanoko Showa A *Showa* with dappled red markings.

Karasu Literally 'crow'. Black (overall colour).

Karasugoi Black koi with white or orange bellies. *(Kawarimono)*

Kasane sumi *Sumi* that appears on the *hi*. (As opposed to *tsubo sumi*, which appears on the white skin.)

Kata moyo A pattern on only one side of the body.

Kawarimono A classification of all non-metallic koi not included in any other group.

Ki Yellow.

Ki Bekko A yellow koi with black markings. *(Bekko)*

Ki Matsuba A yellow koi with black 'pine-cone' *(matsuba)* markings in the centre of the scales. *(Kawarimono)*

Ki Shusui A yellow *Shusui* with a greenish dorsal. A very rare variety. *(Shusui)*

Ki Utsuri A black koi with yellow markings. *(Utsurimono)*

Ki-goi A non-metallic bright yellow koi. *(Kawarimono)*

Kikisui Literally, 'water crysanthemum'. Basically a *doistu* platinum *Kohaku*. *(Hikarimoyo-mono)*

Kin Metallic gold.

Kin Hi Utsuri A metallic *Hi Utsuri*. *(Hikari-Utsurimono)*

Kin Kabuto A black koi whose scales have gold edges. Now considered valueless.

Kin Ki Utsuri A metallic *Ki Utsuri*. *(Hikari-Utsurimono)*

Kin Showa A metallic *Showa* with a gold lustre. *(Hikari-Utsurimono)*

Kin-Fuji See *Platinum Kohaku*.

Kinbo A black koi with a gold metallic sheen. Now considered valueless.

Kindai Showa A *Showa* with a predominantly white pattern. *(Showa)*

Kinginrin A normally scaled koi that has gold or silvery mirror-like deposits on each scale.

Kinsui A metallic *Shusui* with a gold lustre. *(Hikarimoyo-mono)*

Kinzakura A metallic *Goten-zakura*. *(Hikarimoyo-mono)*

Kiwa The definition between *hi* and white markings.

Kohaku White koi with red markings.

Kokesuki Scales that are visible because the colour is thin.

Komoyo Small *hi* markings.

Konjo Asagi A dark blue fish. An early ancestor of the modern *Asagi*.

Koromo Literally 'robed', referring to a group of koi whose *hi* pattern is outlined in a darker colour.

Koromo Sanke A koi with the *koromo* reticulated pattern over the *hi* marking, and the *sumi* markings of a traditional *Sanke*. *(Koromo)*

Koromo Showa A koi with the markings of a *Showa* overlaid with the *koromo* pattern. *(Koromo)*

Koshi-nishiki The result of a cross between an *Ogon* and a *Sanke*. Now known as *Yamato-nishiki*.

Kuchibeni Red, lipstick-like markings.

Kujaku A platinum koi with *hi* markings covering a large proportion of the body and with *matsuba* patterning in the scales. *(Hikarimoyo-mono)*

Kujaku Ogon Another name for *Kujaku*.

Kumonryu Literally, 'dragon fish'. A black *doitsu* koi with white markings in the scales on its head, fins and body. *(Kawarimono)*

Kuro-Ki-Han The original name for *Shiro Utsuri*

M

Madoaki Scales with 'shadows' under the skin.

Magoi A black carp, an early ancestor of modern *nishikigoi*.

Makibara A red pattern that wraps around the body.

Maruten A koi with a separate red marking on the head (e.g. *Maruten Kohaku*). Also used to describe such a head marking (i.e. maruten spot/maruten).

Maruten Kohaku A *Kohaku* with a separate red marking on the head and additional red on the body.

Maruten Sanke A *Sanke* with a separate red marking on the head and additional red on the body.

Matsuba A koi with black markings in the centre of the scales on the body. This matsuba pattern is also known as a pine-cone pattern. Non-metallic Matsuba koi are classed in *Kawarimono*, metallic ones in *Hikarimono (Ogon)*.

Matsuba Ogon Another name for *Kin Matsuba*. *(Hikarimono)*

Matsukawa-bake A non-metallic black and white koi whose pattern changes with the time of year and water temperature. *(Kawarimono)*

Meija era A period in Japanese history, 1868-1912.

Menkaburi An early *Kohaku* with a red head.

Menware The traditional *Showa* head pattern, where the black pattern divides the red marking on the head.

Midori Green.

Midori-goi A very rare koi, bright green in colour, with black or silvery scales. *(Kawarimono)*

Mizu Asagi A very light *Asagi*.

Mono Single.

Moto Or 'original *sumi*', i.e. black markings that are apparent in fry and remain visible on the adult koi.

Muji Self-coloured (literally, 'nothing else').

N

Narumi Asagi The typical light-blue patterned *Asagi*. *(Asagi)*

Nezu Grey.

Nezu Ogon A silver grey koi with a dull metallic lustre. *(Hikarimono)*

Nezumi Grey.

Nibani Secondary *hi*, which appears and disappears depending on such factors as water condition and temperature.

Nidan Two.

Nidan Kohaku A *Kohaku* with two hi markings on its body. *(Kohaku)*

Niigata An area on the northwest coast of mainland Japan, the birthplace and pillar of the koi-breeding industry.

Nishikigoi Fancy or coloured koi (from 'nishiki', a beautiful, coloured linen, and 'goi', meaning fish).

O

Ochiba-shigure A blue-grey koi with a brown pattern. *(Kawarimono)*

Ogon Single-coloured metallic koi. *(Hikarimono)*

Omoyo Large hi markings.

Orenji Orange.

Orenji Hariwake A silver koi with metallic orange markings. *(Hikarimoyo-mono)*

Orenji Ogon A deep orange metallic koi. *(Hikarimono)*

P

Purachina A white metallic koi, also known as a *Platinum Ogon*. *(Hikarimono)*

Pearl Ginrin A solid sparkling area on each scale, also known as *Tsuba-gin* or *Tama-gin*.

Pearl Shusui A *Shusui* with silver scales. *(Shusui)*

Platinum Kohaku A metallic white koi with an overlaying *hi* pattern. Also known as *Kin-fuji*. *(Hikarimoyo-mono)*

Platinum Ogon A metallic white koi, also known as *Purachina*. *(Hikarimono)*

S

Sadazo Sanke One of the better-known *Sanke* lineages, with bright *hi* markings and small *sumi* markings that do not overlap the *hi*.

Sakura Ogon A metallic *Kanoko Kohaku*. *(Hikarimoyo-mono)*

Sandan Three.

Sandan Kohaku A *Kohaku* with three *hi* markings. *(Kohaku)*

Sanke Literally 'tri-colour'. White koi with red and black markings. (Referred to in early literature as *Sanshoku*.)

Sanke Shusui A *doitsu Sanke* whose pattern is underlaid with the blue back of the *Shusui*. *(Kawarimono)*

Sanshoku See *Sanke*.

Sarasa Red spots on the back.

Sashi The underlying black or red markings on a koi. These markings often stabilize when the koi is mature.

Shimis Small black specks, which sometimes spoil the appearance of the white or red markings of koi.

Shiro White.

Shiro Bekko A white koi with black markings. *(Bekko)*

Shiro Matsuba A white koi with a black 'pine cone' *(matsuba)* pattern in the scales on the back. *(Kawarimono)*

Shiro Utsuri A black koi with white markings. *(Utsurimono)*

Shiro-muji A white non-metallic koi. *(Kawarimono)*

Shirogane An early name for *Platinum Ogon*.

Shochikubai A metallic *Ai-goromo*. *(Hikarimoyo-mono)*

Showa Black koi with red and white markings.

Showa Shusui A koi with the strong *sumi* and pattern of a *Showa* and the underlying blue of a *Shusui*. *(Kawarimono)*

Shusui *Doitsu Asagi*.

Sora-goi A grey-blue, non-metallic koi. *(Kawarimono)*

Sui Water (rippling effect).

Sumi Black (markings).

Sumi-goromo An *Ai-goromo* whose *koromo* pattern is overlaid with solid black markings. *(Koromo)*

Sumi-nagashi A koi whose black scales are outlined in white.

T

Taisho era A period in Japanese history, 1912-26.

Taisho Sanke The full name of *Sanke*, which are white koi with red and black markings.

Taki Sanke An *Asagi* whose blue body colour is divided from the red markings on its sides by a white line. *(Sanke)*

Tama-gin See *Pearl Ginrin*.

Tancho A red spot on the head. (Used when the koi has no other red on the body, in contrast to 'maruten'.)

Tancho Kohaku A white koi with a red spot on the head. *(Tancho)*

Tancho Sanke A *Sanke* whose only red marking is a head spot. *(Tancho)*

Tancho Showa A *Showa* whose only red marking is a head spot. *(Tancho)*

Tobihi Small red markings, resembling splashes of paint.

Tora Ogon (Literally, 'tiger' Ogon.) An *Ogon* with black markings. *(Hikarimono)*

Tsubo sumi Black that appears on the white skin (as opposed to *Kasane sumi*, which appears on the red markings.)

Tsubu-gin See *Pearl Ginrin*.

U

Utsuri See *Utsurimono*.

Utsurimono Black koi with white, red or yellow markings.

Y

Yagozen A *Kohaku* lineage, developed in the 1950s.

Yamabuki Literally, a Japonica bush with pale yellow flowers.

Yamabuki Hariwake A silver koi with metallic yellow markings. *(Hikarimoyo-mono)*

Yamabuki Ogon A yellow-gold *Ogon*. *(Hikarimono)*

Yamato The result of a cross between a *Sanke* and a *Fuji Ogon*. One of the two varieties now known collectively as *Yamato-nishiki*.

Yamato-nishiki A metallic white koi with red and black markings, (basically a metallic *Sanke*).

Yondan Four.

Yondan Kohaku A *Kohaku* with four red body markings.

Yotsushiro Literally, 'five whites'. A black koi with white head, pectoral, dorsal and caudal fins. *(Kawarimono)*

Z

Zukinkaburi An early *Kohaku* with a red forehead.

総合索引
GENERAL INDEX

Page numbers in *italics* indicate captions to illustrations. Other text entries are shown in normal type.

種別索引
INDEX TO VARIETIES

種別索引
INDEX TO VARIETIES

写真提供
PICTURE CREDITS

Artists

Copyright of the artwork illustrations on the pages following the artist's name is the property of Salamander Books Ltd.

Bernice Brewster: 18-19(B)

Rod Ferring: 103, 104, 105, 106, 108

Bill Le Fever: 16-17, 19(T), 20-21, 25, 53, 62, 63, 74, 78, 82, 88, 94, 95, 96, 118, 125-198

Janos Marffy: 34, 35(T), 56

Ian Stead: 26, 29, 32, 35(B), 36, 40, 41, 42, 47, 51

Stuart Watkinson: 73, 75, 77, 79

Photographers

The publishers wish to thank the following photographers and agencies who have supplied photographs for this book. The photographers have been credited by page number and position on the page: (B)Bottom, (T)Top, (C)Centre, (BL)Bottom left etc.

Chris Andrews: 57, 73, 102(TR), 103, 105(C,B), 106(BR), 109(TC)

Heather Angel/Biofotos: 79

Bernice Brewster: 98-9, 101, 102(TC), 109(TR,C,B), 110(B), 111, 112

The British Museum: 12

James Chubb: 104(C), 105(CR), 106(CB), 107(TL), 108, 110(T)

Eric Crichton © Salamander Books: Endpapers, Title page, Copyright page, Contents page, 8-9, 22-3, 24, 27, 28, 30, 31, 32, 33, 35, 37(B), 42, 43, 44, 45, 46, 48-9, 51, 54(BL),

55(T), 56, 61, 62, 72, 76, 80-1, 82, 83, 84, 85, 86, 87, 88, 90(TR,B), 91(T), 97(B), 100, 114-5, 116, 117, 118, 120, 122-3

John Cuvelier: 37(T), 70-1, 74-5

Mark Davis: 13(B), 60(T), 92-3, 94

Garden Picture Library: 10-11(Elizabeth Wilkinson), 78(Derek Fell), 89(Ron Sutherland), 90(TL, Marijke Heuff)

Ideas into Print: 14-15

Jonathan Kelly © Salamander Books: 13(T), 54-5, 58-9, 60(B), 64-5, 66, 68-9, 77, 97(T), 139, 144, 147, 152, 153, 155, 158, 160-1, 161, 162, 165, 166, 167, 170, 172, 177, 180-1, 181, 187, 189, 192

Kent Koi Ko: Half title page, 104(B), 121, 124, 125, 128, 129, 131, 133, 134, 135, 137, 138, 141, 142, 143, 145, 148, 149, 151, 154, 156, 157, 163, 168, 169, 171, 173, 175, 176, 178, 179, 182, 183,

184, 185, 188, 191, 193, 201

M. R. Lewis: 34, 38, 39, 41

Peter W. Scott: 107(TC,BR), 113

Harry Smith Horticultural Photographic Collection: 91(B)

Stonecastle Graphics: 50, 52

Acknowledgements

The publishers wish to thank the following individuals and organizations for their help in the preparation of this book:

Chris Ball, Mrs Barret, Nigel Caddock, Stuart Craik (indexes), Philip Edwards, Brian Garner, G.A. Grant, Brian Harman, Kent Koi Ko., Graham Lowe, Alan Mann, Mitaka (Japanese typesetting), Panache (headline setting), Gregory Peck, Mary Riddoch, Peter Tebby, Ken Waterhouse, Helga Watson, World of Koi.

Hyperspace

Hyperspace
our final frontier

John Gribbin

This book is published to accompany the television series *Space*
which was produced by the BBC and was first broadcast in 2001.
Creative Director: John Lynch
Executive producer: Emma Swain
Series producer: Richard Burke-Ward

Published by BBC Worldwide Limited,
Woodlands, 80 Wood Lane, London W12 0TT

First published 2001

First US edition published in 2001 by

DK Publishing, Inc.
95 Madison Avenue
New York, New York 10016

ISBN: 0-7894-7838-2

Commissioning Editor: Joanne Osborn
Project Editor: Helena Caldon
Academic Consultant: Dr Margaret Penston
Design concept: The Attik
Art Direction: Pene Parker, Lisa Pettibone
Art Editor: Kathy Gammon
Design: Bobby Birchall, DW Design, London
Picture Research: Carmen Jones and Miriam Hyman
Illustrations: Mark McLellan and Kevin Jones Associates

Set in Albertina MT and Gill Sans
Printed and bound in Great Britain by Butler & Tanner Ltd, Frome
Colour separations by Radstock Reproductions Ltd, Midsomer Norton
Jacket printed by Lawrence Allen Ltd, Weston-super-Mare

Contents

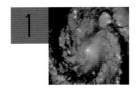

ACROSS THE UNIVERSE   8

Astronomers only began to understand the way the Universe works once they developed techniques to measure distances across the Universe. Without a knowledge of distances, they had no way to measure the sites and brightening of stars and galaxies.

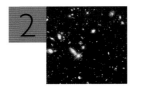

THE FATE OF THE UNIVERSE   76

Will the Universe expand forever? Or will it one day collapse into a black hole? Nobody knows the answer, but 21st century cosmologists at least know where to look for it.

MAKING CONTACT

136

Are we alone in the Universe? Astronomers can now estimate the chances that there are other forms of life out there. But even if there is life, is there any other intelligent life?

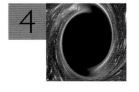

OTHER WORLDS

182

How special is the Universe? It seems to be just right for life forms like us. But is that because it is designed for our convenience, or because we have evolved to fit it?

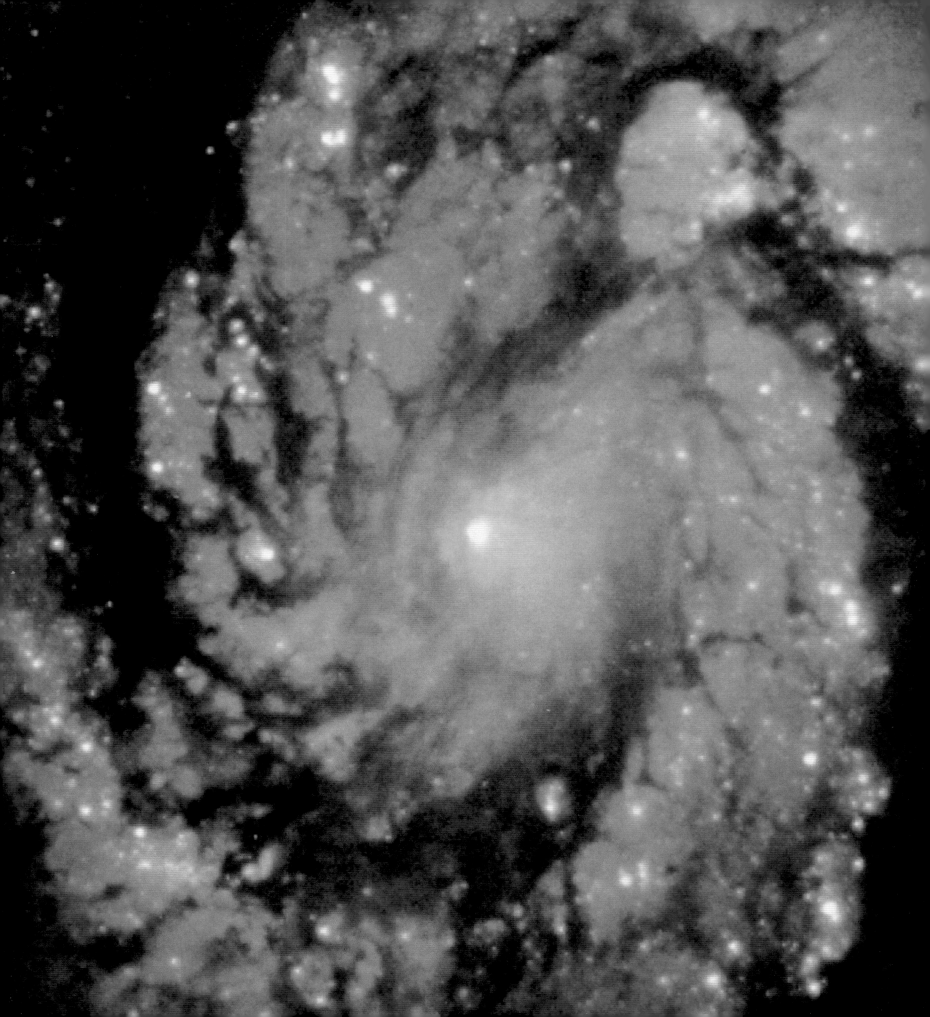

1

ACROSS THE UNIVERSE

STEPPING STONES TO THE UNIVERSE

The travellers in *Star Trek* boldly go where no one has gone before to explore the final frontier – space. No human has yet visited any object outside our own Solar System, but that has not stopped us exploring new worlds – at long range, using telescopes on the surface of the Earth and satellite-based instruments orbiting above the atmosphere. The data from these observations are then compared with what we can infer about stars and galaxies from the laws of physics. In astronomy, theory and observation always go hand in hand – a theory about stars is useless without observations to test the predictions of the theory, and observations of a startling new phenomenon remain a mystery until they can be understood within the frameworks of a theory about the Universe. Together, theory and observation can take us on a journey to the furthest reaches of the Universe, and back in time to when the Universe was born.

Previous page. A spiral galaxy, like the Milky Way in which we live.

MAKING MAPS OF SPACE

Astronomers are interested in the evolution of stars and galaxies (how these objects are born, live and die), and in tracing the origin and ultimate fate of the entire Universe. Putting this type of knowledge together with a knowledge of the distances between cosmic objects enables astronomers to achieve an understanding of their domain similar to a naturalist's understanding of the world – the equivalent of combining biology with geography, and finding out what different kinds of creatures live in different parts of the world.

By studying the light emitted by stars and galaxies, astronomers are able to find out what different kinds of objects exist in different parts of the Universe. But they also need to measure the distances to cosmic objects, so they know where they are in relation to one another. And how can the distances to stars and galaxies that we have no hope of ever visiting, even with an unmanned space probe, be measured? It sounds like an impossible task, but astronomers have found 'stepping stones' that effectively take them from Earth to the furthest reaches of the Universe.

It's all Done with Triangles

As the Chinese proverb says, the longest journey begins with a single step; and the geographical exploration of the Universe starts with a simple piece of geometry involving triangles.

The first step into the Universe uses exactly the same kind of surveying techniques used here on Earth to measure the distances to distant objects (such as mountains) without actually having to go there. The idea itself is not new, but with the aid of new instruments here on Earth and satellites orbiting above the Earth it reaches further than ever before.

It all depends on the geometry of triangles. If you know the length of one side of a triangle (the base) and you can measure the angle each of the other two sides makes with the base, then it is a simple matter to calculate how far it is from the base of the triangle to

1

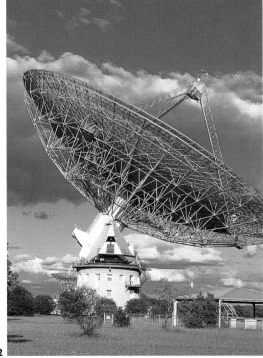

2

1. Human beings have only visited our nearest neighbour in space, the Moon.

2. Exploration of deep space relies on remote observing using instruments such as radio telescopes.

the opposite tip. The process is called triangulation, for obvious reasons.

The trouble with triangulation is that you need a longer baseline to measure the distances to more distant objects.

The Importance of Parallax

Triangulation is not restricted to measuring distances on Earth – it works very well for measuring the distance to our nearest neighbour in space, the Moon. If one observer sees the Moon directly overhead, for example, while another observer, standing on what is the horizon for the first observer, also measures the angle it is in the sky, then it is easy to work out the distance to the Moon – about 384,000 km – from the geometry of triangles.

This is possible because the Moon appears in a different part of the sky to the two observers. It is exactly the same as the way you can make your index finger jump across a distant background if you hold your arm straight out in front of you, point your finger upwards, and look at it with each eye closed in turn. The slightly different views from your two eyes give you different perspectives on your finger; and the slightly different views from two observatories give different perspectives on the Moon. The effect is called 'parallax', and for our two observers it shifts the apparent position of the Moon nearly twice the diameter of the full Moon on the night sky.

But the distant stars are so far away that the background pattern looks the same from anywhere on Earth, and this makes it convenient to measure parallax by measuring how far the Moon (in this case) seems to shift against the fixed background of stars.

MAPPING THE EARTH

Triangulation is a technique that can be used to measure distances to distant objects. A map-maker can plot the location of a hill on a map by first measuring out a baseline, perhaps a kilometre or so long then, using small telescopes (called theodolites), measuring the angle between the baseline and the hilltop – from both ends of the baseline. Using these angles, and knowing the length of the baseline, the map-maker can now calculate the lengths of the other two sides of the triangle, and thus how far the hill is from the baseline. The distance from one end of the first baseline to the hilltop can be used as a new baseline to measure other distances. You can use this process repeatedly to work your way across the surface of the Earth. Indeed, although the technique has now been superseded by satellite mapping, triangulation was used by nineteenth-century surveyors to map India, starting at the southern tip and working their way northward to the Himalayas.

Beyond the Moon

Triangulation and parallax have also been used to measure the distances to the nearest planets, Venus and Mars. This is much harder than measuring the distance to the Moon, because the planets are much further away. It involves making observations from opposite sides of the Earth at the same time, then calculating the geometry of a very tall, thin triangle.

The parallax of Mars was determined accurately in 1671, when the French astronomer Jean Richer led an expedition to French Guyana (in South America) to measure the position of Mars against the background stars at a certain time on an appointed night (actually several nights, to allow for cloud).

On the same nights and at the same times, back in Paris, the Italian-born astronomer Giovanni Cassini also made observations of the position of Mars against the background stars. When Richer's expedition returned, the two teams compared notes and calculated the distance to Mars.

Law-abiding Planets

These measurements were particularly important, because they made it possible to work out the geography of the entire Solar System.

The laws which describe the motion of the planets around the Sun were described early in the seventeenth century by Johannes Kepler, and explained by Isaac Newton with his theory of gravity. They state that, if planet A is twice as far from the Sun as planet B, then the orbital period of planet A (the time it takes to go round the sun: its 'year') is a certain multiple of the orbital period of planet B.

Astronomers thus had to measure at least one planetary distance directly in order to put real numbers into the equations, even though they already knew the orbital periods for the planets. By measuring the distance to just

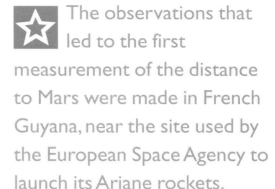

The observations that led to the first measurement of the distance to Mars were made in French Guyana, near the site used by the European Space Agency to launch its Ariane rockets.

2

1. Triangulation and the parallax effect.

2. Once astronomers had determined the sizes of galaxies, they could even use triangulation to estimate the distances between them from how small the galaxies look on the sky.

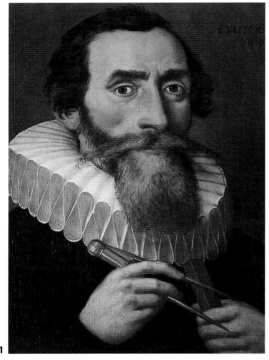

1 and 3. Johannes Kepler discovered the laws of planetary motion by studying the orbit of Mars (right).

2. Kepler's key discovery was that planets in their orbits trace out equal areas in equal times.

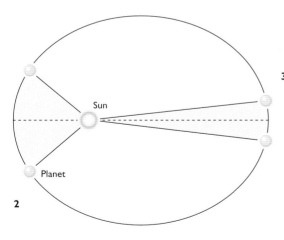

Venus and Mars, they were able to calculate the distance from the Sun to each of these planets. Once they knew these distances, they were able to use Kepler's laws to calculate the distance from the Sun to all the other planets in the Solar System – including the Earth. In addition, they could use Newton's laws to calculate what the mass of the Sun must be to hold the planets in these orbits through gravity.

By the end of the seventeenth century, astronomers were able to calculate the distance from the Earth to the Sun fairly accurately. The observations have been improved since then (we can even measure the distance to Venus directly, by bouncing radar signals off it), and the distance from the Earth to the Sun is now known to be 149.6 million kilometres (almost 4000 times the distance around the equator of the Earth). But even 200 years ago, the calculated distance was 140 million km – an error of less than 7 per cent compared with the modern figure.

STEPPING STONES TO THE STARS

It takes the Earth 12 months to orbit the Sun once. The radius of the Earth's orbit – the distance from the Earth to the Sun – is roughly 150 million km. This distance is called the Astronomical Unit, or AU. It is vitally important in astronomy, because it provides a new baseline with which to measure parallaxes for more distant objects – the nearest stars.

At intervals 6 months apart, the Earth is at opposite sides of a diameter measuring 2 AU (about 300 million km). This is such a long baseline that in photographs of the night sky taken 6 months apart a few of the stars seem to have shifted their position slightly, because of the parallax effect. But the shift is very slight, because the stars are so very far away. To give you some idea how small the effect is, in the 1830s the first star studied in this way (known as 61 Cygni) was found to have a parallax shift of just 0.31 seconds of arc. (There are 360 degrees in a circle, 60 minutes in a degree, and 60 seconds in a minute.) In comparison, the full Moon covers 30 seconds of arc on the sky. So the apparent shift in 61

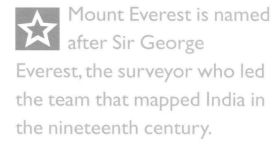
Mount Everest is named after Sir George Everest, the surveyor who led the team that mapped India in the nineteenth century.

4. We live in a spiral galaxy like this one (M65) containing hundreds of billions of stars like the Sun.

4

1

Cygni as the Earth goes round the Sun is equivalent to about one-six-thousandth of the apparent diameter of the Moon.

The distances to the stars are so great that astronomers had to invent new units with which to describe them. If you were so far away from Earth that the distance between the Earth and the Sun (the radius of the Earth's orbit, 1 AU) covered just one second of arc on the sky, then you would be one parsec away from Earth (the term 'parsec' is a contraction of 'parallax second of arc'). A parsec is just over 30 million million kilometres, a number so big that it is hard to visualize – but you can look at it in terms of the speed of light. Light travels at just under 300,000 km per second, and so covers 9.46 million million km in a year, a distance known as a light year. So a parsec is 3.26 light years. Converting the parallax measurement into distance, we find that 61 Cygni is 3.4 parsecs away, or just over 11 light years from us. And, amazingly, this makes it one of the closest stars to our Sun.

Stars Like Dust

When you look up at the sky on a dark and cloud-free night, it seems to contain countless numbers of stars, and poets have waxed lyrical about the view. But the human eye is not very sensitive to faint light: even under perfect conditions, with no Moon or cloud, and far from city lights, the most you can see at any one time is about 3000 stars. Under more ordinary viewing conditions, you are lucky to see a thousand.

The true numbers of stars in the sky only began to be appreciated at the beginning of the seventeenth century, when Galileo Galilei turned his telescope onto the night sky. He found that, what seemed to be a faintly glowing cloud of light was actually a myriad of individual stars, each too faint to be seen by the unaided human eye. He announced his discoveries in a book, *The Starry Messenger*, which was published in 1610.

At that time there was no accurate way to estimate the distances to the vast majority of these stars. Until very recently, only a few stellar distances had been measured directly by parallax. By the end of the nineteenth century, just 60 stellar distances had been measured in this way. At the end of the twentieth century, the situation improved dramatically when the HIPPARCOS satellite, orbiting clear of the obscuring influence of the Earth's atmosphere, measured the distances to a large number of stars with unprecedented accuracy. It pinned down the parallaxes of more than 100,000 stars, to an accuracy of 0.002 seconds of arc. But even this impressive achievement gives the distances to less than one-millionth of the total number of stars in the Milky Way, taking the range of directly measured stellar distances out to a few hundred parsecs (about a thousand light years).

1. The satellite HIPPARCOS, shown here being tested prior to launch, measured the distances to the stars with unprecedented accuracy.

2. The Hyades star cluster and the smaller cluster known as the Pleiades.

Colour, Brightness and Distance

So even with the aid of satellites like HIPPARCOS, astronomers still need other techniques to measure distances to stars outside our local region of space. The most important of these techniques is called the 'moving cluster' method. It gives the distance to a large group of stars, called the Hyades Cluster. These stars are about 40 parsecs (130 light years) away from us, and all move as a group through space (HIPPARCOS has, now, also confirmed the distance to this cluster). Because this cluster contains hundreds of stars with different colours and brightnesses, the fact that they are all at the same distance away helps astronomers to understand how brightness is related to the colour of the light emitted, in subtle ways. The colour of a star has no relation to its distance: it's the brightness that tells us how far away it is. Then, when they

▷ THE STARS ARE SUNS

The Sun is a star or, to put it another way, the stars are suns. Scientists only began to appreciate this in the seventeenth century, and even then they found it hard to believe. Isaac Newton, for example, calculated that if the star Sirius is really as bright as our Sun, then to appear as faint as it does in the sky it must be a million times farther away from us than the Sun. Newton was more or less right, but he was so discomfited by this calculation that he never published it during his lifetime (it appeared in a book, *System of the World*, published in 1728, the year after Newton died). Yet Sirius is actually one of our nearest stellar neighbours, only 2.67 parsecs (8.7 light years) away.

We now know that the Sun is a very ordinary star. It is neither particularly large nor particularly small, not unusually hot nor unusually cool, and it is roughly halfway through its life. This is disappointing for people who like to think that there is something special about our place in the Universe. But it raises a much more exciting possibility. If the Sun is an ordinary star, then it seems likely that other stars like the Sun will have families of planets orbiting them like the Solar System. Could it be that as well as being ordinary in every other way, the Sun is quite typical in having a family of planets that includes a home suitable for life? If so, there may be literally billions of other Earths out there in the Milky Way Galaxy.

SPECTROSCOPY: THE KEY TO ASTRONOMY

The single most important tool of astronomers is the ability to analyze starlight and discover what stars are made of. This depends on the fact that atoms of any particular chemical element radiate energy (if they are hot) or absorb energy (if they are cold) at very precise wavelengths in the rainbow spectrum of light. Each element produces its own distinctive set of lines in the spectrum when radiating or absorbing energy, yielding a pattern similar to a barcode. And, like a barcode, each pattern is unique.

2

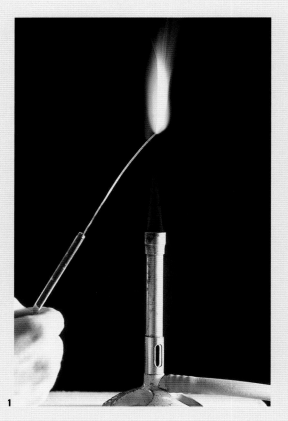

1

The Flame Test

We know which spectroscopic 'barcode' corresponds to a particular element because the light emitted by elements has been studied using simple flame tests. A sample of a known element (perhaps a piece of copper wire) is heated (often using a simple Bunsen burner) and the light it radiates when it is heated is passed through a triangular prism. This spreads the light out and produces a pattern of lines that is unique to that element. By repeating this test with many substances, a huge library of patterns has been built up, and an unknown substance can be identified by examining its spectroscopic pattern and comparing it with the patterns in the library.

Spectroscopy was invented in the middle of the nineteenth century, but there were many gaps in this library of knowledge, which still needed much investigation to fill. The first person to notice that light from the Sun, when passed through a prism to make a spectrum, contained many distinct lines was the British physicist William Wollaston, in 1802. But he had no idea what they were. In 1814, the German Josef von Fraunhofer counted 574 lines in the spectrum produced by light from the Sun, and discovered many of the same lines in light from the stars. But the person who explained that these lines were caused by the presence of different elements in the atmospheres of stars was Gustav Kirchoff. He pioneered the basic principles of scientific spectroscopy in collaboration with Robert Bunsen in Germany at the end of the 1850s.

Secrets of Sunlight

Spectroscopic studies of the light from the Sun's atmosphere, obtained during an eclipse in 1868, showed a distinctive pattern of lines which did not correspond to any known element. The British astronomer Norman Lockyer concluded that there must be an element in the Sun that had never been found on Earth, and gave it the name helium, from helios, the Greek word for the Sun. Helium was actually identified on Earth in 1895, and Lockyer received a knighthood (partly as a result of his famous prediction) in 1897. Spectroscopy had actually found an element in our nearest star before it had been found on Earth.

Moving Stars

There is one other vitally important use of spectroscopy in astronomy. Although the lines corresponding to a particular element are always produced at the same distinctive wavelengths, if the object making the lines is moving, the whole barcode pattern is shifted across the spectrum. If the object is moving towards us, the lines are shifted to shorter wavelengths. Because blue light has shorter wavelengths than red light, this is called a

'blueshift'. Similarly, if the object is moving away from us, the pattern is shifted towards longer wavelengths, a 'redshift'. This is known as the Doppler effect, and it enables astronomers to measure how fast stars are moving through space, how fast galaxies are rotating, and how fast stars in binary systems (where two stars orbit around each other) are moving in their orbits. The last application is particularly useful, because it is a key (along with the law of gravity) to measuring the masses of the stars involved.

So spectroscopy tells us what stars are made of, how fast they are moving, and what mass they have. Without spectroscopy, there would be little more to astronomy than making pretty patterns called constellations out of the arrangement of stars on the night sky.

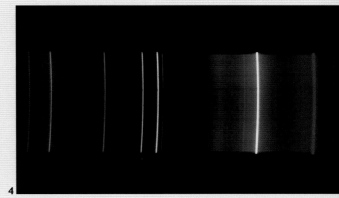

4

1. A bunsen burner being used to heat copper wire in a flame test

2. Solar corona - an ultraviolet image of the sun's outer atmosphere taken by the SOHO satellite. On the left is a prominence being absorbed after a solar flare event.

3. The Stephen's Quartet group of galaxies and NGC 7320. Colour coding shows the different red shift values of the quartet members.

4. The distinctive fingerprint of coloured lines is clearly shown here in the light from hot Helium gas.

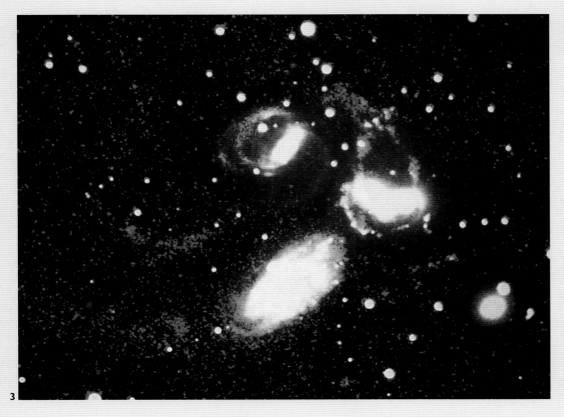

3

see a star with the same colour as one of the types of Hyades stars, they can estimate its distance by comparing its brightness (or faintness) with the Hyades star. Crucially, the subtle differences in the colour of the stars involved are revealed by a technique called spectroscopy – probably the single most important tool used by astronomers.

The result of applying such methods is that we now have a clear idea of distances between stars, and also of their sizes. The distance from one star to even its nearest neighbours is usually tens of millions of times its own diameter (except, of course, for systems where two or more stars orbit around one another). For example, the Sun has a diameter of 1.39 million km (which is typical for a star during the main period of its life). If the Sun were the size of an aspirin, on this scale the nearest star would be another aspirin 140 km away. The distances between stars are absolutely enormous – even compared with the huge sizes of the stars themselves.

AN ISLAND IN SPACE

By using every possible technique for measuring distances to stars, astronomers have been able to map the collection of stars in which we live, an island in space called the Milky Way Galaxy, or just the Galaxy. This is rather like trying to map a forest from the inside by working out the distances and relative positions of the trees in all different directions. The process is aided by the fact that, in parts of the Galaxy, there are great clouds of gas and dust between the stars. These clouds contain large amounts of hydrogen, which can be detected by radio telescopes.

The overall shape of our Galaxy is a flattened disc containing hundreds of billions of stars, all more or less the same as our Sun, with a diameter of about 28 thousand parsecs (28 kiloparsecs). The disc is only 300 parsecs thick at its outer regions (roughly 1 per cent as thick as its width), but it has a bulge in the middle measuring 7 kiloparsecs across and 1 kiloparsec thick. If we could view our Galaxy from the outside it would look rather like a huge fried egg.

Surrounding the whole disc is a halo of about 150 known bright star systems called globular clusters. Each globular cluster is a ball of stars containing hundreds of thousands, or even millions, of individual

If you take a deep breath, you will have more molecules of air in your lungs than there are stars in all the galaxies in the visible universe put together.

1. An impression of the number of stars in our galaxy is given by this picture of part of the Milky Way.

2. The Milky Way has been mapped using star clusters.

3. Our Milky Way Galaxy is a flattened disc of stars embedded in a halo of globular clusters.

stars, so close to one another that there may be 1000 stars in a single cubic parsec of space. From the way stars move, astronomers also infer that there is a great deal of dark matter (material that has mass but cannot be detected directly ▷ p. 96) surrounding the whole Galaxy and holding it in a gravitational grip.

Stars in Spiral Patterns

Viewed from above, our Galaxy has a distinctive structure, with bright trails of stars, called 'spiral arms', twining outwards from the central bulge. This is a very common feature of disc galaxies like the Milky Way, so much so that they are sometimes referred to as spiral galaxies. The most important distinction between the central bulge and the disc proper, however, is that the stars in the bulge (and the globular cluster stars in the halo surrounding the Galaxy) are all old stars. They are perhaps 12 billion years old and are known, for historical reasons, as Population II stars. There is also very little gas or dust in the bulge. The disc, where the spiral arms twine outwards, contains gas and dust and some old stars, but also middle-aged stars and very young ones, which are known as Population I stars (the Sun is a Population I star). New stars are still being formed in the disc all the time.

All the stars in the disc, together with the gas and dust, orbit around the centre of the Galaxy. But the disc does not rotate as if it were a solid object (the way a CD rotates as it is played). Each star moves independently – just as each planet in our Solar System orbits around the Sun independently – and the stars closer to the centre move faster than those near the edge of the disc. The Sun is travelling at a speed of about 250 km per second in its own orbit around the centre of the disc, carrying our Solar System with it; but the Galaxy is so large that even at this speed it takes our Solar System about 225 million years to complete just one orbit, a journey it has made about 20 times since it was born some 4.5 billion years ago.

The Sun and its family of planets orbits the Galaxy at a distance of about 9 kiloparsecs from the centre, two-thirds of the way out to the edge of the disc, on the inside edge of a feature known as the Orion Arm. We are not in the centre; there is nothing particularly special about our place in the Milky Way Galaxy.

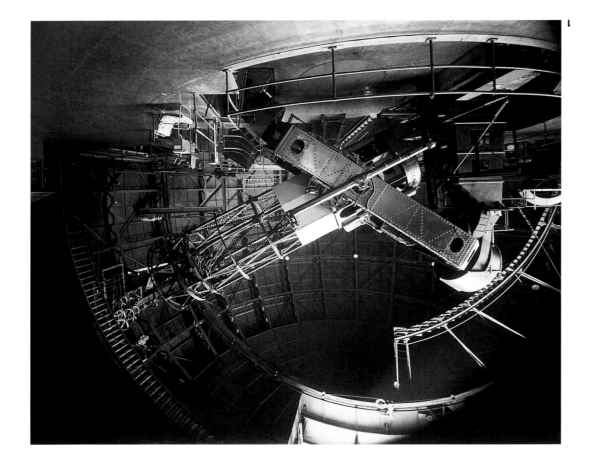

1. The Hooker telescope – used in working out the size of our galaxy.

2. Supernova 1987A,
a huge stellar explosion
photographed in
March 1987.

A MATTER OF PERSPECTIVE

The size and shape of the Milky Way Galaxy were only really described properly in the 1920s. Before then, most people thought that the stars they could see in the sky made up the entire Universe – everything there was to see. But as well as revealing a myriad of stars in the Milky Way, telescopes also showed up faint patches of light in the sky, fuzzy blobs called 'nebulae'. At the same time that astronomers started to appreciate and understand the geography of the Milky Way, some of them began to wonder whether these nebulae might be other islands in space, galaxies like

the Milky Way, but so far away from us that the light from the stars they contained only added up to a faint patch of light like a little cloud on the night sky. This suggestion caused a fierce debate among astronomers at the time, because it would mean that the other galaxies were at enormous distances from us, hundreds or even thousands of kiloparsecs away. This was hard to accept when astronomers had only just discovered that the Milky Way itself was several tens of kiloparsecs across, bigger than anything previously imagined. The other possibility was that the nebulae were indeed glowing clouds of gas within the Milky Way itself, between the stars.

The only way to find out whether the nebulae were actually galaxies was to identify individual stars within them and measure their distances directly. They would be too far away for triangulation to work; but by the 1920s astronomers knew that some kinds of exploding star (called novae) all have about the same brightness, while another kind of star (called 'Cepheids') have a brightness that can be inferred from their other properties. If you know the true brightness of a star, it is easy to work out how far away it is by measuring how bright it appears. So if the astronomers could identify novae and Cepheids in nebulae, they would be able to work out roughly how far away they were.

1. A galaxy like the Milky Way is made up of a central bulge of stars surrounded by a thinner disk.

2. (opposite) The Sun and the Moon both look the same size from the Earth even though the Sun is really much bigger than the Moon. In the same way, galaxies look tiny on the sky because they are so far away.

Beyond the Milky Way

The astronomer who made the crucial measurements was Edwin Hubble. He identified both Cepheids and novae in nebulae that are now known to be the closest galaxies

It turned out to be just possible to make the crucial measurements for stars in some of these nebulae in the 1920s, using what was then the best telescope in the world. The telescope (still in use today) has a 100-inch diameter mirror, and is called the Hooker Telescope, after the benefactor who paid for it. It is located on top of Mount Wilson, near Pasadena, in California.

But it turned out that not all of the nebulae were other galaxies. Some of them really were clouds of gas and dust within the Milky Way, and these objects play an important part in the life cycles of stars and the origin of planetary systems like the Solar System. In order to avoid confusion, astronomers kept the name nebulae for the clouds within the Milky Way, and used the term 'galaxy' to refer to the great star systems beyond the Milky Way. Even with the 100-inch Hooker telescope, it was very difficult to make the observations needed to calculate the distances to galaxies. When Hubble first began to make

If each star were represented by a single grain of rice, a scale model of the Milky Way galaxy would just fit into the gap between the earth and the Moon.

measurements of the distances involved, he found that, although the other galaxies did indeed lie beyond the Milky Way, they did not seem to be as big as ours. It's all a matter of perspective. One of the few things we can actually measure is the area a galaxy covers on the sky. A small galaxy close up will cover the same area as a big galaxy further away, in just the same way that if you hold a small model of a cow up in front of your eye, it looks as big as a real cow on the other side of a field. In the same way, the Moon completely covers the Sun during a total solar eclipse because, although the Sun is almost 400 times bigger than the Moon, it is also almost 400 times further away and so it appears to be the same size.

As telescopes got better and better, astronomers were able to measure the distances to other galaxies more and more accurately. They used many different stepping stones, not only Cepheids and novae, but also comparisons of the brightness of things such as globular clusters in one galaxy with those in another. After more than half a century of effort, they found that the galaxies were about 10 times further away than Hubble had thought, so it followed that they must be that much bigger than he had thought in order to look as large as they did on the sky.

However, Cepheids and novae are still the best indicators of distance. In the 1990s, using Cepheid distances obtained from the Hubble Space Telescope, a team at the University of Sussex finally showed that the Milky Way Galaxy is an average galaxy of its type (if anything it's a little bit smaller than the average disc galaxy in our part of the Universe). Like our position in it, there is nothing special about the Milky Way Galaxy.

Putting Galaxies in Perspective

The result of all these efforts is a clear understanding of the sizes of galaxies and the distances between them.

As well as disc (spiral) galaxies like the Milky Way, there are much larger, elliptical galaxies, which do not have a disc or spiral shape, but are ellipsoidal (like a rugby ball). These are thought to have been built up by a kind of cosmic cannibalism, from mergers between disc galaxies.

There are also smaller elliptical galaxies (resembling the globular clusters ▷ pp. 21-2) and small irregular galaxies which have no distinct shape. The largest elliptical galaxies contain several thousand billion stars. Disc galaxies, such as the Milky Way, have diameters of a few tens of kiloparsecs and contain a few hundred billion stars.

Galaxies are much closer together, relative to their own size, than the stars are to one another. Again, it's a matter of perspective. If we adapt the aspirin analogy to galaxies, and represent the Milky Way by a single aspirin, we find that the nearest large disc galaxy to us, the Andromeda Galaxy, would be represented by another aspirin just 13 centimetres away. And only 3 metres away we would find a huge collection of about 2000 aspirins, spread over the volume of a basketball, representing a group of galaxies known as the Virgo Cluster. On a scale where a single aspirin represents the Milky Way Galaxy, the entire observable Universe would be only a kilometre across, and would contain hundreds of billions of aspirin. In terms of galaxies, the Universe is a crowded place.

1. Most galaxies are grouped together in associations that are called clusters. This is the centre of the Virgo cluster of galaxies, which is a crucial stepping-stone into the Universe at large.

THE CEPHEID SCALE

Variable stars called Cepheids are the key to measuring distances across the Universe. Each Cepheid goes through a very regular periodic change in brightness; some have periods as short as a day, some take 50 days or so, others run through their cycle between these extremes. While they are interesting in themselves, their importance in astronomy derives from the fact that the Cepheids provide a vital stepping stone to the Universe – they give us accurate distances to the nearest galaxies.

Cepheids are large, yellow stars which have an intrinsic brightness between 300 and 26,000 times that of the Sun. They are typically between 14 and 200 times the size of the Sun. The change in brightness of a Cepheid is associated with a rhythmic pulsation, as if it is breathing in and out. A Cepheid is faintest when its outer layer has expanded to its maximum size and has cooled down, and brightest when the outer layer has contracted to its minimum size and is hotter.

First Steps
In the early years of the twentieth century, Henrietta Swan Leavitt was working at Harvard College Observatory, studying Cepheids in a star system called the Small Magellanic Cloud (which we now know to be a small irregular galaxy in orbit around the Milky Way). She noticed that the brighter a Cepheid is, the more slowly it goes through its cycle.

This showed up clearly for Cepheids in the Small Magellanic Cloud because the cloud is so far away from us that the distance from one side of the cloud to the other is such a small fraction of the distance to the cloud, that all the stars in it can be regarded as being at the same distance from us.

So if one Cepheid star looks twice as bright as another, it really is twice as bright, not just closer to us.

Stellar Street Lights
Leavitt's discovery of the relationship between brightness and period for Cepheids

meant that they could be used to measure relative distances within the Milky Way. The period–luminosity relationship might tell you that one Cepheid is intrinsically twice as bright (say) as another, and comparing their apparent brightnesses on the sky would then reveal their relative distances from us. But in order to use this information to measure actual distances across the Milky Way, the distances to at least a few Cepheids had to be measured directly.

At first, this proved possible for just a handful of Cepheids; but crucially there were stars in the Hyades Cluster, whose distance could be measured, that are similar to stars in clusters that contain Cepheids. These provided the calibration, so that the distance to any Cepheid could be worked out simply by measuring its period, calculating its intrinsic brightness, and comparing that with its apparent brightness. The technique only just worked, even as late as the 1980s, because there were only 18 Cepheids with reliably determined distances. However, data from the HIPPARCOS satellite, which became available

1. Henrietta Swan Leavitt, who discovered the value of Cepheid stars as distance indicators.

2. The small Magellanic Cloud lies 20,000 light years away from us and contains many Cepheid variables.

3. Everybody who lives in the Northern Hemisphere has seen at least one Cepheid variable – the bright star in this picture.

4. If we know how bright a star really is we can work out its distance from us by judging how faint it looks – just like street lights.

in the 1990s, provided direct distance measurements to some Cepheids, and improved the accuracy of the distance measurement for the Hyades Cluster, so that the Cepheid distance scale is more solidly based now than ever before.

Into the Universe

Other objects within the same galaxies (most notably supernova explosions) can now be calibrated for brightness against the Cepheid distance scale. Because supernovae are so bright, they can be used as distance indicators in galaxies far, far away.

⬥ TOPIC LINKS

1.1 Stepping Stones to the Universe
p. 24 Beyond the Milky Way

2.1 The Big Bang
p. 80 Beyond the Local Group

2.2 Cosmology for Beginners
p. 95 Einstein's geometry

Stars are not born in isolation, but in nurseries that may contain thousands or even millions of stars forming together. No astronomer has been able to watch a single individual star being born, but because we see stars in all stages of the process, it is possible to work out how it happens. In the same way, an alien visitor to Earth could work out the life cycle of a human being without waiting to watch an individual person being born, living and dying, but by studying a large group of people where all stages of the life cycle are present.

Fortunately for astronomy, our Solar System is located in a densely populated part of the Galaxy, close to a stellar nursery where new stars are being born all the time. This is the Orion Nebula. The nebula is visible through a small telescope or binoculars as a faint patch of light just below the belt of the constellation Orion, the Hunter.

THE ORION NURSERY

The constellation of Orion, the Hunter, is one of the most familiar in the sky. If you look carefully just below the three stars that form Orion's belt, you can see a fuzzy patch of light, which is called the Orion Nebula (it is quite clearly visible with a decent pair of binoculars). This nebula is typical of the clouds of gas and dust that are scattered throughout the disc of the Milky Way Galaxy and are particularly associated with the spiral arms. Most of the known nebulae can only be identified with the aid of telescopes, but the Orion Nebula is visible to the naked eye because it is so close to us, a mere 1500 light years (about 460 parsecs) away.

Because it is so close, when large astronomical instruments, such as the Hubble Space Telescope, are turned on the nebula, they show its structure in spectacular detail, and reveal the presence of hundreds of newly formed, hot young stars. These light up the nebula from within and make the glow that we can see with our unaided eyes or binoculars.

Although the Orion Nebula looks spectacular because it is so close, it is important to appreciate that it is not special in any way; it is typical of the kind of stellar nursery in which new stars are being born in our Galaxy all the time. The Orion Nebula is about 20 light years (16 parsecs) across, and contains four big, bright stars forming a pattern of stars called the Trapezium and many hundreds of smaller stars more or less the same as the Sun was just after it was born.

Turning up the Stellar Heat

Stars start to form in a gas cloud like the Orion Nebula because such clouds cannot be perfectly smooth and uniform. Some parts of the cloud are inevitably more dense than

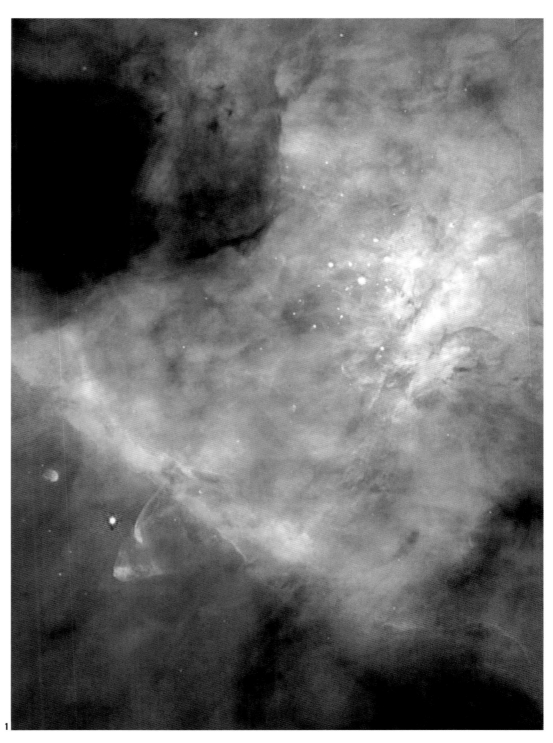

1. The great nebula in Orion is a region where new stars are forming today.

1. The shape of these dark fingers of gas and dust in the Eagle nebula has been sculpted by radiation from young stars. Each finger is about one light year long.

2. Gas in the Orion nebula reflects the blue light of hot young stars.

others, and begin to attract material to themselves and collapse through the attraction of gravity. The more dense such a clump becomes, the stronger its gravitational influence becomes, and the more it attracts material from its surroundings.

As this proto-star collapses, it gets hot inside. This heat makes the young star begin to glow, and the heat clears a bubble of more or less empty space around it within the nebula. At first, the heat of the young star comes from the gravitational energy liberated during its

collapse. But when the temperature at the heart of the star reaches a little more than 10 million degrees Celsius, the nuclei of hydrogen atoms can begin to fuse together to make new helium atoms. This can only happen if the proto-star has more than about one-tenth of the mass of our Sun. Blobs of gas with less mass than this cool off and settle down into objects rather like the giant planet Jupiter (which itself has 0.1 per cent as much mass as our Sun), only bigger. They become failed stars, which are sometimes referred to as 'brown dwarfs'.

Nebulae like the ones in Orion may contain enough gas and dust to make millions of stars like the Sun, but not all of this gas will be turned into stars, because as the first stars begin to form, the light and heat from the star-forming process blows the remaining material away. The material can easily be blown away like this because it is almost entirely made up of hydrogen and helium gas left over from the Big Bang when the Universe was born. In round terms, the material from which stars are made starts out as just under 75 per cent hydrogen and just under 25 per cent helium, which leaves no more than 1 per cent for everything else put together.

Stars like the Sun

For stars with enough mass, nuclear burning occurs when four hydrogen nuclei (protons) combine to make one helium nucleus in a multi-step process. Helium nuclei are so stable, and so important in the process of star formation (▷ p.53), that they are sometimes regarded as individual entities in their own right and called 'alpha particles'. Crucially, the mass of one alpha particle is a little bit less than the mass of four protons added together. The mass that is lost when an alpha particle is made in this way is turned into pure energy, in line with Albert Einstein's famous equation $E = mc^2$. The heat liberated as mass is converted into energy which provides a pressure that counters the inward pull of gravity and stops the star from contracting any more. It settles down as a stable star, burning steadily at the same temperature as long as its supply of nuclear fuel lasts. The stars we can see today in the Orion Nebula stabilized in this way about 300,000 years ago, very recently indeed by astronomical timescales.

Although stars usually form together in a nebula, they do not stay together throughout their lives. Like everything else in the disc of our Galaxy, the Orion Nebula and the stars it contains are orbiting around the centre. As the nebula disperses and the stars continue in their own orbits, they will each be moving at a slightly different speed, and although at first they will seem to move together, as a so-called 'open cluster' of stars, over hundreds of millions of years they will disperse into the disc of the Galaxy. The Sun formed some 4.5 billion years ago and it is now impossible to identify which of the hundreds of billions of stars in our Galaxy were born with it in the same nebular stellar nursery.

 ## HEAT FROM GRAVITY

When a cloud of gas in space collapses under the pull of gravity (if you like, under its own weight) heat is released. But heat is a form of energy, and you can't get energy out of nothing. The heat of a young star is actually gravitational energy that has been converted into heat as the cloud collapses. On Earth, if you drop something from a tall building or into water, an object moves faster and faster until it hits a surface. As it falls, gravitational energy is being converted into energy of motion (kinetic energy). When it hits the surface, the kinetic energy is turned into heat energy, making the atoms and molecules in the object jostle around faster. Heat is a form of kinetic energy, related to the speed that atoms and molecules move.

In a collapsing gas cloud, all the atoms and molecules are trying to fall towards the centre of the cloud, so they move faster and faster until they hit something. The only 'something' around for them to hit is each other. So the atoms and molecules bash together more and more violently as the cloud collapses. Their kinetic energy increases because they are moving faster and the result is that the cloud gets hotter.

The four stars in the Trapezium constellation, are separated from each other by only 0.1 light years, just 2 per cent of the distance from the Sun to its nearest stellar neighbour.

DUSTY BEGINNINGS

It isn't just stars that form in nebulae such as the Orion Nebula – many of the stars forming in the Milky Way today probably have planets forming around them as they collapse and nuclear burning begins in their hearts. This is thanks to that 1 per cent or so of stuff in these nebulae that is not hydrogen and helium. This material is mainly other gases (such as carbon monoxide), but also very fine grains of dust, similar in size to the particles in cigarette smoke, made of carbon, silicon and other substances. All of this material has been produced inside previous generations of stars (▷ p. 67) and has been scattered into space as those stars age and die.

Apart from the presence of the Sun itself, the most important feature of the Solar System is that all of the material in it (with a few tiny exceptions) is orbiting in the same direction. The Sun itself rotates on its axis (once every 25.4 days or so), the planets (including the Earth) orbit around the Sun in the same direction, the various moons in the Solar System orbit their parent planets in this same direction, and so on.

What this tells us is that the cloud of gas and dust from which the Solar System formed was itself rotating in this direction –

1. Young stars in an association known as the Antares-Rho Ophiuchi complex.

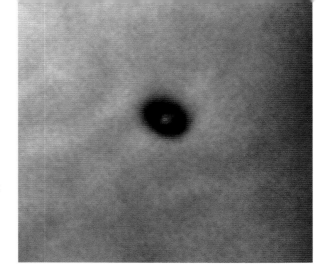
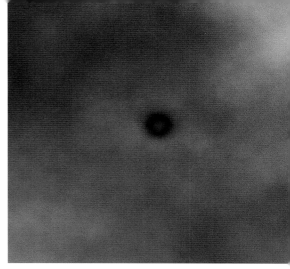

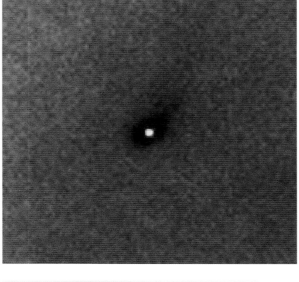
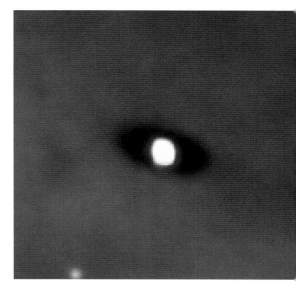

no real surprise, since it is very unlikely that any cloud of gas will just hang around in space without rotating. When the cloud began to collapse, its rotation would have got faster, in exactly the same way that spinning ice skaters rotate faster by pulling their arms in to their sides. This is a feature of something called angular momentum, which all rotating objects have. The amount of angular momentum depends on the mass of the object, how this is distributed, and how fast the object is rotating. If most of the mass is far out from the centre, it will have more angular momentum than if it is concentrated near the centre; and if the object is rotating fast, it will have more than if it rotates slowly. So when a spinning object shrinks in size, it spins faster to keep the same angular momentum.

In a Spin

The collapsing cloud that formed the Sun and planets got rid of some of its angular momentum by throwing material off into space, like water flung from a rotating garden sprinkler. But even so, there was too much angular momentum left to allow all the dust associated with the young star to fall into it. As the star began to shine at the heart of the collapsing cloud, the leftover dust settled into a disc around it, a disc containing only a little of the mass of the system but, thanks to its position far out from the centre, lots of the angular momentum.

From Dust to Pebbles

The planets began to form in the dusty cloud even before it had settled into a disc. The tiny grains of dust in the cloud collided with each other more and more frequently as the cloud collapsed, because the volume of the cloud ▷▷ **3**

2

2. Disks of dusty material (protoplanetary disks) photographed around young stars in the Orion nebula.

3. As stars shrink they spin faster, like an ice-skater pulling in her arms.

FORMATION OF THE SOLAR SYSTEM

1. Collapsing cloud of gas gets hot inside

5. Gravity becomes important as the lumps get bigger

6. Gravity pulls the large lumps into spherical shapes

2. As the star forms, matter settles into a disc around it

3. Matter in the disc begins to clump together

4. Rocks form around the star

7. Planets like the Earth coalesce out of the rocky material

1. Family portrait representing the planets in our Solar System (excepting Pluto).

2. The Solar System also contains many smaller pieces of material – cosmic rubble such as comets.

was getting smaller, and there was less space between the grains. These very gentle collisions allowed the grains to stick together to make fluffy particles a few millimetres across, and these supergrains then collided with other supergrains to make bigger particles. Eventually, so many grains stuck together that objects the size of pebbles, then bigger lumps of rock formed, and gravity

began to play its part. Once the primordial rocks were big enough, gravity would have pulled them together, and then the biggest rocks, by now kilometres across, would begin to dominate, attracting smaller lumps of rubble by gravity and growing bigger still.

As the lumps of rock grew, they collided with other lumps of rock. But because all the proto-planets, as they now were, were moving in the same direction around the Sun, these collisions would be relatively gentle, allowing the rocky lumps to join together, rather than be blasted back into dust. The larger lumps in the dusty disc grew to become planets, sweeping up most of the cosmic junk that still littered the disc. There is a reminder of those days still present in our Solar System. Between the orbits of the planets Mars and Jupiter, there is a band of rubble called the asteroid belt, populated by objects thought to be leftover material from the era of planet formation. There are estimated to be more than a million rocks in the asteroid belt bigger than 1 km across, with countless smaller lumps. The biggest, Ceres, is 933 km in diameter. But the total mass of all those rocks put together is only 15 per cent of the mass of our Moon.

Two Kinds of Planet

This picture of how planets formed neatly explains why there are two main kinds of planet in our Solar System. Close to the Sun, its heat would have driven away volatile material, leaving solid balls of rock with only thin atmospheres, such as Mercury, Venus, Earth and Mars. Further out from the Sun, it would have been cool enough for the rocky cores of planets to hold onto large amounts of gas, forming the giant planets Jupiter, Saturn, Uranus and Neptune. And further out still, there was scope for frozen balls of ice to remain in orbit around the Sun and that's where we find the ice planet Pluto and the comets that occasionally fall into our part of the Solar System from the outer fringes.

Recently, though, this simple picture has been challenged by the discovery of Jupiter-like **2**

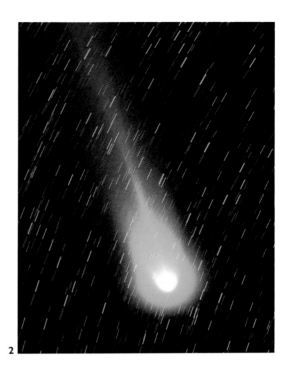

DUSTY DISCS

The astronomical explanation of how planetary systems form is no longer pure speculation, but is based on observations made in the 1990s of dusty discs of material around many young stars. The best studied of these discs is associated with a star called Beta Pictoris (right), and covers a span of at least 1000 AU. This is huge compared to the Solar System (the outermost giant planet, Neptune, is only 30 AU from the Sun), and shows that the disc is in the early stages of settling down, with some material still being ejected and blown away into space.

The Beta Pictoris system is thought to be only about 200 million years old, and the mass of material in the disc today is about one and a half times the mass of the Sun. Most of this will be lost as the system settles down. The inner part of the disc, comparable in size to our Solar System, is warped and distorted, possibly by the gravitational influence of planets forming within it.

The Hubble Space Telescope discovered hundreds of discs like this around young stars. This discovery is of key importance in our understanding of how planets form, and the fact that there are dusty discs around so many young stars suggests that planet formation is a common process. Further investigations of these objects will tell us what the Sun was like when the planets formed.

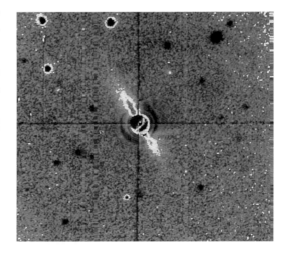

giant planets in Mercury-like orbits around other stars. Astronomers do not yet understand exactly how systems like this can form, although the discoveries are further evidence that solar systems are common in the Universe.

Whatever the details, the important point is that planet formation is a natural consequence of the way a dusty cloud of material collapses to form a single star. However this doesn't necessarily mean that all stars have planets. Multiple star systems have no problem getting rid of angular momentum, because it is stored in their orbital motion around each other, and it is unlikely that there are stable planetary orbits in these more complicated systems. Rather more than half of all stars seem to occur in systems with at least one other stellar

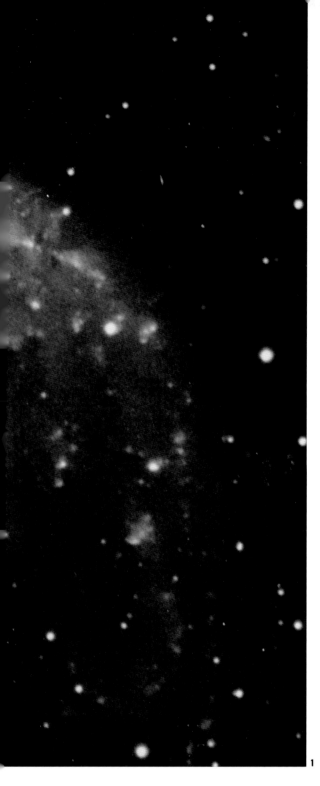

THE COSMIC SQUEEZE

Astronomers have a good understanding of how stars and planets form when a cloud of gas and dust in space begins to collapse. But what is it that triggers the collapse in the first place? In the Milky Way (and other disc galaxies) today, stars continue to be born because of the activity associated with the presence of other stars in the galactic disc itself.

The Orion Nebula is part of a much bigger cloud of gas, called a 'giant molecular cloud', which covers almost all of the constellation Orion on the night sky. Such giant molecular clouds are held together by gravity and can be regarded as single entities, the most massive single entities in our Galaxy, with a mass up to 10 million times the mass of the Sun and diameter of between 46 and 77 parsecs (150 and 250 light years). If a star explodes to create a supernova on one side of such a cloud, it sends out shock waves in the form of ripples moving through the cloud. These shock waves sweep up material in front of them (almost literally in the way that a broom sweeps dust into a heap), and this compresses some of the gas in the cloud enough to start it collapsing to form new stars with a whole range of masses. The biggest blobs of gas in these compressed regions collapse very quickly and form massive stars – tens of times as massive as our Sun which run through their life cycles very rapidly (in less than a million years) and explode in turn, sending more ripples out across the molecular cloud. In this way, a wave of star formation can travel right across a giant molecular cloud over a span of 10 or 20 million years.

companion (some have two or three). But even if just under half of the stars in the disc of the Milky Way are single systems like our Sun, that still leaves scope for well over 100 billion solar systems to have formed in our Galaxy in the way just described.

How Galaxies Make Stars

This is still not the complete picture, because the molecular clouds themselves are associated with the spiral arms of a galaxy like our own. They have come into existence because the thin

1. Planetary systems like our Solar System seem to be a natural part of spiral galaxies like the Milky Way.

gas between the stars has itself been squeezed on its journey around the disc of the Galaxy. Although the pattern made by the spiral arms twining outwards from the nucleus of a disc galaxy looks superficially rather like the pattern of cream stirred into a cup of coffee, there is one important difference. The spiral pattern made by the white cream against the black coffee quickly dissolves into a smooth brown colour as it mixes in. In the same way, the spiral pattern in a disc galaxy ought to get smeared out as the individual stars move on in their own orbits, at their own speeds around the centre. This should happen within about a billion years, a blink of an eye in the lifetime of a galaxy. But the spiral arms are not dissolved by rotation because they are constantly being renewed.

The distinctive pattern that shows up so clearly on photographs of spiral galaxies is caused by the presence of hot young stars along the edges of the spiral arms. These hot young stars are being born there because new clouds of gas and dust are constantly moving through the spiral pattern and being squeezed by a shock wave there. It is the shock wave that is the more or less permanent feature, like a sonic boom spiralling around the Galaxy, with the gas and dust just passing through. A useful way to picture what is going on is to think of a crowded motorway, where a slow-moving, large vehicle causes a kind of mobile traffic jam. Vehicles pile up behind the obstruction, work their way slowly past it, then speed up on the other side. The traffic jam moves along the road at a steady speed, but the individual cars that make up the jam are constantly changing as new cars approach from behind and others escape from the front of the jam. In the case of the spiral arms of our Galaxy, the shock wave itself is travelling around the Galaxy at a speed of about 30 km per second, while the stars and clouds of gas and dust are overtaking the spiral wave at a speed of about 250 km per second, passing through it but getting squeezed in the process. Clouds of gas and dust pile up in the cosmic traffic jam along the inside curve of the spiral arm, and are squeezed there, triggering bursts of star formation like the one going on in the Orion molecular cloud.

How Stars Make Stars

The whole process is self-sustaining. The shock waves are maintained by the stellar explosions going on along the edge of the spiral arm, and the stellar explosions are caused by the squeeze given to clouds of gas and dust by the shock waves. Although giant molecular clouds are constantly forming stars in this process, the explosions of other stars constantly feed raw material back into interstellar space to make new molecular clouds, the raw material for later generations of stars. Each year, just a few solar masses of material are being recycled in this way in the Milky Way Galaxy, but over a few billion years that adds up to a lot of new stars.

At any one time the amount of matter orbiting around the disc of the Galaxy in the form of giant molecular clouds is about 3 billion times as much as there is in our Sun. This is equivalent to about 15 per cent of the total mass of stars in the disc itself. It takes surprisingly few big stellar explosions to keep the recycling process going. There are only two or three supernova explosions in our Galaxy every century, and there hasn't been one close enough to be studied by human observers for nearly 400 years (the closest occurred in 1987 in a small nearby galaxy, the Large Magellanic Cloud). Think of this in terms of the lifetime of a galaxy. Even at a rate of only two per century, there will be 20,000 supernova explosions every million years, and several hundred million have occurred since the Sun was born 4.5 billion years ago.

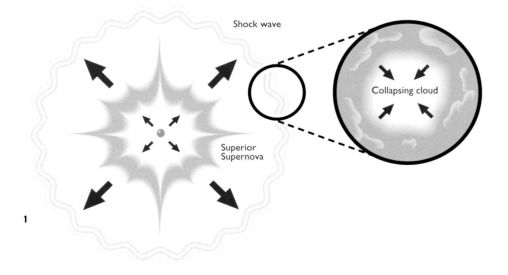

Shock wave

Collapsing cloud

Superior
Supernova

1

1. The expanding shockwave from an exploding star (main picture) squeezes clouds of gas and encourages new stars to form (inset).

2. (opposite) The large Magellanic Cloud is a near-neighbour of our galaxy. It is about 160,000 light years away, and 30,000 light years across.

OUR COSMIC NEIGHBOURHOOD

The Sun and its family of planets lie just inside one of the spiral arms of our Galaxy, passing through it on their endless journey around the Milky Way. This spiral arm is sometimes called the Orion Arm, after the distinctive constellation of Orion. But because the bright stars that form the traditional constellations lie in the same spiral arm, this name is slightly misleading and many astronomers prefer to call our region of the Galaxy simply the 'Local Arm'.

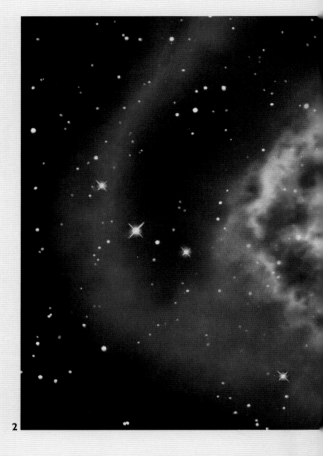

The View from Inside

From our viewpoint within the Local Arm, astronomers see a congregation of stars, nebulae and dark clouds in two opposite directions on the sky. The Local Arm comes outwards from the inner part of the Galaxy from the direction of the constellation Cygnus, as seen from Earth, and

carries on past us in the direction of the constellation Vela. The Orion Nebula and its nursery of stars are slightly offset from this main curve of the Local Arm and lie about 46 parsecs (1500 light years) away from us. The brightest star in the sky, Sirius, is part of the constellation Canis Major, and is also known as Alpha Canis Major, meaning that it is the brightest star in that constellation. But Sirius is not intrinsically very bright; it only looks bright because it is so close to us, 2.5 parsecs (8.7 light years) away, the seventh closest star to the Sun.

Canis Major seems to be part of a huge, faint nebula, with a diameter of 100 light years, which is sometimes called the Seagull Nebula after a fancied resemblance to a bird. But appearances can be deceptive, because of the way objects at different distances are superimposed on the sky. In fact, the Seagull Nebula lies far beyond Sirius, roughly a kiloparsec (3000 light years) away. The nebula is an expanding shell of material produced in a supernova explosion about half a million years ago and is associated with a group of young stars (about 300,000 years old) whose birth was triggered by the shock wave from the supernova.

Local Nurseries

Between us and the Seagull Nebula there are three regions of active star formation, the closest being the Orion Molecular Cloud. All three regions seem to be linked by a thin streamer of gas, only 6 parsecs (20 light years) across but more than 300 parsecs (1000 light years) long.

Apart from the regions of star birth (and the stars themselves), there is another key component of the story of stellar life and death to be seen in our neighbourhood. The Helix Nebula, lying in the direction of the constellation Aquarius, but about 140 parsecs (450 light years) away, is the closest example of a so-called 'planetary nebula'.

1. The constellation Canis Major showing Sirius, the brightest star in the night sky.

2. The Helix nebula, also known as NGC 7293.

3. The constellation Orion.

Overleaf. The Trifid Nebula in the constellation Sagittarius. The pink part is a cloud of hydrogen gas, the blue area reflects the light of bright stars. Dark lanes of dust obscure emitted light.

Planetary nebulae get their name because, when viewed through a small telescope, they look like discs on the sky, just as planets do. But in fact they are huge, expanding balls of gas that have been ejected by a star late in its life. The Helix Nebula is so big that even at a distance of 450 light years it covers half of the apparent diameter of our Moon on the sky. It is a glowing shell of material (nearly a light year across) ejected from the central star about 10,000 years ago.

Every part of the cycle of stellar birth, life and death is represented in our immediate cosmic neighbourhood. This is why astronomers have been able to piece together the life story of a star. If we had not

been in a spiral arm, astronomers might not have been able to do this.

The gas in any part of the disc of our Galaxy is exposed to the squeezing effect of a supernova at least once every few million years, on average, while it takes the Sun more than 200 million years to orbit around the Galaxy just once. However, the average is a little misleading, because most of the explosions, and most of the squeezing, happen near spiral arms, with long quiet periods during the journey of a star around the Galaxy.

The Sun has orbited right around the Milky Way Galaxy about 20 times since the Solar System formed.

TOPIC LINKS

1.1 Stepping Stones to the Universe
p. 21 An island in space

1.2 Star Birth
p. 31 The Orion Nursery

1.3 Stellar Evolution
p. 51 Lifetimes of the Stars
p. 57 Red Giants and White Dwarfs

STELLAR EVOLUTION

Astronomers use the term 'evolution' to refer to the life cycle of a star: how an individual star changes as it goes through its life cycle. This is different from the way the term is used in biology, where it refers to the way a population of individuals changes from generation to generation.

Once nuclear burning begins to occur in their hearts, all stars stabilize and shine more or less steadily as long as their nuclear fuel lasts. During this stable phase of their lives, stars range in size from one-tenth to 10 times of the diameter of our Sun. The size and the external appearance of such a stable star (its brightness and colour), and the amount of time that it can spend burning nuclear fuel steadily in this way, depend on just one thing: its mass. Bigger stars burn their fuel more quickly to hold themselves up; smaller stars can sustain themselves with less rapid consumption of fuel.

THE MAIN SEQUENCE

The process which generates the heat that provides the pressure holding a star up and prevents it from collapsing under its own weight is the conversion of hydrogen into helium. This is a multi-step process (actually, two multi-step processes – ▷ p. 58) in which a little of the original mass is converted into pure energy. The higher the mass of a star, the more weight it has to support. The only way that the star can do this is to burn its nuclear fuel more rapidly, generating a higher pressure in its core. This means that it will use up its fuel more quickly. It also means that more heat is escaping from the surface of the star. So a more massive star is both shorter-lived and brighter than a less massive star.

If two objects are the same size, but have different temperatures, they will have different colours. For example, a red-hot lump of iron is cooler than a white-hot lump of iron. If all stars were the same size, the same simple rule would apply to them, and the colour of a star would immediately tell you its temperature and therefore reveal its mass. But the astronomer's life is not quite that simple.

If one star is bigger than another, it has a larger surface area from which heat can escape. So the same amount of heat can

1. The colours of stars depend on how hot and bright they are, which helps astronomers to work out how far away they are.

escape from the whole surface of the larger star every second, even though each square metre of its surface has a lower temperature than each square metre of the surface of the smaller star; there are more square metres for the heat to escape from. In principle, if the size difference is big enough, a red star can be radiating just as much heat as a white star. And it is the *rate* at which heat is escaping overall which tells us how much heat is being generated in the core of the star, and therefore how massive it is.

The Key to Astrophysics

When, in the twentieth century, astronomers began to study the relationship between the colour of a star and its absolute brightness (the brightness it actually has close up, not its apparent brightness on the sky), they found that many stars obey a simple rule, which shows up clearly when absolute brightness (which astronomers refer to as 'absolute magnitude') is plotted against colour in a kind of graph known as a colour–magnitude diagram. The colour–magnitude diagram is also known as the Hertzsprung–Russell (or HR) diagram, after the two astronomers who discovered the relationship.

The HR diagram is plotted in such a way that the brightness of a star (its absolute magnitude) increases as you go up the page, and the temperature decreases as you go from left to right across the page. So stars at the bottom right of the diagram are faint, cool and red (with surface temperatures below about 3500 Kelvin) while stars in the top left are bright, hot and blue-white (with surface temperatures above about 25,000 K). Most visible stars lie on a band in the diagram (opposite page) running from the top left to the bottom right, and this band is called the 'main sequence'. All stars that, like our Sun, get their energy by converting hydrogen into helium in their hearts, lie on the main sequence.

Large Stars are Hot

From other evidence relating to the masses of stars (in particular, the way that stars in binary systems orbit around each other), astronomers have been able to measure

 ABSOLUTE TEMPERATURE

Like other scientists, astronomers prefer to measure temperatures in terms of the absolute, or Kelvin, scale. Unlike the temperature scales in everyday use (the Celsius and Fahrenheit scales), the Kelvin scale is not based on any arbitrary choice of a zero point, such as the freezing point of water, but on the absolute zero of temperature, the lowest temperature that can ever exist. This temperature was calculated from thermodynamic principles by the British physicist Lord Kelvin (left) in the nineteenth century and corresponds to –273.16 degrees on the Celsius scale. The size of the units on the Kelvin scale has been chosen to match the size of the degrees on the Celsius scale, so the freezing point of water is 273.16 kelvin, or 273.16 K (on the Kelvin scale, the degree symbol is never used). Astronomical temperatures are often so high that it doesn't make very much difference which units you use. The temperature at the surface of the Sun, for example, is 5800 K, which corresponds to 5527 degrees Celsius, a difference of less than 5 per cent. The choice of units is even less important when we describe the temperature at the heart of the Sun – 15 million degrees Celsius or kelvin means much the same. However, it is crucially important to be sure which units are being used when describing the temperatures of cold objects in space, where the temperature can fall to within a few kelvin of absolute zero.

enough stellar masses directly to understand what is going on in the main sequence. A small star, which does not have to burn fuel very rapidly in order to hold itself up, sits at the bottom of the main sequence; while a large star that has to burn fuel rapidly in order to avoid collapse sits at the top of the main sequence. The Sun is a middle-sized star, generating a moderate amount of heat and having a yellow-orange colour; it sits near, but slightly below, the middle of the main sequence.

Although most visible stars lie on the main sequence of the HR diagram, there are exceptions. In particular, there are a few visible stars in the bottom left half of the diagram, and some in the top right half of the diagram. The ones at the bottom left are small, faint and hot, while the ones at the upper right are large, bright and cool. They represent stars which are in the later stages of their evolution. They have left the main sequence.

Lifetimes of the Stars

The amount of time a star can spend on the main sequence depends on its mass, which also determines its position on the main sequence. So the bright stars at the top of the main sequence live fast and die young, like some rock stars. The Sun itself will be able to spend a total of about 10 billion years steadily burning hydrogen in its core as a main sequence star, and is now just under half way through its main sequence lifetime. A cool star with a mass about one-tenth of that of the Sun can sit at the bottom of the main sequence quietly burning its fuel for hundreds of billions of years. But a star with five times as much mass as the Sun only has a main sequence lifetime of some 70 million years, and those with 25 times the mass of the Sun have main sequence lifetimes of only

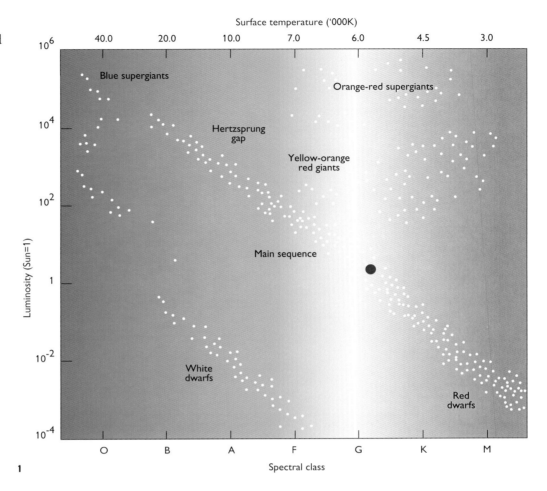

1

2

1. Schematic representation of the HR diagram. The position corresponding to the Sun is marked with a dot.

2. Betelgeuse is a massive red, supergiant star 17,000 times brighter than the sun and with a diameter 300 times bigger than that of the sun.

1

Although the core of the Sun has 12 times the density of lead, its outer layers are so tenuous that the average density of the whole Sun is only 1.4 times that of water.

3 million years. The most massive stars on the main sequence have about 50 times the mass of our Sun, and are perhaps 20 times its diameter, but have lifetimes of less than a million years. Anything much bigger than this that tries to become a star generates so much heat in its core as it collapses that it blows itself apart.

Because of the way bigger stars have shorter lifetimes, when a group of stars of the same age but with different masses is plotted on an HR diagram the main sequence will be incomplete. This can be done for stars in globular clusters, which are groups of thousands (sometimes millions) of stars that were born together from a single cloud of material long ago. In such a cluster, the more massive stars have already left the main sequence, so the top left of the main sequence is truncated. The exact point where the main sequence ends tells you the masses of the oldest stars still on the main sequence in the cluster today, which (since they must be just about to leave the main sequence themselves) reveals their age, and that tells you how old the cluster is.

Brightness and Distance

The HR diagram can also be used to measure distances to clusters of stars, because the position of the main sequence on the diagram is related to the absolute brightnesses of the stars. The further away the cluster is, the lower down on the diagram the main sequence will seem to be, because the stars will look fainter. Astronomers can work out how far it is to the cluster by calculating how much brighter the stars would have to be to lie on the standard main sequence. All of this places the HR diagram and the main sequence among the most important sources of information about the stars.

COOKING THE ELEMENTS

All of the elements in the Universe today, except for hydrogen, helium and a very small amount of light elements such as lithium and deuterium, have been manufactured inside stars and spread through space late in the lifetimes of those stars, either as clouds of gas puffed away gently from the surface of the star or in great stellar explosions. The raw material for the manufacture of those elements is the hydrogen and helium which were produced in the Big Bang when the Universe was born. Some of that hydrogen is being converted into helium today inside main sequence stars, and more was converted into helium in the past. But by far the bulk of the 25 per cent helium that contributes to the composition of a star like the Sun is primordial stuff left over from the Big Bang. All the heavier elements, such as oxygen, carbon, nitrogen, iron, and all the elements in your body, are literally star dust created from this primordial matter.

The fundamental component of an element is, of course, the atom. All atoms of a particular element (such as oxygen) are identical to one another and are made up of a core (the nucleus) containing particles called protons and others called neutrons, surrounded by a cloud of electrons (one electron in the cloud for every proton in the nucleus). It is the number of protons in the nucleus which determines the nature of the

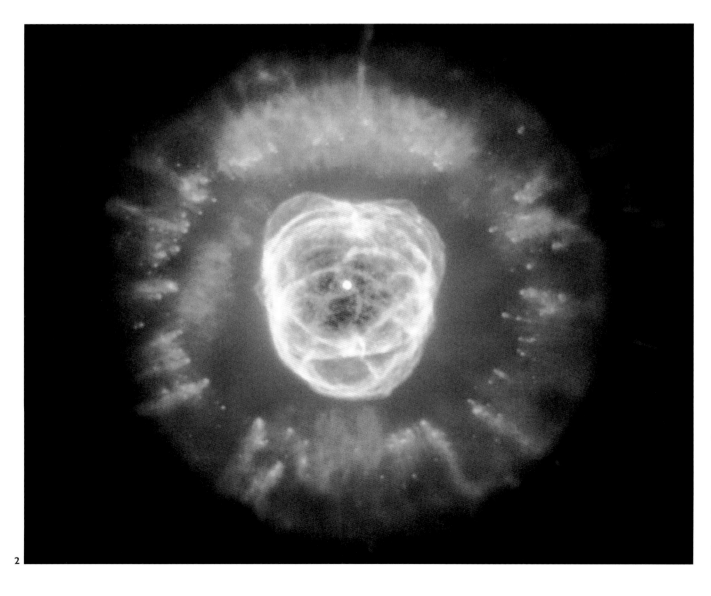

2

1. Eta Carinae is a star about 100 times as massive as our sun, blowing material away into space.

2. The Eskimo nebula is one of the prettiest examples of a planetary nebula.

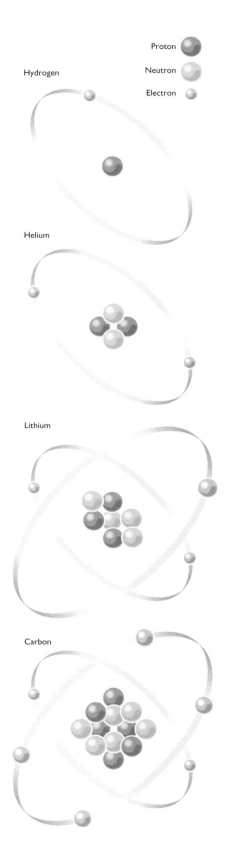

Proton

Neutron

Electron

Hydrogen

Helium

Lithium

Carbon

atom, whether it is an atom of lead, or sulphur, or whatever. The simplest atom of all, hydrogen, has a nucleus consisting of a single proton.

The Stellar Pressure Cooker

Under the extreme conditions that exist in the hearts of stars (temperatures in excess of 15 million K and densities greater than 10 times the density of lead on Earth), the electrons are stripped away from their atoms, and the nuclei are free to move about through a sea of free electrons and collide with one another. Very occasionally, the nuclei interact to make new nuclei, making new elements in the process known as stellar nucleosynthesis.

Making helium out of hydrogen is the first step in nucleosynthesis. Although this mostly happened in the Big Bang, the stellar process is still important in providing the energy that keeps main sequence stars shining. The story of how elements are cooked inside stars really begins later in a star's life, when conditions become extreme enough for helium nuclei to combine with one another to make nuclei of carbon.

The problem with nucleosynthesis is that it is difficult to make nuclei stick together. All nuclei carry positive electric charge, because protons are positively charged and neutrons have no charge at all. If the nuclei can come close enough together (in effect if they touch) then they can interact and (sometimes) fuse to make new nuclei, held together by a strong nuclear force which overcomes the electrical repulsion but which has only a very short range. Slow-moving nuclei are repelled from one another electrically before they can interact in this way; only fast nuclei (which means hot nuclei) can collide powerfully enough to overcome the electrical repulsion. The more protons there are in the nucleus, the stronger the repulsion is and the hotter the

nuclei must be before they can interact.

The extra heat required to initiate stellar nucleosynthesis is provided, paradoxical though it may seem, when the core of a main sequence star has used up all of its hydrogen fuel. Because the core can no longer generate heat by converting hydrogen into helium, the temperature and pressure there fall, and the weight of the star pressing down on the core makes it collapse. But as the core begins to collapse, gravitational energy is released, making the core hotter again. It gets so hot that helium nuclei can move fast enough to stick together. Energy is released (through $E = mc^2$ ▷ p. 58) as they do so and the collapse is halted for as long as the supply of helium lasts.

Cooking up Carbon

Each helium nucleus involved in this process contains two protons and two neutrons (and is known, for obvious reasons, as helium-4). (There is another variety of helium containing two protons and a single neutron (helium-3), but it is not important here.) You might think that the natural result of an interaction between two helium-4 nuclei would be a nucleus containing four protons and four neutrons (beryllium-8). But it turns out that this nucleus is very unstable and breaks apart within 10 millionths of a billionth of a second after it forms. The only way that helium-4 nuclei can combine to form a new stable nucleus is if three of them get together at very nearly the same time to make a nucleus of carbon-12. This step is made much easier by the fact that the carbon-12 nucleus has just the right energy to be stable. The three helium nuclei initially form what is called an 'excited' carbon-12 nucleus, which then gets rid of the excess energy by radiating it away, forming a stable nucleus. This is called the 'triple alpha process'.

Just as a helium-4 nucleus has slightly less

1

1. The atomic structure of some simple elements.

2. Heavy elements such as gold are only made in dying stars.

mass than the total masses of the two protons and two neutrons that make up the nucleus, so a carbon-12 nucleus has slightly less mass than the three helium-4 nuclei that went into it. This loss of mass is what provides the heat to keep a star going during this phase of its life, 'burning' helium into carbon.

Making Heavier Elements

Once carbon-12 has been formed, making the rest of the elements is downhill all the way. When the helium in the core of a star is beginning to be used up, once again the core shrinks a little, gravitational energy is released, the core gets hotter, and a new wave

of fusion begins. This time, alpha particles fuse with carbon-12 nuclei to make oxygen-16. Further steps in the process (for stars which have enough weight to generate the required temperatures in their cores) manufacture the elements neon-20, magnesium-24 and silicon-28. Other elements are produced when the nuclei of these elements are involved in interactions in which they either absorb or emit protons, or in which neutrons are converted into protons, or vice versa.

But the end of the line comes when pairs of silicon-28 nuclei fuse together to make iron-56 and related elements, such as cobalt-56 and nickel-56. At every step, energy has

Every second, the Sun converts 5 million tonnes of matter into pure energy, in line with Einstein's famous equation $E = mc^2$.

1. The variable star Mira is shown here at its maximum brightness.

2. Alpha Hercules is an example of a red giant star.

been released by fusing lighter nuclei to make nuclei of heavier elements. But from the iron-group elements onwards, it takes energy to make the nuclei stick together to make nuclei of even heavier elements. There is no way to liberate energy by making iron-group elements fuse and any star that gets this far has no nuclear source of energy left to draw on.

There are, of course, elements heavier than iron in the Universe at large and on the Earth itself – like gold, lead, and uranium. They must have been made somewhere, and the story of their origin is one of the most dramatic in astronomy. But as far as ordinary stellar nucleosynthesis is concerned, iron and its associated family of elements marks the end of the line. Many stars (including the Sun itself) are not big enough for nucleosynthesis even to proceed that far, and will not be able to manufacture anything more interesting than carbon (indeed, the lightest stars will never get beyond the simple fusion of hydrogen nuclei to make helium). But all this activity in the core of a star has profound effects on its outer layers, and even a star like the Sun is destined to change its outward appearance drastically as its core adjusts to different phases of nuclear burning.

RED GIANTS AND WHITE DWARFS

A star stays on the main sequence of the HR diagram, with very little change in its outward appearance, as long as it is converting hydrogen nuclei into helium nuclei in its heart. But when hydrogen burning ends the appearance of the star changes dramatically.

At this point in its life, the core of the star shrinks and gets hotter, until helium burning begins. The effect of the extra heat coming out from the heart of the star is to make the outer layers (its atmosphere) swell up and expand. So the star gets a lot bigger overall, even though its core has shrunk. Because the star is much bigger, it has a much larger surface area from which the heat coming from the core can escape. This means that although there is more heat escaping overall, less heat is

escaping across each square metre of the surface. So the surface gets cooler, even though the core gets hotter and the star gets brighter. A star like the Sun, which starts out yellow or orange on the main sequence will cool to a deep red colour as it expands in this way. It becomes a red giant, one of the bright but cool stars that lie in the upper right side of the HR diagram, above the main sequence (▷ p. 51).

Wandering Stars

If you could live long enough to watch a single star change as it aged, you would see it wander about in the HR diagram, moving upwards and to the right away from the main sequence at first, but zig-zagging about in the red giant part of the diagram as the conditions in its core changed and different nuclear energy

sources came into play. During part of its time as a red giant, such a star may, if it has the right mass, experience rhythmic pulsations as its atmosphere swells and shrinks in response to the changes going on inside it. It is these pulsations that make some red giants show up as Cepheid variables (▷ pp. 28-9).

In another part of the HR diagram, red giants show a similar and almost equally useful kind of activity: they are known as RR Lyrae variables and are also good distance indicators, even though they are fainter than Cepheids.

A stable red giant star has a core in which helium is being burnt into carbon by the triple alpha process. This core is surrounded by a shell of material in which hydrogen is being converted into helium just as it is in a main sequence star, and this in turn is surrounded by a hugely distended atmosphere consisting ▷▷

 THE FATE OF THE EARTH

Although a main sequence star like the Sun (right) stays roughly the same during its time on the main sequence, even minor changes in solar output can have a big effect on the Earth. Computer simulations of how stars work suggest that the Sun has actually got warmer, slightly, since it was formed some 5 billion years ago. So far, this has been compensated for on Earth by changes in the atmosphere of our planet, which have reduced the strength of the natural greenhouse effect. But if things continue in this way, the Earth may become uninhabitable in about a billion years time. Looking further ahead, there is about another 5–6 billion years before the Sun becomes a red giant. At that time, its diameter will increase to between 150 and 200 times its present size, and its brightness will increase to 2000 times its present value. By then, because the Sun will have lost about a quarter of its mass, loosening its gravitational grip on the planets, the Earth will have drifted out into a larger orbit. However, it will still be close enough to the Sun for the surface layers to be melted. As the Sun blows away its atmosphere to form a planetary nebula and settles down to become a white dwarf, all that will be left of the Earth will be a lump of solidified slag with no atmosphere, orbiting far out from the faint, dying star.

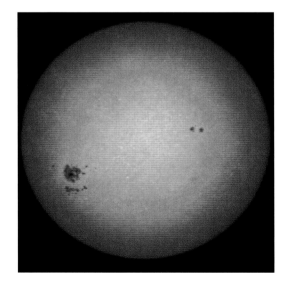

WHY STARS SHINE

Stars on the main sequence of the Hertzprung–Russell diagram (▷ p. 51), like the Sun, shine because they are converting hydrogen into helium (specifically helium-4) in their cores, in the process known as 'nuclear fusion'. The nucleus of a hydrogen atom consists of a single proton. The nucleus of a helium atom is made up of two protons and two neutrons, held together by a short-range interaction called the 'strong nuclear force'. To make a helium nucleus from hydrogen, you start with four protons, persuade two of them to convert themselves into neutrons, and stick the resulting four particles together. This is not easy, but nature has found two ways to perform this trick – and both operate inside stars.

On the Chain Gang

The first process is called the 'proton–proton chain' (or p–p chain) and it is the main source of energy for the Sun and other stars in the bottom half of the main sequence of the Hertzprung–Russell diagram. The process begins when two protons come close enough together to interact in spite of their mutual electrical repulsion. In the interaction, one of the protons spits out a 'positron' (a positively charged counterpart to an electron) and a very light particle called a 'neutrino', thus converting itself into a neutron.

With the positive charge of one of the original protons carried away by the positron, the neutron and proton are no longer repelled from one another and form an entity called a 'deuteron'. A third proton can then collide with the deuteron to form a nucleus of helium-3, which contains two protons and one neutron, held together by the strong nuclear force. Finally, two helium-3 nuclei collide, forming a single nucleus of helium-4 and spitting out two protons.

Each time four protons combine in this way (or any way!) to make one helium-4 nucleus, 0.7 per cent of the original mass is released as energy. Since the Sun formed, about 4 per cent of its original stock of hydrogen has been used up in the process.

Stellar Cycles

Stars with more mass than the Sun are slightly hotter in their hearts, and generate energy through a different process, which is known as the 'carbon cycle'. (A very small amount of the Sun's energy does come from the carbon cycle, but most is produced by the p–p chain.)

The carbon cycle depends on the fact that stars today are made from the debris of previous generations of stars, and contain a smattering of heavy elements produced by nucleosynthesis. It starts when a proton enters a nucleus of carbon-12, which contains six protons and six neutrons. The resulting nucleus (nitrogen-13) is unstable and emits a positron and a neutrino as one of its protons converts into a neutron

1

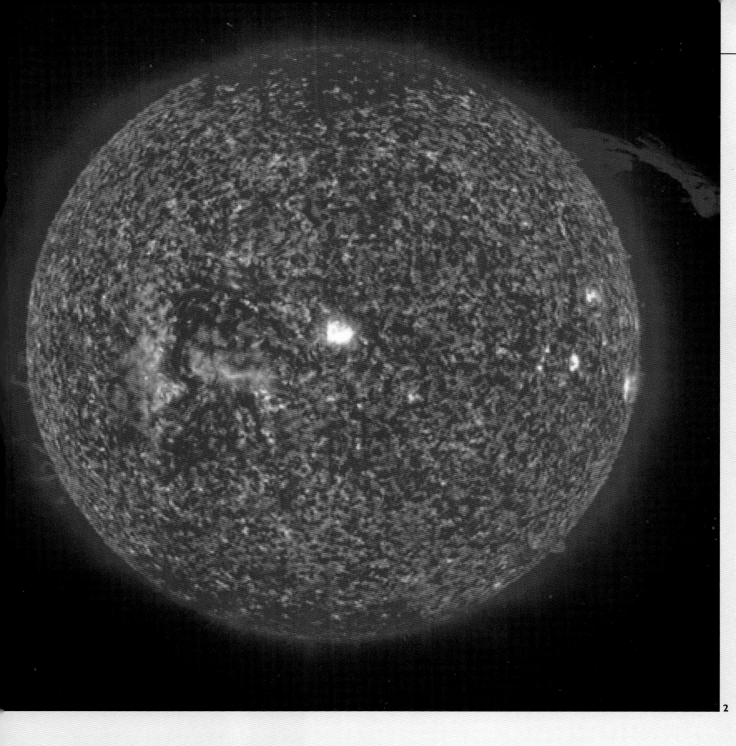

1. The p–p chain, which releases heat inside the Sun.

2. A SOHO ultraviolet image of the chromosphere layer of the Sun's atmosphere, with a solar flare pictured top right.

2

(converting the nucleus itself into carbon-13). If a second proton penetrates this carbon-13 nucleus, it becomes nitrogen-14. A third proton will convert it into oxygen-15, which is unstable and spits out a positron and a neutron as it converts into nitrogen-15.

Now comes the crunch. If a proton penetrates a nucleus of nitrogen-15, it spits out a whole alpha particle (a helium-4 nucleus), leaving behind a nucleus of carbon-12 identical to the one that started the cycle. The net effect is that four protons have been turned into one helium-4 nucleus with energy being released along the way. As with the p–p chain, 0.7 per cent of the mass of the set of four protons is converted into energy each time an alpha particle is made.

⬥ TOPIC LINKS

1.2 Star Birth
p.41 The Cosmic Squeeze

1.4 Out With a Bang
p. 67 A Bigger Blast
p.71 Black Holes and Neutron Stars

mainly of hydrogen and helium. Red giants can have masses tens of times the mass of the Sun, and diameters up to 100 times larger. Because they are so big, the gravitational pull at the surface of such a star is very weak and it is easy for material to escape into space. This is especially true when the atmosphere is being puffed in and out by variations like those we see in Cepheids.

The Fate of the Sun

The Sun itself will become a red giant in about 5 billion years' time, and at its largest it will expand to engulf Mercury and approach the orbit of Venus. You may sometimes hear or read that it will even engulf the Earth, but this prediction is not correct, because it does not take account of the fact that by that stage of its life the Sun will have lost about 25 per cent of its original mass by ejecting material into space.

The overall time that a star spends as a red giant is much less than the time it spends on the main sequence, only between 5 per cent and 20 per cent of its main sequence lifetime, depending on its mass. The Sun will be a red giant for only about a billion years, and will never get beyond the helium-burning stage. Bigger stars, though, may go through successive phases of nuclear burning, ending up with a structure like that of an onion, with different kinds of nuclear burning (and nucleosynthesis) going on in each layer.

Fading Stars

For a star like the Sun, and stars with up to a few times as much mass as the Sun, all the nuclear burning possibilities will eventually come to an end. The star will blow away its outer layers to form a planetary nebula as the core collapses and stabilizes as a solid lump

of material. This dense core of star stuff starts out hot, thanks to the leftover heat of its former glory and the heat generated in its final collapse, but it is very small, about the size of the Earth. It becomes what is known as a 'white dwarf', one of the hot but faint stars that occupy the bottom left part of the HR diagram.

A white dwarf contains anything from about half to one and a half times the mass of our Sun, packed into a solid lump about the size of the Earth. One cubic centimetre of white dwarf stuff would have a mass of about 1 tonne – a million times the density of water.

If all stars faded away quietly, as the Sun is destined to do, there would be very little in the way of heavy elements in the Universe, very few planets (if any) and no life forms like ourselves. But some stars end their lives in events that play a key role in both manufacturing heavy elements and recycling them into the interstellar medium.

However, stars which start their lives with more than about eight times as much mass as our Sun have a different, and more spectacular, fate in store. They are destined to become the supernovae which trigger the next generation of star birth, allowing new stars to arise Phoenix-like from the ashes of the old.

1. The constellation Canis Major showing Sirius, the brightest star in the night sky.

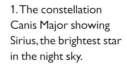

1.4 OUT WITH A BANG

If all stars faded away quietly, as the Sun is destined to do, there would be very little in the way of heavy elements in the Universe, very few planets (if any) and no life forms like ourselves. But some stars end their lives in explosive events that play a key role in both manufacturing heavy elements and recycling them into the interstellar medium. These supernovae have been known from observations since the 1920s, but it took a long time for their significance to be appreciated.

One of the most important discoveries of late twentieth-century science is that we are made of star dust, but it was only in the last decade of the century that astronomers worked out the details of how supernova explosions manufacture the heaviest elements and spread them through space in their death throes, providing the raw material for the formation of new planetary systems.

STARS LOCKED IN A MORTAL EMBRACE

There are two kinds of stellar explosion involved in recycling the elements, and the more common kind occurs in the most common kind of star – the ones which, unlike our Sun, are part of a binary system, with two stars in orbit around one another.

The presence of a companion star has very little effect on the early evolution of a star like the Sun, and it can happily run through its time on the main sequence in the usual way. But things get more complicated when one of the two stars leaves the main sequence and tries to become a red giant. This will happen first to the more massive of the two, since more massive stars burn their fuel faster and leave the main sequence sooner.

Swapping Matter Between Partners

If the two stars are close enough together (as is often, but not always, the case), as the more massive star swells to become a red giant it will begin to dump material from its distended atmosphere onto its companion. The gravitational pull of the companion will tug a streamer of material away from the red giant, and this extra matter will pile up on what was the less massive star in the pair, adding to its mass and speeding up its own evolution. By the time the first star has become a white dwarf, it may be lighter than its companion, which will have gained mass and become a red giant in its turn, dumping material back onto the white dwarf.

This can produce a variety of interesting phenomena, including bursts of X-rays from the point where the infalling material from the red giant creates an intense hot spot on the surface of the white dwarf. But the most important consequence of this kind of binary interaction is that it can produce repeated outbursts which blast matter off into space.

1. Artist's impression of a binary star in which a red giant is losing matter to a small companion.

1

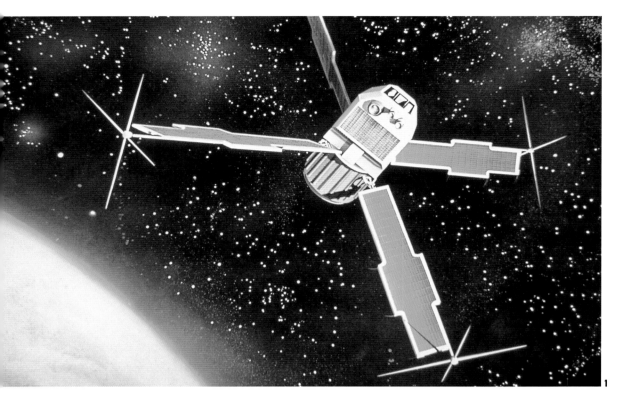

whole process can start again as gas from the giant star continues to fall onto the white dwarf.

New Stars for Old

Such a brightening of the star is called a nova (meaning 'new'). The name derives from the fact that white dwarfs are too faint to be seen with a small telescope in their resting state, and when novas were first observed it was thought that they were literally new stars being born. During a nova, the brightness of the star may increase by 100,000 times in a few days, before fading back to its previous insignificance over a few months. The surface temperature of the star reaches about 100 million K during the outburst and it ejects the equivalent of about one tenthousandth of the mass of the Sun in the form of heavy elements, which enrich the interstellar medium.

In a disc galaxy like our own Milky Way, about 25 novae occur each year. It is thought that all novae are produced by the binary accretion process described above and that all are subject to repeated outbursts of this kind. Some novae have actually been seen to recur in this way. The star T Corona Borealis, for example, flared up in both 1866 and 1946. All novae are believed to follow a similar pattern, but gaps between outbursts are too long for us to have seen them explode more than once since we started watching the skies.

Some white dwarfs in binary systems suffer a more extreme fate. A white dwarf is made of atomic nuclei (atoms stripped of their electrons) jostling together, in a sea of electrons, with one electron for every proton present. This is very nearly the most compact form in which matter exists. But the rules of quantum physics tell us that there is a more dense form of matter, which could be achieved if each proton absorbed one electron and became a neutron. If that happened, all

1. The first x-ray astronomy satellite Uhuru, which discovered evidence for what are now thought to be black holes in our galaxy.

These explosions happen in systems where the separation of the two stars provides a more or less steady rain of gas from the red giant onto the white dwarf, instead of creating a hot spot. This material is mostly hydrogen, from the atmosphere of the giant star, and it builds up on the surface of the white dwarf at a rate of about 1 billionth of the mass of the Sun each year. But the gravitational pull at the surface of a white dwarf is so intense – tens of thousands of times greater than the gravitational pull at the surface of the Earth – that even hydrogen forms a dense layer with an intense pressure at its base. As more gas falls onto the white dwarf, this pressure increases steadily. When a thick enough layer of hydrogen has built up in this way, the pressure at the base of the layer triggers a wave of fusion activity (like the explosion of a huge hydrogen bomb), which blasts the material out into space and causes the star to flare up brightly for a short time. Then the

the matter would shrink down to become a single ball of neutrons, like a single huge atomic nucleus.

Matter at its Most Extreme

The pressure required to make this happen is immense, but it will be reached if the mass of the white dwarf exceeds 1.4 times the mass of the Sun. So if a white dwarf with just a bit less than this critical mass is quietly accreting matter from a companion star, when its mass reaches this limit the inside of the star will collapse as the material in its core is turned into a ball of neutrons. As the star collapses, a huge amount of gravitational energy is released in the form of heat, triggering a wave of nuclear reactions in the material the star is made of. The matter the star contains is blasted away into space. Such an event is called a supernova, because it far exceeds the outburst of a nova. In a supernova, a single star can briefly shine as brightly as a whole galaxy of billions of ordinary stars.

The kind of supernova produced by the disruption of a white dwarf in a binary system is called a 'Type I supernova'; because all Type I supernovae are produced in the same way, from white dwarfs with exactly the same mass, they all have the same brightness. This makes them good standard candles to use in measuring distances to other galaxies. The other important thing about Type I supernovae is that they spread huge amounts of heavy elements through space. A Type I supernova laces the interstellar medium with about half to one solar mass of iron, plus 12–15 per cent of a solar mass of oxygen, and a smaller amount of other heavy elements. But even this is not the most spectacular way in which a star can die.

 THE STAR OF BETHLEHEM

One thing we know for sure about the birth of Jesus Christ is that it did not occur in the year 1. It was only in the sixth century (by the modern calendar) that the idea of counting time from the birth of Jesus was suggested by the Roman scholar Dionysus Exiguus, and he simply made a mistake in counting back to the all-important year. We know this, because King Herod, who played such an important part in the Nativity story, died in 4 BC. But while Herod is an historical fact, is there any truth in the Biblical story of the Star of Bethlehem?

It so happens that Chinese astronomers were keeping records of unusual events in the heavens at that time, and these records include a report of the presence of a 'guest star' in the constellation Capricorn in March of the year we now call 5 BC.

The date fits neatly with the Biblical account – not only the year (before Herod died) but the season (March would be a likely time for shepherds to be out tending their flocks in the lambing season). Intriguingly, a faint nova was seen in the same part of the sky in 1925, and since all novae are thought to be recurrent, it may be that this was the star observed by the Magi. Whether it was or not, the expanding shell of debris from the nova observed by the Chinese should soon be detectable to the latest telescopes, and that will pin down its exact location. Even without that confirmation, however, some astronomers are convinced that the evidence is strong enough to pin down the time of the birth of Jesus not 25 December in the year 1, but late March in the year 5 BC. Which, among other things, means that everybody celebrated the end of the second millennium after His birth five years late!

1 and 2. Supernova 1987 A (left) compared with the same star before it exploded (right).

A BIGGER BLAST

Type II supernovae occur in massive, young stars rich in heavy elements produced by nucleosynthesis. These stellar explosions mainly occur in the spiral arms of disc galaxies (▷ p. 22), because the stars involved are so massive they do not have time to move far from their place of birth before they die. They also occur in other regions where starbirth has been triggered. This happens, for example, when clouds of gas and dust in a relatively quiet galaxy are disturbed by the tidal forces created when another galaxy passes nearby, and collapse to form new stars. Type II supernovae release even more energy when they explode than Type I supernovae, but they are not as bright to conventional telescopes, because most of this energy is released in the form of invisible particles called neutrinos. A Type II supernova produces in a few minutes about 100 times as much energy as the Sun will radiate over its entire lifetime of 10 billion years or more.

The more massive a star is, the more quickly it burns its fuel, and the shorter its life. The progenitors of Type II supernovae can have masses tens of times that of our Sun, but to give an example of how they are formed we must look at the evolution of a star which starts out with a little less than 20 solar masses of material. It is thought to be the mass of a supernova that was seen to explode in the Large Magellanic Cloud in 1987, the supernova known as SN 1987A.

Running Out of Fuel

Such a star has to burn nuclear fuel so fiercely to hold itself up that it shines 40,000 times brighter than our Sun and spends only 10 million years on the main sequence. Burning helium as a red giant supplies it with energy for only another million years or so, and then it runs through the remaining possibilities offered by nuclear fusion at an ever faster rate. Converting carbon into a mixture of oxygen, neon and magnesium provides energy for 12,000 years; burning neon and oxygen sustains it for another 16 years; and fusion of silicon nuclei to make iron-family nuclei keeps it going for about a week. During that last week of its life as a more or less stable star, the inner core of the giant star is like a series of Russian dolls, with each of these nuclear

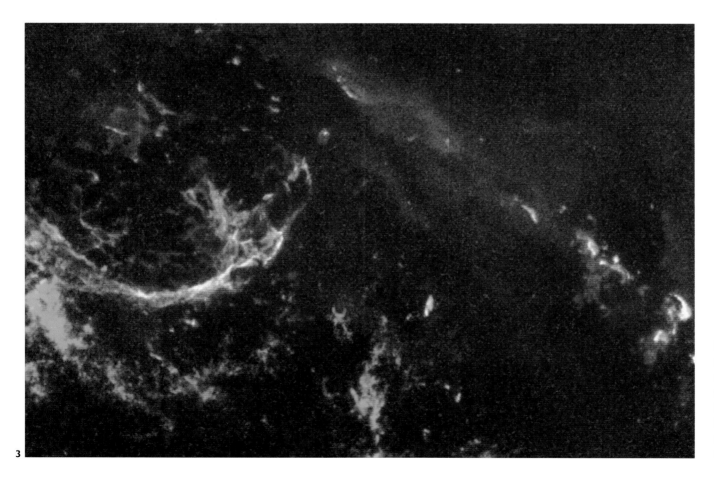

3. The remnant of a supernova that exploded long ago in the Large Magellanic Cloud. The colour indicates the presence of large amounts of oxygen.

1

1. One of our nearby irregular galaxies, NGC 1313.

2. Relative sizes of stars. To help put this into perspective, a white dwarf is about the same size as Earth.

fusion processes going on one inside the other.

Once the silicon in the core has been converted into iron-family elements, there is no longer a source of energy to provide pressure to hold the star up against its own weight. With the rug pulled from under it, the star collapses in spectacular fashion, converting gravitational energy into a heat so intense that it breaks the heavy nuclei apart. This produces a pressure so great that it forces electrons to combine with protons to make

neutrons. The inner core of the star collapses in a few seconds from a sphere of star-stuff bigger than the Sun into a ball of neutrons about 20 km across. This leaves the outer layers of the star, with perhaps 15 times as much mass as our Sun (remember that it will have lost a lot of its original mass during its time as a red giant), plunging inward at about a quarter of the speed of light. But the formation of the neutron star produces a shock wave which ripples out from the core in a kind of rebound, rapidly followed (really rapidly, at almost the speed of light) by a blast of neutrinos. One neutrino is released for every proton that combines with an electron to make a neutron.

The combination of the shock wave and the neutrino blast turns the collapsing outer layers of the star (all 15 solar masses) inside out, and sends them hurtling out into space to form a rapidly expanding, glowing cloud of gas – a supernova remnant.

A Blast of Oxygen

Whereas Type I supernovae eject huge amounts of iron into the interstellar medium, most of the iron in a Type II supernova is converted into neutrons in the core collapse. The material that gets thrown out by a Type II supernova is very rich in oxygen – perhaps as much as 1.5 solar masses of oxygen for a 20 solar mass supernova – but it also contains all the heavy elements produced by stellar

nucleosynthesis, plus a smattering of elements even heavier than iron, produced in the extreme conditions of the supernova itself (particularly in the shock wave). This is where things like gold, zinc, uranium, and everything heavier than iron originate.

The amount of very heavy elements produced, however, is tiny compared with the amount of hydrogen and helium in the Universe. Remember that everything else (all the nuclear matter that is not hydrogen or helium), put together amounts to less than 1 per cent of the matter that is. Of that everything else, all of the nuclei of everything heavier than iron put together add up to less than one thousandth as much matter as all the nuclei from lithium (the third lightest element) to iron family elements put together. Without Type II supernovae, the very heavy elements would not exist at all. Life might still exist, but there would be no radioactivity and no fission bombs.

A thimbleful of neutron star stuff would contain as much mass as there is in the bodies of all the people on Earth put together.

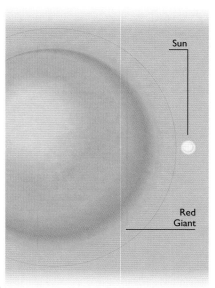

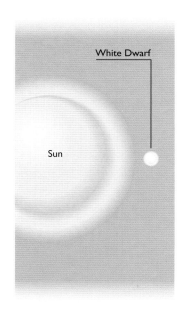

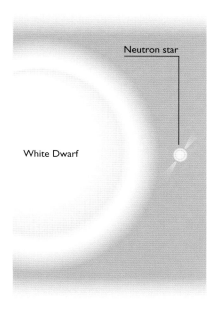

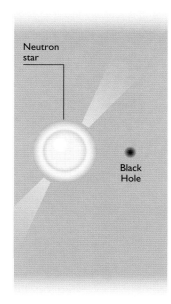

2

1. A detailed view of the Crab Nebula shows how the nebula is still being affected by the activity of the central neutron star.

2. The magnetic field of a spinning neutron star forces radiation out in two beams, like a lighthouse. Such an active, spinning neutron star is called a pulsar.

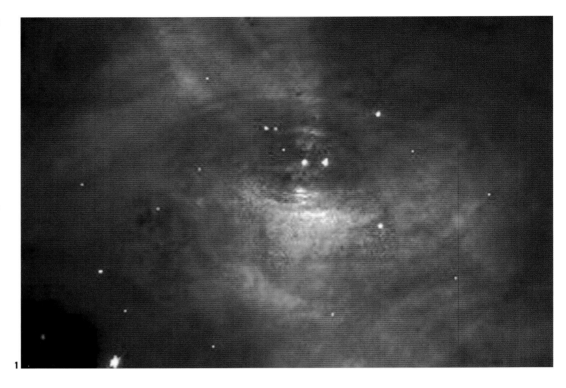

1

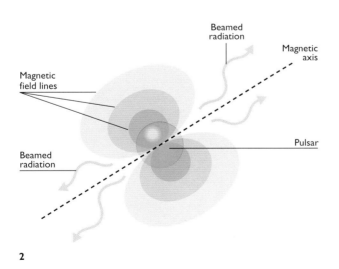

2

▷ PULSARS

A spinning, magnetic neutron star produces beams of radio waves which sweep around as the star rotates. When these beams happen to flick past the Earth (like the beams of a cosmic lighthouse) they produce regular, rapid blips of noise in radio telescopes. Such objects are called pulsars. The first known pulsars were discovered by accident in 1967, by a team at the University of Cambridge that had built a new kind of radio telescope to look at flickering in the radio output of quasars. When theorists realized that pulsars must be spinning neutron stars, it opened the way for a new wave of investigation of very dense objects (neutron stars and black holes) in a classic example of how observation and theory combine in the exploration of the Universe.

Roughly a thousand pulsars have now been discovered, and the number is growing. The magnetic field of a pulsar is about 1000 million times as strong as the magnetic field of the Earth. Most of them spin once every second or so; the slowest pulsar has a period of about 4 seconds, but the fastest yet discovered spins on its axis more than 600 times a second. Imagine a ball of stuff the size of Mount Everest but containing as much mass as our Sun, spinning once on its axis every 1.6 milliseconds and you have some idea what a pulsar is like.

BLACK HOLES AND NEUTRON STARS

The remnant left behind by such a supernova is almost as interesting as the supernova itself. It is a star made almost entirely of neutrons – a neutron star – matter packed into the most compact state possible, with a density the same as that of an atomic nucleus. If such a neutron star had the same mass as our Sun, it would have a diameter of only about 10 or 20 kilometres, the size of a large mountain on Earth. This is far smaller even than a white dwarf which packs about a solar mass of material into a sphere about the same size as the Earth. The density of matter in a neutron star is about 1 million times the density of a white dwarf. If it could be magically transported to Earth and kept in its superdense state, a cubic centimetre of a neutron star would weigh about 100 million tonnes.

Under the extreme conditions of pressure that occur at the heart of a Type II supernova, neutron stars with as little as one-tenth of the mass of our Sun can form. But any neutron star with less mass than this that was formed in such a blast would expand as the pressure was released and turn into an unusual low-mass white dwarf (with some of the neutrons converting themselves into protons).

In the Realm of Speculation

A few astronomers speculated about the existence of neutron stars in the 1930s, soon after the neutron itself was discovered. One team, Walter Baade and Fritz Zwicky, even speculated (in 1934) that the only way to explain the energy output of a supernova would be by the transition of an ordinary star into a neutron star, releasing huge amounts of gravitational energy. But whereas white dwarfs had been identified in 1934, nobody had ever seen a neutron star, and most astronomers could not accept what the equations of physics were telling them. They didn't believe that such superdense objects really existed. Baade and Zwicky's speculation was not taken seriously by most of their colleagues for three decades, until the accidental discovery of pulsars, which were explained as rapidly spinning, magnetic neutron stars.

The Earth would have to be squeezed to the size of a large pea in order to become a black hole.

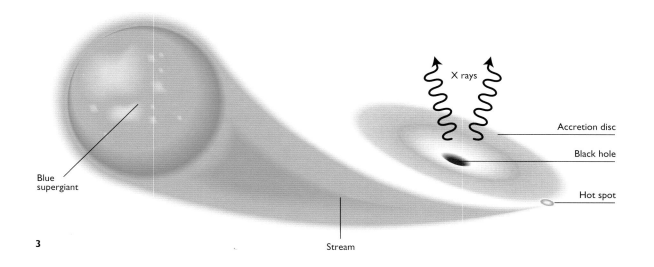

Blue supergiant

X rays

Accretion disc

Black hole

Hot spot

Stream

3. When matter from a giant star streams onto a black hole companion, the material gets hot and emits x-rays.

THE SEARCH FOR BLACK HOLES

Even after the discovery of pulsars started astronomers thinking about the possibility of black holes, there was no proof that they existed. But at the beginning of the 1970s, a satellite called Uhuru pinpointed the position on the sky of an X-ray star (▷ p. 64) called Cygnus X-1. The positioning was accurate enough for optical astronomers to identify the star with their telescopes. (Cygnus X-1 gets its name because it is the brightest X-ray star in the direction of the constellation Cygnus, the swan.)

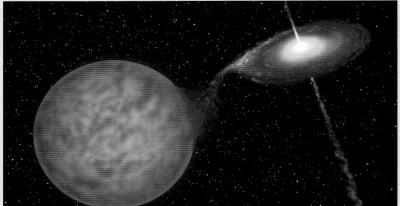

A Dying Swan

When astronomers studied the source of the X-rays from Cygnus, they found that the X-rays were coming from a point near a blue star called HDE 226868, but not from the star itself. The star and the X-ray source orbit around each other once every 5.6 days and the orbit corresponds to an object with a mass of about 20 times the mass of the Sun. This means that the X-ray source cannot be either a white dwarf or a neutron star, and if it were an ordinary star that big, held up by nuclear fusion, it would be bright enough to see (nearly as bright as its blue companion). Theory and observations combined to show that it could only be a black hole – a dead

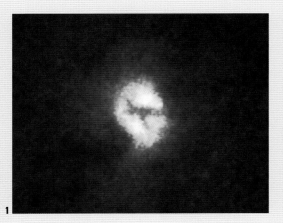

(or dying) star. Several similar objects are now known, and they are referred to as 'stellar mass black holes', because they have masses similar to those of stars.

Stellar mass black holes are difficult to find, because they only show up if they are in orbit around another star, stripping matter away from it and swallowing it in a messy fashion. An isolated black hole is, indeed, black. But using our understanding of how stars evolve, Roger Blandford, of Caltech, has estimated that there may be 100 million isolated black holes scattered across our Milky Way galaxy, and that the nearest one may be only 5 parsecs (15 light years) away.

Bigger Black Holes

From the late 1960s onward, astronomers speculated that quasars must be what are known as 'supermassive black holes', with masses roughly 100 million times the mass of the Sun, because the only way that enough energy can be liberated to explain the output of a quasar is if it is a large black hole swallowing matter from its surrounding galaxy. This was finally proved in the 1990s, when the Hubble Space Telescope obtained images which show the discs of material swirling around some of these black holes. The size of these discs and the speed with which they move (revealed by the Doppler

4

1. Actual photograph of the centre of a system like the ones illustrated here. This is a black hole at the heart of the galaxy M51 taken by the Hubble Space Telescope.

2. Illustration of a super-massive black hole ejecting jets of material from its poles.

3 and 4. Close-up views (artist's impression) of black hole activity.

effect – ▷ p.120) tells us how big the central black holes in these galaxies are.

In a typical example, the galaxy NGC 7052, there is a disc of material 1100 parsecs (3700 light years) in diameter swirling round a black hole with a mass 300 million times the mass of our Sun. The disc itself contains 3 million solar masses of material – enough to keep the quasar shining for 3 million years, because it swallows only one solar mass a year.

Bending Space
The general theory of relativity explains gravity as a result of space being bent by the presence of matter. In a neat aphorism,

physicists say that matter tells space how to bend; space tells matter how to move. In effect, objects moving under the influence of gravity roll along the valleys in a hilly landscape of curved space (strictly, curved spacetime). Using this image, flat spacetime, without any matter in it, is like a stretched flat sheet of rubber (or a trampoline). A heavy weight placed on the stretched sheet makes a dent, and anything rolling across the sheet follows a curved path around the dent. If the object is heavy enough, it stretches the fabric so much that it makes a deep pit with vertical sides, from which nothing can escape – a black hole.

⟡ TOPIC LINKS

1.4 Out with a Bang
p. 71 Black Holes and Neutron Stars
p. 75 Proof of the Pudding

2.1 The Big Bang
p. 87 The Singular Beginning

4.3 Into the Unknown
p. 217 Beyond the Black Hole
p. 230 The Evolution of Universes

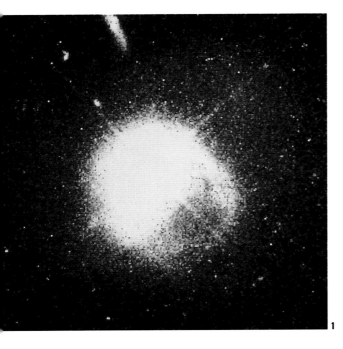

⭐ Gamma ray bursts from space were first identified in the late 1960s by American satellites designed to look for gamma rays from any secret nuclear bomb tests being carried out in Russia.

Singularities

The discovery of pulsars meant that the equations which said neutron stars exist had to be taken seriously. That meant that another, even stranger, prediction of those equations also had to be taken seriously. At the end of the 1930s, Robert Oppenheimer and George Volkoff had shown that the equations which say neutron stars exist also say that there is an upper limit to the amount of mass a neutron star can have. The exact value of this upper limit depends on subtleties in the equations, which the experts still argue about, but it is about three times the mass of the Sun. What would happen to any neutron star that tried to form with more mass than this, or which started out with less mass but crossed the line as a result of accreting material from a companion? The equations said that it would shrink down indefinitely, towards a single point – a singularity.

But on the way to a singularity, a collapsing object would disappear from view, because the gravitational pull at its surface would become so intense that nothing, not even light, could escape. The work of Robert Oppenheimer and his colleagues was not followed up at the time because of the Second World War. Oppenheimer himself worked on the Manhattan Project – to build the first nuclear bomb.

In fact, collapsed objects like this had already been described, using the equations of Albert Einstein's general theory of relativity, by Karl Schwarzschild, in the second decade of the twentieth century. In terms of relativity theory, the collapsed object is pinched off from our Universe because space itself (strictly speaking, 'spacetime') has been bent (or warped) around it, making a hole in space. The interior of the hole is, in effect, a separate, self-contained universe. These objects were only given their now-familiar name, 'black holes', in 1967, just after the discovery of pulsars made everyone begin to take the idea seriously.

Getting to Grips with Black Holes

Any object will form a black hole if it is squeezed into a small enough volume. For a particular mass, the crucial radius at which this occurs is called the Schwarzschild radius, and this becomes, in effect, the radius of the black hole. Once anything is squeezed within its Schwarzschild radius, it will collapse to a singularity, leaving a black hole with that radius as its imprint on our Universe, like the grin on the face of the fading Cheshire cat. For the Sun, the Schwarzschild radius is just 2.9 km, which shows how close neutron stars (with radii of about 10 km) are to becoming black holes. For the Earth, it is only 0.88 cm. But black holes need not necessarily be associated with very high densities. An object with the same density as the Sun (or water) would be a black hole if it were about as big across as our Solar System.

There is now direct proof that black holes exist. Even though nothing can escape from a black hole (so it cannot be seen directly), there may be a great deal of activity going on just outside the Schwarzschild radius (which is also known as the 'event horizon'). If a black hole with a radius of a few kilometres is in orbit around another star, stripping matter away from it and swallowing it up, there will be an intensely swirling maelstrom of stuff orbiting around the black hole in a disc and being sucked in. Gravitational energy released as the matter falls into the black hole will heat this disc to the point where it radiates X-rays. Such X-ray stars have been detected orbiting ordinary stars, and their masses, sometimes exceeding 10 solar masses, have been measured from studies of their orbits.

There is no doubt that some of these X-ray stars are black holes.

Much more massive black holes (perhaps containing 100 million solar masses of material, and as big across as our Solar System) are also thought to reside at the hearts of galaxies, where the energy released as they swallow matter makes the gas around some of them shine more brightly than the rest of the galaxy put together. They are known as quasars. To give you some idea of the enormous amount of energy that can be released when matter falls into a black hole, the energy output of a quasar can be maintained by swallowing only about one solar mass of material each year.

Proof of the Pudding

The best evidence that black holes exist came in the 1990s, when astronomers identified the sources of intense bursts of gamma rays detected by instruments on board satellites orbiting the Earth. These gamma ray bursts had long been known, but it was only at the end of 1997 that astronomers were first able to identify the source of one of these bursts using ordinary telescopes. It turned out to be in a galaxy more than 3 billion parsecs (10 billion light years) from Earth. In order to produce a burst of gamma rays visible to our detectors that far away, for a few seconds the object had radiated as much energy as every star in every galaxy in the visible Universe

put together. In a region about 150 km across, it briefly produced conditions like those which existed in the Big Bang itself. The only way in which to generate such enormous outbursts of energy in such a short time is in a kind of super supernova (a hypernova?) where the core collapse does not stop at the neutron star stage, but goes all the way to a black hole. The power of a quasar (as bright as several hundred billion Suns) comes from swallowing about one solar mass of material in a year; the power of a gamma ray burster comes from swallowing several solar masses of material in a few seconds. It is the ultimate form of stellar death.

1. The quasar PKS2349 photographed by the Hubble Space Telescope.

2. Radiation coming from a region of space where a black hole has collapsed is like the fading grin of the Cheshire cat.

2

THE FATE OF THE UNIVERSE

THE BIG BANG

One of the greatest achievements of the human intellect was the discovery in the twentieth century that the Universe as we know it originated in a hot, superdense state at a definite moment in time (a beginning, if you like), that it has been expanding ever since, and that we can work out when time began – about 14 billion years ago. It is pleasing too that the age of the Universe, determined from cosmology, closely matches the ages of the oldest stars determined by astrophysics.

There is overwhelming evidence in support of both the idea of the Big Bang, as it is known, and when it occurred. At the beginning of the twenty-first century, instead of resting on their laurels, cosmologists are now attempting to answer the other big questions about the Universe: where it is going and how it will all end. The first tantalizing clues that we might soon be able to give definite answers to these questions came at the end of the twentieth century.

Previous page. The Hubble Deep Field. Galaxies seen by light that left them more than 10 billion years ago.

THE LAW ACCORDING TO HUBBLE

The most important thing we know about the Universe is that it is expanding, that galaxies (or rather whole clusters of galaxies) are getting farther apart as time passes. We cannot see the distance increasing between them, because the distance scales and time scales involved are so huge. Even if we watched for a million years, we would scarcely be able to detect the expansion of the Universe directly. But we know for sure that the Universe is expanding, because we can measure both the distances to many galaxies and the speeds with which those same galaxies seem to be receding from us.

The key discovery is that there is a very simple relationship between these two properties, telling us that the apparent velocity recession is proportional to the distance of a galaxy from us. This is known as Hubble's Law, and the constant of proportionality in Hubble's Law is called the Hubble Parameter (or sometimes, Hubble's Constant); it is denoted by the letter H. Hubble's Law does not mean, however, that we are at the centre of the Universe. It is the only velocity/distance law (except for a situation in which nothing is moving at all) which holds wherever you are in the Universe.

Everything is receding from everything else, like raisins being carried away from one another in the rising dough of a raisin loaf as it

To a cosmologist, a galaxy like the Milky Way, containing hundreds of billions of stars, is the *smallest* thing in the Universe worth taking account of.

1. The Andromeda galaxy, also known as M31, is the nearest large spiral galaxy to our own.

cooks. Whichever galaxy you sit on, it will look as if all the other galaxies are rushing away from you with speeds proportional to their distances.

Beyond the Local Group

The first measurements of distances to galaxies beyond the Milky Way were made at the end of the 1920s, using the Cepheid distance scale (▷pp. 28–9). But even with the aid of the best telescopes that were available before the 1990s, it was not possible to detect Cepheids in more than a handful of the very nearest galaxies to our own. However, this was enough to show that the Milky Way and the Andromeda galaxy (also known as M31) are the two largest members of a small group of galaxies which also includes the Large and Small Magellanic Clouds, and is collectively known as the Local Group. The Local Group is actually a very small cluster of galaxies – other clusters of galaxies contain hundreds or even thousands of individual galaxies. In a cluster, the individual members are held together by gravity, and move around within the cluster like individual bees moving within a swarm. But the cluster as a whole takes part in the expansion of the Universe (the swarm of bees moves as a unit).

Right up until the 1990s, measuring distances to galaxies beyond the Local Group depended on using so-called 'secondary indicators' calibrated within the Local Group. Because the distances to galaxies in the Local Group (in particular, the distance to the Andromeda galaxy) are known from the Cepheid method astronomers can study the apparent brightnesses of bright objects in these nearby galaxies and use the known distances to work out how bright they really are. This makes it possible to calibrate the brightness of things like globular clusters, supernovae, and the huge star-forming clouds known as 'HII regions'. Then, by identifying

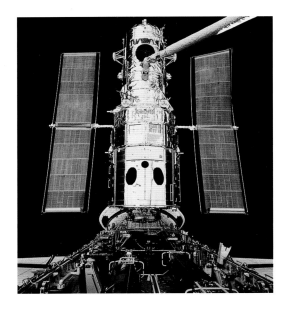

 THE OLDEST THINGS IN THE UNIVERSE

Until the middle of the 1990s, astronomers were slightly embarrassed to admit that their best estimates of the age of the Universe came out at slightly less than their best estimates of the ages of the oldest stars. Obviously, the Universe must be older than the stars it contains, but measurements of the Hubble Parameter using ground-based telescopes gave rather rough and ready estimates. They showed that the Universe was about 10–12 billion years old, while the oldest stars were thought to be 14–15 billion years old. The astronomers weren't too perturbed, however, because both measurements were difficult and plagued with uncertainties, and they expected one or both of them to need adjustment when telescopes were flown above the obscuring layer of the Earth's atmosphere.

In fact, both of them needed adjusting, and in the 'right' way. In the second half of the 1990s, data from the Hubble Space Telescope (left) showed that the Hubble Parameter is a little smaller than had been thought. This meant that the best estimate for the age of the Universe became 14 billion years. At almost the same time, data from the HIP-PARCOS satellite showed that some of the stars used to calibrate stellar ages were a little further away than had been thought, so they must be a little brighter than was thought in order to look as bright as they do to us. And that implies they must burn their fuel faster than anyone had thought, so they haven't taken as long to get to their present state. The best estimate for the ages of the oldest stars came down, as a result, to 12–13 billion years.

1. The way open clusters of stars move through space is like a swarm of bees moving through the air.

2. The globular cluster 47 Tucanae.

the same sort of objects in galaxies beyond the Local Group, and measuring the brightness (or faintness) of those objects compared with their counterparts in the Andromeda galaxy, it is possible to estimate the distances to more remote galaxies.

The key step in all this is working out the distance to the Virgo Cluster, which contains about 2500 galaxies spread over a spherical volume of space the centre of which is about 17 million parsecs (17 Megaparsecs, or roughly 55 million light years) away from us. The Virgo Cluster contains so many different galaxies that it provides ample secondary indicators that can be used (after they have been calibrated from the measured distance to the

cluster) to work out distances to even more remote galaxies.

But the distance to the Virgo Cluster itself was only measured really accurately in the 1990s, when the Hubble Space Telescope was able, for the first time, to pick out individual Cepheids in some of the galaxies in the cluster. That is why the distances to galaxies beyond the Local Group were only finally pinned down in the last decade of the twentieth century. And that meant they could be reliably compared with the velocity measurements to work out the Hubble Parameter, and therefore the age of the Universe, which depends on the Hubble Parameter.

Galaxies on the Move

The 'velocities' of galaxies associated with the expansion of the Universe are measured in terms of redshift , and in some ways they behave like Doppler shifts. But they are not Doppler shifts, and they are not really velocities (this caused a lot of confusion at one time, but is quite easy to understand now that cosmologists have a clear idea of what is going on).

Redshifts in the light from a few other galaxies (then called 'nebulae') were first identified in the second decade of the twentieth century. But they were first studied systematically and put into their modern cosmological context by Edwin Hubble and

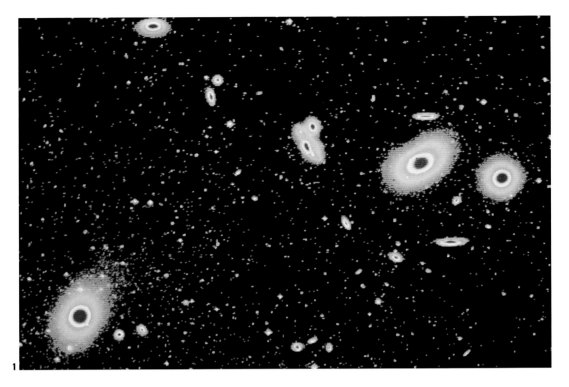

1

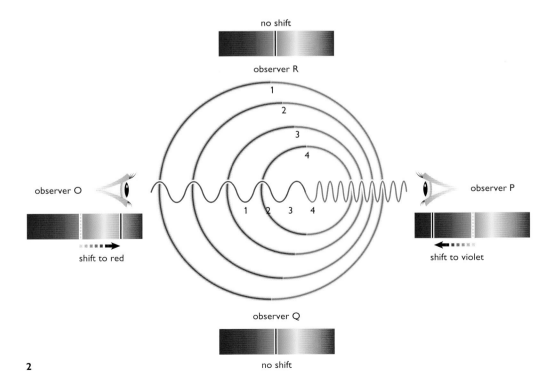

2

no shift

observer R

observer O

shift to red

observer P

shift to violet

observer Q

no shift

Milton Humason, working at the Mount Wilson Observatory in California, in the 1920s and 1930s. They found evidence that the redshift of a galaxy (provided it is outside the Local Group) is proportional to its distance from us.

Because a Doppler redshift would mean that an object is moving away from us through space, at first it was thought that this cosmological redshift was because the galaxies were hurtling apart through space, like pieces of shrapnel from the explosion of a huge bomb. But the recession of the galaxies from one another was quickly explained in terms of Albert Einstein's general theory of relativity, which describes the behaviour of space and time under the influence of matter. Einstein's theory says that space itself (strictly speaking, spacetime) is flexible, and can be stretched and squeezed.

When the equations of Einstein's theory are used to provide a description of the whole Universe (what cosmologists and mathematicians call a 'model' of the Universe), they say that it is possible for either stretching or squeezing to happen naturally, but that it is *not* possible for the Universe to stand still. Since we see other galaxies moving away from us, we know that what is happening is a stretching of space. The space between the galaxies (strictly, between clusters of galaxies) is expanding and taking galaxies along for the ride. The galaxies are not moving through space, so this is not a velocity. But because space is stretching while light from distant galaxies is travelling through it, the light gets stretched to longer wavelengths – it is redshifted. And this redshift mimics the Doppler Effect.

The distances between clusters of galaxies are getting bigger today, at a rate we can measure. This means that clusters of galaxies used to be closer together. If we could wind the expansion backwards for long enough, all

3

the galaxies would be touching one another. Go back further and they would be squashed together into one hot lump. This is the origin of the idea that the Universe was born in a hot Big Bang at a definite moment in time. We can calculate when this happened – about 14 billion years ago – from Hubble's Law. But is there any other evidence that the Big Bang really happened?

Microwaves from the Birth of Time

The discovery that convinced many people that the Big Bang really happened came in 1965, when two researchers at the Bell Laboratories in the United States, Arno Penzias and Robert Wilson, discovered a faint hiss of radio noise coming from all directions in space. This is exactly like the kind of static you hear on a badly tuned radio receiver – indeed, some of that static is radio noise from the depths of space.

This 'cosmic microwave background radiation' had been predicted, using Big Bang theory, by George Gamow and his colleagues in the late 1940s. But Penzias and Wilson didn't know that when they made their discovery, by accident, while testing a new radio telescope.

The Big Bang theory says that the furthest back we can ever 'see' using any kind of electromagnetic radiation is the time when the whole Universe was as hot as the surface of the Sun is today. Before that time it was so hot that electrons were stripped from their atoms, leaving a mixture of negatively charged electrons and positively charged nuclei (called a 'plasma'). Because electromagnetic radiation interacts with charged particles, under those conditions the electromagnetic waves are bounced around like crazy and thoroughly mixed up. This is why we cannot see inside the Sun. For the same reason, we cannot see further back

The name 'Big Bang' to describe the birth of the Universe was coined by cosmologist Fred Hoyle (now Sir Fred) in a BBC radio broadcast in the 1940s.

1. A representation of the COBE satellite in orbit.

2. George Gamow, one of the founders of the Big Bang theory.

1

towards the Big Bang than the time when the entire Universe was as hot as the surface of the Sun is now.

The Very First Light

Once the whole Universe cooled to the temperature of the surface of the Sun today, electrons and nuclei combined to make neutral atoms. By and large, these do not interact with light – they will, but only if the wavelength of the light is just right to match the steps in their spectroscopic energy levels (▷ pp. 18–19). This meant that the light from the Big Bang could at last stream out through the gaps between the atoms, filling the entire Universe. If the time when everything in the entire visible Universe today was piled up in one place is set as 'time zero', this critical temperature (about 6000 K) was reached between 300,000 and 500,000 years later. This is the time of the first light, when matter and radiation are said to have 'decoupled'.

Since then, the Universe has expanded enormously, and the electromagnetic radiation that filled the Universe has been stretched and redshifted accordingly. It is straightforward to calculate the effect this has on the radiation. It turns light, just like the light from the Sun and stars, with a temperature of about 6000 K, into much longer wavelength radio waves, with a temperature of only a few Kelvin. It is exactly like the radiation in a microwave oven, but with a temperature of about *minus* 270 degrees Celsius.

This is exactly what Penzias and Wilson found, and which other radio astronomers soon confirmed: a hiss of cool microwave radiation, coming from all directions in space (from the gaps between the galaxies). This radiation has not interacted with anything at all from 500,000 years after time zero until it fell into the radio telescopes used to detect it.

Over the next two decades, many different radio telescopes, operating at many different wavelengths, identified the cosmic microwave background radiation and confirmed that it has exactly the right properties to be the highly redshifted first light from the Big Bang itself. These measurements also pinned down the temperature of this radiation very precisely (to 2.735 K). By 1978, the evidence that this really was the 'echo of the Big Bang' was so compelling that Penzias and Wilson received the Nobel Prize for their work.

A Smooth Beginning

Apart from the fact that it exists, however, the most important thing about the background radiation is that it is very smooth. To this accuracy (three decimal places, better than 0.01 per cent or 1 part in 10,000), the temperature is exactly the same from all parts of the sky. Matter and radiation were inextricably mixed up until the time of the first light. This meant that when matter and radiation decoupled, the hot gas that later went on to form stars and galaxies was also distributed very smoothly through the Universe, smooth to an accuracy of better than 0.01 per cent.

This tells us that the Big Bang itself was a very smooth event – and gives astronomers the task of explaining how things like stars and galaxies ever did get to clump together from such a smooth beginning.

The Birth of the Universe

In the ten years after Einstein came up with the general theory of relativity in 1916, mathematicians played with the equations, exploring the possibilities allowed by the laws of physics, because that's what they like to do – play with equations. It was only after Hubble and Humason discovered Hubble's Law – that redshift is proportional to distance – that anyone realized that the equations might be describing the actual expanding Universe in which we live. The person who first tried to use the equations to work out how the Universe was born was a Belgian astronomer by the name of Georges Lemaître. This was the beginning of Big Bang cosmology.

A TV screen when it is on, but not tuned in, will show white dots dancing on it. Some of these (about 1 per cent) are caused by cosmic background radiation.

2

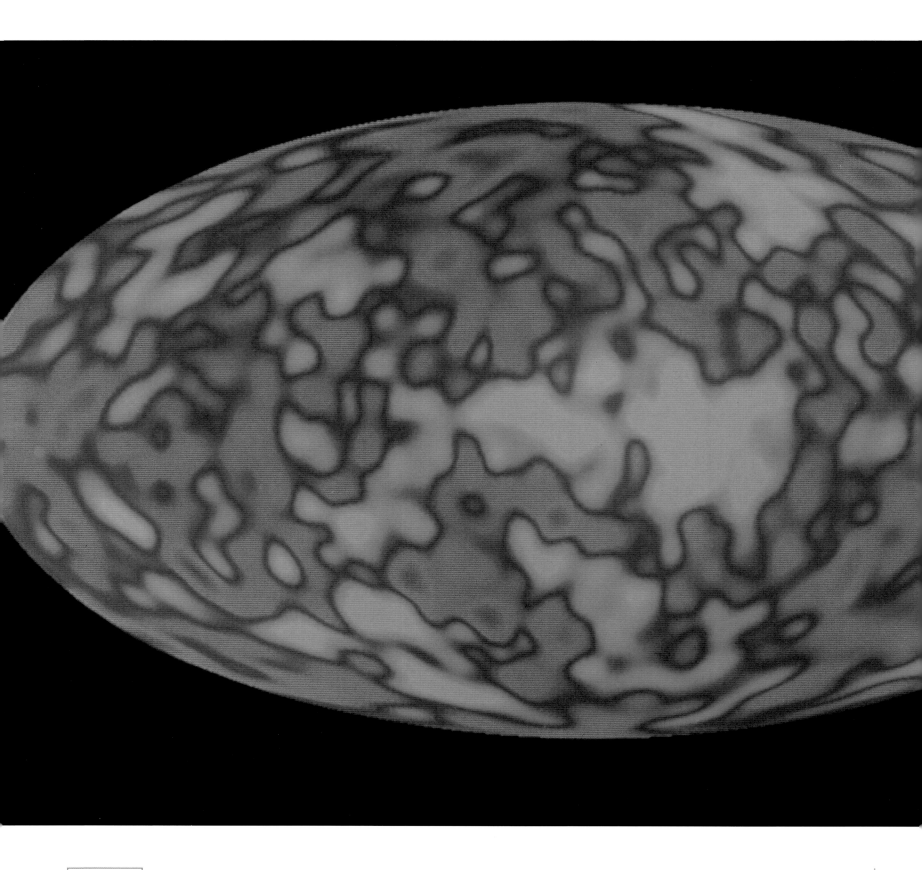

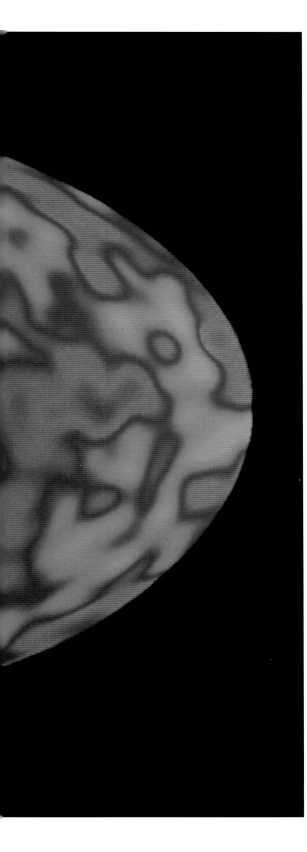

The Cosmic Egg

Lemaître developed his ideas about what we now call the Big Bang in the 1930s and 1940s. He realized that, because the Universe is expanding, with galaxies getting further apart, it must have been in a superdense state long ago, with everything in the visible Universe today packed together in a single lump of stuff with the same density as the nucleus of an atom (or a neutron star ▷ p. 71). He sometimes called this the 'Primal Atom', and sometimes referred to it as the 'Cosmic Egg'. The amazing thing about Lemaître's calculation is that the Cosmic Egg would only have been about 30 times the diameter of the Sun – much smaller than the Solar System. This gives you some idea of just how much empty space there is between the stars and galaxies; it also shows how much smaller than an atom an atomic nucleus is (which is why 'Primal Atom' is a bad choice of name – it should have been 'Primal Nucleus').

Lemaître didn't try to explain where the Cosmic Egg had come from. He had the idea that it was rather like a giant unstable atomic nucleus, and that it had 'split', or decayed, in just the same way that an unstable nucleus of an element such as uranium-235 splits into lighter elements. It is no coincidence that Lemaître developed these ideas at about the same time that physicists were first studying the natural decay of elements like uranium-235, and developing the first so-called atomic bombs. This depends on the process properly referred to as nuclear fission, but which is popularly known as 'splitting the atom' (so an 'atomic' bomb is really a nuclear

bomb). This is why Lemaître, a great popularizer of science, referred to a Primal Atom.

This is an unfortunate analogy in one way, because it gives the impression that the Cosmic Egg was sitting somewhere in empty space for an indefinite time and then exploded outwards into space. Einstein's equations, however, tell us that there was no empty space for it to explode into. The egg contained all the matter in the Universe and all the empty space. The primal stuff, whatever it was, expanded outwards, because space itself expanded.

The Singular Beginning

Einstein's equations also tell us where Lemaître's Cosmic Egg came from. Although the density of an atomic nucleus, or a neutron star, is the most extreme density that matter can exist in today, if it is compressed even further it will shrink down into a point and become a black hole as it does so (▷p. 69). In 1965, the mathematician Roger Penrose proved, using Einstein's equations, that when a black hole forms, all the matter in it must fall into a single point inside the black hole, a point of infinite density and zero volume known, for obvious reasons, as a 'singularity'.

There is only one way in which it might be possible to avoid this happening, and that is if, as the matter falls towards the singularity, conditions become so extreme that the general theory of relativity is inadequate to describe what is going on. Almost certainly, this must happen before the density gets to infinity. But many tests have shown that the general theory of relativity is still a good description of what is going on until everything in the black hole has been squeezed into a tiny volume smaller than a sub-atomic particle, such as a proton or a neutron. This is good enough to take us beyond the Cosmic Egg and back to the

1. This false-colour image based on **COBE** data shows the whole sky in microwave 'light'. Pink shows hotter regions, and blue indicates cooler regions.

The radio telescope which discovered the background radiation had originally been designed and used for early experiments in sending TV signals across the Atlantic by satellite.

moment when time began.

The point is, that something collapsing inside a black hole towards a singularity looks a lot like something expanding outwards from a singularity, if time is reversed. It's easy to guess that the Cosmic Egg might have expanded out from a singularity, in a kind of mirror image of the way matter collapses inside black holes. But it is much harder to prove that this is the way the Universe works. Nevertheless, by 1970, Penrose (in collaboration with Stephen Hawking) had refined his earlier calculations to show that this is the case. The way the Universe is expanding today proves that it started out from a singularity – or at least, from a point so small and dense that the general theory of

relativity breaks down, a point even smaller than a proton or a neutron. By the time it was as big as Lemaître's Primal Atom, the Universe was already expanding rapidly as space stretched, and the simplest description of the Universe we see around us is that it is the inside of a rapidly expanding black hole.

But there is a lot more to cosmology than this simple description. One of the most fertile areas of scientific research in the 1990s and 2000s is the developing understanding of how the very early stages in the expansion of the Universe have imprinted it with the structure we see around us today. The existence of clusters of galaxies can now be seen to match the predictions of our model of the very early Unniverse.

 ## BLACK BODY RADIATION

Because a red-hot object is cooler than an object glowing orange, which is cooler than an object glowing blue-white, astronomers can tell which stars are hotter than others by looking at their colours. They can do even better than this, because there is a mathematical expression which describes very accurately how the spectrum of energy radiated by an object at different wavelengths depends on its temperature. This is called the 'black body curve' (detected by the Bell Laboratories Horn Antenna, left). It may seem odd to describe a glowing object as a 'black' body, but the name derives from the fact that the same mathematical expression describes how radiation is absorbed by a perfectly black object. So 'black body radiation' can come from very hot, bright objects.

With this meaning of the term, the radiation from the surface of the Sun corresponds to radiation from a black body with a temperature of 5800 K. This temperature is measured using the black body curve which matches the Sun's spectrum. In the same way, astronomers can measure the temperature of a star thousands of light years away by comparing its spectrum of light with the appropriate black body curve.

But black bodies need not be hot. The spectrum of microwave radiation coming from all directions in space, the cosmic background radiation, has a curve which corresponds almost perfectly (to an accuracy of about one part in a 100,000) with the radiation from a black body with a temperature of 2.7 K. This is the chilled, leftover radiation from the Big Bang itself.

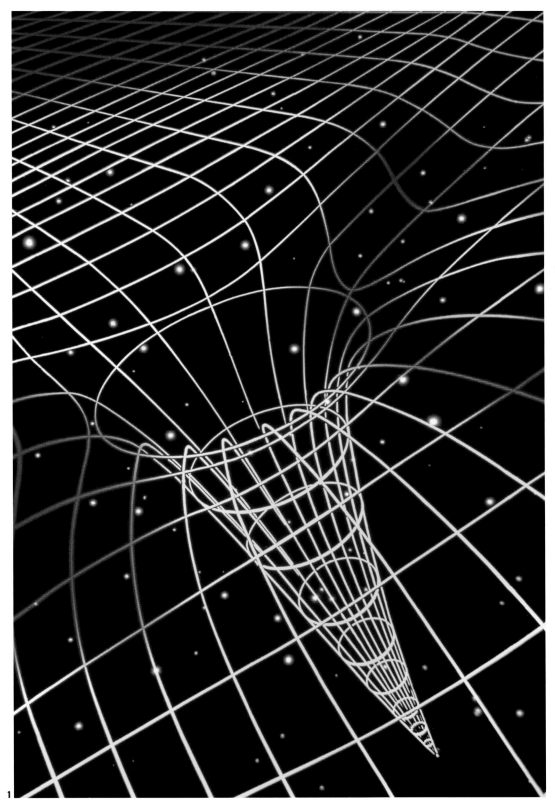

1. Representation of a singularity in space time. The same representation could describe either a collapsing black hole or the expanding Universe.

2. As well as being an astronomer, the Belgian Georges Lemaître was also an ordained priest in the Catholic church.

THE FIRST FOUR MINUTES

Stellar nucleosynthesis describes how all the elements in the Universe except primordial hydrogen and helium were 'cooked' inside stars out of that hydrogen and helium (▷ p. 54). This understanding was essentially complete by the end of the 1950s. But one key puzzle remained: where did the original hydrogen and helium come from in the first place? The greatest triumph of cosmology in the 1960s was the explanation of how interactions taking place in the Big Bang itself produced the primordial elements, with exactly the proportion of hydrogen and helium that we see in the oldest stars today, in the span of just under four minutes.

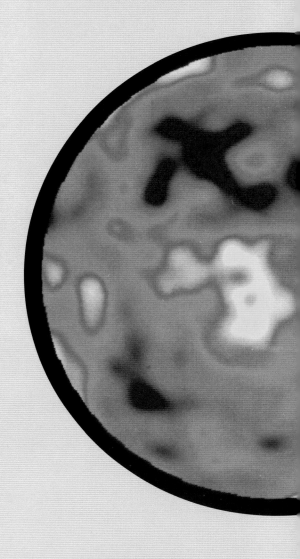

1. Fred Hoyle, whose insight led to an understanding of how the elements were made.

Matter from Radiation

The story of Big Bang nucleosynthesis begins just after the beginning of time. At time zero, the temperature everywhere was 100 billion Kelvin, so hot that most of the energy of the Universe was in the form of electromagnetic radiation, with protons and neutrons being created and destroyed by the radiation in line with Einstein's equation $E = mc^2$.

Matter began to 'freeze out' from the radiation when the temperature fell to 30 billion K, 0.1 s after time zero. At that time, the density of the entire Universe was 30 million times the density of water, but the energy was still mostly in the form of radiation. This radiation, however, could no longer create and destroy particles as easily as before (there was less E around, but the mc^2 needed to make each proton, say, was still the same). In the beginning, the radiation made equal numbers of protons and neutrons (plus lots of electrons), but because neutrons tend to decay, if they are not locked up in nuclei, spitting out an electron and turning into a proton, gradually the proportion of protons increased.

Freezing at Three Billion Degrees

By the time the temperature dropped to 3 billion K, 13.8 s after time zero, nuclei of deuterium (one proton and one neutron together) could form temporarily. They were soon knocked apart in collisions with other particles and conditions were at last starting to resemble what goes on inside stars today. Three minutes and two seconds after time

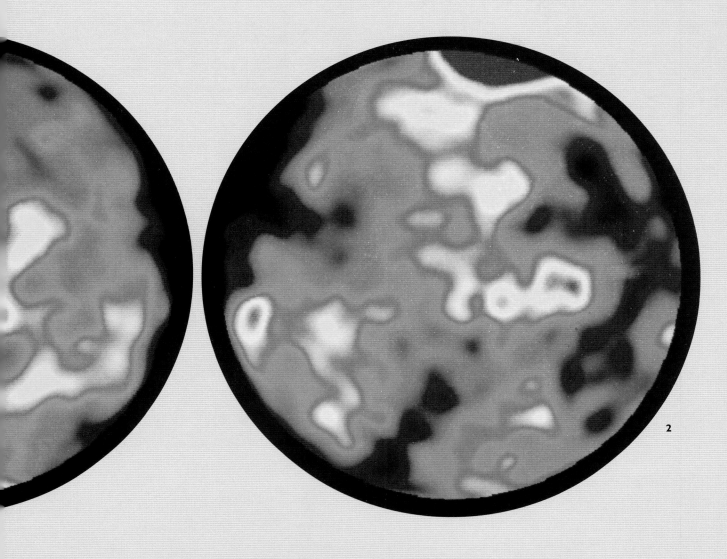

2. Detailed map of temperature variations when the Universe was half a million years old, based on data gathered by COBE over four years.

2

zero, the temperature had fallen to a billion K, just six times hotter than the heart of the Sun today, and the proportion of neutrons to protons had fallen to just 14 per cent. But they were saved from disappearing entirely because at last it was cool enough for nuclei of deuterium, and other light nuclei, to stick together permanently.

Saving Neutrons
In a flurry of nuclear reactions over the next few seconds, almost all the remaining neutrons in the Universe were locked up with protons in nuclei of helium-4, producing a mixture of about 25 per cent helium (in terms of mass), nearly 75 per cent hydrogen, and a trace of very light elements such as deuterium and lithium. This process of Big Bang nucleosynthesis finished about 3 minutes and 46 seconds after time zero – in round terms, four minutes after the beginning.

The standard Big Bang theory predicts exactly the proportion of these light elements actually seen in the oldest stars.

◆ TOPIC LINKS

1.3 Stellar Evolution
p. 53 Cooking the Elements

2.2 Cosmology for Beginners
p. 94 The Steady State Model

2.4 The Accelerating Universe
p. 132 Quantum Fluctuations
pp. 134–5 Balloons and the Background Radiation

COSMOLOGY FOR BEGINNERS

Cosmology started out as a game played by mathematicians who liked to tinker with the equations of the general theory of relativity, which describes the behaviour of space, time and matter. The Universe is the biggest collection of space, time and matter they could think of. The game started soon after Albert Einstein discovered the general theory, in 1916. Before then, any views that people had about the origin of the Universe and its ultimate fate depended entirely on philosophy or religion, and had no scientific basis.

After Einstein's discovery, ideas about the evolution of the Universe abounded, based on his equations. But it was impossible to say which set of ideas matched the real Universe. It was only right at the end of the twentieth century that cosmologists were able to test their calculations with accurate measurements of the way the real Universe behaves.

A VARIETY OF UNIVERSES

Mathematicians can use the equations of the general theory to provide mathematical descriptions of different ways in which space and time interact in the presence of matter – that is, different ways in which a universe could change as time passes. Notice the use of the lower case 'u' on 'universe' there. Cosmologists reserve the capital, Universe, to refer to the real version of spacetime in which we live. They refer to their hypothetical mathematical versions as universes, or as 'models'. There are very many (perhaps an infinite number) of model universes that can be described using Einstein's equations, and the big trick is to find one that looks just like our own Universe.

Fortunately, our Universe turns out to be a very simple variation on the theme, and can be described using a very simple version of the equations. Einstein himself marvelled at this, saying, 'the most incomprehensible thing about the Universe is that it is comprehensible.'

But just how simple *is* the Universe?

Simple Models of Space and Time

The most basic division of cosmological models into categories can be described in terms of the expansion of the Universe. The Universe is expanding today but the gravity of all the stuff in the Universe is tugging on all the stuff in the Universe and trying to slow the expansion down.

The difference between the two main kinds of model can be pictured by imagining the difference between a baseball being hit and a rocket being launched. Even the most powerful baseball player in the world cannot hit the ball hard enough for it to escape from the pull of the Earth's gravity. No matter how high the ball

1

2

1 and 2. No baseball player can hit the ball so hard that it never falls back to Earth. You need a very powerful rocket to escape the Earth's gravitational pull.

flies, it will slow down, stop, and then fall back to Earth. But a sufficiently powerful rocket can launch at such a high speed that it can escape from the bonds imposed by the Earth's gravity, leave the vicinity of the Earth entirely, and never return. It is said to have achieved 'escape velocity' from Earth – a velocity which depends only on the mass of the Earth itself.

The question is, is the Universe expanding fast enough to escape from its own gravity – will it expand forever, or one day slow down and stop like the baseball and re-collapse? It is relatively easy to measure how fast it is expanding, but much harder to measure how much mass there is in the Universe, so it took a long time to find the answer.

Two Complications

This simple picture is not really quite so simple.

First, Einstein's equations also allow for the presence of a number, called the 'cosmological constant', which affects the expansion rate. It is given the Greek letter lambda (Λ) in those equations, but nothing in the equations tells us what value lambda has. Depending on its size, it could act as a kind of antigravity, making the Universe expand faster, or as an extra gravitational influence, slowing down the expansion. This is great fun for the mathematicians, because it gives them lots more models to play with. But studies of the expansion of the real Universe show that even if the lambda term does exist it must be very small, and until the 1990s astronomers usually set the constant as zero, to make life easier.

The other complication is more of an oddity than a complication. If you could throw a ball upwards at *exactly* the escape velocity, and nothing got in the way, it would keep going forever, but it would keep slowing down forever, and after a very long time it would seem to be hovering, high above the Earth (strictly speaking, infinitely far away), never to fall back. This curiosity is interesting, because the Universe itself seems to be very nearly in this state. It can be pictured another way, using geometry.

THE STEADY STATE MODEL

In the 1940s, three astronomers (Fred Hoyle, Tommy Gold and, right, Herman Bondi), came up with an idea to explain the expansion of the Universe without invoking a Big Bang. They pointed out that if new atoms of hydrogen were being created by expanding spacetime at a rate of just one new atom in every 10 billion cubic metres of space each year, enough atoms would be produced to make new galaxies to fill in the gaps as the old galaxies moved apart. At any moment in time (any cosmic epoch), the overall appearance would be much the same as it is in the Universe today. This became known as the 'Steady State' model.

This is a good example of how astronomers explore the Universe in their imagination, by thinking up models that might correspond to reality. When people argued that the continual creation of matter seemed rather an extravagant hypothesis, the supporters of the Steady State model pointed out that it didn't seem any more extravagant than creating all the matter all at once in a Big Bang.

The rivalry between the Big Bang and Steady State models encouraged astronomers to probe the Universe with radio and optical telescopes to find out which one was right. Eventually, this probing produced clear evidence that the Universe has changed as time has passed. It is not in a steady state. The discovery and investigation of the cosmic microwave background radiation then confirmed the reality of the Big Bang. So today we refer to the Big Bang theory (because it has passed the tests), whereas the Steady State is still just a model.

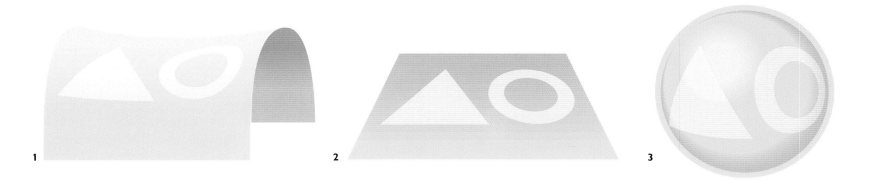

Einstein's Geometry

The general theory of relativity describes gravity in terms of bent spacetime. Around a black hole, the influence of the matter in the black hole bends spacetime round upon itself so that nothing can escape. The space around a black hole is like the surface of a sphere (or the surface of the Earth), and is said to be closed. Just as if you keep going in the same direction on Earth you go round the planet and back to where you started, so in closed space if you keep going in a straight line you go round the universe and back to where you started. The inside of a black hole really is a closed universe. Nothing can escape.

At the other extreme, gravity can bend space in the opposite sense. This is hard to picture, but an analogy would be the surface of a saddle, or a mountain pass, which curves away in all directions. Such a surface is said to be open. A closed universe is one which cannot escape from its own gravitational grip; an open universe is one which is expanding faster than its own escape velocity.

But there is a special case in which space is flat, like the surface of a smooth desktop. In Einstein's geometry, this is the equivalent of the special case where the ball is travelling upwards from the Earth at exactly the escape velocity. It is the only unique kind of geometry allowed by the general theory of relativity – there are lots of open universes, and lots of closed universes, but only one flat universe. And the real Universe seems to have a geometry indistinguishable from this very special case.

Close to Critical

Because the flat universe model is unique, cosmologists use it as a benchmark against which to measure other models. The flat universe model is said to have 'critical density', which means that the density of the universe is exactly right to make space flat. Cosmologists measure the density of the Universe (or model universes) in terms of a parameter called omega (Ω). It is also known as the flatness parameter. For a flat universe $\Omega = 1$. For an open universe, Ω is less than 1, and for a closed universe, Ω is bigger than 1.

The Universe we live in is expanding, and that means that the density is decreasing as time passes. This affects the value of Ω at any moment of cosmic time (any epoch), but it does not affect which side of the critical dividing line Ω sits. Leaving aside some of the more exotic complications that can be caused by a cosmological constant, if the Universe was dense enough to be closed when it

1. In an open universe, the angles of a triangle add up to less than 180°.

2. In a flat universe, the angles of a triangle add up to exactly 180°.

3. In a closed universe, the angles of a triangle add up to more than 180°.

⭐ Alexander Friedmann's application of the general theory of relativity produced a variety of model universes in the early 1920s – before astronomers knew for sure that there was a Universe beyond the Milky Way.

1

emerged from the Big Bang, then it will stay dense enough to be closed. And if it started out open, then it will always be open.

Going to Extremes

Whichever way the Universe started out, the fact is that it shifts further and further from that critical density as time passes. If it started out with Ω just less than 1, as it expands and the density decreases, the value of Ω gets less and less. If i t started out with Ω just bigger than 1, the expansion proceeds more slowly and the value of Ω gets bigger and bigger as time passes. By now, some 14 billion years after the Big Bang, there has been ample time for this effect to have been at work. The Universe should have evolved to one extreme or the other. But when we look at the real Universe, we see that it is still very close to the critical density.

It is hard to measure the density of the entire Universe, but astronomers can make a good stab at it. First, they count all the bright galaxies in a chosen volume of space, and estimate the mass of all the bright stars in those galaxies. Then, from the way galaxies move in clusters under the influence of gravity they can estimate how much 'dark stuff', or 'dark matter' ($\triangleright$ p. 117), there is, tugging on the bright stuff gravitationally, for every galaxy they see. Adding all this up, they find that there is matter to account for at least 10 percent of the critical density of matter around, and probably at least 30 percent. So, based on the dynamics of galaxies, Ω is at least 0. 1 and may be bigger than 0. 3. But for 14 billion years, Ω has been getting further and further away from 1. For Ω to be as big as 0. 1 today means that in the first second of the Big Bang it must have been within one part in 10^{60} (a 1 followed by 60 zeroes) of being precisely 1. This means that the Universe was born flat to an accuracy of 1 part in 10^{60}. The flatness of the Universe in the Big Bang is the most accurately determined parameter in the whole of science.

2

More than Meets the Eye

Many cosmologists believe that this must mean that the value of the flatness parameter Ω in the Big Bang was precisely 1. Because the critical density is the only special density there is in cosmology, it is hard to see how the Universe could have started out so close to critical without actually being at critical density. The fact that the amount of matter we can locate today only corresponds to a value of between 0.1 and 0.3 is not a problem, they say, because our observations of the Universe are incomplete. We cannot claim to have discovered everything in the Universe, so there must be more dark stuff, of one kind or another, which makes Ω bigger.

The important point is that a value for Ω of 1 is the only value that stays the same as the

Universe expands. If Ω is 1 in the beginning then it is always 1. As the Universe expands and slows down, the density decreases at exactly the right rate so that at each epoch the speed with which the Universe is expanding is still exactly the escape velocity from itself. A few cosmologists, however, hope that there is even more mass than this.

The Phoenix Universe

Where did the Big Bang come from in the first place? Until the end of the twentieth century, one attractive idea proposed by the mathematical cosmologists was a model universe in which there was an endless cycle of birth, death and rebirth. Like the mythical Phoenix, which lays a single egg, dies, and then

The average density of the Universe is equivalent to between ten and 100 hydrogen atoms in every cubic kilometre of space.

1

emerges from the egg when it is heated in a fire, such a universe recreates itself. It does so in a fireball like the Big Bang. The mathematics still hold up – a universe (or universes) like this *could* exist according to the known laws of physics. But could this model actually represent the real Universe? One thing it requires is that the density of the universe is higher (preferably a lot higher) than the critical density needed for flatness.

If Ω is bigger than 1, sooner or later the expansion of the universe will stop and then reverse, so that eventually everything in the universe will plunge together into what is sometimes known as the 'Big Crunch' (occasionally, and more pompously, as the 'Omega Point'). In the early stages of the collapse, life could go on pretty much as it does now, but the light from distant galaxies would be blueshifted, not redshifted, as space began to shrink, rather than expand. As time passed, the background radiation would get hotter, but it would take a long time for this to begin to cause problems.

Crunch and Bang

The first real change in the overall appearance of the shrinking universe occurs when it has shrunk to about 1 per cent of the size of our Universe today and the galaxies begin to merge with one another (this reflects the fact that in very round terms the distances between galaxies today are 100 times larger than the sizes of galaxies themselves). Even then, the temperature of

 THE QUANTUM OF TIME

Cosmologists know that actual singularities (points of infinite density and zero volume – ▷p. 89) cannot really exist inside black holes and that the Universe as we know it cannot have been born out of a literal singularity. This is because space and time themselves are 'quantized' – there is a smallest possible length and a smallest possible time, both specified by the laws of quantum physics. The smallest length (called the 'Planck length', in honour of the quantum pioneer Max Planck, right) is 10^{-33} cm, one hundredth of a billionth of a billionth the size of a proton. The smallest possible time (called the 'Planck time') is the time it would take light to cross this tiny distance, which is 10^{-43}s.

Although these are unimaginably small quantities, they are not zero. This is important, because it means that physicists do not have to divide by zero in their equations, so they do not get answers of infinity out of their calculations (for example, when they work out the density of the Universe in the beginning). The implication is that, whatever the event was that created our Universe, the Universe was 'born' with a finite density at an age of 10^{-43}s, and that this was the moment when time began. In a collapsing universe heading for a Big Crunch (see opposite), the 'bounce' that turns the universe inside out would happen not at a singularity, but when the collapse was still 10^{-43}s away from reaching the singularity.

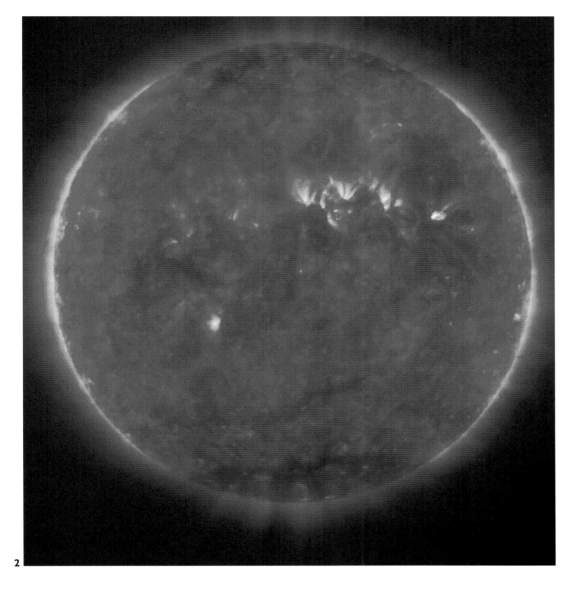

2

1. Like the mythical Phoenix, the universe may not only have been born in fire, but had probably also experienced previous cycles of life and death.

2. In the late stages of a collapsing universe, the blue-shifted light from the whole sky would be as hot as the Sun.

the background radiation would only be about 100 K, and it is entirely possible that life could still exist under those circumstances.

By the time the universe has shrunk to about 0.1 per cent of the size of our Universe now, the blueshifting of the background radiation would make the entire sky as bright as the surface of the Sun is today. The 'background' radiation would have a temperature of thousands of Kelvin and life as

we know it would be impossible. Soon after, about a year before the Big Crunch, the background radiation would be hotter than the inside of a star and all life would be extinct. Stars themselves would be torn apart by the radiation and broken down into their constituent particles. An hour away from the Big Crunch, based on the rate at which spacetime is contracting then, the huge black holes that exist at the centres of galaxies would begin to merge with one another. But

⭐ Alexander Friedmann, who first applied Einstein's equations to a variety of model universes, died of pneumonia after he caught a chill while flying in a balloon to study the weather.

the merging of black holes is an all-or-nothing affair, and instead of the rest of the collapse taking an hour it would happen instantly, as the singularities inside the black holes came together, causing the Big Crunch itself.

What would happen then is largely guesswork. But the most popular guess is that this dramatic mingling of singularities would cause a 'bounce', turning the collapse inside out and making the universe expand in a new Big Bang. According to this picture, our Big Bang may have been the Big Crunch of a previous cycle of expansion and collapse, in an endlessly repeating rhythm.

Reversing Time

There is one extremely curious feature of a collapsing universe – at least, according to some of the mathematicians who explore these possibilities. In the 1960s, the cosmologist Tommy Gold (one of the co-founders of the Steady State model) suggested that during the collapsing phase time might run backwards.

Gold's original speculation was not based on detailed mathematics, but is still intriguing. Because the laws of physics have no inbuilt 'arrow of time', they would work equally well if the direction of time in the equations were reversed. Gold said that, according to those laws, stars in a collapsing universe would soak up radiation from space instead of emitting light. Inside the stars, the incoming energy would drive nuclear reactions that converted helium into hydrogen, while on a planet like our own, ice cubes would radiate away heat and grow

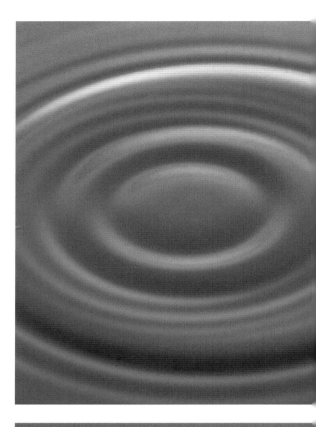

larger, while living things 'grew' from old age to youth.

With time running backwards, you might think that the world would look very bizarre. But the crucial twist in Gold's story is that inhabitants of such a world might never notice. If time is running backwards, the thought processes that make intelligent beings intelligent will also run backwards. Any intelligent being living in the contracting phase of the universe would think 'backwards' compared with us, and would still 'see' heat flowing from hotter objects and into cooler objects and so on. The punch line is that we could be living in a contracting universe and are totally unaware of it!

This intriguing, but infuriating, suggestion has roused several cosmologists, including Paul Davies and Stephen Hawking, to try to find a mathematical description for what goes on in such a universe and prove whether or not time can run backwards. They have not yet succeeded in finding a definite answer to the question of whether time runs backwards when a universe contracts, and you can get some idea of how difficult a problem this is from the fact that Hawking has changed his mind at least twice on the answer to this puzzle. It is probably just as well for the sanity of the mathematical cosmologists that it now seems as if the question will remain a hypothetical one. There may indeed just be enough stuff in the Universe we live in to make it flat, but there is now compelling evidence that there is no more mass-energy than this, and that the Universe will expand forever. One of the big puzzles in cosmology is finding enough mass to flatten the Universe.

1. According to some theorists, in a collapsing Universe, time would run backwards and so drops of water would fall upwards from the ripples in a pond.

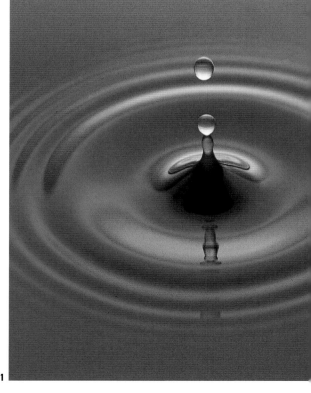

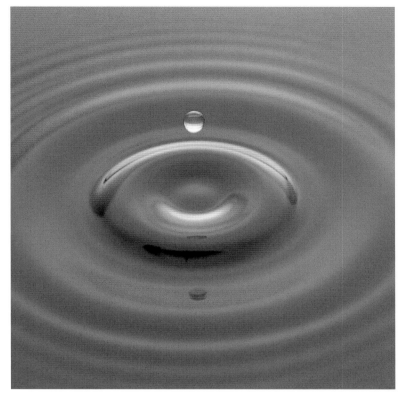

THE ARROW OF TIME

One of the most puzzling things in science is the origin of the 'arrow of time'. We all know that there is a difference between the past and the future, but where does this difference come from? There is nothing in the laws of physics which makes the distinction. In the classic example of two billiard balls colliding and moving apart, the laws of physics 'work' just as well to describe the same collision with time running backwards. However, the arrow of time seems to have something to do with the way very large numbers of things interact with one another. In the break of snooker, for example, it is quite clear in which direction time goes.

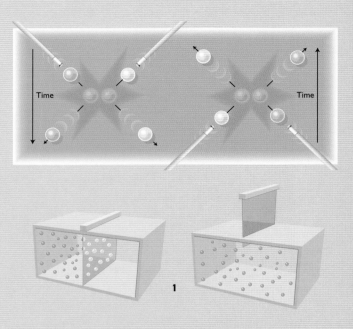

Time in a Box

Think of a simple box, divided in two by a sliding partition, with smoke in one half and empty space in the other. When you slide open the partition, the smoke spreads out to fill up the box. However, no matter how long you wait, you will never see the smoke move back into one half of the box so that you can slide back the partition and trap it. If you saw two pictures of the box, one with smoke in one half of the box and one with smoke in all of the box, you would know which picture was taken first.

Mathematically, the difference between the two situations is that you need less information to describe the full box. There is a pattern (or order) in the half-empty box (half-empty, half-full) that is lost when the box is uniformly full of smoke. Information, or order, is measured by a quantity called entropy, in such a way that a decrease in information (increase in disorder) corresponds to an increase in entropy. Overall, in the Universe at large, entropy always increases as time passes.

Local Order

Left to their own devices, things wear out. Cars rust, glasses break, houses fall down. Disorder increases. We can only make order locally (making cars, building houses and so on) using energy. On Earth, the energy comes, ultimately, from sunlight. But the increase in entropy, caused by the processes inside the Sun which release energy, is much bigger than the decrease in entropy caused by the action of life on Earth. In the Universe at large, entropy always increases, even though it may temporarily decrease on a planet like Earth. Time points in the direction of increasing entropy.

1. Although individual collisions between atoms and molecules seem to be reversible, the behaviour of lots of molecules in a gas reveals the direction of time.

2 and 3. Rusting cars (left) and burning fires (4 and 5 above) both indicate the arrow of time in the real world.

Time and the Universe

The Universe was born in a state of low entropy. Processes going on inside the Sun and stars increase the entropy of the Universe as energy pours out into the cold of space.

Another indication of the arrow of time is that in nature heat always flows from a hotter object to a cooler object. So another way of defining the arrow of time is that it points away from the hot Big Bang and into

a cold future. When all the stars have burned out, everything in the Universe will be at the same temperature. It will be uniform, with no pattern or order, and there will be no way of telling one locality from another. Time will come to an end. This is called the 'heat death' of the Universe and it is inevitable if the Universe is destined to expand forever. The best evidence today is that this will be the fate of our Universe.

◆ TOPIC LINKS

2.1 The Big Bang
p. 87 The Singular Beginning

2.2 Cosmology for beginners
p. 100 Reversing Time

2.4 The Accelerating Universe
p. 129 The Fate of the Universe

4.2 A Choice of Universes
p. 209 Hawking's Universe

MISSING MASS AND THE BIRTH OF TIME

After the 1960s, cosmologists began to accept that the Big Bang idea was more than just a model and offered a good description of the real Universe. But as it stood at the time, this was far from being an exact description of the Universe. The basic idea of the Big Bang seemed sound, but there were problems relating the detailed appearance of the Universe we live in to the physics of the Big Bang itself. These puzzles centre around the observational evidence that the Universe we live in is uniform but nevertheless contains irregularities.

A breakthrough came when particle physicists started to apply their ideas, based on studies of what happens to particles at very high energies, to the physics of the Big Bang. The resolution of those puzzles involved new ideas about what happened in the earliest moments of the existence of the Universe, and new observations to test those ideas. The result was a golden age of cosmology, which is still going on today.

Previous page. Optical image of the Omega Nebula 6000 light years away from Earth in the constellation Sagittarius.

BIG BANG PROBLEMS

Before about 1960, cosmology was still a mathematical game, in which a few experts (probably no more than 20 in the whole world) explored the possible model universes allowed by the equations of the general theory of relativity. In the 1960s, they were delighted, but rather surprised, to find that one of those models, the Big Bang, actually seemed to provide a very good description of the Universe we live in. The discovery of the background cosmic radiation, and the elucidation of how the primordial hydrogen and helium that went into the first generation of stars in the first four minutes of the Big Bang, made people start to take the Big Bang model seriously. But in the 1970s, cosmologists (by now there were hundreds of them) began to realize that there was a problem they had never expected with the Big Bang theory: it was, in a sense, too good to be true.

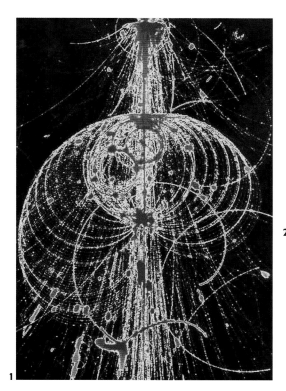

2

1

1 and 2. Photographs showing the interactions between sub-atomic particles in experiments at the high energy accelerators of CERN at Geneva.

It took only 0.000000000001 s (10^{-12}s) for what was to become the entire visible Universe to expand from a size smaller than an atom to the size of the Solar System.

1. On the scale of stars and galaxies, the universe doesn't look smooth. Stars form patterns like the southern cross.

2. Flatness can be a matter of perspective – the ground beneath our feet seems flat even though the Earth is round.

The Flatness Problem

In fact, there were several 'too good to be true' problems that puzzled cosmologists in the 1970s. The first is the question of why the Universe is so nearly (perhaps precisely) flat (▷ p. 95). As we have seen, whichever side of the critical density it started out from in the Big Bang, the Universe should have got further and further away from $\Omega = 1$ as time passed. For the Universe still to be so nearly flat after nearly 15 billion years is about as likely as balancing a pencil very carefully on its point on a table, then going away for 15 billion years and coming back to find that the pencil is still as you left it. The only explanation seemed to be that there ought to be a law of nature which forced the Universe to be precisely flat. But, in the 1970s, nobody could think what that law might be.

The Smoothness Problem

Another big puzzle about the Universe is that it is incredibly smooth. You might not think so, looking at the patterns made by stars on the night sky, or the way galaxies are grouped in clusters across the dark expanse of the Universe. But these are really small-scale effects. What matters is the smoothness of the dark space itself – in Einstein's language, the smoothness of spacetime. From a distance, the surface of the Earth looks smooth and, compared with its diameter, it is. A mountain 12.7 km high is only a pimple corresponding to one-thousandth of the diameter of the planet, even though it looks enormous to us. In the same way, the uniformity of the Universe has to be measured on the largest possible scale, and that means using the cosmic background radiation – the echo of the Big Bang.

The background radiation has the same temperature from all parts of the sky – it is

2

Although nothing can travel through space faster than light, space itself can expand faster than light.

isotropic. This shows that the Universe emerged from the fireball of the Big Bang in a very smooth state. We have to get used to the idea that even clusters of galaxies are like tiny pimples on the smoothness of the Universe.

There's another way of looking at this. The Universe isn't just the same in all directions, it is the same (on average) *everywhere*, once you allow for the effects of expansion. The pimples are distributed at random across the face of space. The buzzword this time is 'homogeneity'. You can see the homogeneity of space by looking at two stunning pictures from the Hubble Space Telescope, called Deep Field North and Deep Field South. These are images of very distant galaxies seen on opposite sides of the sky. But apart from superficial differences, they look exactly the same. The same kinds of galaxies are clustered together in the same kind of way. There is nothing in the pictures to tell you which part of the Universe those galaxies inhabit, although they occupy regions of space billions of light years apart (just as there is nothing in a picture of a pimple to tell you which cheek of an acne sufferer it afflicts). There are no 'lumps' in the Universe, except for the galaxies and clusters of galaxies themselves. It is homogeneous. Or nearly; there are, after all, galaxies. And in the 1970s, this was another problem.

The Problem of Galaxies

As observations of the background radiation got better and its smoothness was measured with increasing precision, it began to be difficult to see how galaxies could have formed at all. Galaxies start out when huge clouds of gas collapse under their own gravitational pull, their own weight. But this collapse can only

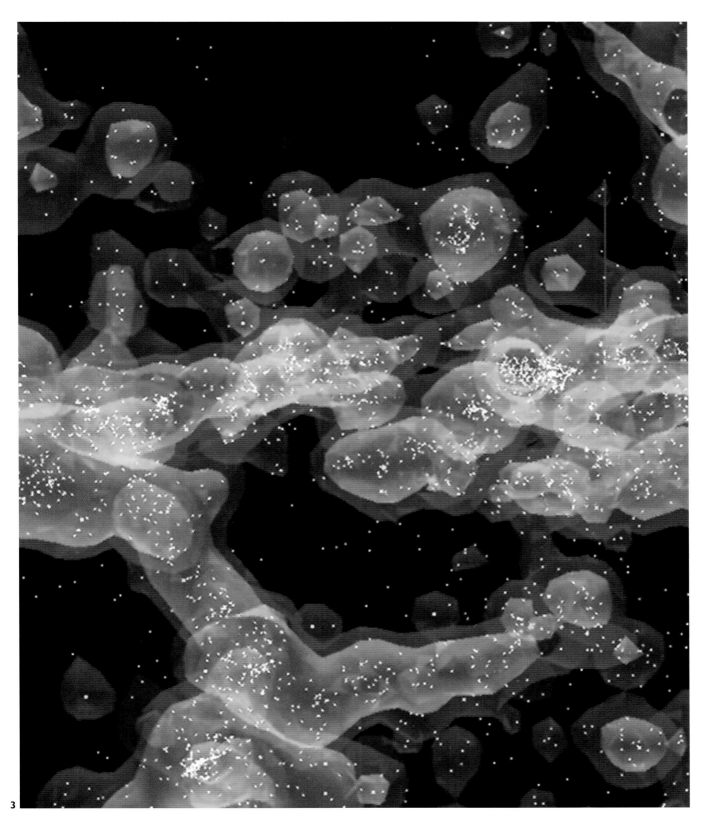

3

1 and 2. The universe looks the same in all directions. The top image is a picture obtained by the Hubble Space Telescope looking north on the sky. The bottom picture is a similar image obtained looking south.

3. The distribution of galaxies on the sky is not entirely random, but forms clumps and filaments.

1. The microwaves used to map the Universe are similar to the ones used in telecommunications.

2. Alan Guth, one of the pioneers of the theory of inflation.

3. (opposite) Computer simulation of the way matter clumps together in the expanding Universe.

begin if some regions of the Universe are more dense than others. If everything were perfectly smooth, gravity would pull evenly in all directions, and everything would get carried along with the expansion of the Universe. Like seeding clouds to make rain, you need some initial lumpiness to provide the seeds on which galaxies can grow. These seeds must have been present at the end of the fireball era of the Big Bang, 300,000–500,000 years after the moment when time began, at the time when the radiation that became the microwave background last interacted with matter.

So the unevenness in the Universe from that time, that led to the formation of galaxies, should have left its imprint on the microwave radiation. Why hadn't this been seen?

The answer was that it was too small. When cosmologists carried the calculations through, they found that the seeds from which galaxies and clusters of galaxies formed should indeed have left a mark on the background radiation, but a mark corresponding to differences in temperature today from one part of the sky to another of only about 30 millionths of a degree. Nothing highlights more clearly just how insignificant galaxies (let alone stars, planets and people) are to the cosmos at large. There was no hope (at that time) of detecting, from the ground, such tiny ripples in the background radiation. In the mid-1970s, a group of astronomers took up the challenge of designing and building a satellite which could look for the predicted disturbances in the background radiation. The result, COBE, did not fly until the end of the 1980s, when it triumphantly confirmed the predictions of the theorists. But by then, the theory of the Universe had itself undergone a radical rethinking that solved the problems of the Big Bang.

Flattening the Universe

The standard model of the Big Bang describes everything that happened in the Universe from about 0.0001 s (10^{-4} s) after 'time zero', when the temperature of the Universe was 1000 billion degrees (10^{12} K), up to the time about half a million years later when matter and radiation decoupled at a temperature of 6000 K. It never pretended to explain what went before that, when temperatures were higher than 10^{12} K. The understanding of physics that existed in the 1960s was inadequate to describe what went on that close to the singularity. But as physicists on Earth

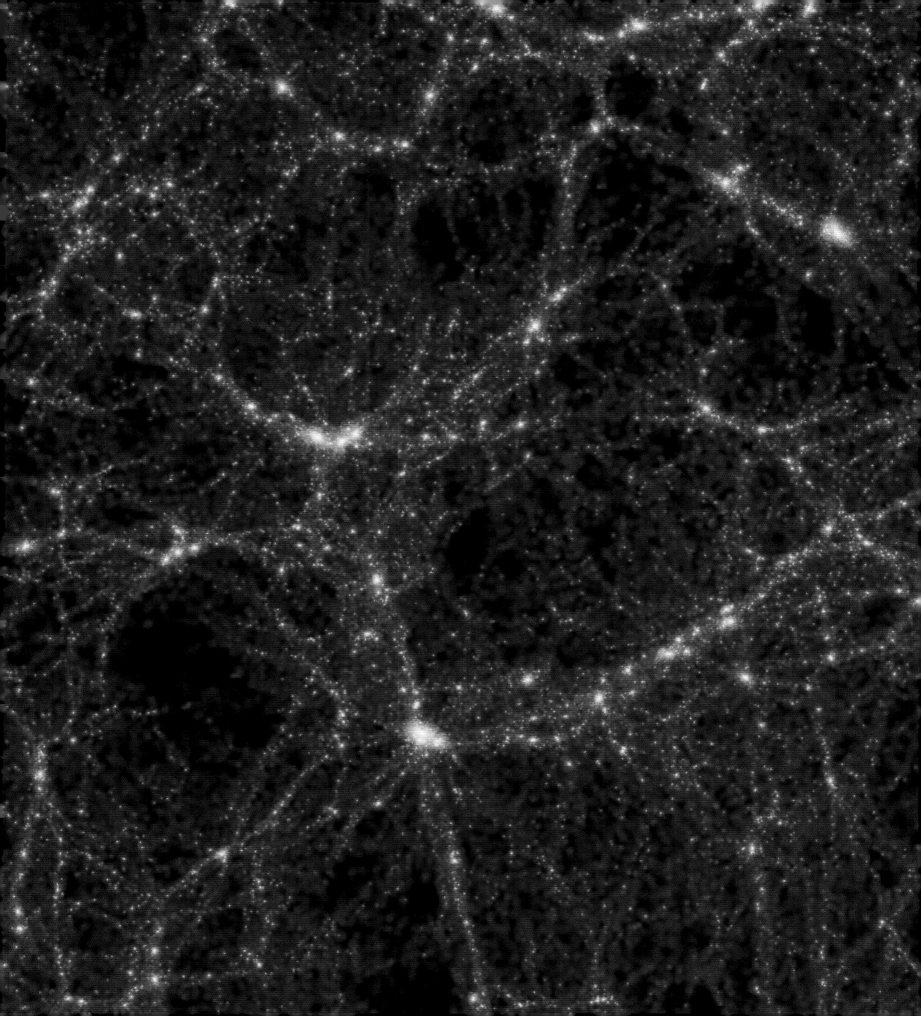

began to explore such extreme conditions, both with their particle accelerators and with new mathematical models and theories, the new discoveries offered a way to explain how the Universe got to be so flat and smooth.

Two New Beginnings

As is usually the case in science, progress in solving the puzzles was made because the time was ripe and both new technology and new ways of thinking about the puzzles became available. It is very rare that progress happens because of the unique insight of a lone genius.

In the late 1970s, cosmology was transformed by an influx of ideas from particle physicists, used to thinking about what goes on at the enormously high energies corresponding to temperatures above 10^{12} K. Two people, on opposite sides of the world, independently hit on the same solution to the puzzles of the Big Bang. This was not a result of a strange coincidence, but because the answer was built into the laws of particle physics that had been unveiled in the 1970s, and because their training in particle physics gave these men exactly the background needed to help solve those puzzles.

The two young researchers who made the breakthrough were Andrei Linde (then working in Moscow, but later in the United States), and Alan Guth (then working at the Stanford Linear Accelerator Center in California). Their ideas involve some very deep physics, but, even without going into the technical details, it is straightforward to see how they solved the problems of the Big Bang.

Universal Inflation

All of the problems of the Big Bang could be solved if the Universe had expanded enormously in the first split-second after time zero, long before the beginning of the standard Big Bang model. In this scenario, during that first split-second, something took

 BENDING LIGHT

One of the first tests of the general theory of relativity measured the way light from distant stars was bent as it passed close by the Sun during the total solar eclipse of 1919. Now, almost 100 years later, astronomers can study the way light from far across the Universe is bent by whole galaxies (or even clusters of galaxies, right) that lie between us and the source of the light.

In the mid-1980s, astronomers discovered two huge, luminous arcs on the sky (they are huge in reality, but look small because they are far away). Each is about 90 000 parsecs long and spanning about 9000 parsecs. More arcs have since been discovered. In the best example, the light from the arc has the same spectrum and a redshift of 0.724, but the arc is along the same line of sight as a cluster of galaxies at a redshift of 0.374. The implication is that the light in the arc comes from an object (almost certainly a galaxy) about twice as far away as the cluster. This light has been bent by the gravity of the cluster in its way to us, forming a magnified and distorted image of the galaxy which produced it.

Calculations using Einstein's general theory show that in all of the arcs investigated so far, the galaxy clusters involved in this lensing process cannot produce such high magnifications unless they contain at least ten times as much mass as we can see in the form of bright stars in the component galaxies. This is powerful independent evidence to support the idea that at least 90 per cent of the matter in the Universe is dark stuff.

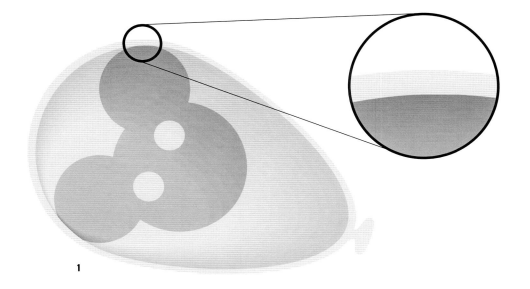

1

hold of the Universe when it was a seed containing all of the mass-energy that was to become the visible Universe, but was still much smaller than an atom, and made it expand dramatically. For obvious reasons, this process became known as 'inflation'.

In everyday language, it is hard to see how there was time between time zero and 0.0001 s for anything much to happen. But remember that there is ten times as much time in 100 s as there is in 10 s. In the same way, there is ten times as much time in 0.0001 s as there is in 0.00001 s, and so on. According to simple versions of inflation theory, during the time of inflation, the seed of the Universe doubled in size once every 10^{-34} s. This means that in the span of just 10^{-32} s there would be time for 100 doublings, because, of course, 10^{-32} is 100 times bigger than 10^{-34}. Only 150 such doublings would be enough to take something that was 10^{20} times smaller than a proton and inflate it into a sphere roughly the size of a grapefruit.

It is hard to grasp what this means, because none of us has seen a proton. The best way to visualize the effect of inflation at work is to imagine the surface of a child's balloon, which is clearly bent around in a curve. Now imagine inflating the balloon to the size of the Solar System without it bursting. From the surface of the hugely inflated balloon it would be very difficult to tell that it was curved – it would seem to be flat. In exactly the same way, inflation in the first split-second after time zero could have flattened the space we live in. At the same time, the seed that inflated to become the Universe would have been too small to contain much in the way of irregularities, which explains why the Universe is so smooth.

The change brought about by inflation was very dramatic – the equivalent of inflating a tennis ball to the size of the entire visible Universe in just 10^{-32} s. Inflation predicted a Universe today that is so nearly flat we can never hope to measure any difference from flatness.

But why should such a dramatic event happen?

The Ultimate Free Lunch

The reason why people took inflation seriously is that the laws of physics provided a natural reason for it to happen. Linde and Guth (and then others) found that inflation fell out of the laws of physics without having to be looked for; it came free with the standard model of particle physics. As Guth put it, the Universe is 'the ultimate free lunch'.

Four Kinds of Force

The particle physics which gave us a free-lunch Universe along with the equations is based on an idea called 'grand unification', and the variations on the theme are known as Grand Unified Theories, or GUTs (it should be 'Grand Unified Models', but the acronym isn't so appealing). These ideas start from the fact that there are four kinds of force known in nature – electromagnetism, gravity, the 'strong force' that holds nuclei together, and another (called the 'weak force') that is responsible for radioactivity and nuclear fission.

The Holy Grail of particle physics is to find one set of equations that describes how all four of these forces behave, as different facets of some single 'superforce'. In the 1960s, physicists made the first step towards this goal by unifying electromagnetism and the weak force in one package, known as 'electroweak theory' (theory, not model, you notice, because it has been tested by experiment and passed). In the 1970s they developed a not-quite-perfect account of how to include the strong force in the package. The key thing about this work is that it showed that the forces become indistinguishable from one another at high enough energies. In everyday language, this corresponds to high enough temperatures. Looking back towards the Big Bang, when the Universe was hot enough, electromagnetism and the weak force would have merged into one force. At hotter temperatures still (by which we mean earlier times), the strong force would have merged in

with them. And the guess is that at the earliest and hottest times, even gravity would have merged into the superforce.

But it is what emerges when you calculate how the forces split apart as the real Universe expanded away from time zero that made cosmologists sit up and take notice of these ideas.

Breaking the Symmetry

If the Universe was 'born' at the Planck time, 10^{-43}s after time zero, gravity would have immediately split off from the other three forces. But the strong force would not have split off until 10^{-35} s after time zero, and as it did so it would have released an enormous

amount of energy. This is what gave the Universe the huge burst of expansion that we call inflation.

The breaking apart of the components of the superforce was the equivalent at this level to the kind of phase transition that occurs when water freezes into ice. A phase transition like this releases energy, which is known as 'latent heat'. This is because the rearrangement of the molecules involved takes them to a lower energy state. So even if the outside temperature is well below freezing, a bucket containing a mixture of water and ice will stay exactly at 0 degrees Celsius until all the water is frozen, even though it is losing heat to the outside world. In the same way, if you heat a mixture of water and ice, as long as there is still some ice

 RIPPLES IN THE BACKGROUND RADIATION

The satellite known as COBE (left) was launched on 18 November 1989 to accurately measure the microwave background radiation from above the Earth's atmosphere. Almost immediately, the satellite measured the overall temperature of the sky more accurately than ever before, and showed that the spectrum of this radiation at different wavelengths matches the appropriate spectrum for a 'black body' (▷p. 88) so accurately that it was impossible to see any deviations from the black body spectrum.

But the main purpose of the mission was to map the entire sky, looking for tiny differences in temperature that would reveal the existence of corresponding irregularities in the material Universe at the time when the radiation last interacted with matter, between 300,000 and 500,000 years after the birth of the Universe. It took more than a year to make the observations and months to analyse the 70 million measurements made. But it was worth the wait. The analysis showed that there are hot patches on the sky just 30 millionths of a degree hotter than average, and cool spots just 30 millionths of a degree cooler than average. These 'ripples in the background radiation' correspond to the way hydrogen and helium (and dark matter) were distributed at the end of the fireball era – the seeds from which clusters of galaxies grew.

COBE showed that the background radiation is just irregular enough to account for the fact that galaxy clusters exist. Even better, the nature of the 'ripples' exactly matches the pattern predicted by inflation.

present the mixture stays at zero degrees Celsius, because the heat is simply being used to melt the ice, not to warm up the water.

In a similar way, the situation when the four forces have broken apart corresponds to a lower energy state of the entire Universe than when they formed the single superforce. It is the latent heat released when the symmetry between the components of the superforce was broken in the first split-second after time zero that drove inflation. And, like all good theories, this made a testable prediction.

The Missing Mass

Inflation says that the Universe we see around us should be so nearly flat that it is impossible for any test we can devise to measure the difference. In other words, $\Omega = 1$ precisely. This solves the puzzle of the pencil standing on its point (▷p. 109), and because the entire visible Universe must have started out, if inflation is correct, from a seed far smaller than a proton it explains why the Universe is so smooth: there was no room for anything except the tiniest irregularities in the seed.

The prediction that $\Omega = 1$ means that there must be a lot more matter in the Universe than we can see, in order to make space flat. Because it has not been seen, this is sometimes referred to as 'missing mass', although really it is the light from the mass that is missing. The alternative name for this stuff is dark matter. There must be a lot of it, because if we look at a chosen volume of space and estimate the mass of all the bright stars in all the bright galaxies, it comes out as only about 1 per cent of the critical density.

The COBE satellite should have been launched by the Space Shuttle in 1986, but was delayed for three years after the Challenger disaster.

1

1. The way galaxies rotate shows that they are embedded in halos of dark matter.

Atoms are not Enough

You might think that a lot of what we call dark matter might in fact be faint stars and planets, or gas and dust, that we cannot see because it doesn't glow brightly. But the standard model of the Big Bang only allows for a little of this. The standard model predicts just the right amount of hydrogen and helium (75 per cent hydrogen, 25 per cent helium) – and this is what we actually do see in the oldest stars (▷ p. 18) – but only if the total density of atomic matter in the Universe is less than 5 per cent of the critical density. If the density were any higher than this, the models tell us, hydrogen and helium would not have come out of the primordial cosmic fireball in the proportions that have been observed. Even without the need for inflation, this is not enough to explain our observations of the way galaxies move in clusters, because those studies show that galaxies are in the gravitational grip of enough dark stuff to account for at least 30 per cent of the critical density.

Ordinary atomic matter (the stuff of which we, the Earth, the Sun and stars are made) is called 'baryonic matter', because the protons and neutrons at the hearts of atoms are members of a family called baryons. The combination of the standard model and observations of galaxies tells us that there could be about three times (and no more than five times) as much dark baryonic matter as there is bright stuff in the Universe, and ten times as much non-baryonic matter as there is baryonic matter (both bright and dark).

Inflation says that, in order to make the Universe flat, there must be even more stuff out there. What is it?

Two Kinds of Dark Matter

Once again, particle physics comes to the rescue. The models of particle physics that describe GUTs and suggest the possibility of

1. A technician working inside one of the detectors at the Large Electron Positron collider (LEP) at CERN.

2. The change from water into ice is a phase transition analagous to the change in the state of the early Universe which drove inflation.

inflation also predict that there should be other families of particles, in addition to those detected in particle accelerator experiments. According to these models, there could be two kinds of – as yet undetected – dark matter produced in the Big Bang.

The first kind of hypothetical dark matter consists of particles which are very light (even lighter than an electron) and which were 'born' in the Big Bang. These travel at very high speeds, a sizeable fraction of the speed of light. They are referred to as 'hot dark matter', or HDM. But although it is quite likely that there is some HDM in the Universe, there cannot be enough to make it flat. The problem with HDM is that the fast-moving particles would blast apart any structure that tried to form in the early Universe, and too much HDM would stop galaxies forming at all.

The second kind of hypothetical dark matter consists of fairly heavy particles (each perhaps about as massive as a proton) which emerged much more slowly from the Big Bang. This is called 'cold dark matter', or CDM. The great advantage of CDM is that the slow-moving, massive particles would clump together as a result of their mutual gravitational attraction, forming gravitational 'potholes' into which baryonic matter would fall and accumulate, and act as the seeds from which galaxies and clusters of galaxies could grow.

There are about 10,000 cold dark matter particles in every cubic metre around us, including 'empty' space, the air that you breathe, and seemingly solid objects such as the Earth.

2

Looking for Dark Matter

There are two ways to test the prediction that the Universe is filled with a sea of dark matter particles. The first is to look for them directly. CDM particles interact with baryonic matter only through gravity or when a CDM particle collides directly with a baryon in the nucleus of an atom, making the atom jiggle about. The effect is tiny, and normally it would go unnoticed because, even in solids, atoms are constantly in motion at room temperature. But if a block of metal is cooled very close to the absolute zero of temperature (0 K), this thermal motion is greatly reduced, and the effect of a CDM impact might *just* be detected as a tiny rise in temperature of the supercold metal. According to the models, there are between one and 1000 such collisions (the exact number depends on details of the models) in every kilogram of matter (cheese, steel, water or whatever) every day. To put this in perspective: a kilogram of matter contains about 10^{27} baryons.

At the higher end of the calculated collision rate, the effect of these CDM impacts could just be detected using modern technology. Experiments searching for dark matter in this way are now underway, buried deep down mine shafts to shield them from interference. Because they are exploring the limits of what is technically possible, nobody will be surprised if they do not produce a positive detection. But if they do, direct evidence for the dark matter that fills the Universe will have been found at the bottom of a hole in the ground.

The second way to test the prediction takes us back out into the exploration of the Universe at large. Computer models are now well able to describe how ordinary baryonic matter clumps together to form galaxies in a variety of different cosmological models, with different mixtures of dark matter in them. These simulations show that if there were only baryons in the Universe, and if the density was just 5 per cent of the critical density (that is, $\Omega = 0.05$), then there is no way that the pattern

 IN THE GRIP OF THE DARK STUFF

The speeds at which different parts of a galaxy rotate can be measured by the Doppler effect, which shows that galaxies like the Milky Way rotate differently from the way planets orbit the Sun. In the Solar System, the outer planets not only take longer to complete a single orbit, but actually move more slowly through space than the inner planets, with orbital speed decreasing as the square root of the distance of a planet from the Sun. In a galaxy, the stars sweep around at the same speed, no matter how far they are from the centre of the galaxy. Stars that are further out still take longer to complete one orbit, because they have further to travel. But they all travel at the same speed.

The only way this can be explained is if all of the visible stuff in a disc galaxy is embedded in some larger dark halo, and is held in the gravitational grip of the dark stuff in the halo. The evidence shows that there must be about ten times as much of this dark stuff as there is matter in the form of bright stars in a galaxy like our own. The way whole galaxies move about in clusters shows that there is even more dark matter present in the seemingly empty spaces between them.

1. (opposite)
The face-on spiral
galaxy NGC1232.

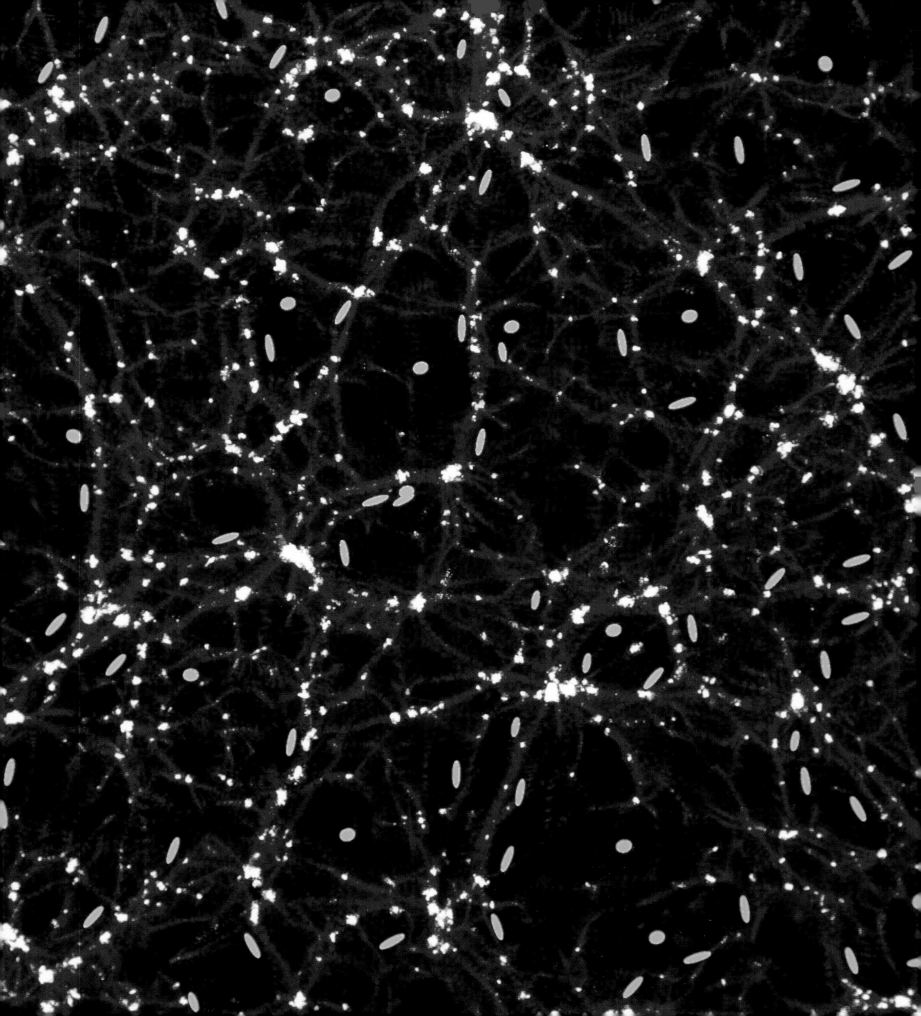

of galaxies and clusters of galaxies that we see around us could have formed in the time available since the Big Bang. Adding enough HDM to flatten the Universe makes things even worse. But if there is at least 30 per cent of the critical density in the form of CDM, then the pattern of galaxies and clusters that emerges from the simulations is strikingly similar to the pattern we see in the real Universe. This is powerful evidence that CDM is the dominant form of matter in the Universe, although these results do allow for the possibility that there is a little HDM as well (perhaps more HDM than there is baryonic matter).

This picture of a Universe dominated materially by CDM was firmly established by the end of the 1990s. But it still isn't quite the last word. In order to make galaxies and clusters that look like those in the real Universe, you need less than half of the critical density in the form of dark matter – but the models still work best if that matter is embedded in flat space. If the density of matter is less than half the critical density, how can space be flat? The answer takes us back to Albert Einstein's original thoughts on cosmology, but also right up to date with key results from the astronomical frontier announced at the beginning of the twenty-first century, seeming to slot the last piece into the cosmological jigsaw puzzle.

The surprising implication of this work, yet to be confirmed, is that the Universe may be precisely flat, but it is also expanding faster as time goes by.

1. (opposite) Computer model of dark matter (red) distribution, the first time the invisible dark matter has been mapped.

2. Experiments designed to detect dark matter particles have to be buried deep underground to minimise interference.

2

WHY THE SKY IS DARK AT NIGHT

You can make one of the most profound observations in the whole of science by going outside and looking at the dark night sky. Why is the sky dark at night? Is it because there are gaps between the stars? But if space went on to infinity, and it was filled with stars, every 'line of sight' out into space would end on a star, and the whole sky would blaze with light. So the Universe cannot be infinite and uniform.

Olbers and the Edge

The puzzle of the dark night sky often goes by the name 'Olbers' paradox', after the nineteenth-century German astronomer who publicised it. But he wasn't the first to ponder the puzzle, and it isn't really a paradox. The simplest way to picture the puzzle is to imagine standing in a large forest. Wherever you look, you will see a tree. But if you are only standing in a small wood, you might be able to see through the spaces between the trees, out to the edge of the forest. In an infinite Universe, everywhere you look you will see a star. The fact that we can see 'out' through the gaps between the stars seemed to imply, to Olbers and others, that there must be an 'edge' to the Universe, beyond which there was only dark, empty space, and no more stars. This reasoning applies even if you think in terms of galaxies rather than stars.

Looking Back in Time

The first person who realized that this need not be the case was Edgar Allan Poe who, alongside his literary activities, was a keen amateur scientist. He gave a lecture setting out the correct resolution to Olbers' paradox in February 1848. But he died a year later and no scientists took up his suggestion.

What Poe pointed out was that by looking further out into space we are looking further back in time, because it takes light a finite time to travel through space. When we look through the gaps between the stars at the dark night sky, we are looking back in time to an era before the stars were born – in Poe's words, to a distance 'so immense that no ray from it has yet been able to reach us at all.'

The Edge of Time

This notion needs only a tiny modification to fit in with the idea of the Big Bang. The point is that the Universe is not infinitely old, and it has an 'edge' in time (the Big Bang) rather than an edge in space. Looking through the gaps between the stars and galaxies, we do indeed look back to a time before galaxies formed.

But modern instruments reveal that the sky is not completely dark. What we 'see' there is the background radiation from the Big Bang fireball itself, once as hot as the surface of a star, but now redshifted by the expansion of the Universe down to 2.7 K.

The darkness of the night sky is evidence that the Universe was born at a definite moment in time. You can see (or rather, not see!) evidence to support the Big Bang model with your own unaided eyes.

1

2

1. In an infinite universe, you ought to see stars everywhere you look, just as in an infinite forest you would see trees everywhere you look.

2. Edgar Allan Poe was the first person to appreciate why the sky is dark at night.

◆ TOPIC LINKS

2.1 **The Big Bang**
p. 83 Microwaves from the Birth of Time
p. 88 Black Body Radiation

2.2 **Cosmology for Beginners**
pp. 102–3 The Arrow of Time

2.4 THE ACCELERATING UNIVERSE

One of the cherished features of the standard Big Bang model that had developed in the 1970s and 1980s was that the gravitational pull of all the matter in the Universe must be making the universal expansion slow down as time passes. Yet, in 1998 the discovery that the Universe is expanding *faster* as it ages earned the accolade 'breakthrough of the year' from the journal *Science*, and was presented to the public as a stunning achievement which overturned conventional cosmological wisdom. But the hype did less than justice to previous generations of cosmologists. The possibility of universal acceleration was already built into the cosmological equations developed by Albert Einstein back in 1916. In fact, to the cosmologists themselves it turned out to be just what the doctor ordered – the last piece in the cosmological jigsaw puzzle. But confirmation had to wait for another couple of years.

EINSTEIN'S UNWELCOME CONSTANT

Albert Einstein tried to describe the Universe mathematically, using his general theory of relativity, in 1917. He wanted to represent the simplest possible model, in which matter is uniformly distributed through space. He also wanted this model to be static, neither expanding nor contracting, to match the fact that the Milky Way (which was thought to be the entire Universe at that time) is neither expanding nor contracting. The only way in which he could achieve this was to include in his equations the term now known as the 'cosmological constant', and denoted by the Greek letter lambda (Λ). The equations said nothing about the value of this constant – they allowed for the possibility that it is zero, or it could have any positive or negative value. Depending on the size of the constant, it could act like antigravity, holding matter up against the inward pull of gravity, or like an addition to gravity, pulling things together even more effectively. Einstein chose a value that held his model still, in a sense cancelling out gravity, and in the very last sentence of his first paper on cosmology, published in 1917, he wrote, 'That term is necessary only for the purpose of making possible a quasi-static distribution of matter, as required by the small velocities of the stars.'

When Hubble and Humason discovered that the Universe was expanding, Einstein said that the introduction of the cosmological constant had been the biggest blunder of his career. But other researchers took the term more seriously.

Exploring the Models

Einstein had been looking for a single solution to the equations of the general theory of relativity, a unique model which

corresponded to the real Universe. But the equations actually offer a variety of models. The first person to appreciate this was the Russian Alexander Friedmann, who was also the first person to incorporate expansion as an integral feature of the cosmological models that he explored mathematically.

Friedmann published his solutions to the cosmological equations of the general theory

1. Albert Einstein's general theory of relativity is the basis of our understanding of the Universe.

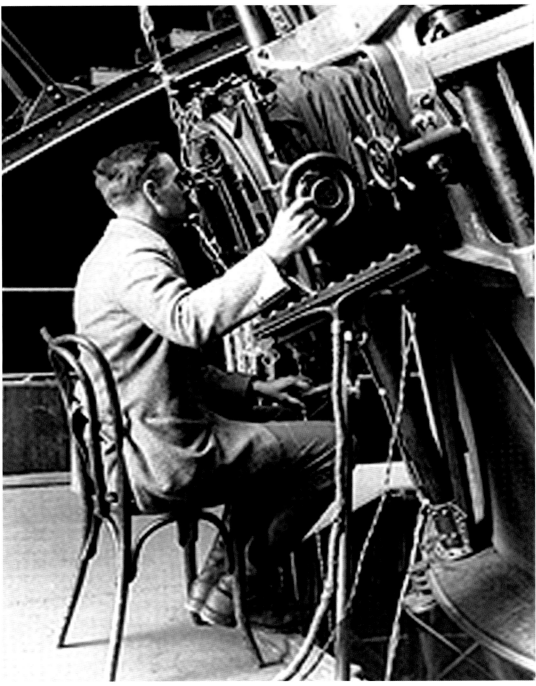

1. Edwin Hubble at the controls of the Hooker telescope.

in 1922. He understood that there is no unique solution to those equations (as Einstein had hoped) but rather a family of models describing different ways in which spacetime could evolve – different model universes. There was no way at the time to tell which, if any, of the models corresponded to our Universe. Significantly, however, all of Friedmann's models incorporated expansion at some phase in their evolution.

In some variations on the theme, space expanded forever. In others, it expanded for a time and then re-collapsed. Sometimes the expansion was fast and sometimes it was slow. It is even possible to find models which start out very big, shrink down to a certain density and then expand. But in all of the models there was at least some phase of the evolution in which the model universe expanded in such a way that from any point in it you would see other points receding with velocities proportional to their distances – exactly what Hubble and Humason found before the end of the 1920s.

Models for All Tastes

Einstein was never really happy with this variety of models, and continued to seek a unique, special case that might describe the real Universe. Together with the Dutch astronomer Willem de Sitter, in the early 1930s (soon after the discovery of Hubble's Law), he developed the Einstein–de Sitter model, which is the simplest variation on the theme allowed by the equations of the general theory. It is the model in which space is precisely flat (the only special case Einstein could think of) and with (= 0. This became the benchmark against which other models were compared.

But there was one embarrassing feature of the Einstein–de Sitter model, that Einstein and de Sitter were careful not to mention. In that model, there is a unique relationship between the rate at which the Universe is expanding today and its age – obviously, the faster it is expanding now, the less time it has taken to reach its present size , but you also have to allow for the way in which the expansion has slowed down since the Big Bang. Using the value of the constant in Hubble's Law (the redshift-distance relationship) found by Hubble himself, this gave the age of the Universe (assuming it really was described accurately by the Einstein–de Sitter model) as just 1.2 billion years, only about a third of the age of the Earth, which was already very well known by the 1930s.

Clearly, something was wrong. We now know that the early measurements of Hubble's Constant were much too big and that the true age of the Universe is about 14 billion years. But in the 1930s (and the decades that followed), there was another way to resolve the dilemma, one favoured by Georges Lemaître. With a suitable choice of the equations described a model which started out from a very dense state and expanded for a while, then 'hovered', neither

 The amount of computer memory needed to analyse the data from a Boomerang flight is 240 Gigabytes. The amount needed to analyse the Planck data will be 1600 Terabytes.

▷ THE FATE OF THE UNIVERSE

The expansion of the Universe is getting faster, because the springiness of space (▷ p. 131) is acting to overwhelm the inward tug of gravity. The effect gets bigger the more space there is, so long ago it had very little influence on the way the Universe expanded. That is why it is not obvious from redshift studies that there is a cosmological constant. But as the galaxies get further apart (like these very distant galaxies, right), it is harder for gravity to pull them back together, and as the Ⅰ effect increases it will eventually dominate, making space expand faster and faster and taking galaxies along with it. Even though the Universe is flat, the very 'dark energy' of the vacuum that makes it flat also ensures that it will expand forever, at an increasingly rapid rate (this could happen even if space were closed, like the inside of a black hole).

Although the amount of matter in the Universe stays the same, as a proportion of the critical density at each epoch (30 per cent today) it decreases, while the proportion of dark energy increases at exactly the right rate to compensate. In the past, gravity dominated. In the future, the Ⅰ will dominate. We live at an unusual moment in the history of the Universe, when the dark energy and the mass energy components are roughly the same size – the mass in dark energy is only twice that in matter. Nobody knows why this should be so, and it may just be a coincidence. It is certainly hard to see how life forms like us could survive in the far future of the Universe, when all the stars have burnt out and all that remains are the ashes, in the form of white dwarfs, neutron stars and black holes, forming black galaxies being carried ever further apart by expanding black space.

1. The two giant Keck telescopes on Mannakea in Hawaii. Each telescope has a mirror ten metres across.

2. Werner Heisenberg, whose uncertainty principle may hold the key to understanding the birth of the Universe.

expanding nor contracting, for an indefinite interval before beginning to expand again. If our Universe were like that, and we lived in the second phase of expansion, it might be much older than implied by measuring the redshift-distance relationship today. Which kind of model you chose to describe the Universe seemed, in the 1930s, just a matter of personal preference.

Taking Λ Seriously

This is just one example of how choosing a value of the cosmological constant could resolve any problem that cropped up in cosmology, such as the age problem. Mathematicians enjoyed exploring the possibilities, but astronomers tried to do

without the term, not least because it seemed too easy to use it as a fudge factor that could be adjusted to match any requirement of the observations. But when the observations of the real Universe began to be good enough to eliminate many of the wilder flights of cosmological fancy, it became clear that even with the up-to-date estimates of the Hubble Constant and the correspondingly extended age of the Universe, something was missing from the Einstein–de Sitter model. The cosmological constant came in from the cold in the 1990s, not so much because astronomers wanted it, but because they had no choice. They had, following the dictum that Conan Doyle put in the mouth of Sherlock Holmes, 'eliminated the impossible', and what they

were left with, no matter how improbable, had to be the truth.

Speeding Supernovae

By the late 1990s, the idea of inflation ($\triangleright$ pp. 114–15) was looking very good, especially in the light of the COBE data and other measurements of the microwave background. The Universe must be flat. But at the same time, studies of the way galaxies move had been unable to come up with firm evidence for more than 30 per cent of the matter needed to make space flat ($\triangleright$ p. 95). One way out of the dilemma, which began to be taken increasingly seriously in the second half of the 1990s, was the Λ term.

Putting a Spring in Space

The cosmological constant actually has two effects on the Universe. First, with the right value of Λ, it makes space springy, producing an antigravity effect, a kind of cosmic repulsion. This is equivalent to an energy of empty space, similar to the way the force of gravity is associated with the energy of matter.

This is where the second effect of Λ on the Universe comes in. Because energy is equivalent to mass, from $E = mc^2$, the Λ term also has a gravitational influence. With the right choice of Λ, it is possible to have a universal energy (associated with the cosmic repulsion) that amounts to 70 per cent of the mass needed to make the Universe flat, and at the same time to have only a tiny effect on the expansion of the Universe, one that is barely detectable today.

Adding the 70 per cent from the Λ term to the 30 per cent in the form of matter gives just the right amount of mass-energy to flatten the Universe. The theorists had explored the possibilities allowed by the models and found the simplest way to make everything fit together if there really is only 30 per cent of the critical density around in the form of dark matter and inflation did occur. It wasn't as simple as many people had hoped and it still looked a bit contrived but, like all good theories, it could be tested by new observations of the real Universe.

The Supernova Story

The role of supernovae in the story is as standard candles that provide a way to measure distances far across the Universe (▷ p. 73). Type I supernovae don't all have precisely the same brightness, but their absolute peak brightness can be inferred from the way they fade away after reaching a maximum. We can see such supernovae in nearby galaxies whose distances are known, so when they are detected in far-distant galaxies their distances can be worked out by comparing their apparent brightnesses with the nearby supernovae. The difficulty is finding supernovae in very distant galaxies, and it was only in 1998 that the technology was good enough to do the job. Then, two teams exploited that technology to make independent studies of the same phenomenon. Happily, they both got the same answer.

Two international teams, one using the Keck telescope in Hawaii and the other based at Australia's Mount Stromlo and Siding Spring Observatories, measured the brightnesses of dozens of Type I supernovae in very remote galaxies and compared the distances they inferred with the redshifts of those galaxies. They found that the recession velocities of those galaxies are a little less than would be expected by applying Hubble's Law, calculated from nearby galaxies, to them.

This means that the expansion of the Universe is accelerating, not decelerating. The point is that we see *nearby* galaxies as they were quite recently, but we see *distant* galaxies as they were long ago, because the light from them has taken so long to reach us. Nearby galaxies are receding from one another faster than distant galaxies are, because the expansion of the Universe is getting faster.

On its own, this discovery would have been interesting enough. What made it spectacular is that the amount of cosmic repulsion required to match the observations is also exactly right to provide 70 per cent of the mass-energy needed to flatten the Universe.

Clinching Confirmation

The one remaining uncertainty was whether the Universe really is precisely flat, **2**

☆ Searches for distant supernovae have to be carefully timed because these objects are so faint that they can only be observed properly at New Moon, when the sky is darkest.

as inflation says it should be. Again, new technology provided a way to test the prediction. Radiation travelling through space is affected by the curvature of space, and the further it travels the more it is affected. The microwave background radiation has been travelling through space for longer than anything else we can detect, and the exact pattern of the variations in that radiation from one part of the sky to another can, in principle, reveal the curvature of space all the way from the Big Bang fireball to us – across 14 billion light years of space.

By the end of the 1990s, instruments carried aloft in balloons were able to monitor fluctuations in the background radiation 35 times smaller than those COBE could detect. Results from two of those balloon flights, announced in 2000, show that the Universe is flat to within 10 per cent – which means that lies between 0.9 and 1.1. With clear evidence that there is only 30 per cent of the mass needed to flatten the Universe around in the form of matter, that meant there had to be 70 per cent around in the form of energy – just as the supernovae suggested. It was compelling evidence that the cosmological constant is real, whether Einstein liked it or not.

Ripples in the Cosmic Sea

The close agreement between all these different elements of the story – the amount of matter in the Universe, the acceleration required by supernova studies, the flatness revealed by measurements of the background radiation – makes inflation far and away the cosmological 'best buy' at the beginning of the twenty-first century. This provides a way to tackle the last great puzzle: why the Universe is not perfectly uniform, but has irregularities big enough to allow us to exist.

Quantum Fluctuations

Where does the energy of empty space come from? According to quantum physics, there is no such thing as truly 'empty' space, because that would have precisely zero energy, and one of the most famous rules of the quantum world, Heisenberg's Uncertainty Principle, says that it is impossible for anything to have a precise value (not just that it is impossible for us to measure things precisely; absolute precision does not exist in the Universe). In this context, in any tiny volume of space there is a tradeoff between time and energy. Particles known as 'virtual pairs' can (indeed, *must*) pop into

 INTO THE FUTURE

The definitive answers to most of the remaining questions in cosmology should come when the instrument technology used in projects such as Boomerang is harnessed to space technology. A new generation of microwave satellites needs to be put into orbit around the Earth. There they will be able to map the whole sky at microwave frequencies, staying in orbit for months or years to pick out the fine details.

The first of these satellites, the Microwave Anisotropy Probe (or MAP, right) was due to be launched by NASA shortly. If successful, it will spend a year mapping the sky. Then the team will spend a year analysing the data. MAP is a quick and relatively cheap mission which will have about the accuracy of Boomerang but will extend to cover the whole sky.

The latest word in microwave mapping yet planned is the European Planck mission (named after Max Planck), which should fly into space before the end of the first decade of the twenty-first century. It is a more ambitious project which, if all goes well, will provide more accurate data than anything that has gone before. Together, these missions should pin down the values of the key cosmological parameters, including Λ, Ω, and Hubble's Constant, to an accuracy of 0.1 per cent.

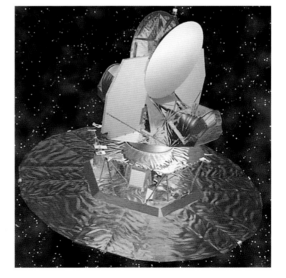

existence out of nothing at all, provided they annihilate one another and disappear within a certain time. The time limit is set by their mass – the bigger the mass, the smaller the time they can exist for – but is measured in tiny fractions of a second. It is as if the particles exist when the Universe isn't looking, but as soon as it has time to notice their presence, they vanish.

The effect of all this is to make space a seething foam of virtual particles, giving it both energy and structure. It is the energy that provides the outward push of the term, and the mass associated with that energy that completes the job of making the Universe flat.

It is no coincidence, by the way, that all the different kinds of mass-energy in the Universe add up to make it flat, with $\Omega = 1$. Inflation drives the Universe to flatness, so there is only so much mass-energy to go round, to be shared among baryons, HDM, CDM and Λ. It's as if you had a variety of different bottles and jars and you poured water into them from a one-litre container. No matter how the water is divided among the different containers, the total amount of liquid has to add up to one litre.

But although quantum fluctuations are usually ephemeral, it seems they have left their imprint on the Universe.

1. In a fractal, each small piece of the pattern can be enlarged to reproduce the whole pattern.

A Matter of Scale

As well as occurring in tiny split-seconds of time, quantum fluctuations also occur on tiny distance scales (not least because the disturbances involved do not have time to travel far before they are forced to disappear). These processes were going on in the earliest phase of the Universe, after the Planck time and before inflation. At the time inflation took a grip on what was to become the visible Universe, all of the mass-energy associated with the visible Universe was tucked inside a tiny seed just 10^{-25} cm across – 100 million times bigger than the Planck length but still 1000 billion times smaller than a proton. Even this ridiculously tiny seed was big enough to contain quantum fluctuations, involving energetic fields (like electromagnetism) rather than particles. So the vacuum had an ever-changing structure, but the structure always matched a certain statistical pattern.

Then inflation happened. Everything in the universal seed was ripped apart and spread out. In the process, whatever fluctuations of the vacuum were going on at the moment inflation began were frozen into the structure of the rapidly expanding seed and also enormously stretched out as space expanded. Space actually expanded faster than light during inflation (this is entirely allowed by Einstein's equations; it is only motion *through* space that cannot exceed the speed of light), and the last quantum fluctuations were imprinted on the pattern of hot gas that emerged from the cosmic fireball.

The statistical pattern of the quantum fluctuations is called 'scale invariance', because it looks the same (statistically) on all scales – if you take a piece of the picture and expand it, it doesn't look precisely like the original, but has the same statistical appearance, in terms of the arrangement of hot spots and cold spots. What COBE and its successors see in the ripples in the background radiation is exactly the same pattern of scale invariance, but 'written' over hundreds of millions of light years, instead of within a sphere 1000 billion times smaller than a proton. We are part of that pattern – life is part of the structure imprinted on the Universe by quantum fluctuations shortly after the birth of time.

BALLOONS AND THE BACKGROUND RADIATION

Technology has improved so much since the time of COBE that, in the absence of any new microwave satellites, the best maps of the microwave background radiation now come from instruments attached to balloons on flights above most of the Earth's atmosphere. Until the next generation of microwave satellites goes up, taking comparable instruments with them right into orbit, the best picture of the microwave Universe comes from one of those experiments, Boomerang.

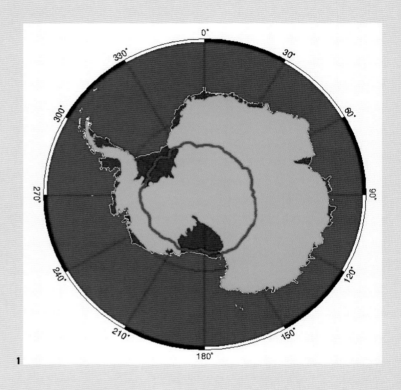

1

Around the World in 10.5 Days

Boomerang gets its name from the fact that the balloon travels in a roughly circular path around Antarctica, carried by high altitude winds. Technically, because it circles the South Pole, this is a round-the-world flight. Its first circumpolar flight started from the McMurdo base at 03:30 GMT on 29 December 1998, and ended when the balloon returned to its starting point at 15:50 GMT on 8 January 1999. It went around the world in 10.5 days.

The microwave telescope used to monitor the background radiation was lifted to an altitude of 40 km by a balloon the size of an American football stadium.

Why Antarctica?

Antarctica is a very good place to operate a balloon mission like Boomerang for several reasons. First, because the path of the balloon is predictable and it returns to its starting point, it can stay aloft for a long time. It cannot stay up as long as a satellite, but similar balloons launched in other parts of the world have to be brought down in a few hours (at most a couple of days) before they become a hazard or get lost.

Secondly, the air above Antarctica is cold and dry, which means that even the remaining trace of atmosphere above 40 km altitude does not have much influence on the incoming background radiation, which can be partly absorbed by water vapour.

Finally, because Antarctica is uninhabited (except by scientists and penguins) the balloon is not going to get in anyone's way, and there are no local radio and television stations to interfere with its microwave detectors.

Supercool Science

Even with all these advantages, mapping the

2

microwave sky accurately is difficult. Basically, the detectors are measuring the temperature of the background radiation from different parts of the sky, and they can only do this accurately if the detectors are even colder than the radiation (the colder the better). The radiation has a temperature of 2.735 K. The Boomerang detectors were cooled to 0.28 K (−272.88 K2, since 0 K is −273.16 degrees Celsius) in a giant Dewar (like a Thermos flask) at the focus of a 1.3 metre diameter telescope.

The Boomerang Dewar contained 65 litres of liquid helium in an inner container and 75 litres of liquid nitrogen in an outer container. Together these are sufficient to keep the detectors at the required temperature for up to 12 days.

Confirmation by Balloon

Although other launch sites are less ideal than Antarctica, other balloon experiments provided valuable confirmation that Boomerang really is detecting fluctuations in the background radiation, and not some spurious 'signals' caused by problems with its detectors. The most important of these complementary balloon programmes was dubbed MAXIMA, from Millimeter Anisotropy eXperiment Imaging Array.

The first flight of MAXIMA took place in August 1998, and lasted for just 4.5 hours. It uses a similar 1.3 metre telescope to the one on Boomerang, cooled to about 0.1 K. On this and subsequent flights, MAXIMA found the same kind of fluctuations as Boomerang, but in the northern sky (it was launched in Texas) not the southern sky. Although the results were not as impressive in themselves as those from Boomerang, they were crucially important because they showed the same pattern from different parts of the sky, confirming that what Boomerang saw is a universal effect.

3

1. Map of the flightpath of the Boomerang.

2. Boomerang's map of the microwave sky. The colour variarions represent varaitions in temperature.

3. The launch of MAXIMA in August 1998.

⬥ TOPIC LINKS

2.1 The Big Bang
p. 83 Microwaves from the Birth of Time
p. 84 The Very First Light
pp. 90–1 The First Four Minutes

2.3 Missing Mass & the Birth of Time
p. 116 Ripples in the Background Radiation

3

MAKING CONTACT

To an astronomer, exploring space (even by proxy) can be a satisfying life's work. Understanding the nature of the stars and galaxies on the basis of the laws of physics determined here on Earth, plus the information gleaned from telescopes, is a breathtaking achievement and a rewarding experience. But at the back of the mind of even the most dedicated astronomer lurks the big question – are there other astronomers out there, looking at the same stars and galaxies from a different perspective, and drawing their own conclusions about the nature of the Universe? Is there life – and in particular, is there intelligent life – beyond the Solar System? After centuries of speculation, it is a question that now seems ripe for the answering. Travelling to the stars may still be a pipe dream; but, for the first time, we have the technology to detect other worlds like the Earth, and perhaps to communicate with them.

Previous page. Ariel view of the Arecibo radio telescope in Puerto Rico.

OTHER WORLDS

As long as we only knew of the existence of one family of planets – the one orbiting around our own Sun – the possibility existed that the Solar System was unique, and that no other planets existed anywhere in the Universe. It seemed unlikely, but it *might* be true. That changed in 1995, when a team of Swiss astronomers discovered a giant planet, not unlike Jupiter, but with about half as much mass, orbiting around a star known as 51 Pegasi. It lies 50 light years from Earth in the direction of the constellation Pegasus. They didn't see the planet directly, but inferred its presence from the way the orbiting planet made the star wobble to and fro slightly, as it was tugged by the planet, moving in its orbit, first in one direction then the other. To measure the wobble of the star they used the two most valuable tools the astronomer has for the exploration of the Universe: spectroscopy and the Doppler effect (▷ pp. 18 and 82).

It's no accident that the discovery was made in the mid-1990s, and not before, because that was when spectroscopic techniques became accurate enough, and the computers used to analyse the spectra became powerful enough, to measure the tiny Doppler shifts involved. What happens is that, when a planet is on 'our' side of a star, it tugs the star towards us, producing a tiny

1. Artist's impression of the giant planet 51 Pegasi B orbiting its parent star 51 Pegasi.

blueshift in the light from the star. When the planet is on the other side of the star, it tugs the star away from us, producing a tiny redshift (▷ p. 82). In round terms, the change in speed of the star that has to be measured in this way is about 10 metres per second – almost exactly the speed of an Olympic-standard 100-metre sprinter. Measuring the Doppler shift in the light from 51 Pegasi is like measuring the speed of the winner of the Olympic 100 metres from a distance of 15 parsecs.

The Big Surprise

The star 51 Pegasi had been chosen for investigation using the Doppler technique because it is a yellow star rather like the Sun. The most important feature of the discovery was that it showed that other Sun-like stars do have planets. In that sense, the Solar System is not unique. But there was a big surprise. Like all explorers entering new territory, the planet hunters had found the unexpected. Although the planet orbiting 51 Pegasi is a giant like Jupiter, it orbits much closer to its star than any giant in our Solar System orbits the Sun (closer even than Mercury), and the heat of its star must raise the surface temperature to 1300 K. Whereas Jupiter takes just over 11 years to orbit around the Sun once, the newly discovered planet takes just over four *days* to orbit its star once.

This was such a surprise that many other astronomers wondered if the Swiss team had made a mistake. But soon their observations were confirmed by a team of researchers in the United States, and then by other observers.

Within the next two years, four more 'hot Jupiters' were found orbiting other stars, as well as four Jupiter-like planets in orbits that seemed more normal, from the perspective of our Solar System. But the questions remained. How could *Jupiter*-like planets get into orbits so close to their stars? And which kind of planetary system really is normal – the Solar System, or systems like 51 Pegasi?

A Profusion of Planets

The best answer to the first question seems to be that giant planets may form far away from their parent star (as in the Solar System) but get dragged in towards it if there is still enough dust around in the disc in which they form (▷ p. 39) to provide enough friction to make them fall inwards. If there is less dust,

 ## THE FIRST 'VISIBLE' PLANET

In the summer of 1999, astronomers from St Andrews University in Scotland and Harvard in the United States announced that they had 'seen' a planet beyond our Solar System for the first time. The planet orbits the star Tau Bootis, chosen for investigation because it is similar in size to our Sun, but rather brighter at certain wavelengths of light. The planet now thought to be orbiting Tau Bootis is too far away to be photographed in any way, but light from the parent star is reflected from the planet, and is detected, mixed up with the raw starlight, by telescopes on Earth. The reflected light from the planet is only one ten-thousandth as bright as the direct light from the star, but it can be picked out from the starlight because the planet is orbiting around Tau Bootis at 150 km per second. This produces a rhythmically changing Doppler shift in the light reflected from the planet.

This first directly observed extra-solar planet has about 1.4 times the mass of Jupiter, the largest planet in our Solar System, and is almost certainly, like Jupiter, a gas giant. If confirmed, this will be one of the most important astronomical discoveries; but confirmation of these claims has not yet come in.

and less friction, they stay where they are.

The honest answer to the second question is 'We don't know'. But there is one point worth bearing in mind. It is easier to detect big planets than little planets, and easier still to detect them if they are in close orbits around their parent stars (the closer they are, the bigger the wobble they cause). So systems like 51 Pegasi are the easiest kind of systems

to find and it should be no surprise that astronomers found them first. Systems like our Solar System are harder to detect; they may be there, but our instruments are not yet good enough to spot them using the Doppler technique. As astronomers are fond of putting it, 'absence of evidence is not evidence of absence'. But so many 'extra-solar' giant planets are now known that it is

hard to believe there are not a few small planets out there as well. By the end of the 1990s, 28 of these giants had been discovered, three of them in orbit around the same star, Upsilon Andromedae. To get some idea of the chances of Earth-like planets being out there as well, we have to take stock of what it is that makes the Earth special in our own Solar System.

1. Artist's impression of planet orbiting the star Tau Bootis. A hypothetical moon has been included in this rendition.

1

2

THE GOLDILOCKS PLANET

Earth is sometimes referred to as the 'Goldilocks' planet, because conditions here are just right for life, just as baby bear's porridge was just right for Goldilocks. The best way to see this is in terms of water (an essential ingredient for life as we know it) and temperature.

In those terms, the Earth lies roughly in the middle of the 'comfort zone' around our Sun. The planet Venus is almost a twin of the Earth in size, but its distance from the Sun is a bit less than three-quarters of the distance of the Earth from the Sun. If Venus had started out a little further from the Sun, it might have formed oceans of water in which life could emerge. But the extra heat present where Venus formed meant that liquid water could not exist there, but built up in the atmosphere as water vapour, helping to contribute to an intense greenhouse effect which, together with the Sun's proximity, sends temperatures soaring above 700 K.

Mars is a lot smaller than the Earth, with only a tenth of the Earth's mass. It orbits one and a half times as far away from the Sun. If the Earth were in the orbit of Mars, it might still be a fertile planet, thanks to the greenhouse effect of its atmosphere. But the gravity of Mars was too feeble to hold onto a thick atmosphere, and the combination of a thin atmospheric blanket and its distance from the Sun sends its night-time winter temperatures plunging below 162 K (minus 111 degrees Celsius).

Stretching things to the limit, you could say that the comfort zone around the Sun extended from the orbit of Venus to the orbit of Mars, with the Earth roughly in the middle of the zone. If this were right, life might be rare. There would be very little

1. The Earth is just right for life, whereas Venus (2) is too hot, and Mars (opposite) is too cold.

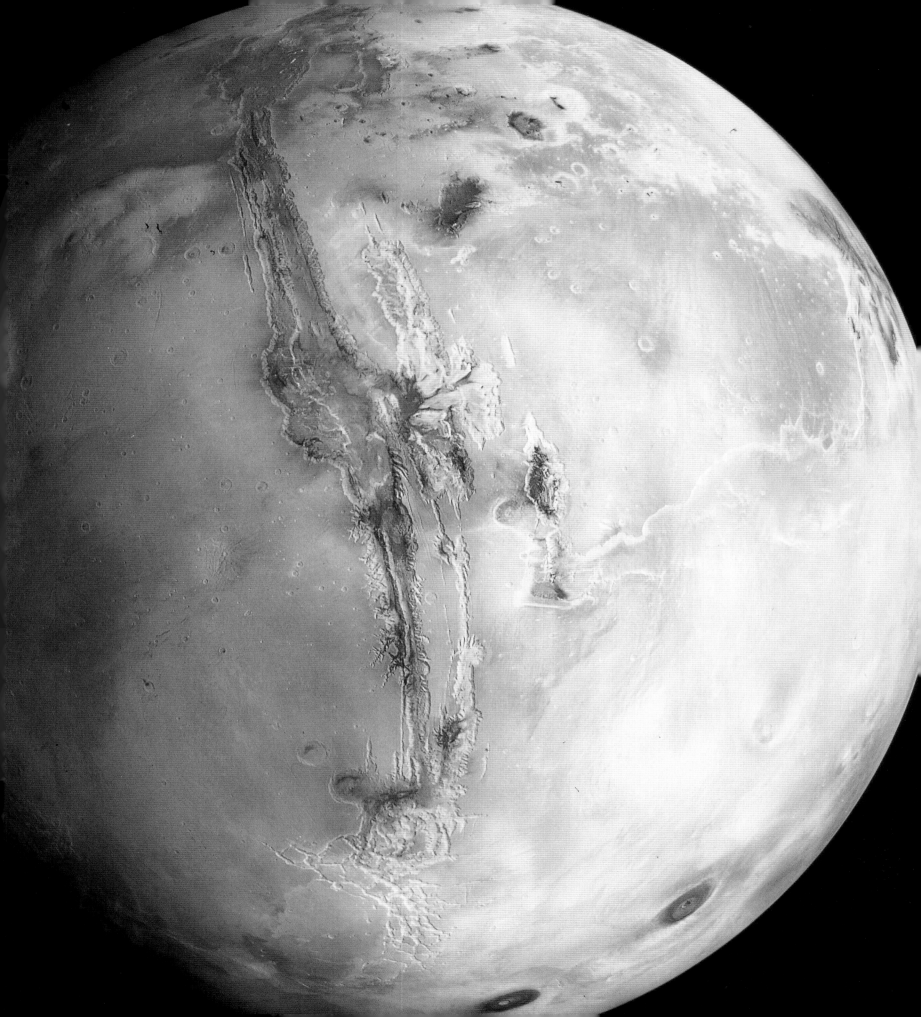

chance of finding more than one planet in the equivalent comfort zone around another star, and all kinds of things might go wrong to prevent life getting a grip on that one suitable planet. But when spaceprobes visited the outer part of our own Solar System, they found that this pessimistic point of view might be wrong.

Extending the Comfort Zone

Assuming that life elsewhere resembles life on Earth (which is the only basis we have to go on), the search for life is essentially the search for liquid water. Without liquid water, there is no life. It is no coincidence that our word for a region on Earth devoid of life, desert, is the same as our word for a region devoid of liquid water.

At first sight, it looks as if the surface of any planet beyond the orbit of Mars should be too cold for liquid water to exist. But in the late 1990s, the space probe Galileo sent back pictures from one of Jupiter's moons, Europa, which revealed that the moon is almost entirely covered by what seems to be a layer of ice floating on an ocean of liquid water, very like pack ice floats on the Arctic Ocean. Although it is smaller than our own Moon, Europa still has a diameter of 3,138 km, making it a respectably sized potential home for life. But what keeps it warm?

The answer seems to be that as Europa follows its orbit around Jupiter, the gravitational pull from Jupiter itself, and from the other moons orbiting around the planet, combine to produce a changing tidal force, constantly 'kneading' the inside of Europa. It is squeezed rhythmically in and out, in the same way that the gravitational pulls of the Sun and Moon cause the tides to move rhythmically up and down the seashore on Earth. This kneading generates heat, enough heat to melt the ice which makes up the bulk

1

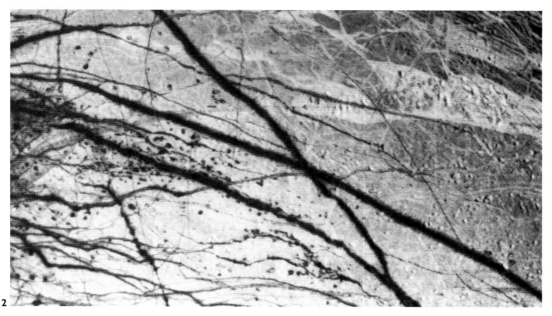

1. Family portrait of Jupiter and its four largest moons.

3. The life zone around the Sun.

2. Close-up view of the icy surface of Europa, one of Jupiter's moons.

2

of Europa. The result might not be comfortable for human beings, but if life can exist in the chilly waters of Antarctica, then in principle it can exist on Europa.

At once, the known comfort zone for life around our Sun doubled in size.

Heat from Inside

There are other ways to generate heat. The Earth itself is hot inside because of radioactivity, which keeps the core molten. If a planet like the Earth formed in the equivalent of an orbit between those of Jupiter and Mars, it might be too cold on its surface for liquid water to flow, but it could have very deep, frozen oceans, because very little of its primordial water would have evaporated. Any ice deeper than 14 kilometres below the surface would be melted by the internal heat of the planet.

At the end of the twentieth century, astronomers realized that they had been far too parochial in their estimates of the chance of finding liquid water elsewhere in

the Universe and, therefore, in their estimates of the chance of finding life. But the Holy Grail still remains: what are the chances of finding other Earths?

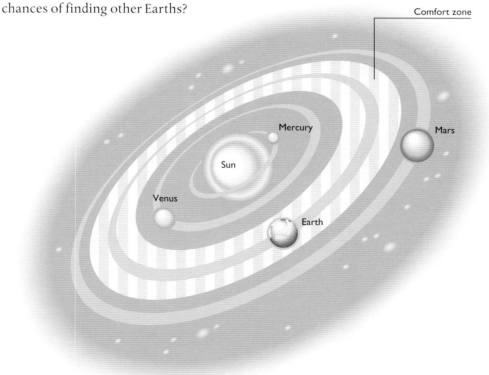

3

LIFE ON EARTH

One of the biggest mysteries in biology is how life got a grip on the Earth so soon after our planet formed. The Earth formed about 4.5 billion years ago, but it was bombarded with debris from space early in its life, and took about half a billion years to cool to the point where liquid water could flow. Yet there is fossil evidence of bacterial life in rocks at least 3.9 billion years old. Could life really have got started from scratch in just a hundred million years or so?

2

Cosmic Rain

Perhaps life didn't have to start from scratch on Earth. Although the bombardment of the Earth eased after about half a billion years, it didn't stop. Even today, the Earth is still occasionally struck by a large object (as the dinosaurs found to their cost 65 million years ago), and more gentle impacts with comets and smaller bits of cosmic debris happen quite often – on a geological timescale, that is. Since the 1960s, there has been a growing awareness that clouds of material in interstellar space contain a variety of complex carbon compounds, the raw materials of life. It now seems likely that cometary impacts when the Earth was young brought some of those raw materials down to the surface of our planet, giving life a kick start.

In 1986, cameras onboard the space probes Giotto and Vega sent back images of dark

1

material coating the surface of the icy core of Halley's comet, and spectroscopy revealed that this is made of a variety of carbon-rich molecules. Ground-based telescopes have shown that the gases which make comets so spectacularly visible are also rich in carbon compounds, including methane and ethane. All this is important, because carbon is the key component of life (so much so that complex carbon chemistry is also called 'organic chemistry'). Microscopic particles of dust from space, much of it comet debris, are constantly falling onto the Earth, and analysis of samples collected at high altitudes tells us that about 30 tonnes of organic carbon compounds reach the surface of the Earth this way each day.

Seeds from the Clouds

The ultimate origin of all this stuff is the interstellar molecular cloud in which our Solar System was born. Spectroscopic studies have revealed the presence of many organic carbon compounds, such as formaldehyde, and ethanol (also known as vodka). But the most important discovery, made in 1994, was that of glycine, the first amino acid discovered in space. Out of more than a hundred molecules known to exist in space, this is the most important, because amino acids are the building blocks of proteins, and proteins are what your body is made of.

It is very hard to see how simple compounds like carbon dioxide and water could have developed into living bacteria in only a hundred million years. But if the young Earth were laced with complex organic molecules things like amino acids, then the whole process would have proceeded much faster.

The problem of the origin of complex organic molecules, the precursors of life, is moved from the Earth and out into space. There, although cold clouds of gas and dust may not seem the ideal places for chemical processes to take place, there was time enough – billions of years – for these first steps to be taken and for the seeds of life to form.

This would have happened before the stars and planets formed from the collapse of those clouds. The implication is that the 'seeds' of life fall upon every new planet, even if they do not always 'germinate' there.

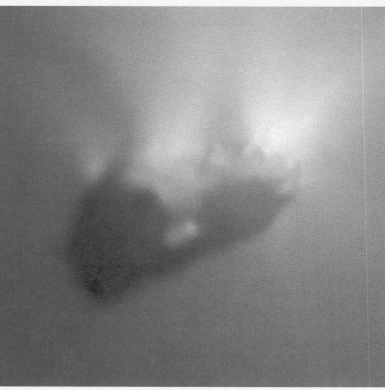

1. Fossils reveal the history of life on Earth. The oldest fossils show that life on Earth existed almost as soon as the planet had cooled.

2. The horse-head nebula is a cloud of dust in space typical of the material from which planetary systems form.

3. The central core of Halley's comet, photographed by the space probe Giotto, is primordial material left over from the birth of the Solar System.

✧ TOPIC LINKS

1.1 Stepping Stones to the Universe
p. 17 The Stars are Suns

1.2 Star Birth
p. 31 The Orion Nursery
p. 39 Dusty Discs

1.3 Stellar Evolution
p. 53 Cooking the Elements

3.2 Talking to the Stars
pp. 164–5 Panspermia

3

OTHER EARTHS?

The technique of detecting planets by the 'Doppler wobble' they produce in the light from their parent stars cannot yet detect the presence of Earth-like planets in Earth-like orbits around other stars. But there are two ways in which astronomers believe they may be able to detect such planets using ground-based telescopes – and other possibilities as space technology improves.

The first technique may already have worked. It depends on the way that light is bent when it passes near a massive object. This phenomenon is called 'gravitational lensing', and it was the technique used by astronomers in 1919 to test Albert Einstein's general theory of relativity. By studying the light from distant stars as it passed close by the Sun during a total solar eclipse, they found that it was bent by the Sun to exactly the degree predicted by Einstein's theory. The effect is bigger for a bending (or 'lensing') object of bigger mass, so it is much smaller for an Earth-sized planet than it is for the Sun. Nevertheless, it should be measurable even for planets orbiting other stars, if conditions are just right.

There are two ways in which conditions may be just right. First, when one star passes exactly in front of another star, as viewed from Earth, the lensing effect of the nearer star makes the more distant star seem brighter for several weeks. If the nearer star has an Earth-sized planet orbiting it, the planet may also pass in front of the more distant star, producing a smaller blip of extra brightness as it passes across our line of sight.

At the end of the 1990s, astronomers working at the University of Notre Dame, in Indiana, observed just such a double blip as one star passed in front of another. From the size of the smaller blip and its duration – just two and a half hours – they calculated that it could have been caused by a planet a few times more massive than the Earth, orbiting its star in the equivalent of the zone in the Solar System where Venus, Earth and Mars orbit our Sun. This single observation is not proof that other Earths exist, and there is no way to take a second look at this possible planet – it was a one-off event. But at least it shows that the technology is good enough for the job.

The Dragon Planet

Other astronomers have looked for the tiny increase in brightness that might be seen in a distant star when a planet in orbit around the star crosses in front of it. This would be a rare event, because there is no reason why the orbit of such a planet should be lined up with the Earth. The effect is also very small. But we would see a repeating pattern of tiny increases and decreases in brightness as the planet orbits round its parent star. Late in 1999, an international team of astronomers reported that they had found just such a pattern in the light from a system known as CM Draconis (which lies in the constellation of the Dragon). The pattern suggests that there is a planet with two and a half times the mass of the Earth orbiting in this system right in the comfort zone, where it receives roughly the same amount of energy that the Earth receives from the Sun. The discovery has yet to be confirmed, but it shows that the technology works, and we can expect more observations like these in the months and years ahead.

As the examples of Venus and Mars show, however, the presence of a rocky planet in (or near) the comfort zone doesn't prove that life exists on that planet. Are there any ways in which astronomers, exploring the Universe with their telescopes without ever leaving the Solar System, might be able to tell whether an object like the Dragon planet harboured life? Astonishingly, the answer is 'yes', and the technology to do the job might exist within 30 years.

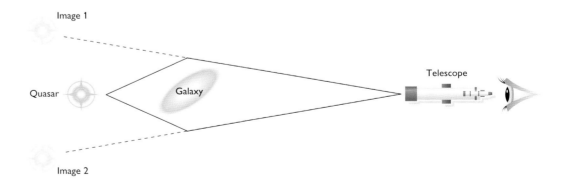

1. A greatly exaggerated example of how the gravity of a galaxy can bend light from a distant quasar.

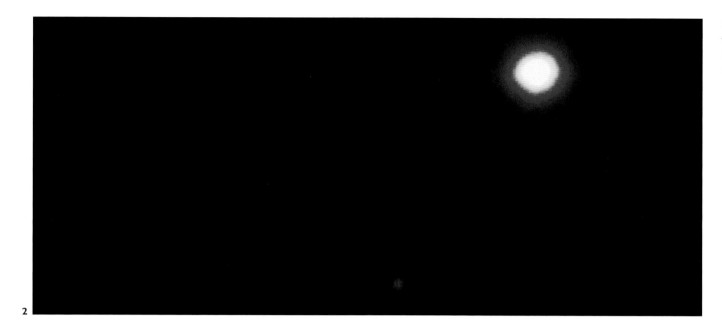

2. The star 51 Pegasi, which is now known to have at least one planet in orbit around it.

The insight on which this possibility is based goes back to the 1960s, when the British scientist Jim Lovelock was designing instruments for NASA to use on space probes that would search for signs of life on Mars. Lovelock realized that this was a waste of time, because spectroscopy had already revealed that the atmosphere of Mars was made up of inert carbon dioxide, which meant that it was a dead planet. On Mars, the chemicals in the air are bound up in low energy states, and nothing interesting can happen to them (the same is true of Venus). On Earth, by contrast, there is a lot of highly reactive oxygen in the atmosphere, which is a mixture of gases in a high energy state, able to react with one another. If chemistry alone were at work, everything would react, producing an inert atmosphere. It is the presence of life, which uses sunlight to break up inert chemicals and release active chemicals to the air, which makes the Earth distinctive.

This insight led Lovelock to develop his idea of Gaia – the Earth as a single living system, with the physical environment and

 A PULSAR WITH PLANETS

To the intense irritation of radio astronomers, what they regard as not only the first extra-solar planet to be discovered, but the first planetary system found outside the Solar System, is almost entirely disregarded by the astronomers who search for planets using optical telescopes. The discovery was made in 1992, from analysis of the radio pulses from a pulsar prosaically named PSR B1257+12. Using the radio equivalent of the Doppler wobble technique, the radio astronomers found the spectroscopic trace of not one but three planets in orbit around the pulsar. Strangely, as far as the orbits and masses of the planets are concerned, this is the most similar system yet found to our own Solar System. The main difference is that the planets orbit their star more closely than the three inner planets of our Solar System – but if the radii of their orbits were doubled they would be close to the orbits of Mercury, Venus and Earth.

The reason why most planet hunters ignore this discovery and regard the planet orbiting 51 Pegasi as the first 'real' discovery is that the planets orbiting PSR 1257+12 must have formed after the neutron star collapsed. Any original planets in the system would have been destroyed in the supernova in which the neutron star was born. So they must be very different objects from the planets in our Solar System, just as the pulsar is a star quite unlike our Sun. Nevertheless, they do orbit a star, and they are planets.

the biological environment interacting to maintain an essentially unstable balance. Forty years on, it has also led to the most promising way to search for life in space.

Seeking Signs of Life

The best way to detect Earth-sized planets will be to put large telescope arrays up into space. These will go far beyond the famous Hubble Space Telescope, both in terms of size and location. The idea is to put systems made up of several large dishes, linked together to act like one huge telescope, far away from the Earth where there will be no disturbances to disrupt their observations. Because planets are much cooler than stars, they radiate energy in the infrared part of the spectrum, with frequencies even lower (and therefore with less energy) than those of red light (▷ p. 18). These space telescopes are being designed to look at that part of the spectrum. If they find an infrared source alongside a star like the Sun, the chances are it will be a planet. But both the European Space Agency (ESA) and NASA hope to do better than that.

ESA already has such a system, called Project Darwin, on the drawing board. NASA's counterpart is the Terrestrial Planet Finder (TPF). It is likely that the two projects will be merged into one, to avoid costly duplication of effort. What makes them so attractive, in spite of the cost, is that the infrared part of the spectrum is just the place where characteristic signatures of chemical compounds associated with life on Earth occur. Oxygen itself, plus the tri-atomic form of oxygen known as ozone, and water vapour all leave their fingerprints in the infrared part of the spectrum. Telescopes like Darwin/TPF could be flown in space as early as the 2030s, and would immediately be able to detect planets in orbit around stars 3 to 5 parsecs away. Obtaining spectra may take a little longer, but if these projects go ahead we should know for sure, within 50 years, whether these planets are dead, like Venus or Mars, or whether they really are other Earths.

1

 ANOTHER 'SOLAR SYSTEM'

In 1997, astronomers discovered a planet with roughly the same mass as Jupiter in orbit around a star in the constellation Andromeda, using the Doppler wobble technique. Two years later, they discovered that there are two more giant planets orbiting the same star. It took so long to work out that there were actually three planets in this system, and to determine their masses and some details of the kind of orbits they are in, because the spectroscopic signatures of the planets in the light from the star interfere with each other. But by the spring of 1999 it was clear that the complicated pattern of Doppler shifts being seen in the light from this star could most simply be explained as the presence of three planets, not one.

The mass of the star is about 30 per cent bigger than that of the Sun, and it is about halfway through its lifetime on the main sequence (▷ p. 51), which will be about six billion years. The system is 13 parsecs away from us. The innermost of the three known planets zips round the star once every 4.6 days. It has about 70 per cent of the mass of Jupiter. The next planet out from the star has a year 242 Earth days long and is twice the mass of Jupiter, while the third takes 1270 Earth days to go round its star once and has four times the mass of Jupiter. There is nothing unusual about either the star or its planets, and this is the first proof that systems of planets, instead of just individual planets, exist outside the Solar System.

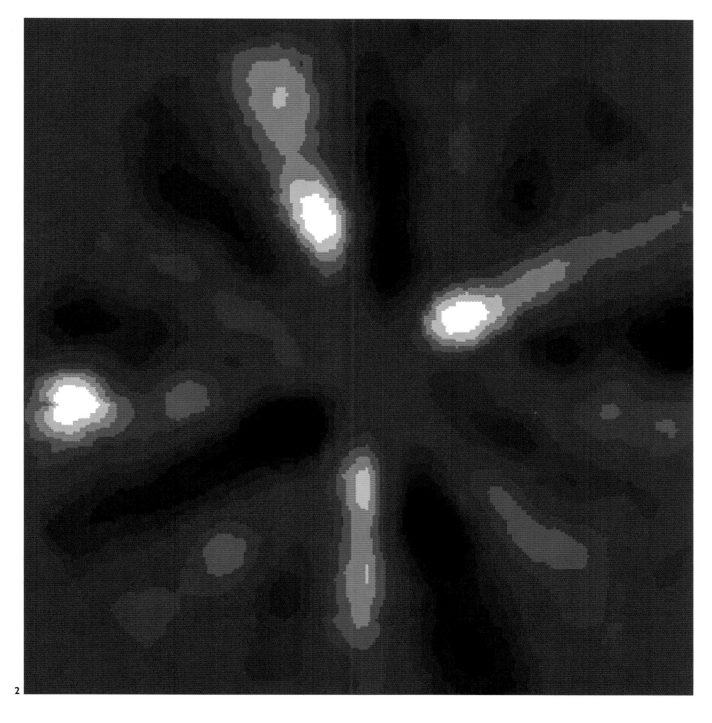

1. Artist's impression of the kind of space telescope needed to obtain images of planets orbiting other stars.

2. A simulation of how the inner part of our Solar System would look to a telescope like the Darwin system.

2

People interested in making contact with other civilizations beyond our Solar System usually talk of the 'Search for Extra Terrestrial Intelligence', or SETI. They assume that we will be able to make contact with such intelligences, if they exist, either by radio communication or by sending space probes to the stars. But what those astronomers are really looking for is evidence of extraterrestrial technologies. Of course, we would have no hope (yet) of detecting a Roman-level civilization on an Earth-like planet orbiting another star, even though the Romans of the first century AD were both intelligent and civilized (in their way). And there may be civilizations that are in some sense more advanced than ours – older and more peaceful, perhaps – that never developed machines and radio communication. But for now, such possibilities remain in the realms of science fiction; the only real prospect of finding extraterrestrial intelligence is by using technology – in particular, one specific piece of technology, radio.

FIRST STEPS

Politicians (and other people) sometimes express concern about the possibility of making two-way contact with alien intelligences. They fear that the experience of encountering a superior civilization might destroy the civilization we already have here on Earth, in much the same way contact with Europeans destroyed the culture of the native Americans. It was for this reason that astronomers hoping to make contact (even if only one-way contact) changed the name of their programme from its original CETI (Communicating with ExtraTerrestrial Intelligence) to SETI, implying that we could listen out for other civilizations without necessarily revealing our presence.

Making Contact by Mistake

But it is already too late – we have been broadcasting to the Universe, more or less indiscriminately, for more than half a century. The first radio broadcasts could not escape into space, because they were reflected back from the ionosphere, a layer of charged particles high in the Earth's atmosphere (they were also very feeble, and would be difficult to detect anyway at stellar distances). The first signals that had both the right wavelength to penetrate the ionosphere and the power to be detected at reasonable distances were the broadcasts made by the BBC from the 1936 Olympics, in Berlin. These were quickly followed into space by early television programmes, radar pulses, and more recently by the powerful radio signals beamed to interplanetary space probes to control their activity.

1. TV camera photographed in 1936 in front of the transmitting mast of the Alexandra Palace.

1. Star cluster in a large magellanic cloud, taken by the Hubble Space telescope.

2. We've already begun broadcasting to the Universe. Given sufficiently advanced technology, aliens in distant star clusters will one day be able to watch *Sergeant Bilko*.

1

The bowl of the Arecibo radio telescope is big enough to hold four billion bottles of beer.

All of these signals travel at the speed of light, in different directions out through space. So the Solar System sits in the middle of an expanding bubble of radio noise (for these purposes, short wavelength electromagnetic radiation such as TV and radar signals are classed as radio waves), extending in all directions out to a distance of about 20 parsecs, and getting bigger by 0.5 parsecs every year. The signals at the outer edge of the bubble are pretty feeble; but the ones following the radio waves from the 1936 Olympics get stronger and stronger as the technology of broadcasting has improved.

This bubble has already spread beyond

scores of stars – there are a couple of dozen within 3 parsecs of the Sun, which have already had the opportunity to experience the Berlin Olympics, *I Love Lucy* (in its original broadcasts), *Monty Python's Flying Circus*, and CNN's coverage of the Gulf War. Because of the time taken for the signals to travel such huge distances, these stars still have the global broadcasts celebrating the start of the third millennium to look forward to.

It is quite possible that our first contact with an alien civilization will come in the form of a communication beamed directly at our Solar System in response to the radio noise we are already making – perhaps even a polite request to turn the noise down a bit.

Shouting at the Stars

There have also been deliberate attempts to attract attention to ourselves – the radio equivalent of shouting, as loud as possible, 'Here we are'. The best way to do this is to use the largest radio telescope in the world, which has been built in a natural hollow in the ground at Arecibo, in Puerto Rico. Because it is built in a bowl in the ground, the Arecibo Radio Telescope can only cover a strip of the sky as the Earth rotates; it cannot be steered to point in other directions. However, it has a diameter of 305 metres, giving it a collecting area bigger than every optical telescope built in the twentieth century put together. This helps it to detect very faint radio noise from space, provided it comes from the right part of the sky. It also makes it ideal (equipped with a suitable broadcast system) for sending a powerful beam of radio waves out into space. In this role, it has been used to bounce radar pulses off Venus and Mars and detect the

2

 ZAPPING THE STARS

Laser beams, which use light instead of radio waves, unlike the Arecibo Space Telescope (right), have much shorter wavelengths and only spread out a little (only enough to cover a whole planetary system) even on a journey tens of parsecs long. The snag is that you can only aim at one star at a time, so you have to know there are planets there before you send out your beam.

At a distance of parsecs, or even tens of parsecs, the light from a powerful laser (broadcast from a space station orbiting the parent star) would merge with the starlight, and would not be detectable as a separate spot of light. But because a laser beam is essentially an intense beam of light all with the same wavelength, any observers with technology as good as our own would see it as a very peculiar feature in the spectrum of the star, shifting to and fro with a distinctive Doppler rhythm. By turning the laser on and off, we could even send messages in binary code. Such a system could be detected by us from a distance of 3 parsecs or more.

The laser required for such a project need not even be very powerful. A few tens of kilowatts would do, provided it is mounted in space, above the obscuring layer of the Earth's atmosphere.

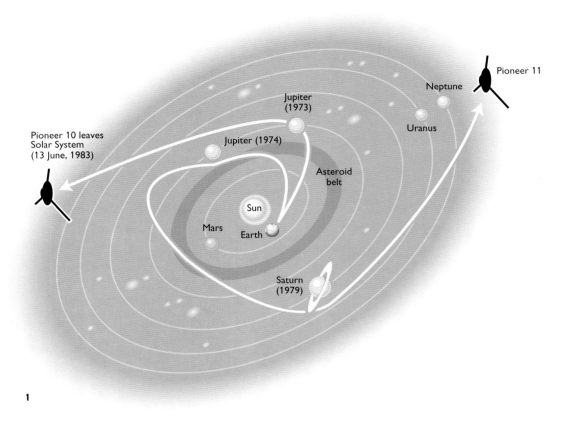

1

1 and 2. The identical space probes Pioneer 10 and Pioneer 11 were the first artificial objects to leave the Solar System.

reflections, measuring distances across the Solar System with unprecedented accuracy.

In 1974, astronomers from Cornell University used the Arecibo Radio Telescope to broadcast the first deliberate message sent by human beings to other stars. This blast of radio waves was beamed in one direction, and will spread out slightly on its way through space. It will not have been detectable from planets orbiting most of the stars in the local volume of space already polluted by the Berlin Olympics, *I Love Lucy* and the rest. In order to give this relatively narrow beam the best possible chance of being picked up by another

technological civilization, the astronomers directed it towards a globular cluster of stars, containing 300,000 individual stars, in the direction of (but far beyond) the constellation Hercules. If there are civilizations capable of detecting radio waves on any planets orbiting any of those 300,000 stars, they could pick up this message, and this hugely increases the chance of a response.

But there's a snag: the cluster actually lies about 740 parsecs away and radio signals travel at the speed of light (there and back). If a civilization in the cluster does pick up the signal from 1974, and responds immediately, we can expect a reply in AD 50,000.

SIGNALLING TO THE UNIVERSE

But how can we hope to communicate meaningfully with alien civilizations, rather than just making a noise? The scientists involved in sending the 1974 signal from Arecibo wanted to send a message that contained information that an alien might be able to decipher, so they used what is considered the universal language – mathematics. One of the scientists involved, Carl Sagan, described the message in words at the time:

'What it said fundamentally was: "Here's the Sun. The Sun has planets. This is the third planet. We come from the third planet. Who are we? Here is a stick diagram of what we look like, how tall we are, and something about what we're made of. There's four point something billion of us, and this message is sent to you courtesy of the Arecibo telescope, 305 metres in diameter."'

It turns out to be surprisingly easy to convey that kind of information in the simplest mathematical language of all – the binary 'on-off' code familiar from computers. Frank Drake, a keen enthusiast for SETI (see later), tested this in the 1960s by devising just such a message (later used as the basis for the Arecibo message) and sending it out to colleagues to see if they could crack the code.

Drake's Message

Drake's message consisted simply of a string of 0s and 1s – binary code – 551 characters (or 551 'bits' in computer language) long. Any mathematician would quickly realize that

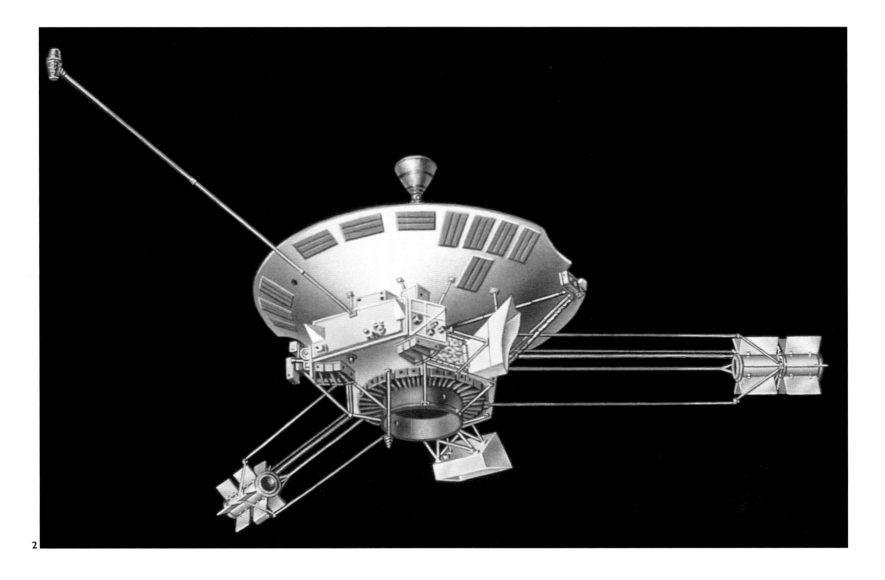

2

⭐ The name 'nano', as in 'nanobacteria' and 'nanometre', comes from the Greek word *nannos*, meaning a mischievous dwarf.

551 is a product of two prime numbers, 19 and 29. The only two numbers that multiply to give 551 are 19 and 29. But 19 and 29 do not divide by any whole number. This suggests (to the mathematically inclined) that the string of os and 1s can be turned into a rectangular 'picture' in either of two ways – a grid with 19 rows of 29 characters, or a grid with 29 rows of 19 characters. Trial and error would quickly show that the first grid is gibberish, but the second produces a distinct pattern if you put a black square everywhere there is a 1 and a white square where there is a 0 (or vice versa).

Drake made up his message as if it came from an alien civilization, so the pattern he made represents the imaginary civilization. The little picture of the alien itself is fairly obvious. Down the left-hand side of the picture there is a representation of a star and its nine planets, with a rough indication of their sizes. The other bits of code are mostly

numbers. The numbers 1 to 5, written in binary, alongside the first five planets, then 11 alongside planet two, 3000 alongside planet three, and 7 billion, alongside planet four. Drake intended this to mean that 7 billion aliens lived on planet four, they had a colony on planet three, and that at the time they sent the message there was a small expedition on planet two. The diagrams at the top right of the picture represent the atoms carbon and oxygen, telling us a little about the aliens' chemistry.

No individual scientist managed to decipher all of Drake's 'alien message' (by the way, he didn't pretend it really did come from aliens; they knew he had made it up as a test). But any real message from the stars would be investigated intensively by high-powered teams of scientists from all disciplines and they would be able to crack any similar code. This shows what an impressive amount of information can be packed into just 551 bits of computer code. With 8 bits making a byte, that is less than 70 bytes of information, and computer memory these days is measured in megabytes and gigabytes.

Messages in Cosmic Bottles

You may think that radio waves take a long time to get to the stars, but space probes, crawling along at a tiny fraction of the speed of light, take vastly longer. Even so, space scientists have already sent messages beyond the Solar System attached to space probes. These were not probes designed for the purpose, but ones that happened to be heading out of the Solar System anyway, after completing their missions of exploration of the outer part of the Solar System. This is the equivalent of throwing a message in a bottle into the ocean, and hoping that it might be picked up by a passing ship; a long shot, but the

1

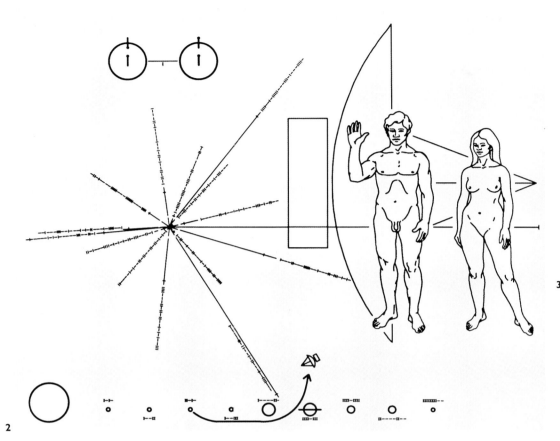

3

1. Frank Drake, with his eponymous equation.

2 and 3. The two Pioneer space probes which flew past Jupiter on their way out of the Solar System, each carried a plaque with scientific information and representations of a man and a woman.

opportunity provided seemed too good to miss.

The spacecraft Pioneer 10 was the first human artefact to leave the Solar System. Launched in 1972, Pioneer 10 and its twin probe Pioneer 11 each flew past Jupiter and then followed slightly different trajectories to provide, between them, our first close-up views of all the gas giant planets. The landmark date was 13 June 1983, when Pioneer 10 crossed the orbit of Neptune and officially left the Solar System (Pluto, which is usually the furthest planet from the Sun, occasionally dives just inside Neptune's orbit, and did so between 1979 and 1999). It became the first message in a bottle from the human race to be launched into the ocean of interstellar space.

Each of the Pioneer 10 and 11 spacecraft carried an identical plaque, designed by Carl Sagan and Frank Drake, as a 'hello' to any intelligent beings that might find it. The plaque includes a representation of the spaceprobe itself, the Sun and Solar System, and a 'map' indicating the location of the Sun relative to some of the pulsars. It also includes a rather stylized drawing of a naked man and woman, which drew an angry response from some American citizens concerned that NASA was polluting the Universe with pornography.

When the next missions to Jupiter and beyond were launched in 1977, they carried a more sophisticated message, in the form of a video disc. Each of the two Voyager craft carried a copy of the disc, sealed in a container engraved with scientific information including instructions on how to play the disc. The disc itself contained images of the Earth, sounds ranging from whale song to Chuck Berry, scientific information, and messages from UN Secretary General Kurt Waldheim and US President Jimmy Carter. In truth, any alien who finds the disc is unlikely to learn any more from its contents than the fact that we exist. All subsequent missions to the outer planets have gone into orbit around them, and only Pioneers 10 and 11 and Voyagers 1 and 2 have left the Solar System (▷p. 156).

TO BOLDLY GO

The Pioneer and Voyager probes are not heading towards any nearby star. Their trajectories out of the Solar System are a result of their encounters with the giant planets, and were not chosen with interstellar travel in mind. But if a probe were to be sent on a voyage of exploration to another star, the obvious place to go would be to the nearest star, Proxima Centauri. Even Proxima, though, is more than a parsec from our Solar System, and some ingenuity (plus considerable financial input) will be needed to send a probe there and get back data. There are two possible approaches that could be put into practice in the twenty-first century if anyone has the inclination and the finance to do it.

Brute Force

The brute force approach is typified by plans drawn up by the British Interplanetary Society (BIS). The BIS carried out a five-year feasibility study of an interstellar probe powered by nuclear fusion. The design calls for the kind of spaceship familiar from fiction, 200 metres long and with a mass of 54,000 tonnes, assembled in orbit around one of the moons of Jupiter. The fuel for the probe is envisaged as compressed pellets containing the heavy form of hydrogen (deuterium) and the light form of helium (helium-3). The design calls for pellets to be injected into a fusion chamber at a rate of 250 per second,

where they would be zapped by beams of electrons, causing them to fuse and release energy in much the same way that nuclear fusion releases energy at the heart of a main sequence star. The rate of the explosions, 250 per second, is roughly the same as the rate at which individual petrol vapour explosions occur in the cylinders of a car while it is

quietly ticking over.

Like the big rockets that launch payloads into space from Earth, the BIS design, dubbed *Daedalus*, is in separate stages, so that one can be discarded when its fuel is exhausted. The first stage of *Daedalus* is designed to run for two years before being dropped behind, with a second stage

1. (opposite) Three superimposed photos taken over a period of four years (the three images forming a dotted line) show Barnard's star moving relative to more distant stars.

2. A representation of the starship *Daedalus*, designed by the British Interplanetary Society.

2

1. Hypothetical depiction of a planet (foreground) orbiting the star Proxima Centauri.

operating for 22 months before the fuel is exhausted. All that effort will have pushed the speed of the 400 tonne payload to about 13 per cent of the speed of light. The target suggested by the BIS for the hypothetical *Daedalus* voyage (because it looks more interesting than Proxima) is Barnard's star, about 2 parsecs away. The journey would take about 50 years, Earth time, and then *Daedalus*, with no means of slowing down, would hurtle through the Barnard's star system in about 20 hours, observing and recording data to send back

at leisure as it continued on its way into the Universe.

Nobody expects that the first spaceprobe will be exactly like *Daedalus*. But the existence of this design study shows what could be achieved using what you might call the conventional approach.

Sailing to the Stars

There is an alternative. American space scientist Robert Forward is the leading proponent of a more subtle approach to exploring the cosmos

– 'starsailing'. The problem with rockets, as *Daedalus* shows, is the enormous weight of fuel required – 54,000 tonnes of rocket to deliver a 400 tonne payload (less than 1 per cent of the original mass of the spaceship). Forward's solution is to leave the power system behind and only send the payload to the stars. He has designed a system that could get a 1-tonne payload to Proxima Centauri or its near neighbour Alpha Centauri in less than 40 years. It does so using a thin 'sail' 3.6 km (2 miles) in diameter, but only 16 nanometers (16 billionths of a metre) thick, made of aluminium. Unfurled in space and attached to the probe at its centre, the sail would be sent on its way out of the Solar System by the beam from a huge laser, also built in space. The laser would give the sail an acceleration of 3.6 per cent of the gravitational force we feel at the surface of the Earth, sending it up to a speed of about one-tenth of the speed of light (at this speed, it would take two days to travel from Pluto to the Sun).

As with *Daedalus*, Forward's probe, which he calls *Dragonfly*, could be left to hurtle through the target system, sending back data. Supporters of this approach to interstellar travel point out that if there are any beings worth talking to in the target systems, they will certainly notice it coming and they may well be able to stop it for themselves.

Starsailing is currently the hot topic in interstellar probe design, with many variations on the theme being developed by Forward and his colleagues. It offers a realistic prospect that a probe could be on its way to the nearest star before the middle of the present century and could be sending back data from its target star before the end of the century. Very possibly, babies already born will still be alive when news from Alpha or Proxima Centauri gets back to Earth.

TIME DILATION

If we ever do send space probes to the stars, we will see an effect predicted by the special theory of relativity at work. The effect is called 'time dilation', because the clocks on a spaceship, moving at a sizeable fraction of the speed of light, will run slow compared with clocks at home. Time literally passes more slowly on the moving spaceship than it does on Earth. The effect only really shows up at very high speeds, but it would already be detectable for a probe like *Daedalus* or *Dragonfly* (right), travelling at about 10 per cent of the speed of light.

The correction factor required is called the Lorentz factor after the Dutch physicist Hendrik Lorentz, who worked on the theory. At 10 per cent of the speed of light, the Lorentz factor is 1.02, which means that for every hour that passes on the spaceship, 1.02 hours (61.2 minutes) pass on Earth. If the journey seems to take 40 years to us, to the spaceship it takes only 39.2 years.

The Lorentz factor gets bigger the faster you go. At half the speed of light, it is 1.15, so that 15 per cent less time elapses for the voyagers than for stay-at-homes. If you could travel fast enough, this would help to make such long voyages more practicable, but the energy required to make the ship go fast enough to make this worthwhile is prohibitive.

If you could travel at half the speed of light, however, and went on a round trip voyage (there and back) lasting 50 years by your spaceship clocks, you would be 50 years older but you would find everything on Earth 57.5 years older than when you left. The effect is real and provides a kind of one-way time travel, into the future.

PANSPERMIA

Human civilization stands on the brink of being able to 'seed' the Universe deliberately. We have already sent four spaceprobes beyond the confines of the Solar System. But, as is often the case, anything people can do Nature can do better. It may be that we owe our own existence to interstellar travellers – not little green men, but bacteria sealed inside grains of cosmic dust.

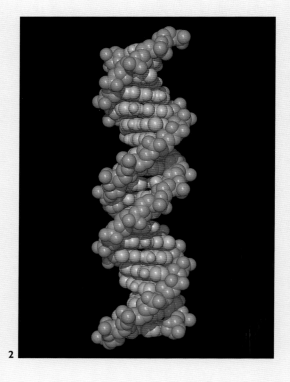

Life is ubiquitous on Earth, and grains of material containing bacteria even float high in the atmosphere of our planet. It is conceivable that such grains could escape into space today, and even be blown right out of the Solar System by the 'wind' of particles and radiation from the surface of the Sun. But, if they did so the DNA of any living things they contained would be destroyed by solar radiation and cosmic rays. Heavier grains of material could shield living microorganisms from the radiation, but such relatively heavy grains could not travel far from Earth, at least, not today.

When the Sun reaches the next phase of its life and swells up to become a red giant, however the amount of energy being radiated from its surface will increase hugely. This will help to blow away a great deal of material from the atmosphere of the Sun into space. It will mix with the material of the interstellar medium to form new molecular clouds. At this stage of its life, the Sun would easily expel material from the inner part of the Solar System, including life-bearing grains of dust from the Earth.

When bacteria are exposed to an extreme environment (particularly one without any water) they are capable of going into a form of hibernation, preserving their core of DNA and other life molecules until warmth and water are available once again.

Everywhere that life exists on planets around Sun-like stars, living material, sheltered inside grains of solid material, will be expelled in this way as the parent star becomes a red giant. It will then lace the molecular clouds from which new planetary systems form. When new stars and planets do form from the collapse of the molecular cloud, the comets that become part of those systems will also contain fragments of living (or once living) material. As the new planets cool, comets and dust from the proto-planetary disc will carry this material, including DNA, and possibly living organisms, down to their surfaces.

This idea, known as panspermia, is the best explanation of how life got a grip on the surface of the Earth so soon after the planet formed. As the proponents of panspermia point out, it doesn't even matter if the living bacteria are killed by the harsh conditions of interstellar space. Even fragments of DNA arriving in the oceans of a young planet like the Earth will give life a head start. If they are correct, the implication is that all of life on Earth is descended from the DNA of cosmic bacteria. It would be quite easy to test the idea by sending a probe to a comet and bringing back samples of its material to investigate for traces of DNA. If the panspermia hypothesis is correct, there should be biological material very similar to that of life on Earth in these fragments. And that would also mean that life elsewhere in the Milky Way Galaxy must be based on the same kind of DNA that we are, although it would undoubtedly have evolved into other forms as superficially different from one another, and from us, as a peony is from a pony.

It would also mean that life is common in the Milky Way, and that the effort of trying to make contact is likely to prove worthwhile.

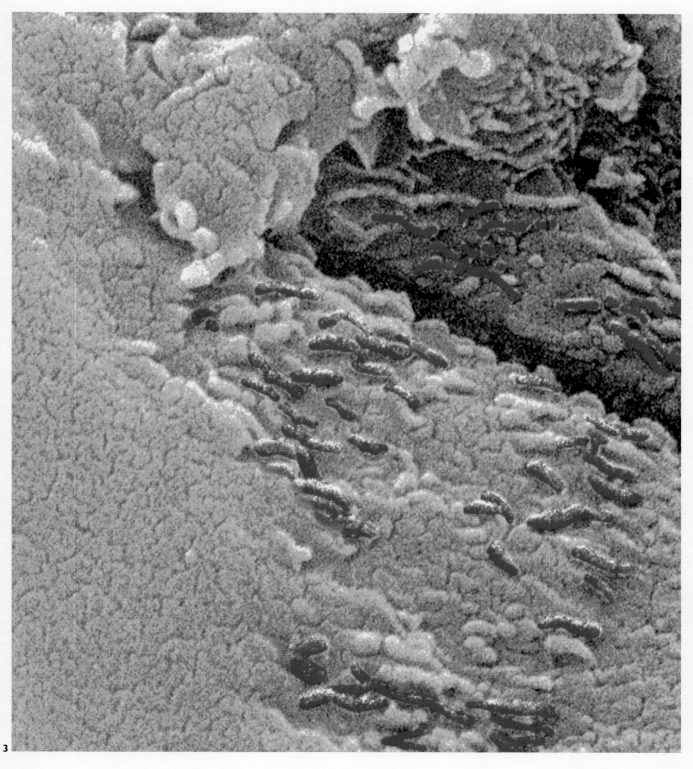

1. If the idea of panspermia is correct, comets like Halle-Bopp, pictured here in 1997, could have brought the seeds of life to Earth.

2. Model of DNA, the molecule of life.

3. Life on Mars? According to some researchers, the tube-like structures shown here, found in a meteorite which originated from Mars, are microfossils of bacteria-like organisms.

◆ TOPIC LINKS

1.1 Stepping Stones to the Universe
p. 22 Stars in Spiral Patterns

1.2 Star Birth
p. 34 Dusty Beginnings

3.1 Life and the Universe
pp. 146–7 Life on Earth

3

From the time when the technology to transmit and receive radio signals was developed (more or less at the end of the nineteenth century) to the time when live TV transmissions were made from the first astronauts to reach the Moon to anyone on Earth who had the right equipment to receive them was less than 70 years – less than a single human lifetime.

Once a technological civilization invents, or discovers, radio, it is likely to move on rapidly to cheap, powerful radio transmissions that are capable of being detected by comparable civilizations at distances of tens of parsecs. To many people this suggests that it makes more sense for us to concentrate on developing technology to listen for alien broadcasts rather than trying to signal to them ourselves. Such efforts to detect extraterrestrial intelligence are already underway.

Previous page. Optical image of comet Hale-Bopp showing both its gas and dust tails. The gas or 'ion' tail (blue) consists of gas blown away from the comet head by a solar wind.

THE INFINITE RADIO SET

Although radio is likely to be invented when a technological civilization is young, a more advanced civilization will still know about radio waves. They will be aware that this is a good way to communicate with people like us, even if they have found better ways to communicate among themselves. The best way to make contact with a newly emerging technological civilization (which, for all our achievements to date, is what we are) is by radio. This is the reason why the first generation of searches for extraterrestrial intelligence, roughly from the early 1960s to the end of the twentieth century, concentrated on the search for radio signals. But where do you search?

The first thing to decide when carrying out a search for extraterrestrial intelligence by listening out for their radio signals is which radio frequencies to listen at.

The important point about all SETI programmes carried out so far is that they are looking for deliberate signals – beacons of some kind designed to attract attention. Our

1. Radio astronomy observatories such as the Very Large Array link several radio telescopes together to mimic the power of a much larger instrument.

technology is not yet good enough to be able to eavesdrop on communications that are not intended to be picked up by people like us – the alien equivalent of *Monty Python*, perhaps. At first sight the search is a daunting task, because the aliens could be transmitting on any one of an infinite number of radio frequencies. It's no good if our radio receivers are tuned in to the cosmic equivalent of Radio 1 if the aliens are transmitting on Radio 4. We'd never hear them. But nature does impose some limits on the possibilities, and astronomers have also tried to get inside the minds of the aliens to work out logically the frequencies most likely they're broadcast on.

Limiting the Options

The first limitation is imposed by the atmosphere of the Earth. The atmosphere blocks out radio waves with frequencies outside the range from about 1000 megahertz (MHz) to 10,000 MHz. We physically cannot listen outside this range (except with instruments flown in space, above the obscuring layer of atmosphere, and no SETI project has yet gone that far).

The first and most important thing that astronomers learned about the Milky Way using radio telescopes is that it is full of hydrogen gas. This gas radiates radio noise at a frequency of 1420 MHz (equivalent to a wavelength of 21 cm). This enabled radio astronomers to map the spiral arms of our Galaxy by looking at where the hydrogen clouds emitting this radio noise were located.

1. The 43-diameter dish antenna of the Green Bank Observatories Radio Telescope.

2. A map of the Milky Way made by radio telescopes studying emission from hydrogen gas.

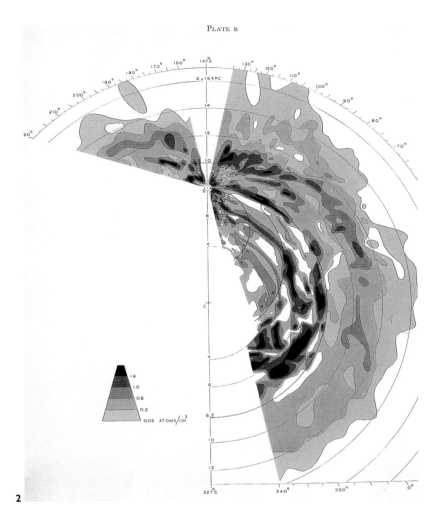

2

Any other radio astronomers in the Galaxy would also have found this frequency invaluable in their work, and would have developed sensitive receivers designed to detect the '21-cm' radiation. Anybody who investigates the nature of the Milky Way must have sensitive receivers capable of detecting the 21-cm radiation, and would realize that other radio astronomers would also have such receivers. So, the argument runs, alien scientists would guess that civilizations like us possessed equivalent detectors, and would therefore broadcast on a frequency close to the natural frequency of hydrogen. For this reason, the first SETI programmes were

carried out using more or less standard radio telescopes, designed to pick up signals near 1420 MHz.

The pioneering example of this approach, headed by Frank Drake of Cornell University, was Project Ozma, named after the Queen in the fictional land of Oz. It looked for signals from several nearby stars in the early 1960s, but without success. Nevertheless, Project Ozma was the inspiration for many other searches that followed in the 1960s and 1970s. In one of these surveys, carried out in the early 1970s using a radio telescope (actually two different antennae) at Green Bank, West Virginia, ten stars were selected for

investigation. One or the other of the antennae of the radio telescope was pointed towards one of the stars whenever this could be fitted into the regular research programme (which actually did involve mapping hydrogen clouds in the Galaxy). At the end of the survey, the team concluded that the study had not revealed the presence of any alien signals, and that substantial improvements in the number of stars studied, the area of sky searched, the sensitivity of the apparatus and the range of frequencies searched would be needed to make SETI worthwhile. Since then, progress has been made on all those fronts.

APPLYING NEW TECHNOLOGY

From the early 1980s onwards, the ability of radio astronomers to listen out at different frequencies was greatly increased by the huge advances in computer power and miniaturization. This made it possible to design compact, relatively simple systems that could automatically search a range of frequencies, looking for the kind of orderly signals that might be produced by intelligent beings. One reason this was an important step forward is that even if aliens were broadcasting at precisely 1420 MHz (21 cm), the signal we receive would be shifted slightly by the Doppler effect (▷ p. 82). In fact, it would be shifted by a combination of Doppler effects caused by the motion of the aliens' planet around their home star, the motion of that star and the Sun relative to one another through space, and the motion of the Earth around the Sun. But in the 1970s, astronomers had also come up with another bright idea to extend their search for extra-terrestrial life, and this too was just right for application of the new technology.

The Best Place to Listen

The region of the electromagnetic spectrum around the 21 cm wavelength is ideal for us to listen on, quite apart from the presence there of the important radio emission from hydrogen. At longer wavelengths (corresponding to lower frequencies), there is a great deal of radio noise, produced by free electrons roaming through interstellar space. At shorter wavelengths (corresponding to higher frequencies), it requires a huge amount of energy to transmit any intelligible information, so it is unlikely that any aliens will be broadcasting in that part of the spectrum. But at so-called 'centimetre wavelengths' (which includes the region from 20 to 30 cm), the Universe is both quiet and dark, so that even a relatively weak signal from another civilization could be heard above the background noise, the hiss of cosmic static that fills the radio band of the Universe.

This may seem surprising, because clouds of hydrogen gas 'broadcast' in exactly this part of the spectrum. But those clouds are

 LIFE AS WE DON'T KNOW IT

One of the most important scientific discoveries of the 1990s was that the interior of the Earth – a dark place where there is no sunlight – is teeming with tiny life forms called nanobacteria (right). The total mass of all these living cells is thought to outweigh the mass of all the multi-celled life forms that we are familiar with. Some of these 'bugs' are living creatures only a few tens of nanometres in size (a nanometre is a billionth of a metre), but there are an awful lot of them.

The discovery was doubly exciting because at about the same time other scientists identified fossil traces of what might be similar life forms in fragments from a meteorite which is thought to have travelled across space from Mars to the Earth. Perhaps there really is life on Mars (or in Mars!), although not 'life as we know it'. Indeed, some people argue that nanobacteria, safely tucked away inside the rocks of a planet, may be the most common form of life in the Universe.

Unfortunately, we cannot communicate with tiny bugs buried deep beneath the surface of a planet, and efforts to communicate with other intelligences in the Universe will have to focus, for the foreseeable future, on attempting to contact technological civilizations similar to our own. But it is worth remembering how restrictive this natural concentration on life as we know it may be.

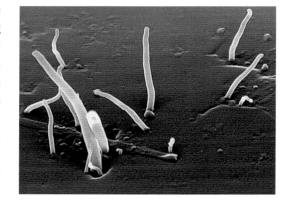

very cold and the radio noise they broadcast is quite feeble. It is only because this part of the spectrum is indeed so quiet that we are able to detect them at all, let alone use them to map the structure of the Galaxy. Any civilization just a tiny bit more advanced than our own would have no trouble 'shouting' loud enough to be heard above this noise.

Listening at the Water Hole

The extra tweak that astronomers came up with in tuning their radio receivers was based on the realization that there is another interesting feature, as well as the radio noise from hydrogen, in this part of the electromagnetic spectrum. Many clouds of gas in space contain the so-called 'hydroxyl radical', written as •OH. It is in effect a molecule of water (H_2O) from which one hydrogen atom has been lost. Under the calm conditions in these clouds, it is stable enough to behave like a molecule in its own right. We know that •OH is there because we detect it by its characteristic radio emission at a frequency of 1,667 MHz. This is close to the frequency hydrogen broadcasts at, but far enough away to be distinctive. Hydrogen plus •OH adds up to water, H_2O, and the region between 1420 and 1667 MHz has been dubbed the electromagnetic 'water hole'. It is a region that would be bound to be interesting to any

A 200-metre diameter antenna operating at a wavelength of about 20–1 cm can detect signals from a similar antenna 1000 light years away.

creatures, like ourselves, for which water is important, and it is smack in the region of the electromagnetic spectrum where the Universe is dark and quiet. So, since about 1980, most searches for extraterrestrial life have concentrated on this part of the electromagnetic spectrum.

The hope is that, just as in semi-arid regions on Earth different species of animal meet when they come to drink at the water hole, so we may 'meet' aliens electronically by signalling (and listening for signals) at the wavelengths corresponding to the radio 'water hole'. There have been about 50 such SETI projects since Project Ozma, and none has found evidence of alien signals. But it is worth going into a little detail of how one of those projects was carried out, just to show how easy (and cheap) the whole thing is.

SETI in a Suitcase

It's worth bearing in mind that even the water hole alone offers millions of different frequencies to search, so it is no real surprise that we haven't struck lucky yet. The only real hope of getting a breakthrough is to automate the search, and that approach was pioneered by the American astronomer Paul Horowitz in the 1980s.

Horowitz designed a system, so compact that he called it 'Suitcase SETI', which could search across part of the band of frequencies in the water hole. One special feature of this search was to look for very precisely tuned bursts of radio noise, at very precise wavelengths (and frequencies), because he

 THE INTERNET SETI PROJECT

Apart from having a radio telescope with which to detect faint signals from space, the big problem with SETI searches is to find the computer time to analyse all the data and pick out anything that might be an intelligent signal. An approach that caught the imagination of the public at the end of the 1990s was the SETI@home project, which hooked up more than a million home computers, via the Internet, to check data coming in from the Arecibo radio telescope.

The Arecibo telescope scans a strip of the sky as the Earth rotates, from the equator up to a celestial latitude of about 35 degrees. Happily, this includes many of the star systems now known to have planets. The SETI equipment is linked up to the telescope and takes advantage of any free time, looking wherever the telescope happens to be pointed while the radio astronomers are using it for their regular work. Over several years, this means that it sweeps across the entire band of the sky covered by the telescope, pulling in a huge amount of data.

This is where the Internet comes in. The SETI@home team offered enthusiasts a screensaver (right) which they could download free into their home computers. This came with a small computer program which downloaded a tiny fraction of the huge mass of data from Arecibo, so that whenever the home computer was not in use it would quietly get on with analysing the data. More than a million people downloaded the software (from www.setiathome.ssl.berkeley.edu), which means that for at least part of the time, every day, over a million home computers are busily searching the Arecibo data for signs of intelligent signals from space.

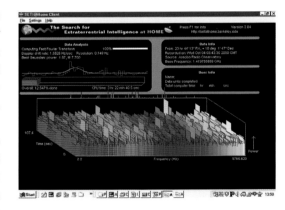

1. The central region of our Milky Way galaxy gives an impression of just how many stars, and therefore potential homes for life, there are in our cosmic island.

reasoned that such precision could only be produced by advanced technology. The computer would search 65,000 radio channels, but each channel would be only 0.015 Hz wide. The project was funded by a private, non-profit organization called The Planetary Society. At first, the idea was to take the equipment from one radio astronomy observatory to another, fitting in with whatever research programmes were going on at the time. The best place to test the apparatus was, of course, the great dish of the Arecibo radio telescope, and the first run of Suitcase SETI listened out for intelligent signals from more than 200 of the nearest stars like our Sun.

After completing his tests (successfully, in that the equipment worked, but unsuccessfully as far as detecting extra-terrestrial life was concerned), Horowitz took his gear back to Harvard University where he worked. There, he discovered that an old 84-foot diameter radio telescope belonging to the university was about to be

The META project could detect a signal as weak as one ten-billionth of a watt of radio power arriving at the Earth.

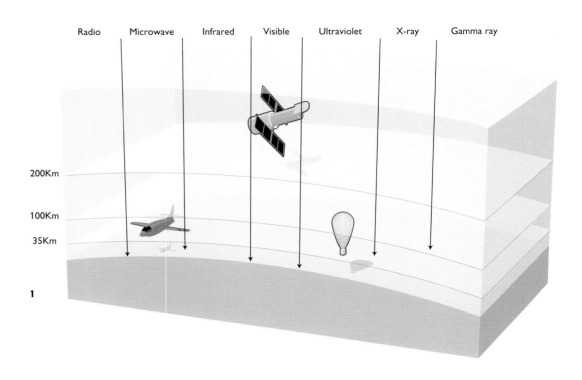

Radio   Microwave   Infrared   Visible   Ultraviolet   X-ray   Gamma ray

200Km

100Km

35Km

1

1. Different wavelengths of radiation penetrate to different depths in the atmosphere.

⭐ The most distant star yet studied directly for intelligent signals is less than 1 per cent of the distance across our Galaxy from us.

made obsolete. The Planetary Society agreed to fund the conversion of Suitcase SETI into a permanent facility, soon renamed Project Sentinel, using this telescope. It became operational in 1983, using a very simple technique to scan the heavens. Each day, the telescope's antenna would point at a chosen angle up to the sky while the Earth rotated. So it swept around a narrow strip of the heavens in 24 hours. Then the angle of the antenna was shifted a little (by half a degree) and the next strip of sky was searched. It covered 131,000 radio 'channels' (upgraded from the original 65,000) – impressive, but peanuts compared with the size of the water hole.

Spielberg's Contribution

The next improvement in the search for detecting extra-terrestrial life came courtesy of Steven Spielberg, director of the movie *ET*. He donated $100,000 to The Planetary Society and with this funding – absolutely tiny compared the cost of the space programme – Project Sentinel metamorphosed, in 1985, into Project META, which stands for Megachannel Extraterrestrial Assay. Technology had moved ahead so rapidly in the 1980s that META was able to search at 8,000,000 channels in the water hole, effectively resolving the problem of Doppler shifts once and for all.

There is still no sign of extra-terrestrial life, but there are still many millions of channels to search. And the standard answer to critics of the project is that it is cheap and funded entirely by voluntary donations. It is, therefore, potentially amazingly cost-effective. But this isn't the only way to search for life beyond the Earth.

BIG IS BEAUTIFUL

Projects such as Sentinel and META only look at a small patch of the sky at a time – the direction the antenna is pointing. The big worry about such an approach is that a signal might arrive from one direction in space while we are looking in another (although we hope that any intelligent aliens would keep broadcasting in the same place for months or years, giving us time to find the signal). One way to scan the whole sky (or interesting regions of the sky) quickly is to use more computer power to look in several directions at once. One way to increase the sensitivity of a detector is to use several different antennae linked together.

This 'brute force' approach was typified by a design study for Project Cyclops, carried out by NASA in the 1970s (the project itself never went ahead). The Cyclops proposal called for an array of 1000 radio antennae, each 100 metres in diameter, spaced 300 metres apart in the desert in the southwestern United States. With sufficient computer power, radio waves coming from different directions in space can be picked out separately by data-processing computers hooked up to the entire array. One processor could look in one direction while another looked in another direction at the same time.

The cost of such a system was clearly so high that there was never any prospect of it going ahead. On the other hand, it would have amounted to just three months of the expenditure the United States actually did pay out in the 1970s for the Vietnam war.

Into the Future

The big difference between the early twenty-first century and the days of the Project Cyclops design study is the huge increase in computing power available combined with the dramatic

THE FERMI PARADOX

If there are intelligent aliens in the Universe, with advanced technology, why aren't they here? This puzzle (it isn't really a paradox, in spite of its name) was put forward as an argument that we are alone in the Universe by the physicist Enrico Fermi (right) in 1950. The point is that the Universe and the Milky Way are billions of years old (at least twice as old as the Sun and Solar System) so there has been ample time for other intelligent civilizations to arise and to develop the means to travel across space. With computers and rocket technology only slightly more advanced than our own, such beings would be able to send probes, travelling at less than the speed of light, to visit every star in the Galaxy in a span of just 300 million years. They could do this because one probe would arrive at a system like our Solar System and use material from the moons and asteroids in it, to build many copies of itself to send on to explore other star systems. For the cost of just one probe (or two if you want a backup), you could explore the Milky Way.

The best answer to the puzzle is that, although the Universe is more than 10 billion years old, that is barely long enough for intelligence to have emerged. It took generations of stars to make the heavy elements that the Earth and its inhabitants consist of, and billions more years for an intelligent species to evolve. The counter to the Fermi Paradox is the argument that there ought to be many civilizations just about at our level, poised on the brink of space travel, but that we are unlikely to meet anyone much more advanced than ourselves. Nobody knows which point of view is correct.

The Arecibo radio telescope featured in the movie *Contact*.

decrease in its cost. This means that even without building such a large array we can still get many of the benefits of Cyclops. Although government funding is still not forthcoming for major SETI projects, they are now well within the means of private funding, as Project META demonstrated.

One system now being built is called, from its size, the One Hectare Telescope, or 1HT (1 hectare is 10,000 square metres). It will use a large number of linked antennae which can not only (thanks to that computer power) look at several dozen stars at the same time, but can also 'view' very many frequencies in the centimetre wave 'window' at the same time.

Even 1HT, though, is not an end in itself – it is a working testbed to prove the techniques that will be used to build the Square Kilometre Array (SKA), an array of telescopes in a grid 1km on each side (covering an area of a million square metres). SKA will be a hundred times more sensitive than any SETI detector yet built, which means that it can look ten times further out into the Galaxy and detect signals from a thousand times more star systems.

These projects are cheap because they use essentially the same data processing systems as home computers. The biggest problem facing the development of systems like SKA is that because technology has become so cheap and ubiquitous, the radio window is rapidly being filled up by the emissions from technology we are coming to regard as indispensable, such as mobile phones. It may be that by the middle of this century we will have to put our antennae on the far side of the Moon in order to find any signals from extraterrestrials without them being drowned by our own radio noise. Alternatively, cheap computers may become so powerful that they will be able to link together several systems such as SKA in different parts of the world and screen out human interference. Or maybe, just maybe, by 2050 that won't be necessary, because we will have already made contact.

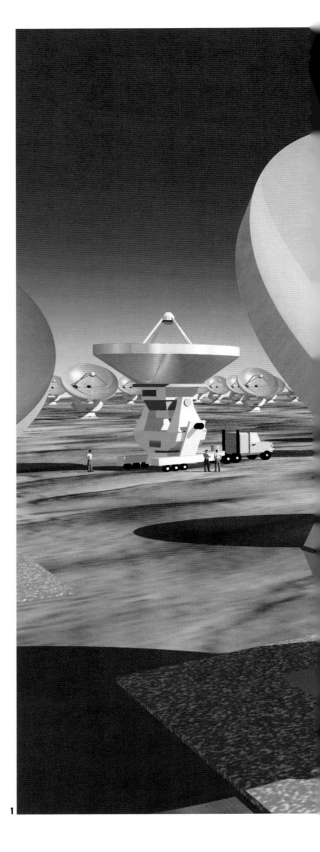

1. An artist's impression of the 1 Hectare Telescope.

THE DRAKE EQUATION

In 1961, astronomer Frank Drake, of Cornell University, developed an equation (the Drake equation) which is a way of expressing the chance of there being other intelligent civilizations capable of communicating with us. It encapsulates a great deal of astronomy in a simple form, although people still argue about what numbers to put into the equation.

1

Counting Suns

The first parameter in Drake's equation is the rate at which new stars are forming in the Galaxy. This is one of the less contentious numbers and most astronomers are happy with a figure of about 20 per year, denoted by the symbol R.

How many of these stars will be similar to our Sun? Drake suggested that as many as one in ten may be sufficiently Sun-like for his purposes, and denotes this by the symbol f_s ('f' for 'fraction').

The next number in the equation assigns a probability that a Sun-like star will have planets (f_p). When Drake suggested a value (f_p) of 0.5, many people thought he was being remarkably optimistic, but recent discoveries of extrasolar planets suggest that he may have been right all along.

Counting Planets

The next item in the equation is pure guesswork: how many planets will there be in each planetary system that are suitable for life as we know it? The number of Earth-like planets (n_e) in our Solar System is exactly 1, of course, but some people argue that this is unusually large and others argue that it is unusually small. Just about the only guess we can make is to set the number at 1 and hope for the best.

What else do we need for technological civilization to arise on a planet? The first requirement is that there is life. The fraction of inhabitable planets which actually harbour life, denoted by f_l, is clearly less than 1, judging from our own Solar System and the barrenness of Mars. But it may not be *much* less than 1, judging from the evidence of complex organic

1. Some civilizations may destroy themselves before they get a chance to communicate.

2. Some aliens may have no wish to communicate. By some criteria, dolphins are intelligent but they have not developed technological civilization.

molecules in interstellar clouds. Again, a guess is all we can come up with.

There are similar uncertainties surrounding the fraction of life-bearing planets on which intelligence arises (f_i) and the fraction of intelligent species that develop technological civilization (f_c).

This piece of the puzzle is particularly interesting. It is quite possible to have a civilization (such as the Ancient Romans, or the Incas) without having the kind of technology needed to communicate across interstellar space, and you can imagine a world in which civilization stays in that state indefinitely. It is also entirely possible to be intelligent without having technological

2

3

4

civilization – in some ways, dolphins are intelligent, but they don't have technology.

Counting Earths

The final piece of the puzzle concerns the longevity of such a civilization – its lifetime, L, expressed in years. In the 1960s and 1970s, the threat of nuclear war made some pessimists set this figure very low – no more than 100 years. Today, many people are more optimistic, but this remains a big uncertainty. Indeed, in the eyes of the pessimists we have simply replaced the threat of nuclear annihilation by the threat that we will destroy our planet through pollution, bringing an end to our present civilization before the end of the twenty-first century.

When you put everything together, you have an equation for the number of advanced civilizations actively involved in communicating across the Galaxy today.

$$N = Rf_s f_p n_e f_l f_i f_c L$$

This is Drake's equation. If R is about 20, and the next six factors multiply up to give a value of about 0.05, which is plausible, what you end up with is the conclusion that N is roughly equal to L. This means that if civilizations do avoid blowing themselves to bits or polluting their planets to destruction, there may be a very large number of them out there trying to make contact with one another, and with us.

3. Even without warfare, technological civilizations may find ways to destroy themselves and the wildlife around them.

4. Intelligent life could exist deep beneath the clouds of a giant planet like Jupiter without even knowing that the rest of the Universe exists.

◆ TOPIC LINKS

3.1 Life and the Universe
p. 139 Other Worlds
p. 148 Other Earths?
p. 150 Seeking Signs of Life

3.3 Listening to the Stars
p. 172 Life As We Don't Know It

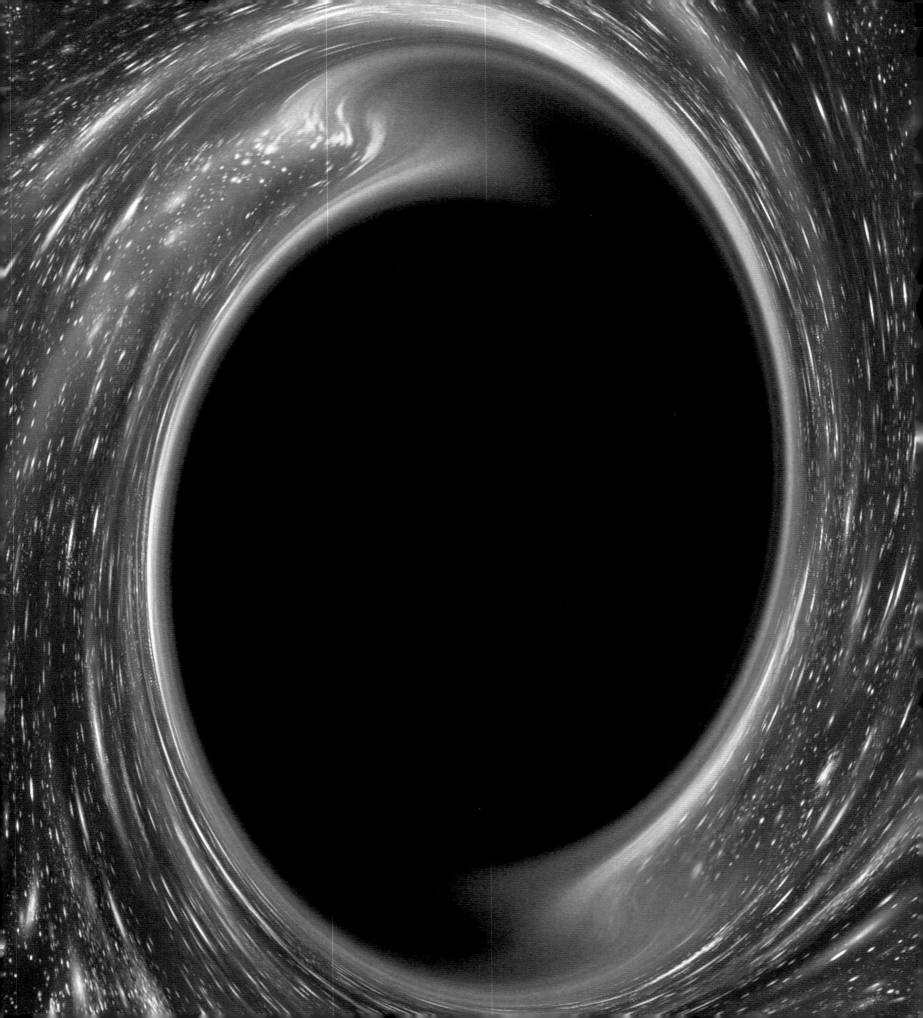

4

OTHER WORLDS

In many ways, the Universe we live in seems to be well suited to the existence of life forms like ourselves. To some extent this must be because we have evolved and adapted to suit our surroundings. But at another level, it turns out that life can only exist because of delicate balances in the fundamental laws of physics. Is this just a coincidence, or is there some deep connection between the way the Universe works and the presence of life in the Universe? Some people think that the answers to these questions lie outside the realm of science, but scientists are forever pushing back the frontiers of their domain. Although these questions are at the cutting edge of cosmological thinking today, and there are no definite answers, scientific exploration of such questions has already begun and science has now answered many questions previously thought to lie in the realm of philosophy.

Previous page. Computer simulation of the appearance of a black hole against a background of stars.

THE GOLDILOCKS UNIVERSE

The Earth is often referred to as the 'Goldilocks planet' because, just as baby bear's porridge was just right for Goldilocks, so the Earth is just right for life. But some astronomers go further than this, arguing that the existence of a planet like the Earth depends on such a precise set of conditions at large that we should think in terms of a 'Goldilocks Universe', set up (by accident or design) to be just right for life. The exploration of the implications of this idea goes by the name 'anthropic cosmology'. It is an exploration which is almost entirely in the mind, since there are very few ways in which the principles of anthropic cosmology can be put to the test.

Life in the Universe

At its simplest, anthropic cosmology is simply a way of inferring what the Universe at large must be like from the fact that we exist. The best example (although it was not thought of in these terms at the time) is the way that Fred Hoyle predicted the existence of the resonance in carbon that allows the triple-alpha process to convert helium into carbon inside stars (▷ p. 54). In effect, Hoyle reasoned, 'We exist, and we are made of carbon compounds. So carbon must be manufactured in stars. So there must be a resonance that allows the triple-alpha process to proceed.' Nobody had ever measured this resonance or predicted its existence until Hoyle came along, and his prediction was based entirely on anthropic reasoning.

In 1957, just after Hoyle's prediction had been triumphantly confirmed by experiments, Robert Dicke pointed out that even the size of the Universe is 'not random, but conditioned by biological factors.'

1, 2 and 3. The Earth seems to be an ideal home for many varieties of life.

⭐ Weak anthropic principle: The observed values of all physical and cosmological quantities take on values restricted by the requirement that there are sites where carbon-based life can evolve.

1. Life on Earth is well represented by a green, lush, moss-covered rainforest.

Dicke argued that, in order for us to exist, the minimum requirement is one star, with one planet, made of a suitable mixture of chemicals. The rest of the Universe, hundreds of billions of galaxies containing hundreds of billions of stars, spread across thousands of billions of light years, seems unnecessary. But remember that only hydrogen and helium (plus dark matter) emerged from the Big Bang (▷ p. 131). It took many billions of years for the first stars to manufacture the heavy elements, explode and scatter them across space, and many billions more years for life to evolve, on a planet created out of that stardust, to the point where it could ask questions about the Universe. All the while, the Universe was expanding. The fact that we are able to ask such questions implies that the Universe is many billions of years old, and many billions of parsecs across.

The Weak Anthropic Principle

Interest in anthropic cosmology only developed in the 1970s, when Brandon Carter elaborated on these ideas and divided them into two categories. The ideas of Hoyle and Dicke fit within the framework of what Carter called the 'weak' anthropic principle. This is based on the idea that the Universe we see around us is not the only universe that could exist. The mathematical models of the cosmologists tell us that it is possible to describe different kinds of universe, where there are different laws of physics (▷ p. 196). In one such model, for example, gravity might be stronger or weaker than it is in our Universe; in another there might be no resonance that allows the triple-alpha process to do its work.

 ## PALEY'S WATCH

The eighteenth-century philosopher William Paley argued that the existence of living things so beautifully fitted to their environment as a human being or a flower required the existence of a designer; just as a man who knew nothing about watches (or marine chronometers, right) but found one lying on the ground could infer from the way everything fitted together inside it to make a working machine that it had been designed by an intelligent being. Just taking a heap of watch components and throwing them together at random, the argument runs, could never produce a working watch. The theory of evolution by natural selection removes the force from Paley's argument, because natural selection acts as the (unintelligent) designer that fits living things so beautifully into their ecological niches.

The important point is that, although evolution is unintelligent, it is not random. Individual changes in living things (mutations) are random, but evolution selects those changes that give an individual an advantage. Given a long enough span of time, this could convert a bacterium into a human being. Paley didn't know about evolution by natural selection, because he died in 1805, 53 years before Charles Darwin and Alfred Wallace published their theory.

A few cosmologists try to use the same argument to say that the Universe it must have been made by a designer. Most, however, think that we are in the same position as William Paley: as yet ignorant of the scientific rules which make the Universe look like a put-up job, even though it has evolved naturally. Hopefully, it won't be another 53 years before we find out what is really going on.

⭐ Strong anthropic principle: The Universe *must* have those properties which allow life to develop within it at some stage in its history.

Where could these other worlds be? If the Universe is infinitely large, there could be regions in which these different laws of physics operate, beyond the range of our telescopes (*forever* beyond the range of our telescopes, in regions of space that are being carried away from us faster than light by the expansion of the Universe). Or, if there have been many cycles in a bouncing Universe, there might have been different laws of physics 'before' the Big Bang.

Whatever possibility you can imagine, the weak anthropic principle says that there are lots of different universes (perhaps infinitely many) separated in space or time (or both) and that life can only exist to notice what is going on in universes very similar to our own.

But there is an alternative, which Carter called the 'strong' anthropic principle. This says that the Universe that emerged from the Big Bang, our Universe, really is unique, and that it had no 'choice' about the laws of physics; they had to be just right for the presence of life – specifically, for human life.

These lead some cosmologists into the strange world of quantum mechanics, where, according to some interpretations of what the equations mean, reality does not exist unless it is observed by intelligent beings. In this (weird) argument, the laws of physics *have* to be what they are, so that we can exist, so that we can notice what the laws of physics are, and make them real. Others see the existence of the 'coincidences' that make the Universe just right for life as evidence that it was designed. This still leaves the question of where the designer(s) came from.

The strong anthropic principle leads us into the realms of philosophy and religion and away from science. Fortunately, however, the weak anthropic principle is all we need to see how cosmological investigations are likely to proceed over the next few years.

A Tailor-made Universe?

The extent to which our Universe is 'just right' for life can best be seen by looking at how different it might be if small changes were made in one or more of a number of key parameters which shape the Universe. Physicists discuss the influence of 20 or more of these parameters, some of them quite exotic by everyday standards. But there are just a handful of more obvious candidates which make the point. None of them does so more forcefully than the force which literally shapes the Universe – gravity itself.

The Role of Gravity

Gravity seems so important to us, and is so important to the Universe at large, because it is always additive. Every atom and subatomic particle in the Earth contributes its tiny influence to the overall gravitational pull of the planet. The same is not true of the other familiar everyday force, electromagnetism. Atoms contain both positively charged protons and negatively charged electrons, so overall both the atoms and the Earth have zero electric charge. But gravity is actually an incredibly feeble force, which can best be seen by comparing the gravitational force between two protons with the electric force between the same two protons.

Because both electricity and gravity obey inverse square laws, the ratio of the two forces is always the same, no matter how far apart (or how close) the two protons are. The electric force that keeps them apart is 10^{36} times bigger than the gravitational force. This large number is so important that the physicists who ponder its implications simply refer to it as N. This number alone explains why stars are so big.

Imagine starting out with a set of objects containing, respectively, 10 hydrogen atoms, 100 atoms, 1000 atoms and so on, packed together. The 24th object would contain 10^{24} atoms and be about the size of a sugar cube. The electric forces that shape atoms would have no trouble resisting the inward tug of gravity, which has a 10^{36} 'handicap' over electricity. The 39th object would be a kilometre across, and still able to hold itself up against gravity.

But the volume and mass of material goes up as the cube of its radius (essentially, as the cube of the number of atoms), increasing the gravity at the centre by three powers of ten, while the inward tug of gravity goes down as the square of radius (two powers of ten) as the object gets bigger. Overall, gravity gains on electricity as a two-thirds power. By the time we reach the ▷▷

1. Even a small amount of electricity can make your hair stand on end, resisting the gravitational pull of the whole Earth.

Overleaf. Multiple bolts of lightning pictured over Tucson, Arizona.

54th object, which would be about as big as Jupiter, gravity will begin to crush atoms into their component parts at the centre, because 54 is three-halves of 36 (▷ p. 31). The 57th object in the collection will be so big that gravity in its heart is enough to make protons bash together hard enough for fusion to occur. Stars like the Sun do indeed contain about 10^{57} protons.

The Big ε

The strength of gravity determines how big stars are. Another fundamental number

determines how long they live. When four protons (hydrogen nuclei) are converted into one nucleus of helium-4, 0.7 per cent of the mass of the protons is released as heat (▷ p. 53). This proportion, 0.007, is a measure of the strength of the strong force that holds nuclei together in spite of the electrical repulsion between protons. All the rest of the nuclear fusion process inside stars, from helium up to iron, releases only a further one-seventh as much energy as the initial fusion of hydrogen into helium, so the lifetime of a star depends almost entirely on the number 0.007

(often written as ε), which determines how much energy is available to keep the star shining.

But E does more than that. If the number were just 0.006, the strong force would be too weak to hold nuclei of deuterium (a proton plus a neutron) together. The first step in the fusion process (the pp chain ▷ pp. 58–9) would not occur, and there would be nothing more complicated than hydrogen in the Universe. Alternatively, if E were just 0.008, the strong force would be so strong that two protons could stick together. Further fusion

▶ FROM ONE EXTREME TO ANOTHER

Not everybody likes the idea of anthropic cosmology. In his book *Perfect Symmetry*, published in 1985, the eminent physicist Heinz Pagels (right) wrote:'Physicists and cosmologists who appeal to anthropic reasoning seem to me to be gratuitously abandoning the successful program of conventional physical science of understanding the quantitative properties of our universe on the basis of universal physical laws. Perhaps their exasperation and frustration…has gotten the better of them…The influence of the anthropic principle on the development of contemporary cosmological models has been sterile. It has explained nothing, and it has even had a negative influence, as evidenced by the fact that the values of certain constants, such as the ratio of photons to nuclear particles, for which anthropic reasoning was once invoked as an explanation can now be explained by new physical laws…I would opt for rejecting the anthropic principle as needless clutter in the conceptual repertoire of science.'

At the other extreme, typifying the kind of argument that annoyed Pagels, Fred Hoyle sees the Universe as 'a put-up job', and wrote in his book *Galaxies, Nuclei and Quasars*, published in 1965, that: 'The laws of physics have been deliberately designed with regard to the consequences they produce inside stars. We exist only in portions of the universe where the energy levels in carbon and oxygen nuclei happen to be correctly placed.'

Both viewpoints may be too extreme. Perhaps we live in a Universe where the energy levels, and other parameters, are indeed 'just right', but by accident rather than design. That would leave scope for Pagels wish 'that fundamental laws which determine the nature of the Universe can be discovered by the traditional methods, but remove the need for a designer.'

1. Is the Universe made for humans, or are humans made for the Universe?

could occur, but there would be no hydrogen in the Universe (only helium-2), and therefore no water – an essential pre-requisite for life as we know it. This is one of the most powerful examples of the Goldilocks effect at work.

The Question of Q

Another way of seeing the special nature of the Universe is to look at its roughness, which is measured by a number the astronomers refer to as Q. If the Universe had emerged perfectly smoothly from the Big Bang, then it would still be perfectly smooth – a uniform sea of gas expanding in all directions.

In fact, when astronomers measure how much energy would be required to break up systems like clusters of galaxies and disperse them, and compare this with the total mass energy ($E = mc^2$) in the same system, they find that the two numbers are in the same ratio – 1:100,000 – right across the Universe. In other words, Q, the roughness of the Universe, is 2^{-5}. When they measure the size of the ripples in the cosmic microwave background radiation, astronomers find the same number. The roughness of the Universe has been 1 in 100,000 ever since the beginning of time.

If Q were much bigger than this, gravity would have pulled clumps of matter together very early on in the life of the Universe, forming supermassive stars and black holes. ▷▷

THE 3-DIMENSIONAL UNIVERSE

Surprising though it seems when you first encounter the idea, one of the most special things about our Universe that helps to make it suitable for life is that it exists in three dimensions of space. Although time is regarded as a fourth dimension, it behaves in a different way to the three space dimensions, and it turns out that if there were either more or less than three dimensions of space life would be impossible.

2

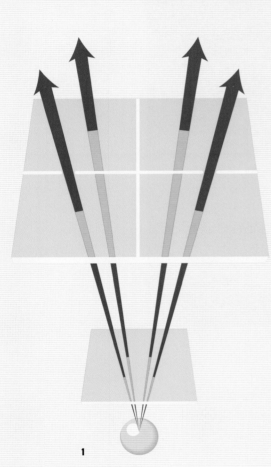

1

Feel the Force

In our three-dimensional Universe, forces such as gravity and electromagnetism obey inverse-square laws. The electrical pioneer Michael Faraday had a nice way of explaining this.

Imagine 'lines of force' reaching out evenly in all directions from a charged particle. If you envisage a sphere surrounding the particle, a certain number of lines will cross each square centimetre of the surface of the sphere. If the radius of the sphere is bigger, its area increases as the radius squared. So we still have the same number of lines of force, the number of lines crossing each square centimetre goes *down* as the radius (the distance from the centre) squared. Electricity obeys an inverse-square law.

Four is Too Many

If there were four spatial dimensions, the area of a 'four-sphere' would go up as the cube of its radius. So electricity (and gravity) would obey inverse *cube* laws. Double the distance and the force would go down by a factor of eight (2^3) not four (2^2).

This is bad news, because an inverse-cube law (or any law apart from inverse square) does not allow stable orbits for planets. In

our Universe, a planet that receives a slight nudge stays more or less in the same orbit, because an inverse-square law exactly balances out the centrifugal force and gravity and the centrifugal force stay in balance over a comfortable range of distances. In a four-dimensional universe, the force changes more rapidly over a short distance (it is said to have a 'steeper gradient'), so that just inside any particular orbit it overwhelms the centrifugal force, while just outside the orbit the centrifugal effect dominates. So a planet that received even the tiniest nudge would either plunge into its sun, or spiral away into the depths of space. And in higher dimensions still, the effect is even stronger.

Two is Not Enough

In a two-dimensional universe, complex life could not exist at all. You might imagine a kind of flat creature, like an amoeba, that could eat by opening a hole in its side and

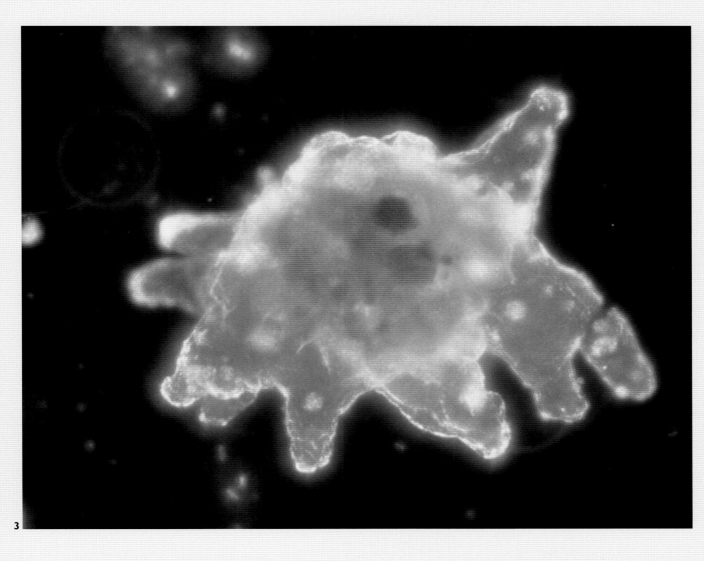

1. One way of visualising the inverse square law. If you double the distance, lines of force are spread over four times (2^2) the area.

2. Michael Faraday, who originated the idea of line of force.

3. An amoeba is the nearest thing on Earth to a two-dimensional life form.

3

swallowing things, then opening another hole to excrete (it couldn't open both holes at once, or it would fall apart). But it could only have a very simple brain, because lines could not cross one another, so there could be no connections between neurons except in the simplest way (and even simple connections would block the flow of food).

The number of space dimensions has to be *precisely* three if intelligent life is to exist in the Goldilocks Universe.

TOPIC LINKS

4.1 Cosmic Coincidences
p. 187 Paley's Watch
p. 188 The Role of Gravity

4.2 A Choice of Universes
p. 211 Geography and Relativity

⭐ There are roughly a billion (10^9) photons (particles of light) in the cosmic background radiation for every single baryon (proton or neutron) in the Universe.

It would have been a very different place from the Universe we live in. The fact that Q is just big enough to allow interesting things to form in the Universe, but that the Universe is very nearly flat (▷ p. 95), is part of the Goldilocks effect. It is also intimately connected with the way the Universe was driven outwards by inflation very early on in its life (▷ p. 115).

WHAT MIGHT HAVE BEEN

Because gravity is such a feeble force, compared with the other forces of nature, you might think that the exact strength of gravity doesn't matter very much. But you'd be wrong. The mass of a star is determined by the balance between gravity and electrical forces, and depends on the square root of the cube of the strength of gravity (a so-called 3/2 power law), because the volume and mass of the star go as the cube, and gravity is an inverse square law. This means that if the strength of gravity were increased by a factor of a million (10^6), the mass of hydrogen needed to make a star would be reduced by a factor of a billion(10^9), because 9 is 3/2 of 6.

Such a change produces a dramatic effect on the kind of conditions that exist in a cosmologist's model universe. Look at what might happen in a universe where the strength of gravity is a million times stronger than it is in our Universe, but all the other key parameters stayed the same.

High-speed Stars

In our Universe, the Sun is a typical star, with a mass defined as one unit (one solar mass) and a lifetime of about 10 billion years (10^{10} years). In our alternative universe less material is required to produce the same pressure and stars will get hotter at lower mass, so stars will typically have masses about one-billionth (10^{-9}) of the mass of the

Sun, which corresponds to about 10^{18} tonnes, a bit less than 1.4 per cent of the mass of our Moon. Everything else going on inside the star (including the nuclear reactions that release the energy to hold it up) is just the same as inside the Sun, and an atomic nucleus at the heart of the star doesn't 'know' much about the strength of the gravitational force in absolute terms, only about the weight of material pressing down on it.

The lifetime of a star is related to its size, not simply to the amount of fuel present, because, by swelling or shrinking slightly as appropriate, it adjusts the rate at which fuel is burnt to compensate for the energy being lost from its surface. So what really matters is how long it takes electromagnetic energy to get from the centre of the star, where it is generated, to the surface, where it escapes. Because the radiation is bounced around inside the star on its way to the surface (rather like the way a ball gets bounced around in a complicated pinball machine), this depends on the square of the radius of the star, not on the radius itself. Mass goes up as radius cubed, so stars with masses 10^{-9} times the mass of the Sun will have radii 10^{-3} times the radius of the Sun, and lifetimes only 10^{-6} times the lifetime of our Sun – about 10 thousand years, rather than 10 billion years.

Could Life Exist?

With all other processes, and in particular chemistry (the way atoms and molecules interact, unchanged in our model universe, it is hard to see how life would have much chance to evolve on a planet orbiting such a star before the star exhausted its nuclear fuel and went through the usual stages of swelling up to become a red giant then fading away to become a white dwarf. Just for fun, however, imagine what life would be like if it did exist on a planet with the same surface gravity as the Earth in such a universe.

1. Inside a star, protons bounce around like balls in a souped-up pinball machine.

The same sizing factor applies, of course, to planets as well as to stars. In order for the gravity at the surface of a planet in the model universe to be the same as it is on Earth, the planet would have to have a billion times less mass than the Earth. It would weigh in at about 5000 billion tonnes (5×10^{12} tonnes) – about the mass of a typical asteroid in our Universe. But just because the pull of gravity at the surface of such an object would be the same as at the surface of the Earth doesn't mean you could walk about there. The mass of your own body also has to be taken into account when working out the force that holds you down on a planet (your weight), and the gravitational pull of your own body would also be hugely increased in the imaginary world. The extra strength of gravity would be enough to crush any human-sized object out of existence. There would be no great mountains or tall trees on such a planet. Any animal life forms that did exist would be low and squat, close to the ground and walking carefully on several stumpy legs to support their own weight. Falling over, even from a height of a few centimetres, would be a disaster.

A Compact Universe

As if that weren't bad enough, it is extremely unlikely that planets could exist in stable orbits in this compact universe we are imagining. Because of the greater strength of gravity, galaxies would form very early on in such a universe, from clumps of gas physically smaller than the clumps which formed galaxies in our Universe, but with the same gravitational attraction. Stars would be much closer together within those galaxies. There would be roughly the same number of galaxies as in our Universe (at least a hundred billion) but each one would be smaller in diameter than the Milky Way by a factor of about a million. Instead of being about 30,000 parsecs across, a typical galaxy would be about 0.03 parsecs across (about 10^{12} km in diameter, less than the distance from the Sun to Alpha Centauri). Instead of stars being separated from one another by distances of parsecs, they would be so closely packed that close encounters between them would be common. The gravitational influence of passing stars would tug any planets that did form out of their orbits and scatter them through interstellar space.

When would all this be happening? Our own Universe is at the stage where the heavy elements have been produced in the first generation of stars and have been converted into interesting things like ourselves. It has also been expanding for some 14 billion years. In that sense, it is 14 billion light years from here to the most distant thing we can see (a number sometimes known as the Hubble radius). In the compact universe, the same interesting stage of heavy element production and distribution (although probably not, alas, interesting things like life) will be reached a million times quicker, after just 14,000 years, when the universe has a Hubble radius of 14,000 light years (a diameter of 28,000 light years). In other words, the high-speed, compact universe would reach the stage our own Universe is at today when it is less than a third of the size of the Milky Way.

There is nothing in the laws of physics to say that such universes, and others even more bizarre, cannot exist. So where are they?

1. (opposite) Could our Universe be just one bubble in a multitude of universes each with its own set of physical laws?

Overleaf. Artist's impression of our Milky Way Galaxy.

If our Universe has not been specifically designed for us (a 'bespoke' Universe), the fact that it is just right for life may be because it is just one universe among many. In the same way, the fact that a suit fits may not be because it is tailor-made just for you but because you have chosen it from a variety of ready-made suits. For this idea to work, our Universe cannot be unique. There must be a huge variety of universes, somewhere in space and time, like the variety of different suits hanging on the racks in a shop. There may be uncountable sterile universes (suits that do not fit), but life can only exist in universes like our own (suits that do fit). To explore this possibility, cosmologists have to get to grips with the strange world of quantum physics. Quantum physics naturally includes the idea of many worlds, existing in some sense side by side. This has long been a source of delight to science fiction writers and their readers, but now these non-commercial ideas have to be considered within the frameworks of science fact.

THE MANY WORLDS OF THE QUANTUM

Quantum physics is strange to us because it describes what goes on on tiny scales, smaller than atoms, and we have no everyday experience of what things are like inside atoms. What we do have are equations that describe what goes on – the equations of quantum mechanics. These equations are completely reliable if they are used to predict how measurable things (like the positions of the electrons used to paint a picture on your TV screen) change. Unfortunately, there are several (at least half a dozen) so-called 'interpretations' of quantum mechanics, which try to explain what is happening to things like electrons when they are not being measured. All are equally valid as aids to human imagination, though none is 'the' truth. The interpretation many cosmologists prefer, for reasons that will become clear, is called the 'Many Worlds Interpretation'.

Particles and Waves

Quantum weirdness is clearly demonstrated by the way things like electrons and photons behave both as particles and as waves. Experiments that are designed to measure the waviness of quantum entities (anything smaller than an atom) clearly show that they are waves. The classic example is the 'two slit' experiment, where a beam of light is shone on a screen with two holes in it. Light spreads out as waves from each of the holes

1. Interference pattern produced by two sets of waves.

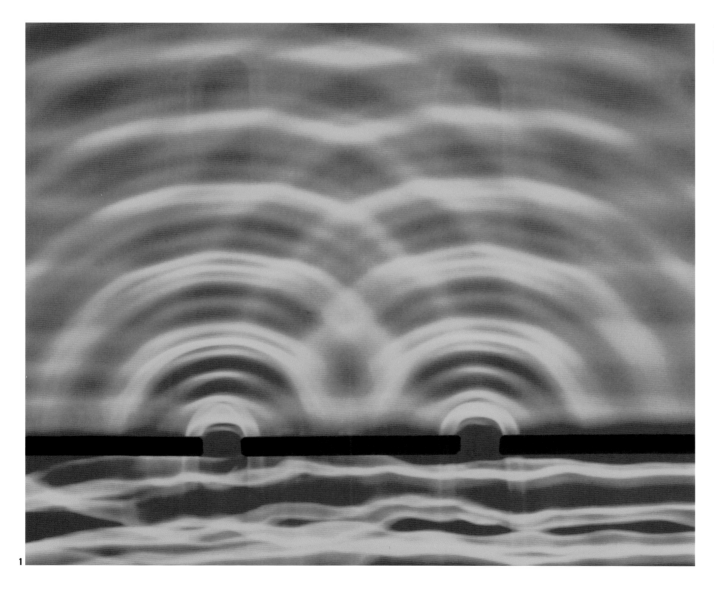

1

and forms a characteristic pattern of light and shade (an 'interference pattern') on a second screen. This exactly echoes the way ripples on a pond interfere with one another. Similar experiments with beams of electrons show them behaving as waves.

But when experiments are designed to measure the particle properties of electrons or photons, recording their arrival at a target like a stream of little bullets, they turn out to be behaving just like a stream of little bullets. Quantum entities are both particle and wave – a phenomenon called 'wave–particle duality'. It seems that quantum entities travel like waves, but arrive as particles. The equation that describes how they move is called a 'wave function'.

Many Worlds

Wave–particle duality is only the beginning of the story of quantum mysteries. The way a travelling quantum entity 'decides' what kind of particle it is when it is observed is also unlike anything in our everyday experience. As a simple example, think of a single electron travelling through space. When electrons are measured, among other things they each have a property called 'spin'. This is not like the spin of a top, or the Earth on its axis. It can best be thought of as a 'label' on the electron. All that matters is that the measured spin of an atom can only have one of two values, called 'up' and 'down'. A measured electron always has one, and only one, of these spins.

What of a travelling electron? The standard interpretation of quantum theory says that when an electron is on its own it does not have a definite spin, but exists in an indeterminate 50:50 state, a mixture of spin up and spin

1. (opposite) A rainbow is produced when lightwaves are refracted and reflected by raindrops.

▷ THE REALITY OF DUALITY

People sometimes think that wave–particle duality is simply a statistical effect. After all, the waves on the ocean are actually made up of billions of tiny particles – atoms. But quantum wave–particle duality is not like that – it operates at the level of individual entities such as photons and electrons, with the 'waves' having about the same size as the 'particles'. Although there had been indirect evidence of this phenomenon since the 1920s, the reality of duality was brilliantly confirmed in the early 1990s, in an experiment devised by a team of Indian theorists and carried out by a team of Japanese experimental physicists. It took so long to provide this final confirmation, because until then the technology was not up to the task. The experiment involved sending single photons (individual particles of light) through a tiny air gap between two blocks of glass (two prisms), and monitoring their behaviour.

The experiment required great precision, not just in producing single photons but targeting them through the gap between the two prisms, with the size of the gap controlled to within a few tens of a billionth of a metre, about one-tenth of the wavelength of the light involved. Because the gap is so small and light travels as a wave, it could cross the gap, but other tests showed that the photons that arrived on the other side of the gap were particles. Individual photons had been observed behaving as both wave and as particle in the same experiment. Dipankar Home, the leader of the Indian team, summed up the implications. 'Three centuries after Newton,' (left) he said, 'we have to admit that we still cannot answer the question "what is light?"'

1. John Wheeler, who encouraged Hugh Everett's work on the 'Many Worlds' idea.

2. According to quantum theory, the Universe is like a many-branched tree, with each branch corresponding to a different reality.

down. This 'superposition of states', as it is called, applies to all quantum properties. It is only when a measurement is made that there is a 'collapse of the wave function' and the electron chooses (at random) which spin (or whatever) to have. Einstein hated the idea of this random behaviour, and famously declared 'I cannot believe that God plays dice.'

But there is an alternative interpretation. Instead of one electron in a superposition of states, the equations work just as well if there are two electrons, one in each possible state, but in two separate universes. Whichever universe you are in, if you measure the spin you get a definite answer, with (in this case) a 50:50 probability of either choice. For more complicated situations (for example, throwing six dice at once), the odds are more complicated, but there is no collapse of the wave function. On this picture, as Dorothy

Parker might have said, 'an electron is an electron is an electron.' The cost is that there is now a separate universe – a separate physical reality – for every possible outcome of every possible quantum measurement. This is where the name 'Many Worlds Interpretation' comes from.

Quantum Physics that Suits Cosmologists

Cosmologists like the idea of many worlds because they have great difficulty with the standard interpretation of quantum mechanics. It is possible to imagine the whole Universe being described mathematically by a single quantum wave function. Such a wave function is sometimes known as the Wheeler–DeWitt equation, after two physicists who studied

the problem, but we don't actually know what the equation is, only some of the properties it must have.

The problem cosmologists then have with the standard interpretation is that the Universe is everything there is, so there is nothing outside the Universe to interact with the wave function and make it collapse – it has to exist forever in a superposition of all possible states. This is essentially the same as saying that all possible universes exist side by side, and all instants of time exist (one in front of the other), with nothing really changing. This literally means that the science fiction idea of alternative histories (a world where the South won the American civil war, a world where Nelson Mandela was never imprisoned, and so on) becomes part (a rather small part) of the quantum mechanical description of reality. What are the implications for ideas such as the Big Bang and the expanding Universe?

Quantum Cosmology

There are two kinds of quantum cosmology. The first kind deals with events that occurred very close to the Planck time (time zero) in 'our' Universe (▷ p. 98), and which led to inflation and the Big Bang in which hydrogen and helium were created out of pure energy in a little less than four minutes (▷ p. 107). The second kind of quantum cosmology deals with the implications of the Many Worlds Interpretation and the Wheeler–DeWitt equation. It is much more speculative and exploring these ideas takes us beyond the frontiers of what is known about the way the world works. But it is this kind of exploration that makes the unknown known, and which has already made the first kind of quantum cosmology a respectable part of astronomical thinking.

After his PhD, Hugh Everett worked on classified subjects for the Pentagon and never published another scientific paper.

2

1. Stephen Hawking, a pioneering quantum cosmologist.

2. To a polar bear standing at the North Pole, all directions are south.

1

In 1906, J. J. Thomson received the Nobel Prize for proving that electrons are particles. In 1937, his son, George Thomson, received the Nobel Prize for proving that electrons are waves. Both were right.

The Cosmic Desert

Accepting, for the moment, the everyday idea of time flowing inexorably forward, we can picture the cosmic version of the Many Worlds Interpretation as implying that the Universe was split into many different branches, like a huge tree (sometimes called the 'Multiverse'), by quantum processes operating at the beginning of time, when what is now the observable Universe was the size of a quantum entity. The different branches of the Multiverse would still be in some sense members of the same family, and governed by some common overriding principles (especially the quantum principles which describe the splitting process and allow the universes to keep branching repeatedly as time passes). But there will be an enormous number of different universes (possibly infinitely many) within the Multiverse, and among that infinite array there will be universes with all possible values (and combinations of values) of the fundamental parameters such as omega and lambda, or the Hubble parameter. There could even be universes with different values of N, or E, or Q.

In the vast variety of all the possible branches of the Multiverse, the combinations of the fundamental parameters will allow life to exist in only a tiny proportion of the universes. (If the Multiverse is infinite, life might still exist in an infinite sub-set of universes, but that infinity would only be a tiny proportion of the bigger infinity.) This is where the weak anthropic principle (▷ p. 187) comes into its own. Most of the Multiverse is sterile – a cosmic desert. Life exists only in a relatively small number of oases scattered across the cosmic desert. But, since we are living things, when we look around us we have to see an oasis, not the desert. These ideas can even predict what kind of oasis we ought to see.

Hawking's Universe

Stephen Hawking developed a version of cosmology based on the Many Worlds idea in the early 1980s. His starting point was the assumption (or guess) that there must be no boundary to the Universe – no 'edge' either in time or space. From the conventional point of view, as we have seen, there is an edge of time at the Big Bang (or, strictly speaking, at the Planck time). Leaving aside the mathematics, Hawking's ingenious way around this can be understood in terms of geometry – specifically, the geometry of a sphere, like the surface of the Earth.

Imagine all of the three dimensions of space represented by a line around the sphere, like a line of latitude. Time can then be represented by a line at right angles to space, measured by the distance from one of the poles of the sphere – say, the North Pole – along a line of longitude. The North Pole itself represents the birth of time, and a tiny circle around the North Pole represents the compact state of the Universe in the Big Bang. As 'time passes', we move to lower latitudes, away from the pole and towards the equator, **2**

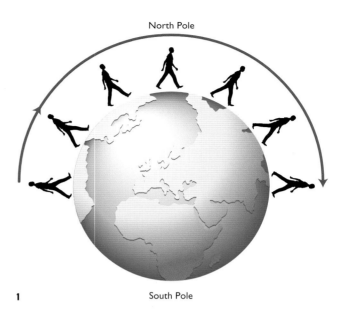

North Pole

South Pole

1

1. If you head due north in a 'straight line' you end up heading south.

and the lines representing space at different times get bigger – the universe expands.

The crucial point is that in this picture there is no edge at the North Pole, just as there is no edge to the Earth at the real North Pole. If you stand at the North Pole, all directions along the surface of the Earth are south. If you stand at the Planck time, all directions of time are into the future. It is as meaningless to ask about what happened 'before' the Big Bang as it is to ask about what exists 'north' of the North Pole.

Bringing Hawking up to Date

Hawking's original model of the Universe carried this analogy beyond the equator, where the line of latitude is biggest, and down into the 'southern hemisphere', with the lines getting smaller towards the South Pole. The implication was that the universe he described must be closed, and space itself must reach a maximum size and then shrink towards a Big Crunch (▷ p. 99). Hawking even considered the possibility that time might run backwards in the shrinking half of the universe.

But the discovery at the beginning of the

twenty-first century that the expansion of the Universe is accelerating because of the lambda term (▷ p. 94) means that although Hawking's model is still a perfectly good one (and might describe a real universe somewhere out there in the Multiverse), it does not describe the Universe we live in. It is easy, though, to adapt Hawking's universe to provide a model like our own Universe. Instead of thinking of spacetime as the surface of a static sphere, it is more appropriate to think of the surface of an expanding balloon. The effect of the lambda term is to make the balloon bigger as time passes, running away so that it becomes impossible for anything starting out from the North Pole ever to reach, let alone cross, the equator.

Everything else in Hawking's model still stands up, and in particular there is still no edge of time at the beginning. The difference is that there is no end of time for a different reason, because of the eternal expansion of the universe. But time is a tricky concept, and some theorists are now exploring the possibility that we should not think of it as flowing from the past into the future at all.

DOES TIME EXIST?

The nature of time is one of the great mysteries in both science and philosophy. We all experience the flow of time, from the past, through the present, and into the future. But where does the past go after the present has happened? And where is the future before the present reaches it? Julian Barbour, an independent physicist based in Oxfordshire, is the latest person to suggest that both past and future really exist 'all the time' (whatever that means) and that all that travels is our conscious awareness of the moment 'now'.

Geography and Relativity

This idea is a natural consequence of the theory of relativity, which sees time as the fourth dimension. Einstein's theory can be expressed in geometrical terms, in which time behaves like a dimension at right angles to the three familiar dimensions of space (up-down, left-right, and forward-back, plus past-future). This is more than a mere analogy. The equations that describe the locations of things in three dimensions of space are an extension of the famous equation derived by Pythagoras regarding the lengths of the sides of right-angle triangles 'the square on the hypotenuse is equal to the sum of the squares on the other two sides'. The equations that describe the locations of things in spacetime are the four-dimensional extension of Pythagoras' equation. And they work perfectly.

This seems to imply that four-dimensional geography is as real as three-dimensional geography or two-dimensional geography. Even if you are somewhere on the surface of the Earth, the Moon is a real place, and you can get to it by travelling through space. In the Einsteinian universe, next Thursday week is always just as real as the Moon, and you get there by travelling through time. The difference is that you have no choice about how fast you travel through time, or where you are going – it's a bit like being on a sealed train travelling at a constant speed through the countryside. At the end of the 1990s, Barbour went further by arguing that there is not even one 'now' (or one 'Thursday week', or one 1914) but an incomprehensible multitude of alternative present moments corresponding to each possible instant of conventional time. He says that the flow of time does not exist, because all times always exist.

Putting the Past in Perspective

Barbour's jumping-off point is the quantum-mechanical vision of reality as an array of parallel worlds, in which every possible outcome of every possible quantum event happens. If I set up an experiment in which an electron has a choice of going through either of two holes, in this picture, the world (the entire Universe) splits into two copies, identical except for the choice of hole the electron goes through. Not very significant – unless I make sure that if the electron goes through hole A it triggers a nuclear bomb which destroys London, while if it goes through hole B London survives. Then, the two alternative realities are quite easily differentiated.

But even this image contains the idea of time flowing, and the Universe(s) evolving. Barbour's Universe (or Multiverse) is utterly timeless. All possible instants in all possible quantum realities always exist. The difference between past and future, in such a picture, is that some instants contain structures that can be called 'records' because they describe accurately what exists in other instants, which we call the past. Those records may be human generated things, like diaries, or natural phenomena, like fossils in geological strata. They define a direction of time, without there needing to be a flow of time. What there is,

2

2. An early time-keeper recorded the passage of the hours by the slowly falling level of oil in a lamp.

though, is a requirement that the records are self-consistent – the records in each instant describe a possible history.

We perceive a flow of time, says Barbour, because in each instant our brain contains an overlapping set of structures (what he calls a 'time capsule') which gives an illusion of time moving, just as an overlapping set of images from a film strip gives an illusion of motion. But consciousness does not move sequentially along the ranks of time capsules in order – every conscious moment, every time capsule complete with its own historical records and illusion of time passing, exists 'all the time.'

Putting the Worlds Together

There is another way of looking at the many worlds idea, which reduces the number of universes to worry about, and makes some people feel more comfortable about it. David Deutsch, another Oxford physicist (who shares Barbour's view that the flow of time is an illusion), has developed the idea that when a single photon approaches the experiment with two holes, the world does indeed divide in two, with a photon going through one hole in one universe, and through the other hole in the other universe. But when the two possible paths for the photons come back together again in the interference pattern, the two

universes merge back together, and that is what makes the pattern. They only exist as separate realities during the time the photon(s) is/are flying through the experiment(s).

According to Deutsch, if we carry out the experiment and allow the interference pattern to form, the splitting and rejoining is a local phenomenon going on in the corner of the lab. But if we look to see which hole the photon goes through, and stop the interference pattern forming, then the world does split permanently into two copies. In a sense, we can make new universes (or new copies of our Universe) on demand. But quantum rules allow universes to be made on a more impressive scale than this.

 AN UNCONVENTIONAL SCIENTIST

The outline of Julian Barbour's work scarcely does justice to ideas which are new, mind blowing, and have taken Barbour (right) 30 years to develop. His own book-length exposition of those ideas (*The End of Time*) pulls few punches, and is often an intellectually demanding read. But apart from its intrinsic interest, the story is fascinating because of the way Barbour worked for those 30 years. Although armed with a PhD in physics, he made a conscious decision to opt out of the 'publish or perish' academic rat race, earning his living as a translator of Russian while working on his unconventional ideas with complete freedom. This doesn't mean either that he was isolated or that he is a crank – he regularly attends scientific meetings, publishes papers (in his own good time) and is held in high esteem by his peers.

All this is a shining example of the power of free will and the result of an independent choice of career. Except that Barbour's ideas raise serious doubts about the concept of free will. As he puts it, in the 'many-instants interpretation' of reality, 'each Now' competes 'with all the other Nows in a timeless beauty contest to win the highest probability.' What I *think* this means is that, although everyone reading this book is experiencing a Now in which Julian Barbour is an independent cuss who has come up with a brilliant and novel idea, there are countless more Nows in which countless versions of Julian Barbour took a conventional academic job in 1969 and published a series of dull but worthy papers on conventional topics. Chance, and chance alone, has made 'our' Julian Barbour special.

1. (opposite) Does time really exist? Or is it merely a succession of frozen instants?

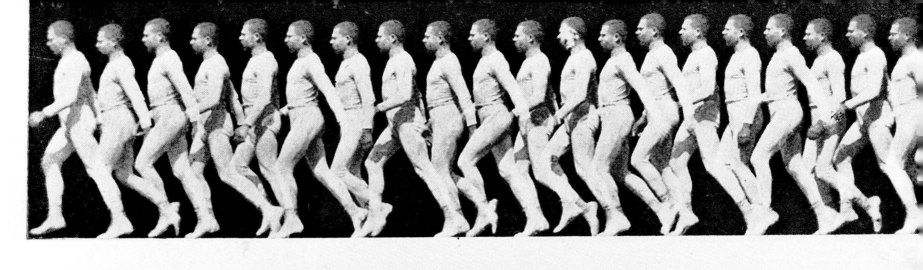

SCHRÖDINGER'S CAT

Erwin Schrödinger, an Austrian physicist, was one of the pioneers who developed quantum mechanics in the 1920s. But by 1935 he was so disgusted with the implications of his own theory that he dreamed up an imaginary experiment to demonstrate its absurdity. It has become the most famous 'thought experiment' in science. A thought experiment is not intended to be carried out 'for real' but it is supposed to have such obvious implications that the result is beyond doubt.

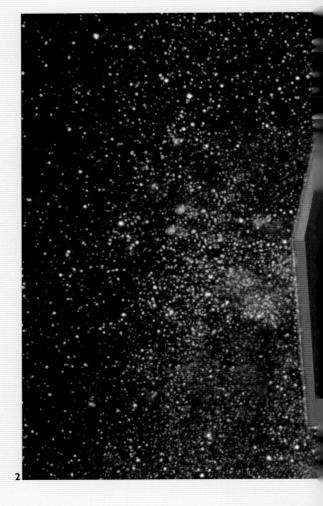
2

1

The Science of Superposition
The basis for Schrödinger's argument is the way that the standard interpretation of quantum mechanics says that a quantum entity exists in a superposition of states until it is measured, and then collapses into a definite state. He used the example of radioactivity, but the 'experiment' works just as well if we think of an isolated electron, which sits in a mixture of two states, spin up and spin down. When the electron spin is measured, it collapses into one of the two states with exactly equal probability. An electron is 'prepared' in such a superposition of states every time one of them is knocked out of an atom, for example, in the electron 'gun' that sends a beam of these particles to paint the picture on a TV screen.

The Cat in the Box
Imagine taking such an electron as it emerges from an electron gun and holding it in a set of magnetic or electric fields, without trying to

measure its spin immediately. The electron trap is inside a piece of apparatus connected to a container of poisonous gas, and everything is sealed inside a large room where a healthy cat lives, supplied with plenty of food and water. When the spin of the electron is eventually measured, an automatic device will release the gas and kill the cat if the spin is up, but will let the cat live if the spin is down. Schrödinger pointed out that according to the standard interpretation of quantum mechanics everything in the sealed room, including the cat, is in a 50:50

1. Edwin Schrödinger, inventor of the 'cat paradox'.

2. The Schrödinger's cat thought experiment devised by Edwin Schrödinger (opposite) says that a live cat and its ghost can both exist at the same time.

superposition of states until somebody looks into the room and notices what has happened. The cat is both dead and alive at the same time.

Parallel Possibilities

There are several rival interpretations of quantum mechanics which try to avoid this unwelcome state of affairs. The one that many cosmologists like involves parallel worlds. In this picture, the moment the electron is released, the entire world splits into two copies of itself. In one, the electron has spin

down and the cat lives. In the other, the electron has spin up and the cat dies. For a human observer in either world, there is still a 50:50 chance of finding a live cat when you look into the room — but neither cat is ever in a superposition of states.

Extending this example, the entire Universe is multiplied into an infinite number of branches, and anything that can possibly happen does happen in one (or more) of the branches of reality. (This experiment really is 'all in the mind'. Nothing like it has ever been tried with a real cat!)

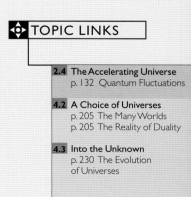

◆ TOPIC LINKS

2.4 The Accelerating Universe
p. 132 Quantum Fluctuations

4.2 A Choice of Universes
p. 205 The Many Worlds
p. 205 The Reality of Duality

4.3 Into the Unknown
p. 230 The Evolution of Universes

INTO THE UNKNOWN

The idea that alternative worlds might exist somewhere in a quantum Multiverse, combined with the weak anthropic principle, is a neat way of explaining why the Universe we see around us seems to have been designed for life, without invoking a Designer and becoming embroiled in the infinite regress of who designed the Designer, and so on. But all this is rather abstract and philosophical.

The quantum rules do, however, allow for a much more direct relationship between universes, suggesting that they may be physically connected, and that one universe may grow out of another, through a black hole. According to these ideas, Universes reproduce, producing baby universes which grow and have babies in their turn. These ideas come from research at the far frontier of science, and have not yet been tested. But they show where cosmological thinking is taking us in the twenty-first century.

BEYOND THE BLACK HOLE

The equations of the general theory of relativity (a very well established theory that has been tested by many experiments) tell us that the entire contents of a black hole must collapse towards a mathematical point, a singularity ($\triangleright$ p. 87). The equations of quantum physics (an equally well founded theory) tell us, however, that there is no such thing as a mathematical point, and that nothing can be smaller across than the Planck radius.

Combining these two well-established ideas, physicists conclude that something happens to matter (mass-energy) falling inwards inside a black hole when it reaches the Planck radius. The most likely result is that the material bounces, and expands outwards again. But it doesn't come bursting back out into the universe it fell in from; instead, it is shunted sideways into a new set of dimensions, forming a new expanding universe in its own right.

To put these ideas in perspective, we need to remind ourselves what kind of objects black holes are.

Black Holes Revisited

A black hole is formed by any concentration of matter which has a gravitational field so strong that spacetime is bent right around to form a closed surface. There are two ways this can happen. If any lump of matter is squeezed into a ball so that, although its mass stays the same, its density increases, at some critical density it will become a black hole. This is the kind of black hole left behind by some supernovae. Alternatively, if you keep the density constant and keep adding more mass, at some critical mass it will become a

1. A jet of material in the galaxy M87 being shot out by a super-massive black hole at the heart of the galaxy.

black hole. This is the kind of black hole that powers a quasar.

The crucial radius at which an object becomes a black hole is called the Schwarzschild radius, in honour of the German scientist who first realized that the equations of the general theory of relativity predicted the existence of black holes. One way of thinking of the Schwarzschild radius is that the escape velocity from a surface with the Schwarzschild radius is the speed of light. Nothing can escape from inside the Schwarzschild surface, because within it the escape velocity exceeds the speed of light.

To see how the different ways of making black holes work, think of the Sun. If the Sun were squeezed within a ball just 2.9 km across (the Schwarzschild radius for an object with one solar mass), it would become a superdense black hole. But if you could add more matter to the Sun without it collapsing (think of a bag containing a lot of marbles, each representing a star like the Sun), it would become a black hole when it had the mass of a few million Suns, and about the radius of our Solar System – the Schwarzschild radius for an object with a few million solar masses. The density of matter needed to make such a supermassive black hole would only be a little more than the density of water – but the matter would then fall inward towards the centre and be crushed out of existence at the Planck radius.

Einstein's Wormholes

Although black holes were only given their modern name in 1967 (by John Wheeler),

THE MAN WHO INVENTED BLACK HOLES

The first person to suggest the existence of black holes was an eighteenth-century English parson, the Reverend John Michell. But he wasn't just a country parson. Michell, who was born in 1724, became one of the leading scientists of his day before he took Holy Orders, and made his reputation from a study of the disastrous earthquake that struck Lisbon in 1755 (left). He was elected a Fellow of the Royal Society in 1760, and Professor of Geology at the University of Cambridge in 1762. In 1764, he left the university to become the rector of a parish in Yorkshire, but he maintained a keen interest in science and published several important astronomical papers. Among other achievements, he was one of the first people to publish a reasonably accurate estimate of the distance to a star. Using an argument based on its apparent brightness, he calculated that the star Vega is 460,000 times further away from us than the Sun is. In 1783, in a paper read to the Royal Society by his friend Henry Cavendish, Michell pointed out that there could be 'dark stars' in the Universe, so big that light could not escape from them:

'If there should really exist in nature any bodies whose density is not less than that of the Sun, and whose diameters are more than 500 times the diameter of the Sun, since their light could not arrive at us…we could have no information from sight; yet, if any other luminiferous bodies should happen to revolve around them we might still perhaps from the motions of these revolving bodies infer the existence of the central ones.'

These are exactly the kind of black holes now thought to be associated with quasars, and we do indeed infer their existence from the way bright stuff orbits around them.

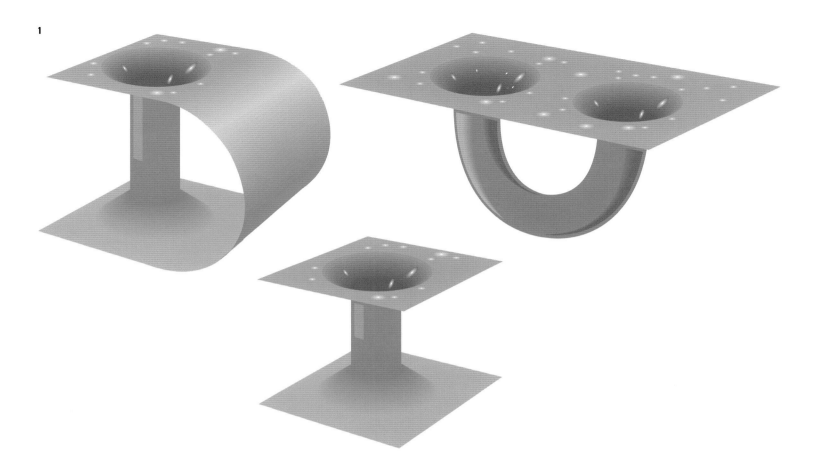

Karl Schwarzschild predicted their existence in 1916, and the mathematical description of black holes was studied by Albert Einstein himself in the 1930s. Working with Nathan Rosen, at Princeton University, Einstein discovered that the solutions to the equations of the general theory discovered by Schwarzschild actually described not a single 'hole in space' but a pair of holes connected by a tunnel linking two separate regions of spacetime. This tunnel became known as an Einstein–Rosen bridge, but more recently physicists have taken to calling them 'wormholes'.

An Einstein–Rosen bridge, or wormhole, joins two black holes in different locations in spacetime. Originally, people thought

that if such entities were real they could link different parts of our Universe, like a cosmic subway. This is still true; but because space*time* is involved not just space, a wormhole might also, in principle, link two different times in our Universe – it could be a kind of time machine. And now cosmologists speculate that if other universes exist, then wormholes may provide links between different universes.

Quantum Foam

Don't get too excited, however, about the possibility of travelling through a wormhole to some other place, or time, or some other universe. It would be extremely difficult (for all practical purposes, it may be

1. 'Wormholes' may join different regions of a single universe, or even separate universes.

impossible) to build a large wormhole through which people could travel. Natural wormholes, if they occur at all, exist on the scale of the Planck length, whatever the size of the Schwarzschild radius of the black hole that acts as the gateway to a particular cosmic subway.

Physicists who study the mathematics of such entities are still intrigued by wormholes, however, because quantum processes operating on the Planck scale may produce vast numbers of tiny (sub-sub-microscopic) wormholes, and these could provide the structure of spacetime itself. The quantum wormholes would be like the strands of a carpet, woven together to make the seemingly solid structure of spacetime (the carpet) itself. And they could be the seeds of baby universes.

1

1, 2 and 3 (opposite): The surface of the sea looks less and less smooth the closer you get to it.

2

HOW TO MAKE A UNIVERSE

The idea that spacetime may be woven together out of quantum-scale wormholes is related to another of John Wheeler's suggestions, which portrays spacetime as a 'foam' of quantum entities, popping in and out of existence at the scale of the Planck length. This could include black hole pairs and the wormholes that connect them. An analogy Wheeler makes is with the appearance of the surface of the sea. From a high-flying aircraft, the sea looks smooth and flat. Closer up, it looks rough, and closer still the surface dissolves into a constantly changing foam of bubbles and tiny waves. Spacetime may only seem smooth to us because we are so much larger than the Planck scale – remember that the Planck length, 10^{-33} cm, is 10–20 times the size of a proton.

Virtual Reality

Wheeler's idea is based on the prediction from quantum mechanics that quantum entities such as pairs of particles can appear out of nothing at all for a short time ('virtual pairs'). We met this idea in Chapter 2, in the

1. A pair of interacting galaxies known as the antennae.

2. A gamma ray burster pictured by the Hubble Space Telescope.

1

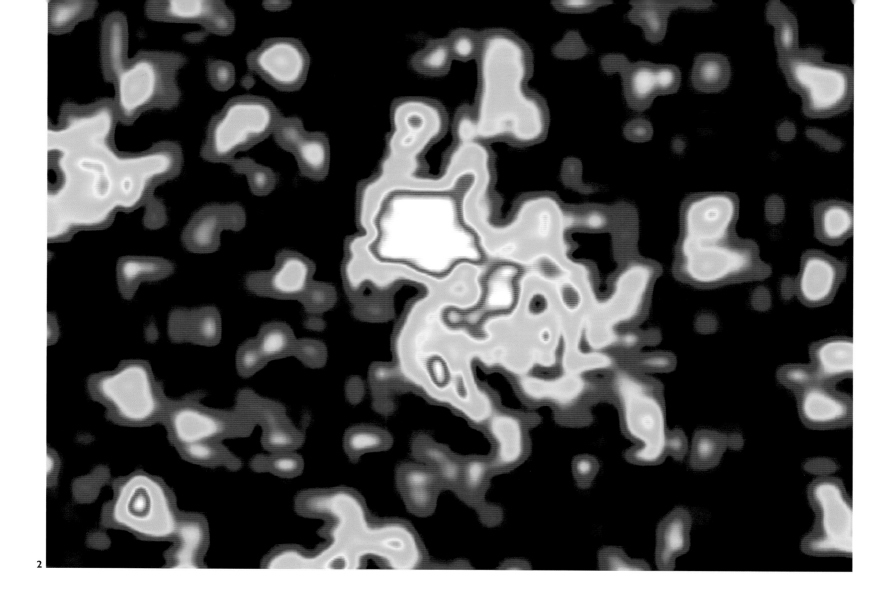

2

context of the term that drives the acceleration of the Universe. But this is not just a speculation floated by the cosmologists to explain their observations of distant galaxies. Such quantum fluctuations are an integral part of quantum mechanics, and give a structure to the vacuum (to 'empty space'), with consequences that can be measured in the laboratory.

Particles made out of nothing in this way always come in pairs (called virtual pairs) with opposite quantum properties. For example, a virtual electron is always accompanied by a virtual positron, a particle like an electron but with positive charge rather than negative charge. Close to a real charged particle, such as a permanent electron, even during the brief

lifetime of the virtual pair there will be time for the virtual positron to move towards the real electron and the virtual electron to be repelled from it. This produces a shielding effect around the real electron, and reduces the effect of its charge, as measured by the influence on another real electron. The consequences of this shielding can be predicted by quantum theory, and exactly match the measured behaviour of charged particles such as electrons. There is no doubt that quantum fluctuations are real.

Something For Nothing

There is nothing in the quantum rules, however, which says that only particles can be created temporarily out of nothing at all

Astronomers estimate there are at least 100 million black holes in our Galaxy. With over 100 billion galaxies, that means our Universe may already have had ten thousand million billion (10^{19}) offspring.

THE NEGATIVITY OF GRAVITY

The idea that gravity corresponds to negative energy is one of the hardest scientific concepts for a non-specialist to come to terms with. But it is also one of the most important, for without the negativity of gravity the Universe probably would not exist.

1. It takes a lot of energy to lift anything out of the gravitational well of the Earth.

Extending to Infinity

Without delving into the equations of the general theory of relativity, the best way to get a handle on this is to imagine disassembling something (anything!) and dispersing its component parts to infinity. This is only a 'thought experiment', so you can do this at the level of atoms, or particles such as protons and neutrons, but the analogy works just as well for a pile of bricks.

Remember that gravity obeys an inverse square law. So the force of gravity between any two bricks is proportional to one divided by the square of the distance between them. If the bricks are infinitely far apart, the force must be zero, because anything divided by infinity (let alone by infinity squared) is zero.

Storing Energy

The amount of energy that is stored in a gravitational field depends on the force between the objects involved. This isn't only true for gravity. Think of a spring. When the spring is relaxed, loose and floppy, it stores no energy (except, of course, its mc^2). When you stretch it, the force pulling the spring inwards gets bigger, and more energy is stored in the spring. But with gravity, there is *less* force when things are stretched apart. If you could stretch a spring to infinity without breaking it, there would be a huge force pulling it inward, and it would store a huge amount of energy. With gravity, though, there is a huge force when things are very close together. When

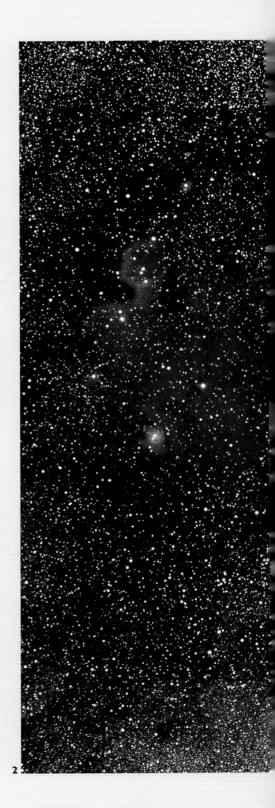

the components are at infinity, there is zero force, so there is zero energy in the gravitational field.

Extracting Energy

But we know that when things fall together, gravitational energy is released. That's how stars get hot enough inside to start burning their nuclear fuel. Imagine all your bricks, dispersed to infinity, given a gentle nudge so that they start falling together. As they fall, they release energy. But they start out with zero energy – so after releasing some, they are left with less than nothing. It's like writing a cheque when you have no money in your bank account – suddenly you have *negative* amounts. In all real objects, the energy of their gravitational field is negative.

If your bricks fall all the way from infinity down to a point (or the Planck length), then, the equations of the general theory tell us, the amount of energy released is equal and opposite to their total mass-energy, $-mc^2$. Turning this around, a universe destined to expand to infinity can appear out of nothing at all at the Planck scale, because its mass-energy is precisely cancelled out by its negative gravitational energy.

2. The Lagoon nebula, about 3500 light years away from us, is a stellar nursery where thousands of new stars have recently been formed.

◈ TOPIC LINKS

1.2 Star Birth
p. 31 Turning up the Stellar Heat

1.4 Out with a Bang
pp. 72-73 The Search for Black Holes

2.1 The Big Bang
p. 87 The Singular Beginning

2.4 The Accelerating Universe
p. 132 Quantum Fluctuations

4.3 Into the Unknown
p. 227 Einstein's Surprise

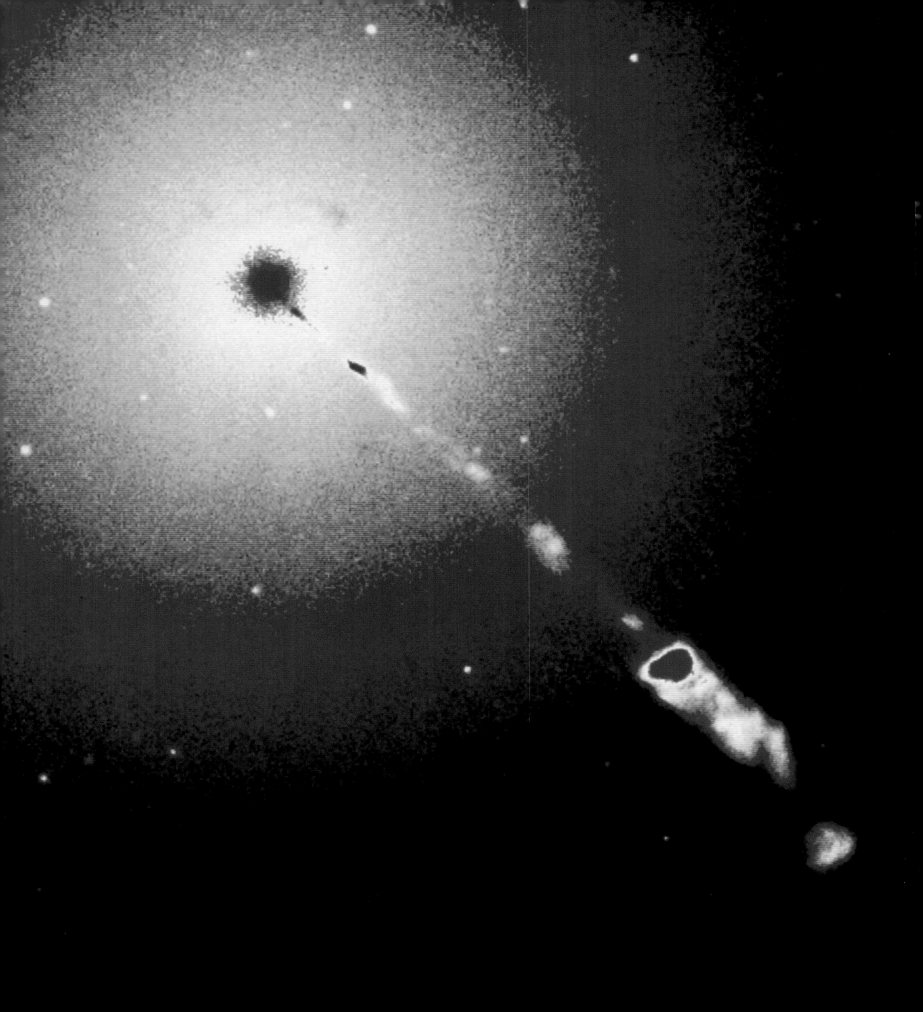

in this way. Little packets of pure energy (bubbles with a radius roughly equal to the Planck length) can also appear out of nothing at all, provided that they disappear within the time allowed by Heisenberg's uncertainty relation. But that time can be very long indeed.

Remember that the less energy a quantum fluctuation contains, the longer it can live. The energy of a little packet of mass-energy actually comes in two forms – from its mass, but also from its gravity. Curiously, the energy of a gravitational field is actually negative. This means that for a bubble with just the right amount of mass-energy the two effects cancel out, and the overall energy of the bubble is zero. In that case, it could last forever. 'Just right' means that the bubble contains just enough mass to make it flat, on the edge of being a black hole. If our Universe is flat, it also contains zero energy overall.

As long ago as 1973, Edward Tryon, of City University in New York, pointed out that as far as quantum physics was concerned the entire Universe could be nothing more or less than a quantum fluctuation of the vacuum.

Blowing Bubbles

The big snag with Tryon's idea was that quantum fluctuations occur on the Planck scale. There was, indeed, nothing in the

 ## EINSTEIN'S SURPRISE

The idea that the negativity of gravity can precisely cancel out the mass-energy $E=mc^2$ in a lump of matter (or the Universe) is so surprising that even after you have had it explained to you, or studied the equations for yourself, it is hard to believe. If you feel that way, you are in very good company.

The first person to realize this possibility was the physicist Pascual Jordan, working in the United States in the 1940s. At that time, Albert Einstein (right) worked as a consultant for the US Navy, assessing schemes for new weapons sent to the military by well-meaning civilians. Einstein was very good at this – in the first decade of the twentieth century he had worked as a Patent Officer in Switzerland, so he was used to finding the flaws in inventions. Every fortnight or so, George Gamow, who was based in Washington DC and also involved in war work, would take the latest batch of ideas up to Einstein in Princeton.

On one of these visits, as Gamow later recalled in his autobiography *My World Line*, the two physicists were walking from Einstein's home to the Institute for Advanced Study, where Einstein worked, when Gamow casually mentioned that Jordan had told him that a star could be made out of nothing at all, because at the point of zero volume its negative gravitational energy would precisely cancel out its positive mass-energy. 'Einstein stopped in his tracks,' Gamow tells us, 'and, since we were crossing a street, several cars had to stop to avoid running us down.'

quantum rules to forbid a bubble containing as much mass-energy as our entire Universe to appear on the Planck scale. But it would have an enormous gravitational pull, which would crush it out of existence immediately. Tryon's idea lay dormant until the 1980s, when inflation theory provided the mechanism which can take a superdense quantum seed and blow it up to the size of an observable object in our world. The enormous push given by inflation acts like antigravity, flattens spacetime, and prevents the baby universe crushing itself out of existence as soon as it forms.

There is no reason, however, to stop at one universe. In this picture, universes of all sizes should be produced by quantum fluctuations, some with just enough strength to expand a little way, others where the term is powerful enough to keep the universe expanding forever, and with all possible intermediate values. Each universe is like another bubble in the foam of spacetime, expanding in its own way with no contact with its neighbours, and we are back to the weak anthropic principle to explain why the Universe we live in is as it is.

But Tryon's ideas, inflation, and the mathematics of black holes can be combined to give a more intriguing insight into how we got here.

Black Holes and Baby Universes

The seed of a universe like our own could come into existence as a concentration of mass-energy containing all the mass-energy of the observable Universe in a volume with the Planck radius, 'born' at an age of 10^{-43} seconds, the Planck time (▷p. 98). Inflation could drive the expansion of such a baby universe up to a large size, and this could be happening anywhere in the vacuum of space around us (or, indeed, in the space between

the atoms of the page you are now reading). If so, these other universes wouldn't explode outwards in your face, filling up our own region of spacetime, but would exist in their own sets of dimensions, all of them at right angles to the dimensions of our spacetime. But it would also be possible, in principle, to make a universe, deliberately.

Universes on Demand

Several physicists, including Alan Guth, one of the pioneers of inflation theory, have explored this possibility mathematically. One of the key points in their argument is that even in order to make as large a Universe as the one we live in, you do not need a lot of mass-energy to start with. Because of the negativity of gravity, nature can make universes out of nothing at all. We cannot quite do that, because we would have to put energy in to trigger the process of inflation. But the amount of energy required is surprisingly small, compared even with the output of a star like the Sun.

The requirement to kick-start inflation is a temperature equivalent to about 10^{24} K and a very high density. The energy required to produce these conditions is no more than could be produced by a few hydrogen bombs; the problem is confining that energy, even if only for a split-second, in a tiny volume of space, about the size of an atom. If this could be done, the equations studied by Guth and others show that under some circumstances inflation will occur in the compressed region.

1. The technology of the hydrogen bomb almost gives us the ability to make black holes – and perhaps baby universes.

There is another way to make a universe, equally impractical as far as present-day technology is concerned, but allowed by the laws of physics, and that is to build a black hole. The stuff inside a black hole must, as Roger Penrose proved nearly four decades ago, fall towards a singularity. At the place where the infalling matter is squeezed into a Planck volume, quantum processes take over and shunt the infalling stuff sideways into a new set of dimensions, forming a new expanding universe. Once again, however, it doesn't matter how much or how little mass-energy goes into the black hole, or whether it is in the form of water, or hydrogen, or peanuts, or anything else. Thanks to the negativity of gravity, a universe as impressive as our own can be made from a black hole with any amount of mass.

But in another twist to the tale, there is nothing to say that the laws of physics need be exactly the same in the baby universe as in the universe which gave it birth.

THE EVOLUTION OF UNIVERSES

Lee Smolin, of Pennsylvania State University, has come up with one of the most spectacular speculations in science. He has made the guess (and as yet it is no more than a guess) that every time a baby universe buds off from another universe through a black hole/wormhole 'umbilical cord', the laws of physics in the new universe are slightly different (but not dramatically different) from the laws in the parent universe. This would echo the way in which children are slightly different from their parents, but horses always give birth to horses, cats to cats, and so on.

Provided this is the case, when new universes are produced by quantum fluctuations, they will come in all varieties, some expanding more than others. But when new universes are born out of old universes, they will have a family resemblance to their parent. If a quantum fluctuation doesn't grow big enough to have very many black holes, it will leave few offspring (perhaps none at all). But the bigger a universe grows, the more black holes it will produce, and the more babies it will have – crucially, those babies will share the propensity of the parent universe to grow big and have lots of babies in their turn.

Smolin sees this as leading inevitably to the production of big universes in which the laws of physics are fine-tuned to make the maximum number of black holes. Universes like our own should, in this picture, actually be the most common kind of universes in the Multiverse, and we don't even need to invoke the weak anthropic principle to explain why we live in such a universe. But if the Universe is the result of a kind of evolutionary process that favours the production of black holes, why are we here at all?

1

People are Parasites

Smolin's answer is that we are at best a by-product of the processes that produce black holes, and at worst parasites on the Universe. This happens because size isn't the only thing that matters if a universe is to have lots of babies – the laws of physics have to be just right for making black holes in that universe.

The most efficient way to turn matter into new universes is to have lots of small black holes, because you get one new universe for each black hole. A hundred million black holes each with the mass of the Sun are much better (a hundred million times better) than a single black hole with a hundred million solar masses. Stellar mass black holes are, of course, made from stars, as part of the natural cycle of starbirth and stardeath. And that natural cycle depends crucially on the presence of elements such as carbon and oxygen, as one example illustrates.

When a cloud of gas and dust (a giant molecular cloud) starts to collapse to form stars, it gets hot inside. As the first stars form, they radiate a lot of ultraviolet radiation and visible light, which tends to blow the cloud apart, and this would stop stars like the Sun forming unless the cloud could get rid of the heat. It does so because compounds such as carbon monoxide (CO) and water (H_2O) absorb the ultraviolet and visible light, and re-radiate it at infrared wavelengths which can penetrate the dusty cloud and escape into space. This allows the cloud to collapse and produce many more stars, including supernovas, the birthplaces of black holes.

Without the carbon and oxygen, only a few stars would form (but at least a few would form, which is how the first carbon and oxygen was made in our Universe). As we have seen, the laws of physics seem to be fine-tuned to allow carbon and oxygen to be formed inside stars, and this benefits carbon-based, oxygen-breathing life forms like ourselves. But if Smolin is right, the 'coincidences' that allow carbon and oxygen to exist have happened neither by accident nor by design, but as part of a process of natural selection among universes. Carbon and oxygen are an integral part of the reproductive cycle of the Universe, and we just go along for the ride.

It is a sobering removal of humankind from the centre of the cosmic stage – but the upside is that if these ideas are correct, there are countless other universes, all relatively rich in carbon and oxygen, where organic beings like ourselves can thrive.

Further information

Aczel, Amir, *Probability 1* (Harcourt Brace, 1998). Arguing the case that we are not alone in the Universe.

Christianson, Gale, *Edwin Hubble* (Farrar, Straus & Giroux, 1995). Definitive biography of the man who discovered that the Universe is expanding.

Crick, Francis, *Life Itself* (Macdonald, 1982). Nobel prizewinner discusses the puzzle of the origin and nature of life.

Croswell, Ken, *Planet Quest* (Free Press, 1997). The most accessible account to date of the discovery of alien 'solar systems'.

Gamow, George, *Mr Tompkins in Paperback* (Cambridge UP, 1967). Classic stories of the dream world in which Mr Tompkins experiences the mysteries of the Universe. An updated version by Russell Stannard is also available.

Gribbin, John, *In Search of Schrödinger's Cat* (Black Swan, 1984). Classic explanation of the 'many worlds' interpretation of quantum mechanics.

Gribbin, John, *The Birth of Time* (Phoenix, 1999). Up-to-date discussion of the evidence for the Big Bang.

Gribbin, John, *Stardust* (Allen Lane, 2000). The most accessible account of the way the elements were manufactured inside stars.

Henbest, Nigel, and Couper, Heather, *The Guide to the Galaxy* (Cambridge UP, 1994). Lavishly illustrated and accurate introduction to the geography of the Milky Way.

Longair, Malcolm, *Our Evolving Universe* (Cambridge UP, 1996). An overview of cosmology from one of Britain's leading astronomers.

Malin, David, *The Invisible Universe* (Bulfinch Press, 1999). Large format collection of spectacular astrophotographs of objects that cannot be seen by the naked eye.

Mallove, Eugene, and Matloff, Gregory, *The Starflight Handbook* (Wiley, 1989). Describes in detail the prospects for interstellar flight.

Murdin, Paul and Lesley, *Supernovae* (Cambridge UP, 1985). A clear account of what goes on when stars explode.

Petersen, Carolyn, and Brandt, John, *Hubble Vision* (Cambridge UP, second edition,1998). Spectacular images from the Hubble Space Telescope, with accompanying explanatory text.

Rees, Martin, *Just Six Numbers* (Weidenfeld & Nicolson, 1999). Britain's Astronomer Royal looks at the cosmic coincidences which define the Universe and life.

Ridpath, Ian, *Book of the Universe* (Dragon's World, 1991). Excellent beginner's guide to the cosmos.

Smolin, Lee, *The Life of the Cosmos* (Weidenfeld & Nicolson, 1997). Controversial but intriguing account of the 'baby universes' hypothesis.

Shklovskii, I. S., and Sagan, Carl, *Intelligent Life in the Universe* (Holden-Day, 1966). Still the best book about the search for ET.

Weinberg, Steven, *The First Three Minutes* (Deutsch, 1977). Nobel prizewinner discusses the puzzle of the origin and nature of the Universe.

Zuckerman, Ben, and Hart, Michael (editors), *Extraterrestrials: Where Are They?* (Cambridge UP, second edition, 1995). Is there intelligent life in the Universe anywhere except on Earth?

WEBSITES:

NASA websites:
www.nix.nasa.gov, www.photojournal.jpl.nasa.gov

Views of the Solar System
www.solarviews.com

Society of Popular Astronomy
www.popastro.com

Sky and Telescope Magazine
www.skypub.com

Hubble Space Telescope
www.stsci.edu

Satellite predictions
www.heavens-above.com

Picture credits

BBC Worldwide would like to thank the following for providing photographs and for permission to reproduce copyright material. While every effort has been made to trace and acknowledge all copyright holders, we would like to apologise should there have been any errors or omissions.

AKG London pages 127, 131, 227; **Brian and Cherry Alexander** page 209; **Allsport** page 93 *above*; **Anglo-Australian Observatory** pages 15, 20 *below*, 21, 23, 32 *right*, 40, 66, 68, 81 *right*, 120, 222; **Art Archive** pages 65, 193; **AT & T Bell Laboratories** page 88; **BBC Worldwide Ltd** pages 36, 42, 51 *above*, 54, 58, 69, 70 *above*, 70 *below*, 71, 82 *below*, 95, 102 *above*, 115, 117, 145 *below*, 148, 156, 176, 194 *left*, 200, 208, 210, 219; **Boomerang Collaboration** pages 134 *left*, 134 *right*, 135; **British Film Institute** page 155; **Corbis** page 124; **European Space Agency** page 16; **Galaxy Picture Library** pages 17, 20 *above*, 22, 26, 27, 28 *below*, 29 *above*, 34, 35, 45, 49, 56 *left*, 56 *right*, 61, 74, 79, 91, 111, 113, 121, 129, 147 *below*, 151, 154, 169, 171, 175, 217, 223, 231; **Genesis Space Photo Library** pages 76, 80, 143, 144, 145 *above*, 224, 232; **Hulton Getty Picture Collection** pages 153, 218; **Imagebank** pages 35 *below*, 199; **Images Colour Library** pages 29 *below*, 33, 102 *below left*, 185 *above left*, 204; **Mary Evans Picture Library** pages 75, 98 *above*, 187, 211; **Mount Wilson Observatory** pages 128; **NASA** pages 14 *right*, 32 *left*, 52, 53, 67, 132, 142 *below*; **Oxford Scientific Films** pages 81 *left*, 119, 146, 173, 180 *top*, 180 *below left*, 180 *below right*, 185 *above right*, 185 *below*, 220 *below*; **Pictor International** pages 112 *left*; **Popperfoto** page 229; **Princeton University** page 206; **Robert Harding Picture Library** pages 103 *left*, 207, **Rockefeller University Archives** page 192, **Royal Society** page 50, **Science Photo Library** pages 2, 5, 8, 11, 11 *right*, 13, 18 *left*, 18 *right*, 19 *below*, 24, 25, 28 *above*, 31, 39 *above*, 39 *below*, 43, 44, 44 *right*, 46, 51 *below*, 55, 57, 59, 63, 64, 72 *above*, 72 *below*, 73 *left*, 73 *right*, 82 *above*, 83, 84, 86, 89 *left*, 89 *right*, 90, 93 *below*, 94, 96, 97, 98 *below*, 99, 100, 100 *below*, 101 *above left*, 101 *above right*, 101 *below left*, 101 *below right*, 104, 107 *left*, 107 *right*, 108, 109, 110 *above*, 110 *below*, 112 *right*, 114, 116, 118, 122, 123, 125, 130, 133, 136, 139, 141, 142 *above*, 147 *above*, 149, 155, 157, 158, 159 *left*, 159 *right*, 160, 161, 162, 163, 164 *left*, 164 *right*, 165, 166, 170, 172, 177, 181, 182, 189, 190, 194 *right*, 195, 203, 205, 212, 214, 215, 220 *above*, 221, 225, 226, 230, 234; **Science and Society Picture Library** pages 141, 213, **Search for Extraterrestrial Intelligence Institute** page 174; **Shout Picture Library** page 103 *right*; **Telegraph Colour Library** pages 102 *below right*, 186, 197, **University of Colorado** page 85.

Index